TOTA ITALIA

TOTA ITALIA

Essays in the Cultural Formation of Roman Italy

Mario Torelli

CLARENDON PRESS · OXFORD

1999

OXFORD

UNIVERSITY PRESS

Great Clarendon Street, Oxford OX2 6DP
Oxford University Press is a department of the University of Oxford.
It furthers the University's objective of excellence in research, scholarship,
and education by publishing worldwide in

Oxford New York

Athens Auckland Bangkok Bogota Bombay Buenos Aires Calcutta
Cape Town Chennai Dar es Salaam Delhi Florence Hong Kong Istanbul
Karachi Kuala Lumpur Madrid Melbourne Mexico City Mumbai
Nairobi Paris São Paulo Singapore Taipei Tokyo Toronto Warsaw
and associated companies in Berlin Ibadan

Oxford is a registered trade mark of Oxford University Press
in the UK and certain other countries

Published in the United States
by Oxford University Press Inc., New York

British Library Cataloguing in Publication Data
Data available

Library of Congress Cataloging in Publication Data
Tota Italia : essays in the cultural formation of
Roman Italy / Mario Torelli.
Chiefly revised versions of texts prepared between 1987 and 1993.
Includes index.
1. Italy—Civilization—To 476. 2. Italy—Civilization—Roman
influences. 3. Acculturation—Italy—History. I. Title.
DG77.T595 1998 937—dc21 98–15866
ISBN 0–19–814393–1

1 3 5 7 9 10 8 6 4 2

Typeset by Graphicraft Limited, Hong Kong
Printed in Great Britain
on acid-free paper by
St. Edmundsbury Press Ltd., Bury St. Edmunds

In Fond Memory of

Ettore Lepore

Foreword

This volume does not aim to be a general book on Roman Italy, but simply an extended essay consisting of seven shorter ones on the social, religious, and cultural routes which led to the Augustan consensus expressed in the famous phrase 'Tota Italia in mea verba iuravit'. The social meaning of such an expression in the momentous years of the confrontation between Octavian and Mark Antony has been explored on various occasions, from Ronald Syme's 'Roman Revolution' onwards; but the complex machine that created the 'unified' class behind the Augustan expression of *Tota Italia* through centuries of social and economic exploitation of the allies by the Romans and of reciprocal cultural influence benefits from a fresh approach, drawing above all upon the immense, but largely underutilized, archaeological evidence.

The essays composing the volume were the subject of a series of lectures I delivered in Oxford as Nelly Wallace Lecturer during the Trinity Term of 1988. I greatly enjoyed this magnificent opportunity and I am grateful to Fergus Millar and Oswyn Murray, who generously supported this task of mine, and to the many graduate students, who attended the lectures. Since then I have published partial or different Italian versions of the text of all chapters, with the exception of Chapter 1, which reproduces faithfully my Oxford inaugural lecture. The substance of Chapter 2 appeared as 'Aspetti ideologici della colonizzazione romana più antica', in *DArch*, 3rd ser., 6 (1988), 65–72; Chapter 3 as 'Paestum romana', in *Atti Taranto 1987* (Naples, 1988), 33–115; Chapter 4 as 'Aspetti materiali e ideologici della romanizzazione della Daunia', in *DArch* 3rd ser., 10 (1992), 47–64; Chapter 5 as ' "Fictiles Fabulae". Rappresentazione e romanizzazione nei cicli figurati fittili repubblicani', in *Ostraka* 2 (1993), 269–99; Chapter 6 as 'La «Sedia Corsini», monumento della genealogia etrusca dei Plautii', in *Mélanges Pierre Lévêque*, 5 (Besançon, 1990), 355–76; and the Epilogue as 'Alle radici della nostalgia augustea', in M. Pani (ed.), *Continuità e trasformazioni fra repubblica e principato. Istituzioni, politica, società* (Bari, 1991), 47–67. In the present English version I have made various improvements to the original texts, incorporating critics and discussions of several friends and colleagues, whom it is difficult to remember individually; to all however I am greatly indebted. The English text of Chapter 6 has been read by Claire Lyons, whom I warmly thank for emendations and suggestions. It is also difficult to enumerate individually all those who helped me in collecting the illustrations; their assistance has been really invaluable. I want however to express particular thanks to my friends Angelo Bottini, Marina Cipriani, and Pier Giovanni Guzzo: without their help many pages of the present book simply would not have been written. And above all the book owes an immense debt to my wife Concetta, who not only supported the creation of the text, reading it as a benign, though critical colleague, but also helped me every single day as a loving and patient mate.

M.T.

Perugia
November 1994

Note: The abbreviations of periodicals are those of the Année Philologique; to these I have added only the abbreviation *Atti Taranto* followed by the year to signify the publication of the Convegni di Studi sulla Magna Grecia, held yearly in Taranto since 1961.

Contents

List of Plates

List of Figures

I

THE ROMANIZATION OF ITALY

1. The Construction of Roman Italy and Modern Italian Historiography

The Lucanians were lovers of justice, order and hard work, but jealous of their independence. In addition, they were valiant and warlike, always showing their indomitable valour in the wars they waged, now against the Greeks, now against the Bruttians, now against the Romans. After Lucania had fallen prey to the latter, after a long and stubborn resistance, it soon fell from its early state of grandeur and splendour and the decline became more and more obvious under the Emperors' rule. After hordes of Barbarians and ferocious peoples had swept through Italy, Lucanian soil for a long time was a theatre to be pitied for its cruel massacres and devastation. In this period, cities which had hitherto been spared disappeared and with them the monuments, the glory and even the very word 'Lucania'. In about the tenth century the modern Basilicata grew up on the ruins of this famous region.

THIS LONG QUOTE FROM THE DETAILED ARTICLE on Lucanian antiquities, which appeared in 1836 in the *Bullettino dell'Instituto di Corrispondenza Archeologica* and was written by the patriot and antiquarian Andrea Lombardi,[1] might well serve as an epigraph to a hypothetical essay on the history of historiography dedicated to the problem which I should like to call 'The problem of denied history'; that is, the history of the Romanization of Italy.

Andrea Lombardi (1785–1849)[2] is only a minor figure in nineteenth-century historical and archaeological research, but for this reason he may be taken as a symbol of a certain intellectual climate which gave birth to a substantial part of the research on the subject now under scrutiny. Judges, lawyers, royal civil servants, gentlemen farmers with decurional posts, all members of that class which Antonio Gramsci so aptly called 'the South Italian humanistic petite bourgeoisie' were among the leading figures of this great intellectual effort made by scholarly Italians, especially those in the Kingdom of Naples. These men, between the end of the eighteenth and the mid-nineteenth century, tried to digest in an acceptable form the great mass of archaeological discoveries made in those years, to lay the foundations of a 'national history', and exalt the exploits of the Italic *ethne* crushed by Rome.[3] This is a very old tradition which links two works and two men with exceptionally diverse personalities. The first is the well-known philosopher and historian Giambattista Vico, seventeenth-century author of *De antiquissima Italorum sapientia*, and the second is the much more modest Francesco Micali, father of the main work on this theme, *L'Italia avanti il dominio de'Romani* (Italy before Roman Rule), which he finished printing in 1832 and thus shortly before the archaeological masterpiece of Andrea Lombardi. As can be seen from the latter's words, the young Italian liberal middle class tended to identify itself with the pre-Roman peoples, whether these were Lucanians, Samnites, or Etruscans. They deliberately put the Greek presence and contribution into the shade and pointed to the Romans, frequently guilty of outright genocide, as being responsible for the tragic decline of their regions, of their peoples, and of the civil life of Italy itself. The Risorgimento, for patriots such as Andrea Lombardi, meant the rescue from a decadence begun with the Roman conquest. Parallel to this, the neo-classicism of the reactionary Restoration regimes also sanctioned, on a cultural level, the identification of the heralds of the neo-classical doctrines with the hated Romans, an identification which was

---

[1] A. Lombardi, *Bullettino dell'Instituto* (1836), 3 (= *La corona di Critonio* (Venosa, 1987), 15).   [2] Short biography in *La corona di Critonio*.

[3] On this subject, see A. Momigliano, 'Ancient History and the Antiquarian', *JWI* 13 (1950), 285 f.

widespread in the liberal clubs of the first Romantic period.

The South Italian bourgeoisie, therefore, looked with great interest at their Apulian, Samnite, Bruttian, Campanian, Lucanian, and Oscan ancestors just as the North Italian bourgeoisie looked with much greater relevance and historical coherence at their true ancestors, the heroes of the Italian Communal (and mercantile) Middle Ages. All that, however, had a very short life. Once Italy was unified, the opinion of the leading figures in the Piedmontese conquest, which was understandably similar to that of the prefects introduced half a century earlier by Napoleon, tended towards the idea of the 'pacifying' unification guided by Rome. While Giosuè Carducci was singing the praises of the newly established Italian kingdom's Roman heritage,[4] the Italic peoples were mentioned less and less and even with reluctance. From this moment on, in Italy the history of its Romanization was paradoxically held fast on the reefs of two antinomies: the mythical perfection of the pre-Roman civilization of Italy, brutally wiped out by the Roman legions on the one hand, and the equally mythical national unity achieved by Rome on the other, each position held by the two opposing leaders of the political struggles of the late Risorgimento and the first few years of political unity of Italy. All this can be readily attributed to the climate (no longer a purely national one) of the great nineteenth–twentieth-century debate on the role and idea of Rome in the construction of Italy[5] and on the essence of Romanization, in which, as Santo Mazzarino has taught us, contrasting ideological stands clash, stands according to which 'Rome gives all or takes all'.[6] However, the specific nature of the Romanization of Italy with its archaeological and methodological aspects deserves further consideration.

Outside Italy, the question of the national unity and identity, archaeological research on and historical evaluation of pre-Roman cultures went ahead and continued to go ahead in one way or another tightly linked[7]—one calls to mind the Chair of 'Antiquités Nationales' at the prestigious Collège de France. In Italy instead, as has already been said, the national problem had run aground first on the pre-Roman sandbank and then on the Roman one, thus breaking the unity of the Romanization problem. In fact, today, with the decisive divorce created by assigning the pre-Roman world to the Italicists, the vast majority of whom are archaeologists, and leaving the control of the Roman world mainly in the hands of the historians, the unnatural division of the problem has been further reinforced. As I pointed out in my paper on Romanization at the Second International Etruscan Congress,[8] it often happens that pre-Roman specialists by reason of their unconscious 'classicism', give preference to the peak moments of the civilization they are studying and deliberately dismiss the Romanization phase as one of total gloom and decadence, just as did Andrea Lombardi. Likewise, the Romanists pay attention mostly to the aspects of integration and assimilation, and generally show more interest in the results than in the nature and forms of the process.[9] As a consequence of such a climate archaeological research directed towards the 'classical' monuments of pre-Roman culture no longer nourishes historical research into Romanization; historians in their turn seem to become more and more caught up in extremely traditional themes of either a juridical or 'événementielle' nature. Yet the contribution which archaeology can make to the solution of such a problem is quite considerable and the time for attempting to unify the historical approach and archaeological documentation is surely ripe.

2. The Ethnic and Cultural Change

As has been realized for a long time, the roots of the problem on the Roman side lay in the tremendous economic, social, and political growth of the city of Rome following the conquest of Veii, and in the subsequent and related settlement of the conflict between the patricians and the plebeians. It is well to remember here (and rarely does this happen) that the effort of Roman imperialism in the hundred years between the

[4] [D. Manacorda] and R. Tamassia, *Il piccone del regime* (Rome, 1984), 84 f.

[5] P. Treves, *L'idea di Roma e la cultura italiana del secolo XIX* (Milan and Naples, 1962).

[6] S. Mazzarino, *Dalla monarchia allo stato repubblicano* (Catania, 1945), 173 f.

[7] A brief discussion by M. Pallottino, *History of Earliest Italy* (London and Ann Arbor, 1991).

[8] M. Torelli, 'Problemi di romanizzazione', *Atti del Secondo Congresso Internazionale Etrusco*, i (Rome, 1989), 393 ff.

[9] A good picture of the socio-economic impact of Roman conquest on foreign populations, but from the Roman perspective, is by provided by K. Hopkins, *Conquerors and Slaves* (Cambridge, 1978).

Licinio-Sextian laws and the beginning of the First Punic War was in fact sustained by two cities—Rome and Veii—separated by only 17 km.[10] These, by reason of their extensive territories and urban centres, had practically no equals, not only in Italy, but in the more advanced regions of the Mediterranean. It is quite clear from a comparison of the surface areas of Greek, Etruscan, and Roman cities of the classical period that the 242 hectares of Veii and the 285 hectares of Servian Rome, even if they were not densely and simultaneously inhabited, once added together made these two cities the largest human settlement in the Mediterranean area and one of the most awe-inspiring concentrations of productive and military manpower in the classical world.

But the greatest tool first of social and military control, and afterwards of Romanization, is represented by the Latin colonies. These colonies were perhaps the most successful weapons used by Rome to take possession of Italy and guarantee a rational exploitation of the agricultural resources offered by the vanquished areas. The researches of E. T. Salmon[11] and Frank Brown[12] have provided us with a useful picture of this original form of conquest, the first from a general historical point of view and the second using the concrete example of Cosa, one of the Latin colonies most extensively excavated.

However, there are many other examples of Latin colonies which have been investigated in recent years: Alba Fucens explored by the Belgian team led by J. Mertens; Fregellae excavated by British and Italian archaeologists; and Paestum which has been the subject of careful study by D. Theodorescu and E. Greco.[13] From these excavations not only new and interesting data for understanding the phenomenon emerge, but also new or partially new aspects of colonization and the relationship between the colonies and the Italic world which deserve a more thorough investigation than in the past. I am thinking especially of the possible enlistment of native elements in the Latin colonies, a question on the whole rarely debated, but crucial for getting to the heart of the problem of the Romanization of Italy. Indeed, no one can be unaware of the enormous political and cultural differences between colonies peopled by Romans and Latins only, and similar foundations with a mixed population. In the latter case, the native elements admitted into the colony clearly acted as intermediaries between it and the local population which had been excluded, and availed themselves of the fact that they not only shared the same language and culture but also had marriage bonds and economic interests in common with their former fellow countrymen.

Regarding this last point, significant and important data have been derived in the first place from onomastic evidence. G. Bandelli's cautious evaluation of the republican *nomina* of Aquileia[14] show that the local ruling class of the last Latin colony of Italy, in addition to elements of Latin origin, above all from Praeneste, included a number of high-ranking colonists enlisted from the Celtic and Venetic worlds. Some preliminary onomastic research seems to give similar results for Bononia.[15] For this other late Latin colony confirms what the same ancient tradition recorded for the entire Po Valley, i.e. the joint presence of but discrimination against, even at the threshold of the Imperial era, the different ethnic elements, Etruscan, Celtic, and Latin. For example, recently discovered evidence from the excavation of the Gallic settlement of Monte Bibele near Monterenzio,[16] which flourished in the Bologna hinterland between the fourth and second centuries BC, shows that a close and frequent marriage trade existed between the chieftains of Celtic village society and what survived of the ancient Etruscan population. Indeed, some tombs of the Monterenzio necropolis, which can be attributed to the *principes* of the site on account of obvious signs of wealth and distinction in the grave contents, have produced Etruscan inscriptions engraved on black glazed bowls—the names of Etruscan women, *Petnei* (tomb no. 87 and tomb no. 14)

---

[10] See Ch. 2.

[11] See the two general volumes E. T. Salmon, *Roman Colonization under the Republic* (London, 1969), and *The Romanization of Italy* (London, 1982).

[12] F. E. Brown, *Cosa: The Making of a Roman Town* (Ann Arbor, 1980).

[13] See the Colloquium of Acquasparta, published in *DArch.* 3rd ser., 6 (1988), 2.

[14] G. Bandelli, 'Per una storia della classe dirigente di Aquileia repubblicana', in *Les 'Bourgeoisies' municipales italiennes aux II et I siècles av. J.-C.* Acts of the Conference; Naples, 1981 (Rome, 1983), 175 f.

[15] I am preparing a separate study on the case of Bononia.

[16] The valuable excavation of this exceptional Gallic settlement of the tribe of the Boi was first published in the volume by D. Vitali (ed.), *Monterenzio e la valle dell'Idice. Archeologia e storia di un territorio*, Catalogue of the Exhibition; Monterenzio, 1983 (Monterenzio, 1983); see also by the same author, *Monte Bibele und andere Fundstellen der keltischen Epoche im Gebiet von Bologna*, Kleine Schriften Marburg, 16 (Marburg, 1985) and, above all, 'Monte Bibele fra Etruschi e Celti: dati archeologici e interpretazione', in D. Vitali (ed.), *Celti ed Etruschi nell'Italia centro-settentrionale dal V sec.a.C. alla romanizzazione*, Acts of the Conference; Bologna, 1985 (Bologna, 1987), 309 f.

and *Tataia* (tomb no. 40), matched by an inscription discovered in one of the houses of the village, and revealing another Etruscan woman, a certain [*Ca*]*via Ataia*.[17] However, it is also significant that one tomb (no. 103) in the necropolis, containing bronze athletic instruments instead of the usual arms of other tombs of the Celtic rite, has given us the name of a genuine Etruscan of the Po Valley, *Laθialu*.[18] The case is very similar to that of a tomb in a Gallic cemetery at Bologna, no. 968, a burial again without weapons but with the owner's inscription, mentioning an Etruscan named *Titie*.[19]

A mixing between the various ethnic groups in the border areas or those of ethnic overlap frequently preceded Roman colonization. Another interesting case is that of Paestum, which we shall deal with thoroughly in a later chapter; here we need only to quote the results of the onomastic study. Paestum was a colony almost a century older than those of Aquileia and Bononia, which allows us to make some interesting comparisons. As we shall see,[20] the Paestum onomastics of the republican era are fairly well known and in the colonial élite not only do nobles of a Lucanian matrix abound (such as the Cepii, the Digitii, the Egnii, the Mineii, and the Vennei), but aristocrats of an unquestionable Latin origin (such as the Claudii, the Cocceii, the Ligustii, the Sextili, and the Valerii) also produce at times *praenomina* of a no less unquestionable Lucanian origin, as for instance in one of the famous inscriptions of republican *quaestores* mentioning a *quaestor* Tr(ebius) Claudius. It must also be added that the oldest senatorial family which Münzer attributed to Paestum, that of the Digitii, already known from 200 BC onwards, was undoubtedly of Lucanian origin. Local Lucanian natives were therefore enlisted in the colony, obviously chosen from the pro-Roman members of the proud equestrian aristocracy immortalized in the famous painted tombs of the pre-Roman period[21]. But along with these, the members of another

ethnic group, for many centuries close to Poseidonia-Paestum on the other bank of the Sele, entered the colony lists. These were the Etruscans settled since the early Iron Age between Pontecagnano (possibly identifiable with the ancient Marcina) and Fratte di Salerno, an Etruscan city, which perhaps preceded also in name the Roman colony of Salernum. The best example of these *nomina Tusca* in the list of the early Paestan *nomina* is that of Numonii, in Etruscan *numna*, to which a famous Horatian character, P. Numonius Vaala, belonged, twice honoured at Paestum as *patronus* and significantly owner of *praedia* at Salernum.[22]

We may conclude that the foundation of Paestum, besides elements from Rome and from old Lucanian stock, also brought with it the transfer within the colony walls of the last Etruscans of Campania from Fratte and Pontecagnano, cities which seem to have been abandoned between the end of the fourth and the beginning of the third century BC. A famous passage attributed to Aristoxenus from Tarentum on the barbarization of Poseidonian Greeks can only be understood after 273 BC (actually after 272 BC, the year of the fall of Tarentum to Roman hands), since during Lucanian rule, the language used in the city continued to be Greek, as the frequent graffiti of the period between 400 and 275 BC show. The Lucanian language was only (and very rarely) used for official inscriptions, to be precise just one text is known to us, the very formal dedicatory inscription of an altar to Jupiter (possibly the equivalent of Zeus Boulaios or Zeus Agoraios) in the *ekklesiasterion*. The change in language and customs and the 'transformation into Tyrrhenians or Romans' of the Greek element—to follow the (Pseudo-) Aristoxenus' text—are instead events that only happened when the Latin colony was founded. Particularly important seems to me the change 'of personal names' mentioned in this passage: yet another event that can be understood only if we are dealing with a Latin colony. The Greek element, therefore, seems to be the one which was really sacrificed within the Roman colonial context. The Lucanian aristocracy, already in contact and partially on good terms with the Romans, in the text of the (Pseudo)-Aristoxenos was assimilated by them. The new ethnic component in the Latin colony seems to be the Etruscan one, but even in this case it is only relatively new, since the Poseidonian

[17] The epigraphic evidence from the village is collected by F. Lenzi, in Vitali (ed.), *Monterenzio*, 183 f.

[18] D. Vitali, in Vitali (ed.), *Celti ed Etruschi*, 370 f.; for the origin from the Po Valley of Etruscan names ending in -*lu*, see G. Sassatelli, 'La situazione in Etruria Padana', in F.-H. Massa Pairault (ed.), *Crise et transformation des sociétés archaïques de l'Italie antique au Ve siècle av. J.-C.*, Acts of Conference; Rome (Rome, 1990), 51 f., esp. 67 f.

[19] On these tombs, M. Torelli, 'I Galli e gli Etruschi', in Vitali (ed.), *Celti ed Etruschi*, 1 f.

[20] See Ch. 3.

[21] A. Pontrandolfo and A. Rouveret, *Le tombe dipinte di Paestum* (Modena, 1992).

[22] For all these Paestan examples, see Ch. 3.

inscription of about 500 BC discovered in a tomb of the nearby Etruscan city at Pontecagnano, which I recently published,[23] and the constant presence of Paestan votive statuettes between 450 and 350 BC in children's tombs of Pontecagnano[24] are witness to a close and continuous relationship between the two adjoining societies from the earliest times of the Greek city onwards. Even more interesting appears the fact that the Romans exerted the most effective oppression only on the Greek element, which had survived, we might say, 'in good health' for more than a century under the rule of a small Lucanian oligarchy, perhaps as a free or semi-free urban population able to use its own language and culture and active as a lively middle class of merchants and craftsmen. Unlike their Lucanian predecessors, the Romans dispossessed the Poseidonian Greeks of their culture and caused their rapid disappearance as an ethnic entity. Later we shall discuss the another interesting detail of the (Pseudo)-Aristoxenos passage, concerning the survival of just one Greek religious festival in Roman Paestum.

All this gives us an inkling not only of the similarity of fate between the Greeks of Poseidonia and the other Greeks of the democratic, anti-Roman factions in the surviving Hellenic cities of Magna Graecia, such as Tarentum, Locri, or Croton, wiped out by the Romans to the advantage of their local allies, the weak and corrupted Greek oligarchies. More generally, as the case of Paestum fairly shows, the policy fostered by the Romans in connection with the social struggles in the Greek and Etruscan cities led, when setting up the colony, to the substantial preservation (or re-establishment) of pre-existing property and class relationships.

3. Roman Italy and the Hierarchy of Exploitation

This leads us to the socio-economic aspects of the Romanization process. There is no doubt that Roman conquest caused severe trauma in the economic system of Italy, even before the military defeats or massacres suffered by the civilian populations, with the confiscation of the vanquished's best land. Prior to conquest, the socio-economic balance in the territories

of each single city or of each ethnic group and between the various Italian regions seems, even if not guaranteed, to have beeen to some extent assured. Even in the most mountainous and inhospitable parts of Italy, where rather limited economic growth did not allow urban centres to emerge, but only a type of *vicatim* settlement (Fig. 1, area 6),[25] as in Sabina and Samnium, valley bottoms or plateaux existed which were fertile enough to permit an agriculture capable of supporting the main economic activities, that is to say stock-raising and related industries. It is these lands or a great part of them that Rome seized, devoting considerable portions of them to Latin or to viritane colonists (those who held their land on an individual basis), i.e. the backbone of the colonies founded and populated by the Romans prior to the second century BC. This obviously caused difficulties for the local economies, already tendentially underdeveloped, thus speeding up the processes of impoverishment and underdevelopment. But as we all know, growth needs underdevelopment[26] and the process which the Roman conquest triggered off in the country is no exception to this golden rule.

Even before the Roman conquest and from the beginning of the proto-historical period onwards, an area of Italy was developing where the favourable environment and an adequate organization of production permitted considerable economic growth. This area essentially coincides with central and southern Etruria, Latium, and Campania (Fig. 1, area 2), that is the wide strip of land along the Tyrrhenian sea where cities sprang up long before others in Italy and where the archaic civilizations of Italy reached their maximum splendour. It is here too after the Roman

---

[23] M. Torelli, 'Un'iscrizione posidoniate nella necropoli etrusca di Pontecagnano', *AION Arch* 6 (1984), 277 f.

[24] I thank Prof . L. Cerchiai for this piece of information.

[25] [P. Gros] and M. Torelli, *Storia dell'urbanistica: Il mondo romano* (Bari and Rome, 1988), 46 f.

[26] Some Italian historians seem to have not liked this idea of developed and underdeveloped areas of ancient Italy, which I have already expressed elsewhere (M. Torelli, 'Le popolazioni dell'Italia antica: società e forme del potere', in A. Schiavone and A. Momigliano (eds.), *Storia di Roma*, i (Turin, 1988), 53 f.) and which they consider affected by the dangerous approach named 'modernism'. As an archaeologist, I was able to demonstrate it simply by taking the quantitative and qualitative aspects of the material culture of the various regions of Italy and using them to reconstruct very different qualities of life: the result was that I could (and everybody using the same material could) reconstruct the existence of two radically different areas, i.e. areas where climate was better, food was better and more abundant, luxury merchandise was more numerous and attractive, and areas where all that was virtually lacking. I would suggest to those historians to try to live just one month in conditions similar to those of the region I describe as underdeveloped and to prove to have enjoyed them more than the conditions of my 'developed' regions.

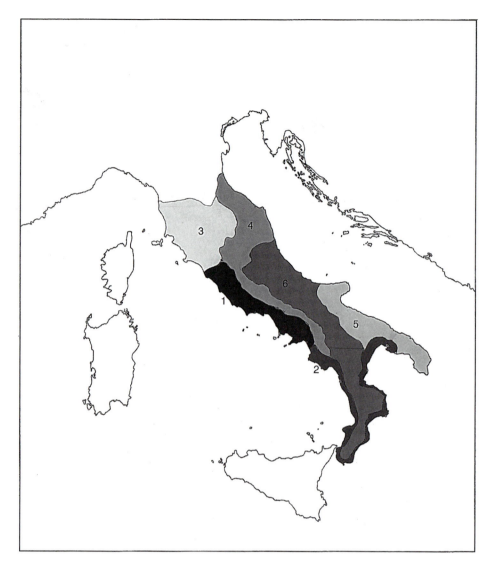

Fig. 1. Map of the urban development in pre-Roman Italy: 1. the area of Greek colonies; 2. the area of the earliest urban Italic develoment (south Etruria, Latium, Campania); 3. the central and northern Etruscan area; 4. the Umbrian and Picene area; 5. the Apulian area; 6. the area of *vicatim* settlement (Samnium, Lucania, and Bruttium) (drawing A. Trapassi).

conquest that a system of agricultural production developed which, by the mid-second century BC, Cato was to describe in his *De agri cultura*: agriculture based on the small and medium-sized farm worked by slave labour.[27] These are the areas for the most part occupied by *ager publicus* or by lands belonging to Latin cities and to ancient Latin colonies or distributions of land on an individual basis: a rough estimate of the percentage of highly productive soil—plains and gentle hills, suitable

for olive-trees and vines—has calculated that in the middle of the third century BC more than 65 per cent of the whole arable land of this zone was controlled by the Romans directly or indirectly, through Latin colonies. The lands conquered in the less-favoured areas referred to above could also develop a similar economic regime; however, for various reasons the Catonian or the Varronian slave-run villa hardly filtered through into these areas, only sometimes transforming the old indigenous, familial farm into a 'Catonian' villa, as is perfectly documented by the Montone di Tolve villa in Lucania (Fig. 2).[28]

---

[27] In general on this period, see A. Giardina and A. Schiavone (eds.), *Società romana e produzione schiavistica*, 3 vols. (Rome and Bari, 1981); on the early 'Catonian' villa, see M. Torelli, 'La formazione della villa', in A. Schiavone and A. Momigliano (eds.), *Storia di Roma*, ii: 1 (Turin, 1990), 123 f.; on the later 'Varronian' villa, see A. Carandini, 'La villa romana e la piantagione schiavistica', in A. Momigliano and A. Schiavone (eds.), *Storia di Roma*, iv (Turin, 1989), 101 f.

[28] A. R(usso), 'Montone di Tolve—Complesso residenziale', in L. de Lachenal (ed.), *Da Leukania a Lucania*, Catalogue of the Exhibition; Venosa, 1992 (Rome, 1992), 39 f.

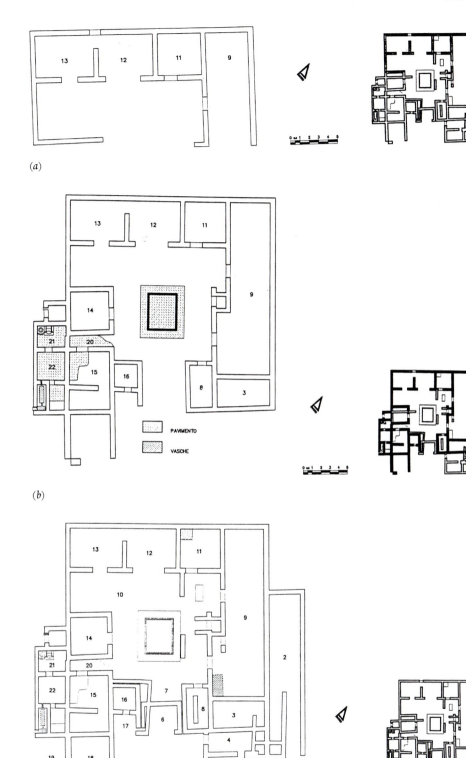

Fig. 2. The Montone di Tolve farm: phase I, late fourth century BC (*a*); phase II, third century BC (*b*); phase III, late second century BC (*c*) (after *Da Leukania a Lucania*).

Anyhow, the different rates of economic growth of the individual zones accelerated the economic growth process on the one hand, but on the other also accelerated impoverishment. Slave labour tended to develop in the Tyrrhenian region, whilst small and middlesized property tended to remain intact (though impoverished by the exaction of *vectigalia*) for the whole of the third century in the flat and fertile plains of the interior, mostly confiscated by Rome. However, in the mountainous areas of the Pre-Appenines and the Appenines, the phenomenon of the concentration of wealth in the hands of very few aristocratic groups became more marked, and, parallel to this, the impoverishment and expulsion of free manpower became the rule. These events, moreover, were very old scourges as demonstrated first by the ancient Italic religious custom of *ver sacrum*[29] (the periodic emigration of an entire generation in case of famine or starvation) and later by the large share of Italic soldiers among the mercenary forces active on various fronts in the fourth and third centuries BC.[30]

Ever since Arnold Toynbee's monumental work, it has become customary to find the reason for the economic transformation of late-republican Italy in 'Hannibal's legacy'.[31] There is no doubt that the bloody ten-year war waged on Italian soil left a very deep scar on the social set-up in Italy: 'war means revolution' as a great theoretician of the twentieth-century revolutions so rightly puts it. However, in this long period, the influence of the war on Italy's real economic life, both on the Roman side and on that of the allies, can best be assessed using as a model Capua, which was so well investigated by M. W. Frederiksen.[32] The city was dismembered and politically annihilated because of its betrayal of Rome in the conflict with Hannibal, but, as is shown by the energetic activities of its *magistri*, in the second half of the second century BC became again one of the wealthiest centres of the Italian world, one of the most imposing cities in Italy with a fully renewed urban form, notwithstanding its juridical and political status as a 'non-city'. Likewise, a closer analysis of the archaeological evidence more and more shows that much of the south Italian destruction previously attributed to Hannibal is more likely to be the work of the Roman conquest sixty or seventy years earlier. This is the case, for instance, in the desertification of many of the territories in the Lucanian interior and of the cities of Magna Graecia such as Metapontum, whose abandonment—despite the assertion of Livy[33]—can be linked better to Pyrrhus' than to Hannibal's campaigns.[34]

4. The Arrival of *Luxuria* and the Economic Areas of the Peninsula

The true revolutionary innovation in the socio-economic sphere is represented by the appearance on the scene of production and politics of the disruptive and disintegrating effect of *luxuria*, of opulent consumption borrowed from the economy and culture of the Hellenistic world and financed by the great imperialistic conquests of Rome. That this was the real driving force behind the great transformation of the second century BC was very present in ancient minds, in the ethical–political logic peculiar to them, as many texts illustrate, from the famous pages of Sallust on contemporary moral decadence to the synthetic but no less famous lapidary judgements of Pliny the Elder on the same subject. Archaeology shows that the massive production of amphoras of the Dressel IA type began then together with the diffusion of the Catonian villa model in the most economically progressive areas of the peninsula (Fig. I, area 2), together with the zone invested by Greek colonization (Fig. I, area I).[35] The local aristocracies of the Latin colonies and the allied cities of Oscan Campania were the richest in Italy in this century and reflected fairly closely the growth brought into the capital city of Rome by Hellenistic *luxuria*, sometimes even anticipating certain forms of private *luxuria* which developed in the capital only later, during the turbulent years of the Civil Wars and the early Augustan period. In the public sphere, the monumentalization of Pompeii (or that of Alba Fucens, Cumae, or Praeneste) is, in its various ways, the concrete

[29] J. Heurgon, *Trois études sur le 'Ver sacrum'* (Brussels, 1957).

[30] G. Tagliamonte, *I figli di Marte: Mobilità, mercenari e mercenariato italici in Magna Grecia e Sicilia* (Rome, 1994).

[31] A. Toynbee, *Hannibal's Legacy: The Hannibalic War's Effect on Roman Life*, 2 vols. (Oxford, 1965).

[32] M. W. Frederiksen, 'Republican Capua: a Social and Economic Study', *PBSR* 14 (1959) 80 f.

[33] Liv. 27. 16. 11–14.

[34] See however the new data given by A. D(e) S(iena), 'Metaponto e il Metapontino', in de Lachenal (ed.), *Da Leukania a Lucania*, 114 f.

[35] C. Panella, 'La distribuzione e i mercati', in Giardina and Schiavone (eds.), *Società romana e produzione schiavistica*, ii. 55 f.

though indirect proof of the colossal building programmes of Rome,[36] known to us mostly through literature and only episodically through archaeology. From archaeological evidence in Pompeii and other sites F. Pesando[37] has argued that in the late second century the *privata luxuria* of the richest Italian cities was much more lavish than that displayed by the great aristocratic families in Rome, where social control and sumptuary legislation were still hampering factors for private expenditure. The huge amount of resources, booty, slaves, and tributes which poured into Rome seeped through the cracks of the geo-economic stratification of Italy in direct proportion to the degree of political and economic uniformity they shared with the capital. Of course, the greatest beneficiary after Rome was the territory which had already experienced a high growth rate, where the Roman productive and political model had already operated to a very considerable extent. This acted as a great impetus to the policy of public benefactions and to the spread of prestige building, which, closely following the capital's example, is recorded in south Etruria, Latium, and Campania,[38] the only area of Italy truly characterized by the slave mode of production and by the slave-run villa.

Bordering on this area, we have the northern Etruscan territories (Fig. 1, area 3), virtually untouched by the Roman pillages at the time of the conquest, and the surviving cities of Magna Graecia. In the ancient Etruscan cities, the former socio-political order based on *servitus* was irreparably shattered and occasionally substituted by forms of small-farmer properties, as we learn from the archaeology and epigraphy of Clusium and Perusia.[39] However, in these, as in the surviving Greek *poleis*,[40] the great wealth of the very few families which made up the oligarchies of local government and the heart of the alliance with Rome remained

unquestioned, as their tombs especially prove.[41] But the economic system of the majority of the ancient Etruscan cities was no doubt extremely archaic and their agriculture usually based on cereals grown in sprawling and badly worked fields. In this area grandiloquent building policies were systematically refused; the attitude was the fruit of the oligarchic austerity as much as that of the generally shorter supply of money, which was due to the primitive state of the agriculture and the lack of interest in the Romano-Italic exploitation of the east, as the absence of names of these areas from the Delos merchants' list shows.[42] The relative economic sluggishness of these older civilized areas had a precise equivalent on the social level. Not only is the ruling oligarchy a very small one, but the Roman conquest practically wiped out a large part of the middle classes in town and countryside, as archaeologists working in southern Italy well know. Here the farms and smaller villages of Apulia, Lucania, Bruttium, flourishing in great numbers between the second half of the fourth century and the first one or two decades of the third century BC, had soon drastically disappeared during the third century BC, leaving huge voids throughout all the territories.[43] The latent or open conflict on a local level which developed in Greek cities during the fourth century BC between the aristocracy and the middle classes of both urban and peasant origins, was radically settled by Rome to the benefit of the aristocracy, leaving or handing back an archaic or in any event torpid social and economic order.

A third area is that of the *socii* in direct contact with the oldest developed areas of ancient Italy (Fig. 1, area 4). These are the Picenian and Umbrian territories and the part of the Samnite areas most close to Etruria, Latium, Campania, or Magna Graecia, where the urban phenomenon—with all that this means in

---

[36] P. Zanker, 'Pompeji. Stadtbilder als Spiegel von Gesellschaft und Herrschaftsformen', 9. *Trierer Winckelmannsprogramm* (1987), 5 f.

[37] F. Pesando, *'Domus'. Edilizia privata e società pompeiana fra III e I secolo a.C.*, Ministero per i Beni Culturali ed Ambientali, Soprintendenza Archeologica di Pompei, Monografie, 12 (Roma, 1997).

[38] M. Torelli, 'Edilizia pubblica in Italia centrale tra guerra sociale ed età augustea: ideologia e classi sociali', in *Les 'Bourgeoisies' municipales italiennes aux II et I siècles av. J.-C.*, Acts of Conference; Naples, 1981 (Rome, 1983), 241 f.

[39] See W. V. Harris, *Rome in Etruria and Umbria* (Oxford, 1971), and M. Torelli, *Storia degli Etruschi* (Rome and Bari, 1981), 251 f.

[40] See the general reassessment of funerary evidence from 2nd-cent. BC Tarentum presented in E. De Juliis (ed.), *Gli ori di Taranto in età ellenistica*, Catalogue of the Exhibition; Milan, 1984 (Milan, 1984).

[41] We lack a general standard work on the Etruscan funerary architecture of the 2nd cent. BC; though oriented towards a different perspective, see J. P. Oleson, *The Sources of Innovation in Later Etruscan Tomb Design (ca.350–100 BC)* (Rome, 1982).

[42] As I noted many years ago in the brief study 'Contributo dell'archeologia alla storia sociale—L'Etruria e l'Apulia', *DArch*, 4–5 (1970/1), 431 f.

[43] A good example of this situation is now provided by the Canadian survey of the Roccagloriosa area, in the territory of a major Lucanian settlement near the modern village of Roccagloriosa (the Lucanian Pyxous?), published by H. Fracchia, M. Gualtieri, and F. de Polignac, 'Il territorio di Roccagloriosa in Lucania (provincia di Salerno)', in *MEFRA* 95 (1983), 345 f.; on the main site of Roccagloriosa see now M. Gualtieri and H. Fracchia, *Roccagloriosa* (Naples, 1990) and M. Gualtieri (ed.), *Fourth Century BC Magna Graecia: A Case Study* (Jonsered, 1993).

economic and social terms—had a relatively recent history, in most respects similar to that of Apulia (Fig. 1, area 5).[44] Despite the scarce archaeological data available, it is obvious that the zones in close contact with the centres of economic growth (for example the Umbrian territories which gravitated towards the Tiber valley and therefore to Rome or the areas of the Sidicinian or Hirpinian tribes near the fertile plains of Campania) were economically very active, as we can see from the rich tombs, such as those of the Umbrian[45] or of the Pelignan[46] centres. This activity was accompanied by attempts to give an urban shape to the old *oppidum*, both in a monumental, physical way and in a political sense, especially during the late second century BC, as well documented in Asisium[47]. This latter phenomenon is very obvious in several well-known cases, such as that of Bantia on the border between Apulia, Samnium, and Lucania (we shall return to this later) and is aimed at a 'self-Romanization' with the very clear purpose of politically legitimizing the local ruling classes.[48] The promotion of the local aristocracies, which were rather more recent and culturally less evolved than the Greek and Etruscan ones, could only be achieved through the adoption of the formal categories of the *urbanitas*, which until then had hardly been realized in concrete terms or only outlined in vague terms. The size of the urban centres is often quite small, with a contrasting concentration in rather limited areas: in this regard we may quote emblematic cases in Umbria and Picenum such as the easternmost section of the southern Umbrian valley, characterized by the presence—after 90 BC—of eight *municipia* in an area of scarcely more than 200 square kilometres (Fig. 3).[49] This leads us to suspect that this urbanizing

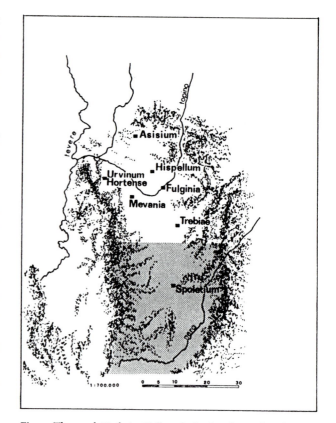

Fig. 3. The south Umbrian Valley: the Latin colony of Spoletium (territory in grey) and adjoining *municipia* of Umbrian origin (drawing M. Monella).

impetus meant that each single aristocratic group dug itself in around a future urban nucleus.

The last level in this economic system of the Italian peninsula, which could be defined as a 'hierarchy of growth', is found in zones which are more truly Appenine, i.e. those from the Umbrian hinterland to the inaccessible mountainous area of Lucania and Bruttium, crossing lands inhabited by the Samnite and Lucanian tribes of Samnium proper, of Lucania, and of Bruttium (Fig. 1, area 6). We have already spoken of this traditionally underdeveloped land organized on the village model of the *pagus* and the *vicus* and hard hit by the conquests and by the Latin colonial foundations. Here even the traditional local aristocracies suffered a drastic reduction in number and in finances of their members. As the senatorial lists of the first century BC show,[50] after the Social War we can often count only

[44] [Gros] and Torelli, *Storia dell'urbanistica*.

[45] Though scandalously unpublished, Umbrian tombs from the 5th to the 2nd cent. BC have yielded some significant Etruscan or Greek luxury goods, such as the Meidiac vase from the necropolis of the Vittorina at Gubbio published by D. Manconi, in *Antichità dell'Umbria a New York*, Catalogue of the Exhibition; New York, 1991 (Perugia, 1991), 324 f. As a whole necropolis, badly published, but extremely rich, we may also cite the 5th–2nd-cent. cemetery of Todi, the finds from which have been assembled by M. T. Falconi Amorelli, *Todi preromana (Catalogo dei materiali conservati nel Museo Comunale di Todi)* (Perugia, 1977), with my comments 'La società della frontiera', in *Verso un Museo della Città*, Catalogue of the Exhibition; Todi 1981 (Todi, 1982), 54 f.

[46] A good survey of the archaeological evidence is in F. Van Wonterghem, *Superaequum, Corfinium, Sulmo*, Forma Italiae 4: 1 (Florence, 1984), 144 f.

[47] F. Coarelli, 'Assisi repubblicana: riflessioni su un caso di autoromanizzazione', *Atti Accademia Properziana del Subasio—Assisi* 6th ser., 19 (1991), 5 f.   [48] See Ch. 4.

[49] [Gros] and Torelli, *Storia dell'urbanistica*, 51 f., fig. 28 here reproduced.

[50] See the lists by M. Torelli, 'Ascesa al Senato e rapporti con i territori d'origine. Italia: Regio IV (Samnium)', in S. Panciera (ed.), *Epigrafia e ordine senatorio*, ii (Rome, 1982), 165 f.

one family of that rank from the territory of each tribe or from pagan sections of a tribal area.

The economic picture which Italy shows us in the second century BC is that of a very complex hierarchical system of micro-economies susceptible to being utterly exploited by Roman imperialism. The majority of the resources deriving from the enormous amount of money and manpower carried by the second-century BC conquest converge on the privileged area of economic growth. These resources were transformed partly into sumptuary expenditures ranging from *ludi* to public and private luxury building projects, both essential for the system's political and economic reproduction, and partly into new investment in agriculture and in collateral activities which had already evolved through slave-run economic forms, a mode of production that became increasingly 'scientific'.

The other economic areas did not know and were never to know (or only in a belated, limited, and fleeting way) agriculture using extensive slave labour. In these territories, as we have already said, what had been developed continued to develop and what previously had been economically marginalized continued to become more and more marginalized and subordinate. Thus, we are facing a dominant mode of production identified with the slave mode of production, which was practised within the geographical and political borders of south Etruria, Latium, and Campania, as described above, and which, to a large extent, was under Rome's direct political and economic control. This dominant mode of production uses residual modes of production surviving in the rest of Italy, whose subordination (and potential and real wealth) is proportionate to the growth level reached in pre-Roman times and which showed an obvious tendency to grow hand in hand with the progressive domination of the more advanced productive forms.

5. Factors of Social and Cultural Cohesion and Tendencies Towards Unification

The entity, depth, and precociousness of the Romanization process depended just as much on these complex socio-economic machines as on the level of ethnic, political, and cultural cohesion and uniformity already achieved in pre-Roman times. The alliance between the ruling Roman classes and the local aristocracies was able to guarantee the necessary and expected control over the subordinate classes for a large part of the second century BC up until the last decades of that century, between the Fregellae War and the *Bellum Marsicum*. This sort of social control, together with the associated Romano-Italic alliance, failed when the economic, social, and political mid-republican balance between social classes in Rome and between Rome and Italy broke down, bringing to the surface all the problems which were already looming at the beginning of the century. A greater and greater importance was assumed by some of these problems, namely the crisis in the Latin and Roman colonization of Italy and with it the old model of the small farmer, the increase in the urban populace and some dramatic movements of very numerous groups, according to the paths mapped out by the political differences imposed by Rome. I am thinking here of the repeated expulsions of the Latins from Rome (206, 187, 177, 172, 126, and 122 BC)[51] or of the presence of *Samnites inquolae* at Aesernia[52] or of the immigration of over 4,000 families of Italic *socii* to Fregellae in 177 BC reported to us by Livy.[53] In short, there was a vast movement of the Italian population involving social classes of varying degrees of subordination, which well described the crisis in social control referred to above. Archaeologically, all this is manifest in the impoverishment of the fringes of the more developed areas and of the poorer areas of Italy. A good instance of this could be the decline suffered by many elegant and better-off houses belonging to the upper class of the Latin colony of Fregellae, with their conversion into *fullonicae* and tanneries, an obvious result of the movement towards Rome of the Latin allies and of the substitution of them by the immigrant families from the adjoining Samnitic area,[54] whose number, 4,000, makes this movement almost equal to that of an entire town; no wonder if Fregellae began to pose problems for Rome and if a revolt broke out there in 125 BC, bringing the old, faithful Latin colony to an end.[55]

[51] Liv. 28. 11. 1 f. (206 BC); 39. 3. 4 f. (187 BC); 41. 9 (177 BC); 42. 10 (172 BC); Cic. *Off.* 3. 11. 47; Cic. *Brutus* 28. 139 (126 BC: *peregrini*); Appian. *Bell.civ.* 1. 23; Plut. *C. Gracch.* 12. 1 (122 BC: *peregrini*).
[52] *CIL* I², 3020.   [53] Liv. 41. 8. 6–12.
[54] See F. Coarelli, 'I Sanniti a Fregellae', in *La Romanisation du Samnium aux IIᵉ et Iᵉʳ siècles av. J.-C.*, Acts of the Conference; Naples, 1988 (Naples, 1991), 177 f.
[55] Best account by G. Tibiletti, 'La politica delle colonie e delle città latine nella guerra sociale', *RIL* 86 (1953), 45 f., esp. 55 f.

The second factor that favoured Romanization is represented by the gigantic effort to fashion everything on urban models which was made throughout Italy in the second half of the second century BC and particularly towards the very end of the same century. It was during this period that almost every corner of Italy, from the artificial urbanization of the small community of Bantia[56] to the surprising architectural achievements of Praeneste,[57] reacted to the economic and ideological pressure of Rome and threw itself into public works often well beyond the economic possibilities of the single local societies. There was an undeniable ideological component in this impressive phenomenon (for which we perhaps need to attempt a new analysis and a catalogue twenty years after the momentous Göttingen Conference):[58] in other words, there was the political need for the Italian allies to prove their own conformity to the ethics of *urbanitas* together with a kind of a flickering attempt to resist the imposition of Roman cultural forms in restoring cult places of 'national' interest and of documented *antiquitas*.

In fact, the most sacred places of local memories, the most prestigious and ancient local shrines were at the centre of the building activity of the Italian allies. As we shall see in a separate chapter,[59] it is not difficult to read into this activity the need to reassert one's ethnic and civic identity at the very moment one realized that it was being lost as a result of the socio-economic, political, and cultural pressure of Rome. The great sanctuaries of Latium, Campania, Samnium, Lucania, Picenum, Umbria, and Etruria from this crucial moment in the late second century BC onwards, were restored and embellished with monumental additions and this state of affairs was to continue throughout the whole of the first century BC until it became part of the obsessive climate of the Augustan *pietas*. This is very important, because it helps us to understand the continuity which binds the last decades of Italic independence to the entire first century BC for the final completion of a Romanization which already existed in the material life of the second century. The culture of *pietas*, the ideological cement of Romanization and a fundamental tool of Augustus' rule, was already firmly rooted in the very old bond of *mos maiorum*. However, the *mos*

maiorum, that is to say the automatic conformity to restrictive tenets of behaviour implicit in the permanent and pervasive presence of a tradition, is radically different both from the yearning toward antiquity and from the nostalgic archaeology of past values at the root of the Augustan *pietas*; the attitude of *pietas* in fact implied a break with that *mos* and the anguish of its revival. It is important, therefore, to understand that the precedents for this *pietas* were firmly entrenched in the climate of Cato's *Origines* and Varro's encyclopaedic works. National myth and rites served as a very reassuring purpose for the Roman and Italic leading figures of the late republican tragedy, in a climate of disruptive *luxuria* with its retinue of *avaritia* and *sumptus*. In spite of the evident differences in context, we can call to mind a clear analogy with the cherishing of the thousand old myths and rites of the many Greek towns by the Callimachean culture of the *Aitia* and by the innumerable studies of local histories in the upheaval caused by the destruction of the values of the *polis* and the triumph of the cosmopolitan culture of the Hellenistic ruling classes.

But the crisis of national identity (in the sense of the individual 'nations' or *ethne* of ancient Italy) and the crisis of social identity (in the sense of the self-awareness of their own role among the local aristocracies) which accompanied the definitive cultural Romanization of Italy until Augustus' reign (after the political Romanization of 90 BC) found a point of reference not only in the great monuments of the past but also in family tradition. The craze for creating fictitious Trojan, Greek, and Sabine lineages, a well-known phenomenon in the aristocracies of the capital and continuously emphasized by coins from the late second century BC on, overtook the *domi nobiles* of the late Republic and archaeology gives us more than one piece of evidence for this. It is sufficient here to recall only a few of the more unusual: the colossal cenotaph of C. Memmius at Ephesus[60] celebrating the *origines Troianae* of his *gens*; the enigmatic Corsini throne, which will be analysed in a special chapter;[61] the inscriptions celebrating the historical ancestors of the Tarquinian Spurinnae.[62] Between 120 BC and the Augustan era, the whole of Italy followed this antiquarian obsession, trying its best

[56] See Ch. 4.
[57] Cf. F. Coarelli, *I santuari del Lazio in età repubblicana* (Rome, 1987), 35 f.
[58] P. Zanker (ed.), *Hellenismus in Mittelitalien*, AGAW 90 (Göttingen, 1976).
[59] See Ch. 5.

[60] M. Torelli, 'Il monumento efesino di Memmio. Un capolavoro dell'ideologia nobiliare della fine della repubblica', *Scienze dell'Antichità*, 2 (1988), 403 f.
[61] See Ch. 6.
[62] M. Torelli, *Elogia Tarquiniensia* (Florence, 1975).

to find in the past the impossible confirmation of an unchanged and unchanging destiny. When we come to think about it, this is really what Andrea Lombardi was doing when he proclaimed himself an heir of the ancient Lucanians at the very moment when he surrendered with patriotic passion to the deathly embrace of the Piedmontese conqueror whom he failed to recognize disguised as a Roman.

2

RELIGIOUS ASPECTS OF EARLY ROMAN COLONIZATION

1. Introduction

THE ROLE THAT ORGANIZED RELIGION PLAYED IN the most important and influential colonization in antiquity prior to the Roman era—this being, of course, that of the Greeks of the archaic age—is well known to all ancient historians and archaeologists. The study of colonial Greek religious practices has occupied and rightly continues to occupy an important place in modern research,[1] focusing in the first place on the circumstances accompanying the act of the *apoikia*; second, on the different origins of the eventual contingents making up the colonies and their relations with each other; third, on the impact sustained by the indigenous tribes as a result of colonization; and finally, on the development therein of both urban and political forms.

It would indeed be difficult to understand the archaic flavour of the economy and society of Locri Epizephyrioi, including the rise and fall of the local aristocracy of the 'Hundred Houses', without the major Locrian sanctuaries of Persephone at Mannella and of Aphrodite at Marasà and Centocamere.[2] In the buildings and *anathemata* of these cult places, is impressed the written and unwritten history of both ruling and subordinate classes, their different mentalities and multiform interchanges, from the foundation of the colony to its decline in the Hellenistic era. Similarly, the Demeter cults of Gela and *in primis* that of Bitalemi,[3] with its well-known international con-

tacts, provide a comprehensive framework in which to place both the extraordinary rise of the Dinomenids and the late Classical and early Hellenistic fortunes of the middle and small agrarian classes, backbone of Sicily in the age of Timoleon and Agathocles.

Naturally, public and private religion, including funeral rites and customs, do not exhaust the ideological implications of colonizations of the ancient world. Without dealing with the more truly political aspects, different formulations of a symbolic, mythical, or semi-mythical nature, even when expressed in a tangible way, come together in this concept and recall or justify various stages in the process of colonization. They actually enable us to reconstruct both the *imaginaire* of the colonization and the more explicitly propagandistic attractions of the various actions which precede, accompany, or follow a colonial movement. Again recalling the better-explored aspects of Greek colonization, there is no doubt, for example, that the model for the Achaean penetration of the Italian peninsula was based on the most popular themes of the legend of Troy;[4] nor is there any doubt that the desperate attempt of Dorieus (an offspring of the Spartan Herakleidai) was conceived by the author, felt by contemporaries, and presented by the historians in the aura of Herakles' deeds.[5] Even the very act of the foundation of a colony may be based upon highly symbolic models; take, for instance, the case of the foundation of

[1] On this subject, see I. Malkin, *Religion and Colonization in Ancient Greece* (Leiden, 1987).

[2] D. Musti, 'Problemi della storia di Locri Epizefirii', *Atti Taranto* (1976), 23 f.; M. Torelli, 'I culti', ibid. 147 f.

[3] D. White, 'Demeter's Sicilian Cult as a Political Instrument', *GRBS* 5 (1964), 261 f.

[4] See M. Nafissi, in G. Pugliese Carratelli (ed.), *Magna Grecia* (Milan, 1985), 189 f.; more in general, M. Osanna, *Chorai coloniali da Taranto a Locri. Documentazione archeologica e ricostruzione storica* (Rome, 1992).

[5] On Dorieus and Herakles, see C. Jourdain-Annequin, 'Être un Grec en Sicile: le mythe d'Héraklès', in *Kokalos*, 34–5 (1988–9), 143 ff., esp. 151 f. (with previous bibliography).

Selinus, which I have dealt with elsewhere.[6] Located on two adjoining hills, that of the Acropolis and that of the Eastern Hill, Selinus aims to reproduce the topographical setting of its ultimate mother-city, Megara Nisaea. In fact all of the major sanctuaries of Megara have been accurately duplicated in Selinus, in the same location and reciprocal relationship on each of the two hills as in the double acropolis of the mother-city, placed on the hills of Caria and Alkathoos;[7] even the temple of Demeter Malophoros was erected outside the city on the banks of the river port, in perfect imitation of the namesake sanctuary of Megara, placed on the shore of the *epineion* of Nisa. And this is not the only example of its kind.

In the case of Roman colonization, however, hardly any of the ideological and symbolical aspects surface in the modern literature, which is much more concerned with the military aspects of colonial expansion. As a result we are faced, for instance, with a redundant discussion of the latter aspects (especially apparent in the commonplace comparison between town plans of colonies and *castra*) or with the vague notion of colonies as *simulacra Romae*.[8] Even the fine summary by F. Brown on Cosa, dealing with the urban history of that town, succumbs in the opening pages to a reconstruction of the foundation of that colony inspired by a 'Romulean' prototype.[9] The 'Romulean' character of colonial foundations actually reproduces a theoretical model created for understandable propaganda reasons by a relatively late literary tradition of republican times. In other words, modern historiography, in blindly following the lines traced by the antiquarians of the late Republic, has envisioned the ideological components of colonization as confined within the limits of the ritual canonized by the legend of the *conditor urbis*. Worse still, some contemporary historians have even viewed the ideal legitimization of colonial expansion—especially in the earliest period—in the logic and rhetoric of a 'passive' imperialism, precisely that which our sources yearned to credit, in depicting that colonization as

unaware and obedient soldier-colonists, unwillingly dispatched to the defence of remote frontiers.

No wonder then that very little attention has been given to the religious dimension of Roman colonization. Instead, research on such matters has usually focused on *Capitolia* and the Capitoline cult or on the possible congruences between a local religious lexicon and that of the *urbs*. Yet, as a norm, this has taken place more in the spirit of typological analysis than a serious inquiry into the history of religion. Furthermore, the reconstruction of the religious phenomena in the earlier (fifth–second centuries BC) colonization has been modelled on the situation prevalent in the latter days of the Republic and in imperial times—periods of dominant official cults, cold formalism, and external respect for tradition. On the contrary, at the time of the earliest colonization and at least until Hannibal's war, the religious mentality of both the ruling classes and especially the lower classes may be seen as an extension of the archaic one (even if somewhat modified, at times indeed in a macroscopic way) rather than as the first step toward what became the official religion between the second century BC and the first century AD.

The same goes of course for the application of the model of the *simulacrum Romae*. First it should be noted that the significance or acceptance of such a model between the first century BC and the first century AD has still to be fully explored. My attempt to reconstruct the ideological framework behind the layout of the Augustan forum of the Roman colony of Iulia Laus Corinthus[10] seems to show that in the choice and distribution of spaces destined for cult buildings, as well as for others also imbued with powerful symbolical and ideological significance (such as basilicas and political spaces), the salvaging of ancient local cults (from Artemis to Aphrodite and from Apollo to Poseidon) was a major determining factor, albeit accomplished in a hierarchy strongly impregnated with politico-religious messages of a typical Augustan flavour. The Roman colony of Corinth demonstrates the power of the concept of the *simulacrum Romae* in the ideology of Roman colonies, producing an early second-century AD image of *Roma aeterna* seated on a rocky base inscribed with the names of the Seven Hills.[11] And we know that the Seven Hills, ideally present in the little Rome of the

---

[6] As reconstructed by [F. Coarelli] and M. Torelli, *Sicilia*, Guide Archeologiche Laterza (Rome and Bari, 2nd edn. 1988), 94 f.; I gave a more detailed presentation of the same reconstruction in 'Intervento (Colloquium on "Mégara Nisaea, Mégara Hyblaea et Sélinonte")', *DHA* 9 (1983), 329 f.

[7] See L. Beschi and [D. Musti], *Pausania—Guida della Grecia, i. L'Attica* (Milan, 2nd edn. 1989), 420 f.

[8] On this concept, see [P. Gros] and M. Torelli, *Storia dell'urbanistica. Il mondo romano* (Rome and Bari, 1988), 127 f.

[9] F. Brown, *Cosa. The Making of a Roman Town* (Ann Arbor, 1980), 15 f.

[10] M. Torelli, in D. Musti and M. Torelli, *Pausania—Guida della Grecia, ii. Corinzia e Argolide* (Milan, 1986), 217 f.

[11] H. S. Robinson, 'A Statue of Rome at Corinth', *Hesperia*, 43 (1974), 470 f.

Isthmus, was still to be a crucial issue in the foundation of the *Deutera Rhome* on the Bosphorus.

However, we should question to what extent this same model influenced early colonization, assuming that the model as such was already in place and operating. The example of Cosa would seem to demonstrate that the parameters of the third-century BC were for the most part greatly different from those evident two centuries later. This is not so much because the urban reality at the base of the model (that of Rome, I mean) presented itself in a manner that appears to be radically different, but mostly because the ideological image of the *urbs*, if and when working, acted at levels that were greatly dissimilar to those of the succeeding eras.

A further complication with respect to this problem is the way in which any study undertaken in this field comes up against not only the relatively scant attention payed to those problems by historical and archaeological research, but also the scarcity and fragmentary nature of the available evidence. There are few colonial centres that have been extensively explored—among these the Latin colonies of Fregellae, Cosa, Paestum, Alba Fucens, and the *coloniae maritimae* of Ostia and Minturnae—and even in these cases the evidence concerning the foundation period, which is of utmost interest to our subject, appears only intermittently beneath the transformations and reconstructions of later times. Very often also, the cults celebrated in surviving temples remain nameless due to lack of related inscriptions or of other archaeological subsidiary evidence, such as votive materials, figured architectural decorations, or even structural or planimetrical forms, from which we might deduce elements for identifying the deity worshipped in the temple. In other cases, the evidence for a cult is represented by a sole inscription of imperial date, removed from any early archaeological context, or by a coin type—so that it is rarely possible to judge either the antiquity of the cult or the value of the evidence. In spite of these and other palpable limitations, some dates emerge from many and varied situations and offer opportunities for a more detailed consideration of the topic under discussion.

2. Antecedents and Models of Early Roman Colonization

It is, first of all, opportune to reflect briefly on the possible ancestry of the general model of coloniza-

tion adopted by Rome before the dissolution of the Latin League in 338 BC. As tradition had it, and as F. Coarelli has recently reasserted on good archaeological grounds,[12] a phase of Roman colonization existed in Latium, including important cities such as Fidenae, Cora, Signia, Pometia, Tarracina, Velitrae, and Norba, between the last decades of the monarchic age and the beginning of the Republic. The memory of this earliest colonial experiment was then so coloured by the annalistic tradition through a collection of multifarious and not always unambiguous anecdotes, that the real significance of the phenomenon has become progressively blurred and modern historical criticism has often ended up rejecting not only the colourful collection of anecdotes, but also the general reliability of the tradition itself. It is impossible to go into great detail about the subject here and I shall limit myself to examining a few elements useful to a better understanding of this important phenomenon, so as to verify the eventual relationship between the more distant period and the theme at the centre of our discussion.

The fundamental mistake committed by modern hypercritical historians lies in conceptualizing the archaic phenomenon in the same terms, both sociopolitical and material, as those under which fourth- and third-century colonization was brought about. The discovery of the *Lapis Satricanus*, apart from the controversial literal meaning of the text,[13] has shown that in this very early colonization a principal role was played by warlike groups—the *suodales* of the Satricum inscription—under the command of leading figures —*Poplios Valesios* in the *Lapis Satricanus*—of tyrannical type, be these Caelius or Aulus Vibennae, Servius Tullius, both the Tarquinii, the Priscus or the Superbus, or Valerius Publicola.[14] I am inclined to believe, in the wake of Coarelli's brilliant reasoning,[15] that pre-Volscian Satricum must be identified as Suessa Pometia, Satricum being the name given to it by the Volscian conquerors (Strabo duly registers the fall of

---

[12] F. Coarelli, *Lazio*, Guide Archeologiche Laterza (Rome and Bari, 2nd edn. 1985), 244 f.

[13] See the excellent *editio princeps* of this crucial document by C. M. Stibbe (ed.), *Lapis Satricanus. Archaeological, Epigraphical, Linguistic and Historical Aspects of the New Inscription from Satricum* (The Hague, 1980).

[14] A more detailed description of the dynamics of such phenomena is in M. Torelli, 'Dalle aristocrazie gentilizie alla nascita della plebe', in A. Momigliano and A. Schiavone (eds.), *Storia di Roma*, i (Turin, 1988), 241 f.

[15] F. Coarelli, 'Roma, i Volsci e il Lazio antico', in F.-H. Massa Pairault, *Crise et transformations des sociétés archaïques de l'Italie antique au Vème siècle av. J.-Chr.* (Rome, 1990), 135 f.; rather different views are to be found in the collective volume *I Volsci*, published in the series Archeologia laziale II: I (1992).

Pometia at the hand of the Volsci).[16] Like the majority of scholars who have dealt with the *Lapis Satricanus*, we may consider the *Poplios Valesios* of the inscription as one and the same as the notorious figure of Publicola, in every respect a king manqué.[17] The occupation of the city of Pometia by the second Tarquinius and the subsequent reoccupation recorded by Livy[18] and Dionysius,[19] share the same socio-political background of the age, dominated by gentilitial power, by individual attempts at tyrannical rule, and by the movement of *gentes*,[20] well attested in Latium between the end of the sixth and the beginning of the fifth century BC. In particular, such a transfer of entire gentilitial clans is well attested by the arrival in Rome of the Claudii from Sabina in 495 BC[21] and probably by that of the Veturii from Praeneste in 499 BC,[22] not to speak of the well-known *nomina Tusca* of the earliest part of the Roman consular list.[23]

It is impossible to separate the archaic colonization of Latium from the meaning of the word *suodales* (with the significant adjective *Mamartei*, in my opinion to be understood as *Martii*, *Martiales*), crucial in the Satrican text. We are dealing with *condottieri* (an appropriate term introduced by J. Heurgon)[24] surrounded by ἑταῖροι, noble or less noble *suodales*, companions of warlike enterprises and lately voted to the funerary cult of one of these *condottieri*, in this case P. Valerius, known in the annalistic tradition with the cognomen of Publicola[25] and belonging to a Sabine *gens* which was, not by chance, specifically connected with a famous chthonian (and funerary) sanctuary—the Tarentum in Rome. In this connection we might compare such a cult with the genesis of the *sodales Augustales*, according to a famous text of Tacitus[26] and with the *ludi Taurei*[27]

and the cults performed at the gentilitial sanctuary known as *Tarentum*,[28] from which we may readily conclude that the archaic *sodalitas* was a social institution, possibly recognized as such and cemented by a special religious tie, which may have been in some way similar to the warlike Germanic companies described in Tacitus' *Germania*[29] and produced by an aristocratic world comparable to archaic Roman society. It is, furthermore, useful to remember that in the *Tabulae Lugdunenses* the emperor Claudius[30]—whose political lexicon appears not only refined, but also substantially supported by erudite research—calls Servius Tullius *sodalis fidelissimus* of Caelius Vibenna. On the other side, the annalistic tradition (Piso?) handed down to us by Plutarch[31] actually remembers the foundation of a 'colony' by Publicola, named Sigliuria, most likely identical with Dionysius' Σιγνούριον,[32] a city conquered by Porsenna and to be identified with Signia, significantly not far from Suessa Pometia-Satricum. Yet another annalistic tradition accepted by Livy[33] registers the 'defection' of the 'colony' of Suessa Pometia (again, significantly together with the neighbouring Cora) in 502 BC, immediately after the death of Publicola (503 BC), and the parallel 'reconquest' of Satricum from the Volsci by the consul Servilius in 495 BC.[34]

If this was the socio-economic nature of archaic colonization, then the political forms of the phenomenon are to be sought in the still rather nebulous reality of the oldest Latin League. Indeed, many of these colonies are labelled as 'Roman' by the sources, and as such they should be considered in the light of the formulation of the first Romano-Carthaginian treaty.[35] This document, which I consider authentic and datable to the beginning of the Republic, presupposes a definite Roman supremacy over the Latin ὑπήκοοι.

[16] Strabo 5. 231.

[17] On this figure, see the interesting perspectives put forward by A. Mastrocinque, *Lucio Giunio Bruto. Ricerche di storia, religione e diritto sulle origini della repubblica privata* (Trento, 1988), 103 f. (with bibliography).

[18] Liv. 2. 17. 1.   [19] Dion. Hal. 6. 29.   [20] See n. 14.

[21] Main annalistic source: Dion.Hal. 2. 46 (cf. Suet. *Tib.* 1; Virg. *Aen.* 7. 707 f.); other ancient literature in *RE* III 2 (1899), c.2662 f.

[22] M. Torelli, 'L'iscrizione latina sulla coppa argentea della tomba Bernardini', *DArch* 1 (1967), 38 f. (= *La società etrusca. L'età arcaica, l'età classica* (Rome, 1987), 131 f.).

[23] On the ethnic aspects of early Roman *gentes*, see C. Ampolo, 'I gruppi etnici in Roma arcaica: posizione del problema e fonti', in *Gli Etruschi e Roma*, Acts of Conference; Rome, 1979 (Rome, 1991), 45 f.

[24] This term has been widely used by this historian: see e.g. J. Heurgon, *Rome et la Méditerranée occidentale jusqu'aux guerres puniques* (Paris, 1993), 244 f.

[25] See A. Mastrocinque, 'Il "cognomen" Publicola', *PP* (1984), 217 f.

[26] Tac. *Ann.* 1. 54; cf. *Hist.* 1. 95.

[27] Varro L. L 5. 154; Fest. 441–8 L; Serv. *Aen.* 2. 140; see J.-P. Thuillier, *Les Jeux athlétiques dans la civilisation étrusque* (Rome, 1985), 95, 448.

[28] Cf. F. Coarelli, 'Il Campo Marzio occidentale. Storia e topografia', *MEFRA* 89 (1977), 807 f.; E. LaRocca, *La riva a mezzaluna. Culti, agoni, monumenti funerari presso il Tevere nel Campo Marzio occidentale* (Rome, 1984), 3 f.

[29] Tac. *Germ.* 13 f. This view has been extensively developed by H. S. Versnel, in Stibbe (ed.), *Lapis Satricanus*, 108 f.

[30] *CIL* XIII 1668 = *ILs*; cf. Tac. *Ann.* 11. 24.

[31] Plut. *Pobl.* 16; cf. S. Boscherini, 'Una fonte annalistica su Valerio Publicola', in *Gli storiografi latini tramandati in frammenti*, Studi Urbinati di Storia, Filosofia e Letteratura, 49 (1975), 141 f.

[32] Dion. Hal. 3. 61.   [33] Liv. 2. 16. 8.

[34] Ibid. 24 f.; Dion. Hal. 6. 29.

[35] Bibliography on this subject is simply immense; see however A. Aymard, 'Les Deux Premiers Traités entre Rome et Carthage', *REA* 59 (1957), 277 f.; F. Hampl, 'Das Problem der Datierung der ersten Verträge zwischen Rom und Karthago', *RhM* 101 (1958), 58 f.; F. Cassola, *I gruppi politici romani nel III sec.a.C.* (Trieste, 1962), 84 f. (with extensive bibliography); lastly, D. Timpe, 'Das Kriegsmonopol der römischen Staates', in W. Eder (ed.), *Staat und Staatlichkeit in der frühen römischen Republik* (Stuttgart, 1990), 381 f.

Actually, I am convinced that these episodes of early colonization, guided by *condottieri*, supported by *suodales* and in fact brought about *per clientelas* (thence their ephemeral nature, misunderstood by modern hypercriticism), were conceived of as issuing from an ethnic-religious context. Evidence for this can be drawn from the uncertainty between the *Latinitas* and *Romanitas* of some of the archaic colonies. This is the case, for instance, with Velitrae, which in Dionysius of Halicarnassus[36] in the late sixth century BC presents as a member of the Latin League, whereas later in Livy,[37] in Plutarch,[38] and again in Dionysius[39] the same town is taken to be a Roman colony dating from the beginning of the fifth century BC. And we do not lack archaeological evidence (such as architectural terracottas and some diagnostic pottery) to support the idea of Roman presence in many of the early sites of Latium, like Norba, Satricum, and Signa, before the Volscian invasion. A more convincing argument, however, can be drawn from the perfect similarity between this earliest Roman expansion and the other archaic model of colonization in the Italian peninsula, absolutely contemporary with this—the second Etruscan colonization of the Po valley.

The strong analogies between the two phenomena have never been taken into serious account and it is worthwhile exploring this Etruscan movement towards the lands of the basin of the river Po, rich in water (frequently marshy) and in grain, comparable to the Pomptine marshes where we see the major development of the Latin colonization of the late sixth / early fifth century BC. Both trends of expansion reveal a strong interest in grain-producing lands, i.e. an intense need for grain due to the astonishing expansion of the great cities in the sixth century BC.[40] Around 520 BC,[41] or perhaps even a few decades earlier, Etruria launched a widespread colonization of the eastern section of the Po valley, the second one after the splendours of the Villanovan colonization. The inspiration for this initiative appears to have come from the League of the *XII populi Etruriae*, whose reunion sanctuary was the Fanum Voltumnae near Volsinii.[42] The reproduction in the Po area of the original system of the religious federation of the Twelve Cities at the Fanum Voltumnae in Volsinii is confirmed by various sources and rendered even clearer by the recent discoveries around Mantua.[43] These reveal the origin of the event, since the capital city of the Etruscan part of the Po valley received the same name—*Felsna i.e. Felsina, later Bononia—as the federal centre in Etruria proper, Volsinii—*Velzna*.[44] Yet the few fragments of local historical tradition, all conceivably concerning Mantua and handed down to us because of Vergil's origins,[45] emphasize the role carried out in the foundation by a specific town of Etruria, Perusia, and of its *rex*, Ocnus;[46] and now the discovery of the possible names of the two gods of the acropolis temples of Volaterrae,[47] *Apa* the 'Father', and *Ati*, the 'Mother', appears to give other clues to the understanding of a well-known passage of Servius relating the dedication of all northern Etruscan colonies to Dis Pater.[48] We can conclude that the Po valley saw two different arrivals of Etruscan colonists from the south. The earliest Etruscan colonization of the Po valley, dating still within the early Iron Age, around the ninth century BC, is marked by the initiative of Tarquinia, as both literary sources and archaeological evidence indicate,[49] and is likely to have had a less definite political character, in keeping with with the very primitive stage of political development reached in the motherland at that time. The second wave of colonization was led instead by the towns of the hinterland, from Perusia to Volaterrae, and had the more definite character of a movement directed by *gentes*, by familial clans. It had the formal aim of reproducing the urban features achieved by mother cities at that time within a religious and political structure of a league similar to that which developed in historical times in the south around Volsinii.

---

[36] Dion. Hal. 5. 61. [37] Liv. 2. 31. 4 and 34. 6.

[38] Plut. *Coriol.* 12. [39] Dion. Hal. 7. 12 f.

[40] See [Gros] and Torelli, *Storia dell'urbanistica. Il mondo romano*, 81 f.

[41] M. Torelli, *Storia degli Etruschi* (Rome and Bari, 1981), 189 f.

[42] On the League, its meaning and composition, see M. Torelli, 'I "duodecim populi Etruriae"', *Annali della Fondazione C.Faina*, 2 (1985), 37 f. (= *La società etrusca*, 99 f.).

[43] L. Malnati and V. Manfredi, *Gli Etruschi in Val Padana* (Milan, 1991), 229 f.

[44] Cf. Plin. *NH* 3. 151.

[45] Discussion and bibliography by P. Tozzi, in *Enciclopedia Virgiliana* i. 164 f., s.v. Andes.

[46] Virg. *Aen.* 10. 198 f.; Serv. auct. *Aen.* 10. 198; cf. Sil. It. 5. 7.

[47] M. Bonamici, 'L'acropoli di Volterra: primi risultati della campagna 1987', in *Volterra '88. Un progetto*, Acts of Conference; Volterra, 1988 (Volterra, 1988), 113 f.

[48] Cf. Schol. Veron. Virg. *Aen.* 10. 198 (from Caecina): 'Tarchon cum exercitu Appenninum transgressus primum oppidum constituit, quod tum Mantuam nominavit, voca[tumque] Tusca lingua a Dite patre est nomen. Deinde undecim dedicavit Diti patri . . . ibi constituit annum et item locum consecravit quod duodecim oppida condere . . . nem.'

[49] Verrius Flaccus, *Rerum Etruscarum I*, fr. 1P; Strab. 5. 219; cf. Torelli, *Storia degli Etruschi*, 41 f.

The model followed by early Roman colonization was then analogous to that developed by late Archaic Etruria; similarly, from what happened at Capua, the main city of Campanian Etruria (the second zone of the peninsula which attracted Etruscan colonial movement) we may better understand the sources of inspiration for Roman colonial politics of that time and of the following century. The double date for the foundation of Capua, 800 BC in Velleius[50] and 471 BC in Cato,[51] can only be derived from the same phenomenon of double colonization; a protohistorical one led by south Etruscan groups in the ninth century BC, and a late Archaic one sponsored by the Volsinian League around 520 BC, but in a different historical and political, as well as geographical context. Campanian Etruria was never organized on a dodecapolis scheme; the second 'foundation' of Capua in 471 BC most likely represents the initiative of a single town of Etruria proper (I wonder if we could not give it to Veii, apparently the mover in the ninth-century BC colonization), totally independent of the Volsinian League; we know from Livy[52] how difficult relations were between the anomalous Veii and the federal council in the fifth century. Etruscan policy of double colonization in the late sixth century BC, one enacted in the federal context and the other organized by a single *polis*, may, I believe, represent, together with contemporary Romano-Latin practice, the model to which Roman late fifth / early fourth-century colonial policy was to conform, until the dissolution of the Latin League in 338 BC. However, Roman colonial policy was naturally conditioned by the actual hegemony exerted by Rome on the *socii Latini*, a circumstance that varied considerably all through the fifth and the early fourth century BC, and in light of this we should also reconsider all the different oscillations of our sources in defining the status of many colonial cities, which are sometimes called a Latin colony, sometimes a Roman colony, and sometimes even an independent town.

Another important example of such gentilitial 'colonies' of these first, unrestful years of the Roman Republic might be seen in the foundation of the *colonia Latina* of Vitellia. We have mention of it in Livy's description of the conquests made in 493 BC by the renegade Q. Marcius Coriolanus as a chieftain of the Volscians,[53] a very important mention for the correct location of the town. Coriolanus, after the conquest of Satricum, Corioli, Lavinium, and other minor sites, moves from the Pomptine plains to the Via Latina through lateral mountain trails, 'in Latinam viam transversis tramitibus transgressus', and seizes, in a row, the towns of Corbio, Vitellia (*codd*. Vetelia), Trebium, Labici, and Pedum, whence he reaches Bola[54] and finally the Fossae Cluiliae on the outskirts of Rome. Given the location of Vitellia on the Via Latina and its position in the Livian itinerary of Coriolanus before the known sites of Trebiae (Trebium), now Trevi nel Lazio, Labici (modern Monte Compatri), and Pedum, near Praeneste, we may propose, here for the first time, its identification with the anonymous, extensive town near Artena excavated by the Belgian Academy in Rome (Fig. 4).[55] The site dates mainly to the early fourth century BC, but, like Norba,[56] has undeniable traces of an earlier occupation dating from the beginning of the fifth century. Its political and urban history is strikingly similar to that of Norba (Fig. 5), a colony founded in 492 BC, but possibly destroyed soon after by the incoming Volscians[57] and then reconstructed only after the Roman reconquest of Circeii (393 BC) and Satricum (385 BC). But Vitellia offers a more interesting history for the religious implications of its origins, according to our sources connected with the name of a very archaic *numen* and of an old *gens*. In fact Suetonius, referring to an erudite book by the orator and rhetorician Q. Eulogius who lived in the late Augustan age, gives us a detailed account of the ancestry of the emperor Vitellius:

Vitellios Fauno Aboriginum rege et Vitellia, quae multis locis pro numine coleretur, ortos toto Latio imperasse; horum residuam stirpem ex Sabinis transisse Romam atque inter patricios adlectam; indicia stirpis mansisse diu viam Vitelliam ab Ianiculo ad mare usque, item coloniam eiusdem nominis, quam gentili copia adversus Aequiculos tutandam olim depoposcissent; tempore deinde Samnitici belli praesidio

---

[54] Plut. *Coriol.* 28, where we find mention of Tolerium, Labici, Pedum, and finally Bola and the Fossae Cluiliae (ibid. 29 f.); Dion. Hal. 8. 17. 3–22. 1, drawing from another source with strong religious interests and ideological aims (Marcius camps at the Fossae Cluiliae, moving against Rome from Lavinium), builds up an impossible itinerary, mentioning in a row Circei (Monte Circeo, in the extreme south-west area of Latium Adiectum), Bola (very close to, or even located on, the Alban Hills), Labici, Pedum (both connected with Praeneste and Tibur), Corbio (unknown site, but placed at the beginning of the list of the Via Latina towns in Livy), Corioli (location unknown, but between Aricia and Ardea), Bovillae (very close to Rome on the Alban Hills).

[55] Good survey of these excavations in *La Civita di Artena—Scavi belgi 1979–1989*, Catalogue of the Exhibition; Artena, Rome, and Louvain-la-neuve, 1989–90 (Rome, 1989). [56] Coarelli, *Lazio*, 265 f.

[57] [Gros] and Torelli, *Storia dell'urbanistica. Il mondo romano*, 134 f.

---

[50] Vell. Pat. 1. 7. 2.   [51] Cato, fr. 69P.
[52] Liv. 5. 1 ff.   [53] Liv. 2. 39. 4.

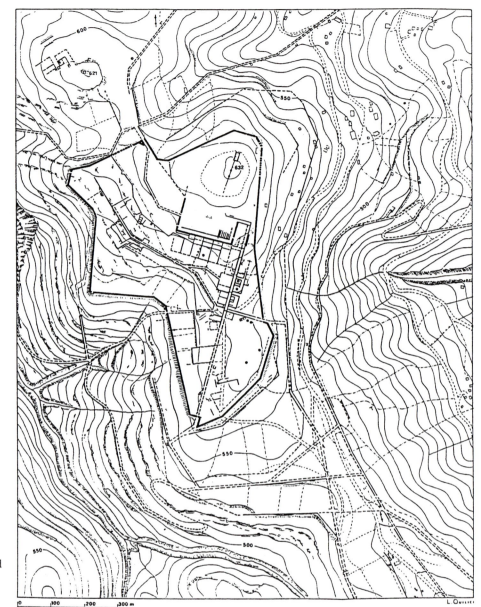

Fig. 4. Plan of the unidentified mid-republican town near Artena (after *La Civita di Artena*).

in Apuliam misso quosdam ex Vitellis subsedisse Nuceriae eorumque progeniem longo post intervallo repetisse urbem et ordinem senatorium.[58]

3. Early Republican Colonization: Ardea, Veii, Ostia

After these late archaic episodes of colonization *per clientelas* and before 338 BC, we have to place three noteworthy episodes within the context of our discourse. The first is the Latin colonization of Ardea in 442 BC,[59]

a town of the old Latin group of the Rutuli, but recently conquered by the Volscian newcomers. The political and ideological importance of the event is now matched archaeologically by the discovery of the great temple of Colle del Noce (Fig. 6), built *ex-novo* immediately after the colonial settlement,[60] a discovery to add to those already made in the 1930s, from the temple of Juno to the necropolis with its extraordinary painted tomb.[61] The event has a central position in the age

---

[58] Suet. *Vitell.* 1.   [59] Liv. 4. 9 f.

[60] L. Crescenzi and E. Tortorici, in *Archeologia Laziale*, 5 (Rome, 1983), 38 f.

[61] A convenient summary of the archaeological evidence of the city of Ardea is now assembled by C. Morselli and E. Tortorici, *Ardea (Forma Italiae*, 1. 16) (Rome, 1980).

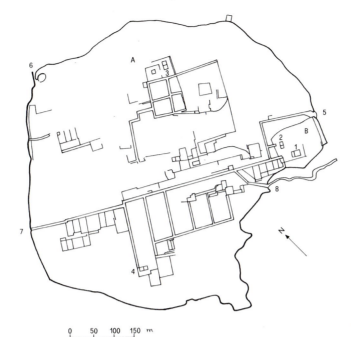

A - Acropoli maggiore
B - Acropoli minore
1 - Tempio maggiore
2 - Tempio minore
3 - Tempio di Diana
4 - Tempio di Giunone Lucina
5 - 8 Porte urbiche
▭ Strade

0   50   100   150 m

Fig. 5. Plan of the Latin colony of Norba (drawing A. Trapassi).

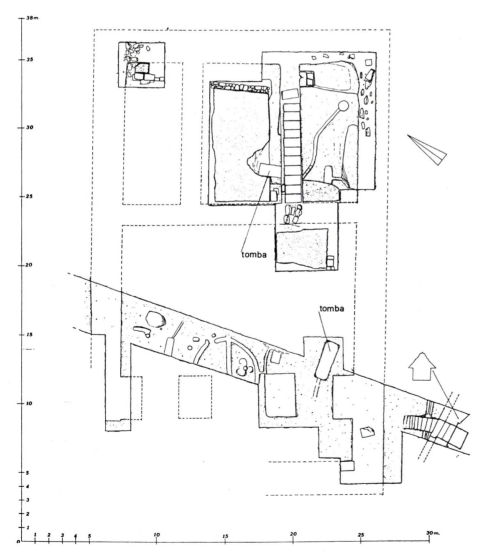

tomba

tomba

Fig. 6. Ardea, plan of the temple of Colle del Noce (after *Archeologia Laziale*).

of fifth-century crisis. Isolated as it is in this sort of intermediate period which the central decades of the fifth century represent for the question we are dealing with, the choice of *Latinitas* as the colonial formula for Ardea may be explained by the function that the city carried out (and continued to carry out) as town-in-charge with control of the Lavinian Aphrodision, well documented by a celebrated passage in Strabo,[62] and therefore in control of inter-Latin *connubia*, as I have tried to demonstrate elsewhere.[63] As a group, the colonists included a strong contingent of native Rutuli, themselves of old Latin stock, who largely outnumbered the true Latins in the enrolment, as Livy asserts,[64] thus proving also the military, anti-Volscian character of the settlement. In this regard, it is difficult to separate the foundation of Ardea from the other isolated fifth-century (418 BC) foundation of a Latin colony, that of Labici,[65] near the modern town of Montecompatri, since it guarded the Algidus pass, the gate into the Latin territory for the dangerous Aequians.

The second episode is represented by the second foundation of a Latin colony at Cercei in 393 BC,[66] after the (perhaps wrongly questioned) settlement of the early republican period, which had been destroyed by Coriolanus exactly one century before, in 493 BC.[67] While in the case of Ardea the colonized territory had an undoubted (if disputed) proximity to Latin lands, the new colony of Cercei arose right in the middle of Volscian territory, though perhaps the territory was still considered an original Latin area, only looted a century before by the incoming Volscians. If not in 393 BC at Cercei (still an old Latin town), certainly ten years later the foundation of Sutri and Nepet in land never in Latin hands signified an experiment with a new formula, which would then dominate the whole of the fourth and most of the third century BC. As is well known, the formula consisted of sending considerable contingents of colonists of Roman or Latin origin into conquered territories far from the Latin area and giving them the status of Latin citizens, with the task of self-sustenance and self-defence. In 383 BC this Latin formula was in fact used to colonize and garrison the *claustra Etruriae* at Sutrium and Nepet[68] well beyond the original limits (even those of the Old Latium of the late sixth century BC) of the Latin ancestral land. It is however significant that, mainly due to its religious importance, Ardea was the sole experiment of that kind conducted as a 'federal' enterprise: from that time on, until the dissolution of the Latin League, we have no more Latin colonies.

The model experienced at Sutrium and Nepet became the rule after 338 BC, with a long list of foundations, Cales in 334,[69] Fregellae in 328,[70] and Luceria in 314 BC,[71] to name just some of the earliest ones. So, the only certain example of the mid-fifth century, the colony of Ardea, clearly still belongs to the early practice—the reconquest of land traditionally in Latin possession with all its religious implications. It is only at the very beginning of the fourth century that it is possible to see a real turning point in the colonial policy hitherto adopted by Rome and by the Latin allies—and it is not by chance that it all happens after the conquest of Veii, which truly represents a big qualitative leap in the opening phase of Roman imperialism, and the third important episode in our short history of Roman colonization.

The conquest of Veii was not the mere victory of one city over another, which gave the winner a battle booty and the right to impose terms on the defeated town: it was a total subjugation, which implied the elimination of the political, economic, and military power of a totally different ethnic group (from now on, in spite of the enfranchisement of the *desertores* into the four new tribes created after the conquest of the town,[72] only Latin is spoken in Veii), the substitution of an Etruscan *polis* by a Roman city. The episode in this regard matches strikingly similar conquests of a few decades before, the Campanian take-over of Etruscan Capua (and of the other Etruscan towns in the Campanian plain) in 425 BC,[73] the Lucanian conquest of the Greek city of Poseidonia around the same time,[74] and the Samnite conquest of the oldest Greek colony of Italy, Cumae,[75] which may be counted among the major events of the great unrest that changed the old, protohistoric order of the peninsula.[76] Up to now two great colonial powers, the Greeks with their

---

[62]   Strab. 5. 232.

[63]   See M. Torelli, *Lavinio e Roma. Riti iniziatici e matrimonio fra archeologia e storia* (Rome, 1984), 216 f.

[64]   Liv. 4. 11. 4.   [65]   Liv. 4. 47. 6, 49. 6; Diod. Sic. 13. 6. 8.

[66]   Diod. Sic. 14. 102; cf. Liv. 6. 12. 6.   [67]   Dion. Hal. 8. 14. 1.

[68]   Liv. 6. 3. 2, 21. 4; 9. 31. 1; Diod. Sic. 14. 117; Vell. 1. 14. 2.

[69]   Liv. 8. 16. 14; Vell. 1. 14. 3.

[70]   Liv. 8. 23. 6, cf. 9. 28. 3; Diod. Sic. 19. 101.

[71]   Liv. 9. 26. 3; cf. Diod. Sic. 19. 72; Vell. 1. 14. 4.

[72]   Liv. 6. 5. 8.   [73]   Liv. 4. 37. 1 f.

[74]   Liv. 4. 44. 12; Diod. Sic. 12. 76. 5; Dion. Hal. 15. 6.

[75]   See M. Torelli, 'Le popolazioni dell'Italia antica: società e forme del potere', in Schiavone and Momigliano (eds.), *Storia di Roma*, i. 53 f.

[76]   On this theme see the Acts of the Colloquium *Le Vème Siècle et la crise des sociétés archaïques de la peninsule* (Rome, 1992).

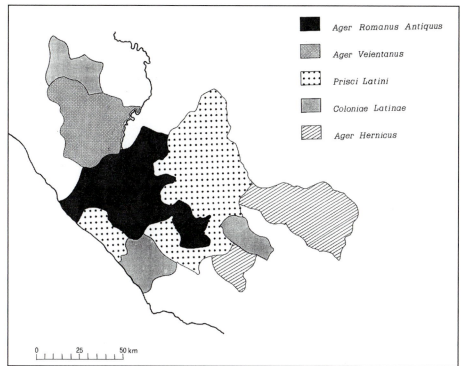

Ager Romanus Antiquus

Ager Veientanus

Prisci Latini

Coloniae Latinae

Ager Hernicus

0 25 50 km

Fig. 7. Map of the *ager Romanus* and territory of the allied Latins after the conquest of Veii (drawing A. Trapassi).

colonization between the eighth and the sixth century BC and the Etruscans with their colonizations of the ninth and the sixth centuries, had dominated the scenario of Italy and kept under control the other ethnic groups of the peninsula, the small, but warlike tribe of the Latins and the numerous Sabellian tribes scattered in the mountain hinterland. The fatal decades around the turn of the fifth to the fourth century BC saw the rapid decline of the old order and the surfacing of new political, economic, and social conditions, that were about to prepare for the rise of Rome.

The annexation of Veii, as I have repeatedly argued elsewhere,[77] can be regarded as one of the main causes —if not the main cause—for the gigantic expansion of Rome in the subsequent 150 years. The Roman conquest of Italy ought to be considered the achievement of two joined towns, of Rome and Veii, and the chief socio-economic device that allowed the solution of the patricio-plebeian conflict, thanks to the enormous amount of fresh land now in the possession of Rome. Because of this land, the extension of the *ager Romanus* rose to *c.* 2,200 km², a figure that it is useful to compare to the 2,650 km² of the remainder of the Latin cities

(Fig. 7). The conquest of Veii, with its retinue of Trojan-like legends investigated by J. Gagè,[78] M. Hubaux,[79] and M. Sordi,[80] for the first time allows the ideological–propagandistic dimension of colonization to emerge in a perceptible manner, even in the field of archaeology. Until then, the bitter struggle against the Volscians and the Aequians and the foundation of colonies at Signia, Setia, and Norba had acquired the flavour, historically justified, of a reconquest. Those territories had been Latin and it was the duty of every Latin to recover them. So there had been no need to legitimize these three colonies, as they could be in fact considered a 'return'. Unfortunately the archaeological evidence is not conspicuous in these instances, but it would be interesting to look for continuity and discontinuity in cult places elsewhere. The sole possible instance is the above-mentioned temple of Colle del Noce at Ardea, which seems to have been built entirely in connection with the settlement of the Latin colony of 442 BC. However, the record of the published archaeological material from this excavation is far from complete, and

[77] Cf. M. Torelli, 'Veio e la colonizzazione plebea', in M. Cristofani (ed.), *Civiltà degli Etruschi*, Catalogue of the Exhibition; Florence, 1985 (Milan, 1985), 314; id., 'Aspetti della società romana tra metà del IV e metà del III sec.a.C. La documentazione archeologica', *AIIN* 36 (1989), 19 f.

[78] J. Gagè, *Apollon romain. Essai sur le culte d'Apollon et le développement du 'ritus Graecus' à Rome des origines à Auguste* (Rome, 1955).

[79] J. Hubaux, *Rome et Véies, recherches sur la chronologie légendaire du Moyen Age romain* (Liège, 1958).

[80] M. Sordi, *I rapporti romano-ceriti e l'origine della 'civitas sine suffragio'* (Rome, 1960).

we have no secure evidence on which to assert that this temple was really only built for the first time at the moment of the Roman conquest; as I have noted,[81] the temple was erected so as carefully to include in its perimeter the remants of a prehistoric hut, a circumstance which has strong parallels with the sixth-century BC temple of Mater Matuta of Satricum[82] and which might suggest the existence of an intermediate building phase between the ninth–seventh-century BC hut and the mid-fifth-century BC massive temple. It is therefore wiser to wait until the authors of this important discovery provide us with a detailed report of the find.

Coming back to our analysis, we may start by observing that in Veii the presence of Roman colonists is fairly well attested in the three major sanctuaries—that of *Menerva*/Minerva at Portonaccio,[83] that of *Vei*/Ceres at Campetti,[84] and that of *Uni*/Juno Regina at Comunità[85]—with rites and cult forms substantially continuing the former Etruscan ones. The double Latin dedications to Ceres at Campetti and to Minerva at Portonaccio given by a *Tolonios*/Tolumnius,[86] patently a former client of the great royal family of Veii, the *Tulumnes*/Tolumnii,[87] is concrete proof both of the inclusion of the Veientan *desertores*, as stated by Livy,[88] in the four new tribes created to populate the conquered territory, and of the continuity of all the sanctuaries of the town,[89] including the recently excavated shrine of *Menerva* near the Caere Gate.[90] Yet, a clear sign of the new situation is given by the widespread appearance, in almost all the major sanctuaries of Veii, of the famous terracotta statuettes representing Aeneas and Anchises (Pl. 1):[91] these simple offerings bear

Plate 1. Rome, Museum of the Villa Giulia. Aeneas carrying his father Anchises: statuette from the Roman phase of the sanctuary of Portonaccio (courtesy of the Museo di Villa Giulia).

---

[81] M. Torelli, 'I culti', *Archeologia laziale*, 6 (Rome, 1984), 412 f.

[82] C. M. Stibbe, in *Archeologia laziale*, 3 (Rome, 1980), 172 f.; cf. G. Colonna, in *Archeologia laziale*, 6. 396 f.

[83] G. Colonna, 'Note preliminari sui culti di Portonaccio a Veio', *ScAnt*, 1 (1987), 419 f.

[84] A. Comella and G. Stefani, *Materiali votivi del santuario di Campetti a Veio, Scavi 1947 e 1969*, Corpus delle stipi votive in Italia, 7: 2 (Rome, 1990).

[85] Cf. M. Torelli, 'Veio, la città, l'arx e il culto di Giunone Regina', in *Miscellanea archeologica Tobias Dohrn dedicata* (Rome, 1982), 117 f. (= *La società etrusca*, 117 f.).   [86] *ILLRP* 64, 237.

[87] Liv. 4. 17–20; see also D. Briquel, 'Entre Rome et Véies: le destin de la "gens Tolumnia"', in *Miscellanea etrusca e italica in onore di M. Pallottino* (= *AClass* 43, 1991), i. 193 f.   [88] Liv. 6. 5. 8.

[89] A good survey by J. B. Ward Perkins, 'Veii: The Historical Topography of the Ancient City', *PBSR* 29 (1961), 25 f.

[90] A description of the votive deposit and of the structures, which include a cistern, by I. Pohl and M. Torelli, in *NSA* (1973), 41 f.

[91] L. Vagnetti, *Il deposito votivo di Campetti a Veio* (Florence, 1971), 88, pl. 48 (with my review in *DArch* 7 (1973), 396 f.); M. Torelli, 'Veio e la colonizzazione plebea', in Cristofani (ed.), *Civiltà degli Etruschi*, 314 f.

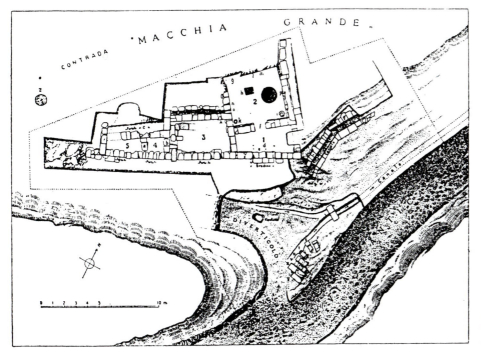

Fig. 8. Plan of the Macchia Grande sanctuary at Veii (after *Notizie degli Scavi*).

witness that the Trojan myth, which fed the epic annalistic narrative of the ten-year siege,[92] also substantiated the plebeian propaganda message, crediting Veii as a new Rome after the burning of the second Troy at the hands of the Celtic hordes.[93] It is of little importance that this message became an element of propaganda used by both the patrician and the plebian faction in the heated political debate concerning the reconstruction of Rome after the Gallic fire; it is more important to emphasize that the colonization of Veii was brought about in the mythical framework of the Trojan legend and that the awareness of such an ideological stimulus spread to the lowest levels of society, to which we must ascribe the dedicators of the statuettes. The Trojan legend acted not only as an ideological stimulus but indeed as a self-representation of the new condition of the colonist. As we shall soon see, the myth of Troy had a specific function from the earliest stages of Roman expansion, long before Pyrrhus, as Perret thought,[94] or the extremely refined mythical propaganda played by the Attalids.[95] It could even work as a reverse message,

as it appears for example just a few years later than the Veii statuettes, in 340–330 BC, in the mirror-like opposition on the walls of the François Tomb, where the Greek conceals the Etruscan and the Trojan the Roman.[96]

Yet another cult complex in Veii, that of Macchia Grande (Fig. 8), presents some interesting elements, inasmuch as it does not seem to have been the site of a previous, Etruscan cult. In an area, apparently *sub divo*, a group of six inscribed and two not-inscribed altars[97] marked a row of divine presences. The chronology of the earliest inscriptions does not go back further than the end of the third century BC, but it cannot be doubted that the creation of the sacred area is connected with the earliest Roman presence in the town. The inscriptions are the following:

> *dis deabus* (Fig. 9)
> *Victorie* (Fig. 10)
> *[M]inerv<i>a* (Fig. 11)
> *Apoline* (Fig. 12)
> *Ive [L]ib(e)rt(ati)* (Fig. 13).

If one dedication includes all the gods (*dis deabus*), the other altars commemorate Olympian deities, such

[92] Hubaux, *Rome et Véies*, 121 f.; Sordi, *I rapporti romano-ceriti*, 8 f.

[93] M. Torelli, 'Il sacco gallico di Roma', in *I Galli e l'Italia*, Catalogue of the Exhibition; Rome 1978 (Rome, 1978), 226 f.

[94] J. Perret, *Les Origines de la légende troyenne de Rome* (Paris, 1942).

[95] An outstanding example is the case of the *stylopinakia* at Cyzicus thoroughly explored by F.-H. Massa Pairault, 'Il problema degli *stylopinakia* del tempio di Apollonis a Cizico. Alcune considerazioni', in *Annali della Facoltà di Lettere e Filosofia di Perugia—Studi Classici*, 19 (1982), 149 f.

[96] See the analysis by F. Coarelli, 'Le pitture della tomba François di Vulci. Una proposta di lettura', *DArch* NS 3 (1983), 43 f.

[97] *ILLRP* 27–31 = *CIL* I², 2628–32.

(a)

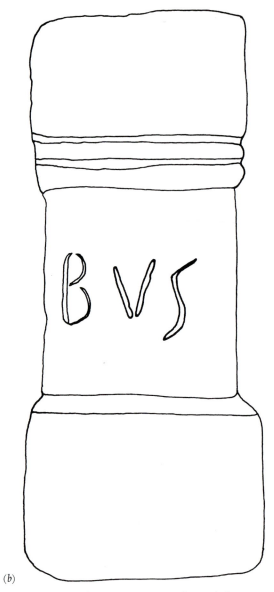

(b)

Fig. 9. Macchia Grande sanctuary at Veii, altar with the dedication *dis deab | <b>us* written on two faces (*a*, *b*) (drawing A. Trapassi).

as Apollo, Minerva, and other late arrivals in the Roman pantheon, in particular Victoria (whose cult in Rome dates from 295 BC) and Jupiter Libertas. The latter is of special interest, because the Roman sanctuary was

in Aventino. As Gilbert[98] almost a hundred years ago concluded from the text of the *Res Gestae divi Augusti*, this Roman temple had a close topographical connection with those of Minerva and Juno Regina. The first of these two temples was apparently built after an *evocatio* from Falerii,[99] and the second is safely a Camillan foundation after the *evocatio* from Veii.[100]

[98] O. Gilbert, *Geschichte und Topographie der Stadt Rom im Altertum*, iii (Leipzig, 1890), 78, 444 f.   [99] Torelli, *Lavinio e Roma*, 52 f.
[100] Liv. 5. 22. 6–7, 23. 7, 31. 3; Dion. Hal. 13. 3; Plut. *Cam.* 6; Val. Max.1. 8. 3.

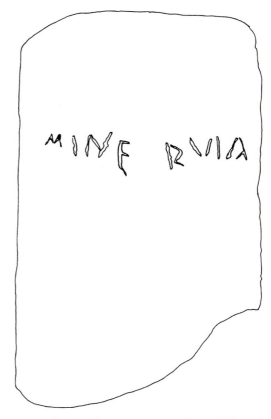

Fig. 11. Macchia Grande sanctuary at Veii, altar with the dedication *[M]inerv<i>a* (drawing A. Trapassi).

Fig. 10. Macchia Grande sanctuary at Veii, altar with the dedication *Victori(a)e* (drawing A. Trapassi).

We are evidently in the presence of a rather complicated interlacing of the religious and topographical situation of Rome with traditions of the Falisco-Veientan area. Even if it is not easy to reach clear-cut solutions, it is nevertheless evident that the Macchia Grande sanctuary aims to be a sort of religious 'recapitulation', so to speak, with respect to the city of Rome and to the atmosphere of conquest. Apollo and Minerva recall the Veientan cult at Portonaccio;[101] Jupiter Libertas, another Aventine foundation, is the plebeian face of the father of Gods particularly at home in the plebeian

'foyer' of Veii;[102] Victoria evokes the atmosphere of conquest and is the goddess introduced in Rome by the great plebeian general L. Postumius Megellus;[103] finally, the *dii deae(que)* appear to be a necessary complement to the assembly of gods more specifically connected with the place.

But this is not all. The recent discovery, in the same area, of another altar belonging to the same series[104] provides us with another precious detail of this important and disregarded Veientan sacred area. The altar is dedicated to Pitumnus—*Pitumno* says the text (Fig. 14) —and the god must be a divine figure in some way inseparable from the couple of Picumnus and Pilumnus. According to Virgil's commentator Servius,[105] these were brothers who belonged to the rather obscure and promiscuous group of the *dei coniugales*,[106] for whom a *lectus* used to be prepared in the house[107] and who had

---

[101] M. Torelli and [A. La Regina], 'Due sortes preromane', *ArchClass*, 20 (1968), 221 f.; Colonna, in *Scienze dell'Antichità* 1.

[102] S. B. Platner and T. Ashby, *A Topographical Dictionary of Ancient Rome* (Oxford, 1929), 296 f.   [103] Ibid. 570.
[104] I owe this precious information to Dr F. Boitani Visentini, whom I warmly thank.   [105] Serv. *Aen.* 9. 4.
[106] Serv. auct. *Aen.* 9. 64.   [107] Non. p. 528M.

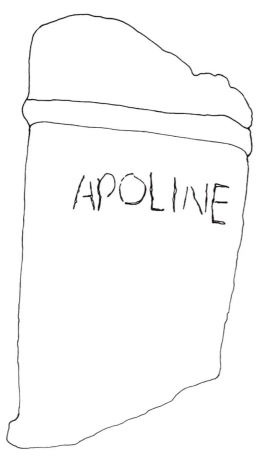

Fig. 12. Macchia Grande sanctuary at Veii, altar with the dedication *Apoline* (drawing A. Trapassi).

Fig. 13. Macchia Grande sanctuary at Veii, altar with the dedication *Ive [L]ib(e)rt(ati)* (drawing A. Trapassi).

Fig. 14. Macchia Grande sanctuary at Veii, altar with the dedication *Pitumno* (drawing A. Trapassi).

the duty of protecting the *infantes*[108] against the threats of Silvanus.[109] It is not necessary to produce here the complex linguistic and religious analyses from which it would emerge with relative clarity that Pitumnus is one and the same as Picumnus, *lectio facilior* of Roman antiquarians for the name of Pitumnus, connected with *stercus* (Sterculinius is the synonymous form for Picumnus according Fabius Pictor),[110] just as Stercutius is a synonym of Picus,[111] the king of the Laurentes, son of Saturn, and father of Faunus.[112] But if we add to this singular dossier the circumstance that Pilumnus is an ancestor of Turnus[113] and is a god specifically from Ardea, we gather a precious detail which helps us to detect the origin of a part of the colonists and to better define the θεῶν ἀγορά of Macchia Grande as a genuine representation of the religious climate of early Roman Veii. But Macchia Grande is significant for yet another reason—it represents a replica of those large Latin sanctuaries with a plurality of worshipped gods connected with a specific religious function. The prototype of these cult places is the famous 'Sanctuary of the Thirteen Altars' (Fig. 15), i.e. the Aphrodision, at Lavinium; their colonial late descendant might be considered the mysterious extra-urban sanctuary which housed the well-known *cippi Pisaurenses*,[114] almost the final *summa* of the original Latin devotion, at that stage (the beginning of the second century BC) in steady decline.

Unfortunately the urban decline of Veii and the very agrarian nature of the colonial settlement prevent us from seeing the developments of this religious situation in the long run and above all on an urban scale. Nevertheless, the religious situation in Veii represents a paradigm for those Latin colonies founded in an already existing urban centre. One may note a widespread survival of local cults with their specific 'reuse' according to the needs of the community, as is documented in Veii by the statuettes of Aeneas dedicated in older, Etruscan sanctuaries; but there are also some remarkable religious innovations, with a specific emphasis on the ideological aspect of the plebeian status of the conquest and of the origin of at least part of the colonists (Ardea), as it is shown by the Macchia Grande sanctuary.

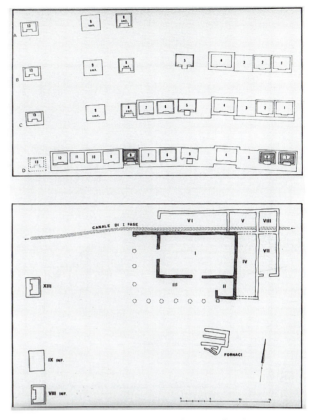

Fig. 15. Plan of the 'Sanctuary of the Thirteen Altars' at Lavinium (after *Lavinium I*).

On the opposite side of the picture we have the Roman colonies of both a more ancient and more recent date. The most significant case is that of Ostia, a settlement of the royal age rebuilt, in the present location and in the form (wrongly) considered similar to that of a *castrum*, in 435 or 426 BC on the occasion of the destruction of Fidenae (Fig. 16):[115] the walls of the Ostian so-called castrum are in fact built of Fidenae tufa and we even hear of the transferral to Ostia of rebellious *iuvenes* from Fidenae in addition to new Roman colonists in 428 BC.[116] The scanty archaeological evidence of the oldest colonial period[117] may be partly supplemented by literary and epigraphic sources. Up to now the site of both the principal cults of the city—that of Vulcanus, from which the local high priest got his name of *pontifex Volcani et aedium sacrarum*, and

---

[108] Piso, fr. 44P.   [109] Varro, *ap.* Aug. *De Civ. Dei* 6. 9.
[110] Fabius Pictor, *Iur.Pont.*, fr. 6P.   [111] Serv. auct. *Aen.* 10. 76.
[112] Virg. *Aen.* 7. 48.   [113] Virg. *Aen.* 9. 4; 10. 76, 619.
[114] *ILLRP* 13–26.

[115] Liv. 4. 22. 2, 33–4.
[116] Liv. 4. 30. 5–6; on the chronology of the Ostian *castrum*, see F. Coarelli, 'I santuari, il fiume, gli empori', in Momigliano and Schiavone (eds.), *Storia di Roma*, i. 136 f.
[117] List of finds by F. Z(evi), in *Roma medio-repubblicana*, 343 f., nn. 494–523.

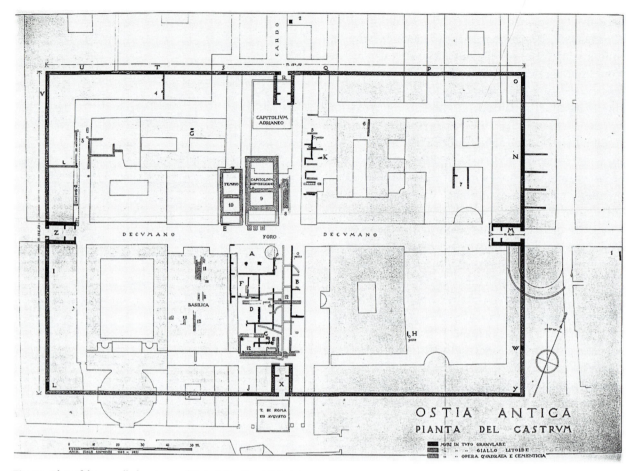

Fig. 16. Plan of the so-called castrum of Ostia (after *Scavi di Ostia*).

that of the Dioscuri—has not been precisely located. We can have doubts about the cult enshrined in the couple of little republican temples in the Ostian forum which preceded the imperial Capitolium,[118] but their identification with the shrines of Vulcanus and of the Dioscuri is anyway most unlikely, since they disappeared to give room to another temple, precisely the Capitolium, which seems to be their heir. It is a far better idea to identify the larger one[119]—the so called republican Capitolium—with the temple of Jupiter mentioned by Livy in the year 199 BC,[120] and the smaller one—a temple structure adjoining the previous one on the west side—with a cult place of Juno, the sole cults, together with that of Minerva, that could be substi-

tuted by the worship of the Capitoline triad without religious traumas.[121]

It is very likely instead, according to Coarelli, that the temple of Vulcanus should be identified in the large public area of monumental character, immediately outside the Porta Marina of the Sullan walls, where so many fragments of the *Fasti Ostienses* have come to light and where at least one other temple has to be located, the shrine of Bona Dea.[122] Whatever we may think of the character of the royal and mid-republican

---

[118] Synthesis of the archaeological evidence: C. Pavolini, 'Ostia', in *DArch* 3rd ser., 6: 2 (1988), 119 f.

[119] So R. Meiggs, *Roman Ostia* (Oxford, 2nd edn. 1973), 346, 352; C. Pavolini, *Ostia* (Rome and Bari, 1983), 99 f.

[120] Liv. 32. 1. 10.

[121] The find of 4th–3rd cent. BC architectural terracottas in the southern side of the forum (*Scavi di Ostia*, i (Rome, 1963), 96; A. Andrén, 'Un gruppo di antefisse fittili etrusco-laziali e la questione dell'esistenza di un abitato ostiense anteriore alla colonia romana', in *SE* 48 (1980), 93 f.) has no counterpart in the actual remains brought to light during the excavations in the republican levels of the area (a recent appreciation of these finds by Pavolini, 'Ostia', in *DArch* 3rd ser., 6: 2, 121); it is wiser to consider these terracottas as a part of a dump, and not as a direct evidence of the existence of a temple in this side of the forum, whose orientation (to the N) would be absolutely contrary to the rules of Roman religion.

[122] On this subject F. Coarelli has an important study in preparation.

colony,[123] the two cults of Vulcanus and of the Dioscuri are nonetheless revealing with regard to the conception of the earliest Roman colonies. In the cult of Vulcanus we may see a specific desire to duplicate in the Ostian *apoikia*, following a Greek spirit one might say, the great political centre of urban religion, the *Volcanal* and the *oikistes'* tomb—the tomb of Romulus —in the *Comitium* of Rome.[124] The royal colony could not have found a better way to stress, by means of religion, the political link with the mother city, significantly ignoring the Capitoline cult, which made its appearance in the colony only very late, in the Sullan age. The cult of the Castores is also a valuable document of the earliest religious history of the town. Administered by the urban praetor with sacrifices and *ludi Castorum*,[125] the cult appears to form an interesting parallel to that of Hercules *in foro Boario* in Rome, also entrusted to the care of the urban praetor, who celebrated sacrifices *Graeco ritu* along with the solemn *ludi Romani*.[126] The antiquity of the Castores in Latium has been proved by the famous Lavinian inscription, a dedication *Castorei Podlouqueique | qurois*. The latter document, found in the context of the *Frutinal*, the sanctuary of Aphrodite-Frutis (identical to the Aphrodision of Strabo)[127] which shows some of the unmistakable signs of a mercantile cult, allows us to place the Ostian cult in the context of an archaic *emporium*,[128] for which the twin gods seem particularly suited since the date of the sacrifice can be associated with the reopening of the earliest type of navigation, i.e. coastal. Compared with the mercantile foundation of the Royal period, the so-called *castrum* qualifies as a settlement of military nature, carried out between the late fifth and the early fourth centuries BC and aimed at a new form of

occupation of the territory. Other centres in the *ager Romanus* of that period can be classified in a similar way, such as the settlement of La Giostra,[129] all sites normally deprived of a real religious and political autonomy. The fact that cult buildings of this period in the Ostian *castrum* are confined to one, identified by the fourth–third-century BC architectural terracottas from the south side of the forum, tallies perfectly with the absence of a real forum and of other buildings of political function, a feature which is presupposed by the status of the early *coloniae civium Romanorum*, notoriously deprived of autonomous judicial administration or military independence.

4. Religion and Colonies after 338 BC: Luceria, Alba Fucens, Cosa

In the following period the most significant example is that of Luceria where, as we shall see later,[130] we find evidence of the fervour inspired by the Trojan cult of Athena Ilias. The grand theme of Trojan propaganda for Roman expansionism, already tried out at Veii, is strengthened by the fact that the Lucerian cult was considered to be identical with the very old one of Lavinium;[131] but in Luceria we are also faced with the momentous event of the assumption—a real phagocytizing—of the non-Roman myth of Diomedes into Roman propaganda. To Diomedes, abductor of the Trojan Palladium, Greek tradition appropriately credited the establishment in Daunia of the cult of Athena Ilias and a solid heroic reputation among the indigenous Daunians, who also exploited the Diomedean saga as a depiction of their great reputation for horse-breeding and of their own social system based on a powerful mounted aristocracy.[132] For the first time, Roman propaganda found a way to take over a specific foreign myth and the related figure of a Greek hero, in

[123] Discussion by I. Pohl, 'Was Early Ostia a Colony or a Fort?', *PP* (1983), 123 f., P. Cicerchia, 'Ostia: considerazioni e ipotesi sul primo impianto urbano', *Xenia* 6 (1983), 45 f. and Pavolini, 'Ostia' loc. cit.

[124] On these cults and monuments of the regal period, see F. Coarelli, *Il Foro Romano*, i (Rome, 1983), 161 f., 188 f.

[125] Sources in Meiggs, *Roman Ostia*, 342 f.

[126] Discussion by F. Coarelli, *Il Foro Boario* (Rome, 1988), 127 f.

[127] See Torelli, *Lavinio e Roma*, 163 f.

[128] The main archaeological finds of the early period from the area of Ostia (survey by Pavolini, in *DArch* 3rd ser., 6: 2, 117 f.), apart from scattered material of the Final Bronze Age, include a few architectural terracottas of the 6th cent. BC from the area of the *castrum* (G. Bartoloni, 'I Latini e il Tevere', *Archeologia Laziale* 7: 2 (1986), 98 f.), which could belong to the early phase of the Vulcanus temple. However, very important to understand the character of this earliest Ostian settlement is the independent Greek tradition, which surfaces in the text of the Massaliote historian Trogus: 'temporibus Tarquinii regis ex Asia Phocaeensium iuventus ostio Tiberis invecta amicitiam cum Romanis iunxit' (Justin. 43. 3. 4).

[129] J. Rasmus Brandt, 'La Giostra: un esempio di urbanistica medio-repubblicana?', *Archeologia Laziale* 2 (1979), 50 f.; see also, by the same scholar, his more general evaluation of this site in relation with the republican Roman colonies, 'Ostia, Minturno, Pyrgi. The Planning of Three Roman Colonies', in *AAAH* 2nd ser., 5 (1985), 25 f.

[130] See Ch. 4.

[131] G. Pugliese Carratelli, 'Lazio, Roma e Magna Grecia prima del IV sec.a.C.', *PP* (1968), 321 f.; Torelli, *Lavinio e Roma*, 19 f.

[132] D. Musti, 'Il processo di formazione e diffusione delle tradizioni greche sui Daunii e su Diomede, in *La civiltà dei Dauni nel quadro del mondo italico*, Acts of Conference; Manfredonia 1980 (Florence, 1984), 93 f.; E. Lepore, 'Società indigena e influenze esterne con particolare riguardo all'influenza greca', ibid., 317 f.

order to present him as friendly to the Trojan–Roman expansion, a detail that surfaces centuries later in the verses of Virgil's Aeneid.[133]

The cult of Diomedes even became part of the ideological paraphernalia of the Latin colonization in the eastern half of the peninsula, in the territories affected by the influence of Greek colonization and commercial presence in the Adriatic Sea, a complex cultural and economic phenomenon that L. Braccesi has appropriately called 'Grecità adriatica' (Adriatic Hellenism).[134] Diomedes emerges in all Latin colonies of the area, at Luceria,[135] at Brundisium,[136] at Venusia,[137] at Beneventum,[138] at Hatria,[139] and perhaps as far away as Ariminum, if one may fairly connect two different issues, the tradition of the Umbrian origin of the town[140] and that of the cult bestowed by the Umbrians upon Diomedes.[141] The persistence of this element of Greek ideological and religious tradition, in Daunia, Samnium, and Umbria cannot be explained merely as an anti-quarian, fossilized conservation of an archaic Italo-Greek heritage, which from the protohistoric past to the classical period spread the myth and the cult of the great Homeric hero all along the Adriatic coasts of Italy up to Venetia, but rather as a conscious exploitation of local memories aiming at a successful integration of indigenous élites enlisted into Latin colonies. We shall discuss later the particular cases of Luceria and Venusia and how this peculiar Trojan atmosphere surrounding both foundations played a role even in internal policy at Rome. Here I shall simply limit myself to stressing the fact that with Venusia we are faced by another novelty, the first instance of an innovative name for a Latin colony, which until the foundation of Venusia seem all to have drawn their names from those of the previous settlements they came to substitute.[142]

We shall also see later the complexity of the case of Paestum, itself of extreme importance in reconstruct-ing Roman behaviour in relation to a major city, already occupied by a barbarian élite of Lucanian stock, but still densely populated by Greeks. The Paestan situation in a way recalls the case of Veii, with its extensive conservation and remodelling of the previous religious setting. At this point, however, it is of some interest briefly to scrutinize instead what happened in two cases where the Latin colonies of the age of the Italian conquest were planted in an area not previously occupied by a town—the cases of Alba Fucens, founded in 303 BC, and of Cosa, a settlement of 273 BC.

The 6,000 Latin colonists of Alba Fucens (Fig. 17) were planted in 303 BC in a land traditionally inhab-ited *vicatim* and with no major pre-existing religious settlement, with the task of controlling the defeated Sabellian tribe of the Marsi, and the mountain passes between Latium and the eastern coastlands, still unsub-dued. The town has been extensively excavated by the Belgian archaeologists, to whom we owe thanks for information on the general topography and the main urban layout, though the cultic situation in the republican period is unfortunately known only in a very partial and fragmentary way.[143] One of the main features of the religious topography of the colony is the presence of two virtually identical temples on top of the two substantial heights, the Pettorino Hill (Fig. 18) and the San Pietro Hill (Fig. 19), which limit the urban area respectively to the east and to the south.[144] The almost twin temples belong to the Italic type on a high podium and have four columns in the prostyle front and a decorated terracotta roof, all details normal in the era of their construction, the first decades of the third century BC, but show a rather unusual plan—the cella is not single, as is the norm for most the *aedes* of the Roman tradition, or triple, as is expected for *Capitolia* or more in general for cults of triads, but double. In one fortunate instance, the temple of San Pietro, a late graffito informs us that the building was an *Apollinar*, a temple of Apollo, which, because of the double cella, we may easily conclude belonged also to his sister Diana. The San Pietro temple was oriented towards the north-east, which helps us to detect the

---

[133] It is to be noted however that a trace of a Latin tradition hostile to the hero survives in the otherwise inexplicable piece of information given to us by Servius (Serv. auct. *Aen.* 8. 9): 'hunc (*scil.* Diomedes) alii Lavinii imperasse olim tradunt'; cf. Torelli, *Lavinio e Roma*, 191, 201. It should also be considered whether this particular tradition conceals local, Lavinian appreciation of equestrian values, which might also be reflected in the early cult of the Dioscuri at Lavinium.

[134] L. Braccesi, *Grecità adriatica* (Bologna, 1977).

[135] Strab. 6. 284.   [136] Justin. 12. 2. 7.

[137] Serv. auct. *Aen.* 12. 246.   [138] Solin. 2. 10.

[139] Plin. *N.H.* 3. 110.   [140] Strab. 6. 217.   [141] Strab. 6. 284.

[142] We might argue that a precedent for Venusia could be found in Alba Fucens, which on the grounds of the inscription *ILLRP* 42, *Albesi patre*, could derive its name from an otherwise unknown and perhaps local deity. However, as we have seen, we have to dismiss the hypothesis of a local character of this *Albensis pater* being sharply contradicted by the more likely Latin origin of the god, i.e. the Jupiter of the Mons Albanus and at the same time by the relationship of the name of the Latin colony in the Marsian land with that of the old mother-city of Rome on the Alban Hills.

[143] Summary of the evidence for the early period of the colony in the brief, but good guidebook by J. Mertens, *Alba Fucens* (Brussels, 1981); more detailed is the article by the same author 'Alba Fucens', in *DArch* 3rd ser., 6: 2 (1988), 87 f.

[144] J. Mertens, 'Deux Temples italiques à Alba Fucens', in *Alba Fucens*, ii (Rome and Brussels, 1969), 6 f.

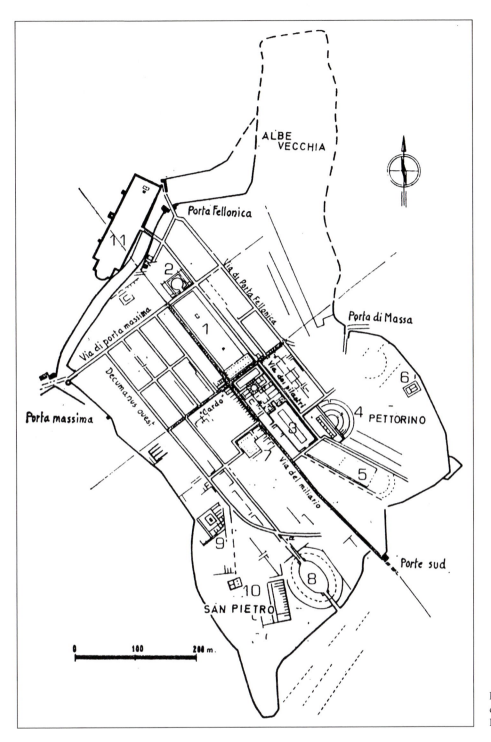

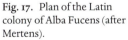

Fig. 17. Plan of the Latin colony of Alba Fucens (after Mertens).

original chthonian character of this local Apollo and his similarity to the Roman Apollo Medicus, whose shrine originally had the same name as that at Alba: *Apollinar.*[145] The healing character of the god at Alba is confirmed by the discovery of a substantial group of anatomic ex-votos near the temple.[146] Since the example of the San Pietro cult teaches us that a double cella was not intended to shelter a marital couple, whose cult might normally be accommodated in a single cella of a normal temple, it is tempting at this

[145] Liv. 3. 63.

[146] Mertens, in *DArch* 3rd ser., 6: 2. 99.

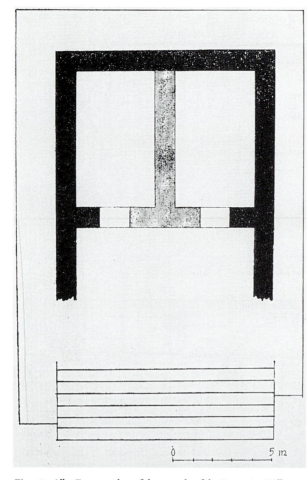

Fig. 18. Alba Fucens, plan of the temple of the Pettorino Hill (after Mertens).

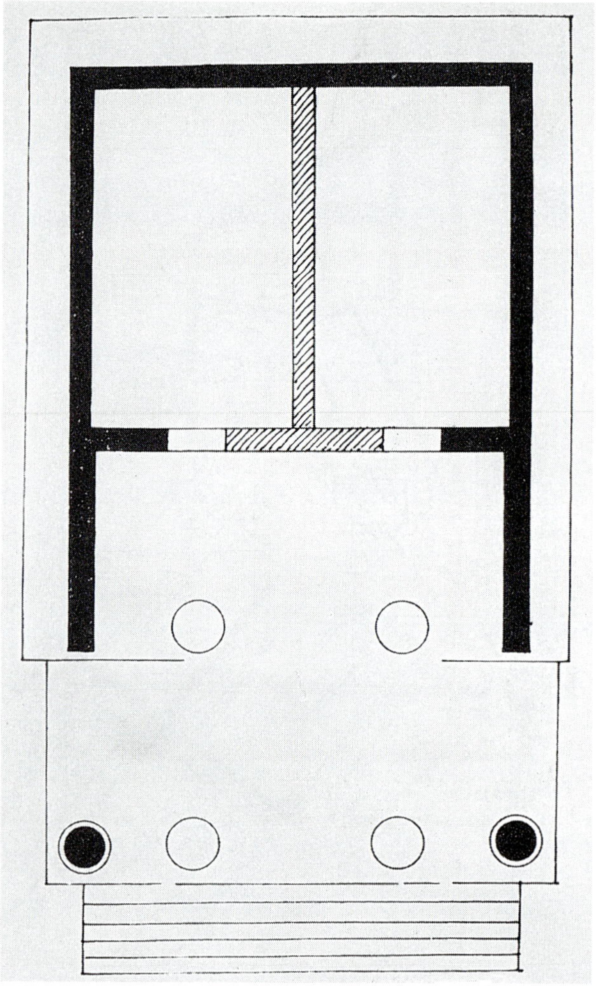

Fig. 19. Alba Fucens, plan of the temple of the San Pietro Hill (after Mertens).

stage to formulate hypotheses as to the second couple of divinities worshipped in the other temple on the Pettorino Hill. It is rare in early Roman religion to find gods associated in pairs and therefore, also taking into account the south-west orientation of the temple, we might perhaps conjecture at identifying the cult with that of Ceres and Liber (we know of the somewhat collateral, less prominent position of Libera in the early cult);[147] but, considering the very archaic name given to the temple of Apollo, other earlier associations of divinities could be vouchsafed also, such as Mars and Ops, a cult coupled in the Roman Regia[148] and certainly of the most venerable antiquity for all the Latins.

[147]   On this point see H. Le Bonniec, *Le Culte de Cérès à Rome* (Paris, 1958), 213 f.; cf. also Torelli, *Lavinio e Roma*, 91 f.

[148]   See P. Pouthier, *Ops et la conception divine de l'abondance dans la religion romaine jusqu'à la mort d'Auguste* (Rome, 1981), 59 f.; Coarelli, *Il Foro Romano*, i. 56 f.

The colony of Alba, itself placed on a plateau 950–975 m above sea level, had its own *arx*, a hill on the north-east side of the town, dominating the whole settlement from the even more pronounced height of 1,022 m. The *arx* has not been explored, since the area is occupied by the ruins of a village abandoned after the tragic earthquake that in 1915 destroyed the neighbouring modern town of Avezzano. It is not difficult to imagine that this area housed a cult of high significance for both the religious and the political life of the town, the cult of Jupiter. His presence from a position dominating the town below guaranteed the correct performance of the *auspicia* and at the same time his eminent position reminded everybody of the god of the mons Albanus, from which the town took its name Alba. Fortunately we have an inscription which refers to the god calling him precisely with the name that appeared to be the legitimization of the colony—*Albesi patre*.[149] The supreme god of the Latins could be named Albanus on the sacred peak of the Alban Hill; or Capitolinus, from the name of the Capitol, the Roman duplicate of the sacred Alban hilltop; or Arcanus, the Jupiter of the *arx*, the acropolis of Praeneste on top of the high mountain of Castel San Pietro;[150] or, finally, *Albensis Pater*, the Father both of Alba Fucens and of the Mons Albanus, to evoke the pan-Latin climate of the sacred festivals of the *populi Albenses* and of the triumphs *in monte Albano*.

The religious atmosphere of Alba, so full of references to old Latium and primitive religion, appears to be archaic more than conventional, and to some extent very poor. Though sketchily explored, the forum area has revealed not a single important temple, while a great emphasis is given (as happens thirty years later at Cosa and Paestum) to primary political structures, such as the circular *comitium* built in ashlar masonry, and the elaborate arrangements of the *diribitorium*, with its stone-walled pits for the placement of the electoral *pontes*.[151] Despite the lack of systematic exploration, we may even doubt that a major temple was ever built in the forum, since we have the almost contemporary cases of Cosa[152] and Paestum,[153] both colonies where no substantial building of a sacred nature was erected on the main public square before the late third century BC.

The rest of the town, with only one possible exception,[154] preserves few other traces of possible temple structures attributable to republican times: a rather mysterious building at the centre of the San Pietro Hill,[155] a monumental Isaeum of the second half of the first century BC,[156] and the extraordinary sanctuary of Hercules, dominating in its actual form of the late second/early first century BC the central area of the town, south-east of the forum. This last building in its present form seems to be the creation of the period of major splendour of the Latin colony, here as elsewhere the second half of the second century BC (Fig. 20). Yet, thanks to the trial trenches carried out by the Belgian archaeologists, we now know that the cult of Hercules was founded contemporarily with the foundation of the colony:[157] we learn that from a group of votive objects (among which a bronze club and some typical objects of the Hercules cults, namely black-glaze paterae[158] marked in white overpaint with the alphabetic letter H) and from fragments of a monumental altar (?) found in the third-century BC levels below the actual building. This datum has a remarkable significance for our problem. In fact, Hercules at Alba Fucens shows a very interesting epithet, *Hercules salarius*, attested by an imperial inscription[159] dedicated by the local *cultores*.[160] The *epiklesis* reveals the function of the god, who has been entrusted with the care, i.e. the storing and the circulation, of a product crucial in the economy of these inland, mountain areas—salt. As has long been recognized,[161] the economy of the Sabellian tribes who populated the whole inland area of the Italian peninsula relied strongly upon cattle-breeding and the raising of large flocks and herds as the main form of wealth accumulation, as opposed to the merely self-sustaining husbandry possible in the mountainous landscape of the Apennines. Transhumance—mostly, but not exclusively of large flocks of sheep—must have played an important role in this pastoral activity from remotest times[162] and salt was a commodity which

---

[149] *ILLRP* 42.

[150] On this identification and in particular for a reconstruction of the main lines of the topography of the sacred places in Praeneste, see M. Torelli, 'Topografia sacra di una città latina—Praeneste', in B. Coari (ed.), *Urbanistica ed architettura dell'antica Praeneste*, Acts of Conference; Palestrina 1988 (Palestrina, 1989), 15 f.

[151] M. Torelli, 'Il "diribitorium" di Alba Fucens e il "campus" eroico di Herdonia', in *Comunità indigene e romanizzazione*, Acts of Conference; Rome, 1990 (Brussels and Rome, 1991), 39 f.

[152] Brown, *The Making of a Roman Town*, 31 f.

[153] See Ch. 3.

[154] I allude to the colossal building, whose scanty traces are to be seen near the eastern section of the walls on the same axis as the basilica: it is marked in the guidebook by J. Mertens, *Alba Fucens* (Brussels, 1981), fig. 15, with the letter N and considered as a possible cult building.

[155] The building, brought to light by Promis long before the Belgian excavations, has never been fully published. Its plan is suitable for a Romano-Italic temple and its position, at the centre of the hill, facing the main *cardo* of the town, appears to be extremely convenient for a major sacred building.

[156] Summary of the archaeological evidence of this sanctuary again in the guidebook by Mertens, *Alba Fucens*, 45 f.

[157] F. De Visscher, J. Mertens, and J. C. Balty, 'Le Sanctuaire d'Hercule et ses portiques à Alba Fucens', in *MonAL* 46 (1963), 360 f.; Mertens, in *DArch* 3rd ser., 6: 2. 94 f.

[158] Important discussion of the evidence by J. P. Morel, 'Artisanat et colonisation dans l'Italie romaine aux IVe et IIIe siècles av. J.-C.', in *DArch* 3rd ser., 6 (1988), 59 f.   [159] *CIL* IX 3961.

[160] We may even detect the place for the meetings of this *collegium*: the room, originally connected with the porticoes of the sanctuary, which adjoins the west side of the shrine housing the colossal cult-statue of the god; cf. Visscher, Mertens, Balty, *MonAL* 46, 344 f.

[161] On this subject the standard work is that by E. T. Salmon, *Samnium and the Samnites* (Cambridge, 1967); cf. also M. Torelli, 'Le popolazioni dell'Italia antica: società e forme del potere', in Momigliano and Schiavone (eds.), *Storia di Roma*, i. 53 f.

[162] A good summary of the evidence on transhumance by M. Corbier, in *La Romanisation du Samnium aux IIe et Ier siècles av. J.-C.*, Acts of Conference; Naples, 1987 (Naples, 1991), 149 f.

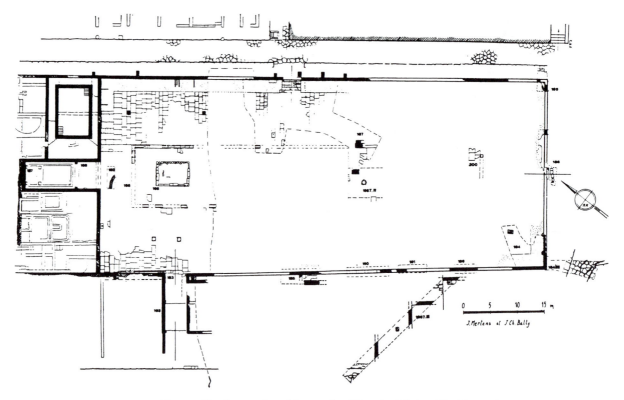

Fig. 20. Alba Fucens, plan of the temple of Hercules Salarius (after Mertens).

occupied a crucial place among the needs of these peoples, for the preparation of cheese and for the pickling of all sort of meat and fish.[163] The Via Salaria notoriously was the road that connected the salt-works of the Tiber with the Sabine hinterland,[164] and a backbone in the archaic road system of Rome, as F. Coarelli has recently stressed.[165] The Hercules of the Ara Maxima in the Forum Boarium, the most archaic god of the area, is undoubtedly connected with a local branch of the *Salinae* and with the earliest commercial traffic in the area of the future Roman harbour, the *portus Tiberinus*.[166]

Although we have to remind ourselves that a perfectly identical cult is known in two other major Latin cities that had analogous strong contacts with the Sabellian hinterland, Tibur[167] and Praeneste,[168] the Hercules of Alba Fucens is a duplicate of the Roman sanctuary and the very iconography of the colossal

marble cult statue retrieved in the Belgian excavations confirms it. The interesting late Hellenistic Greek sculpture (Pl. 2)[169] must be considered a 'replica' (precisely in the late Hellenistic way, different from a copy) of the Roman cult statue of the Forum Boarium, of which a significant echo is to be seen in the so-called 'Heraklesschalen', the third-century BC black-glaze cups of Roman manufacture.[170] Coarelli has rightly pointed out[171] the connection of the iconography of this so-called 'Epitrapezios' Hercules with the local, Roman myth, centred on the *coena* of the god and his playing dice with the priest. The archaic character of the whole cult is to be understood as an unmistakable sign of a mercantile origin of the cult along the lines of the brilliant suggestion by D. Van Berchem, who recognized in several details of the myths and worship the traces of a very old Phoenician Melqart.[172]

[163] A. Giovannini, 'Le sel et la fortune de Rome', *Athenaeum* 63 (1985), 373 f.; M. Torelli, 'Gli aromi e il sale. Afrodite ed Eracle nell'emporia arcaica dell'Italia', in A. Mastrocinque (ed.), *Ercole in occidente* (Trento, 1993), 104 f.

[164] On the Tiber salt-works, most recently, G. Algreen-Ussing and T. Fischer-Hansen, 'Ficana, le saline e le vie della regione bassa del Tevere', *Archeologia Laziale* 7 (1985), 65 f.

[165] Coarelli, *Il Foro Boario*, 109 f.   [166] Ibid.

[167] On the great Tiburtine sanctuary, see F. Coarelli, *I santuari repubblicani del Lazio* (Rome, 1988), 85 f.

[168] Lastly, see Torelli, in *Urbanistica e architettura dell'antica Praeneste*.

[169] F. De Visscher, 'Heraclès Epitrapezios', *ArchClass* 30 (1961), 67 f.; H. G. Martin, *Römische Tempelkultbilder* (Rome, 1987), 62 f., 225 f.; O. Palagia, in *LIMC* IV 1. 776; the Alba statue, however, did not hold the Hesperides apples, as Palagia thinks, but a cup, of which the lower part is quite visible in the hollow of the god's hand.   [170] Morel, in *DArch* 3rd ser., 6: 57 f.

[171] Coarelli, *Il Foro Boario*, 129 f.

[172] D. Van Berchem, 'Sanctuaires d'Hercule-Melqart. Contribution à l'étude de l'expansion phénicienne en Méditerranée, III. Rome', *Syria* 44 (1967), 307 f.

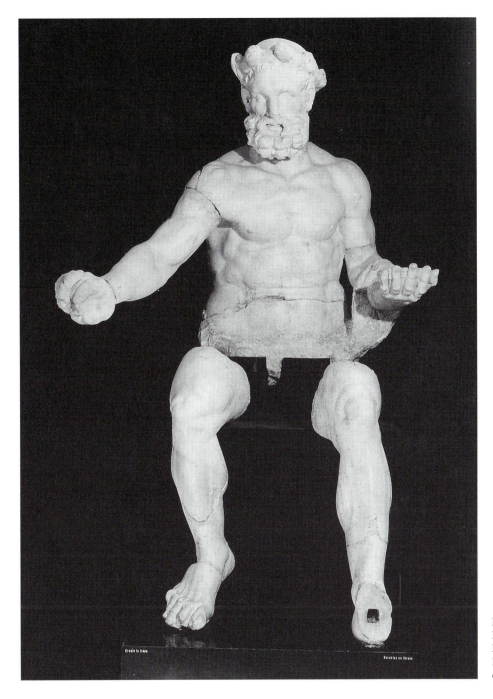

Plate 2. Chieti, Museo Nazionale. The cult statue of Hercules Salarius from Alba Fucens (courtesy of the Museo di Chieti).

The Hercules of the Forum Boarium was then the *Hercules salarius* of Rome, and the adjoining *salinae*[173] are one of the various elements that contribute to explaining the presence of the cult in the area. But Hercules was also a divinity who enjoyed an immense popularity in the Sabellian world, as the many shrines of the god, the huge quantity of bronze ex-votos and the inscriptional evidence from the Italic areas witness.[174] The Italic Hercules is one of the most remarkable loans from Greek religion to the native pantheon and as such still awaits a full, comprehensive study to clarify the motivations of the enthusiastic welcome that the Greek heroic and divine figure received among

---

[173] These *salinae*—Coarelli, loc.cit., has shown—are however different from the great salt-works on the right bank of the Tiber, the *ripa Veientana*, where the Via Campana extended, cf. Dion. Hal. 3. 29 f.

[174] Torelli, in Mastrocinque (ed.), *Ercole in occidente*, 108 f.

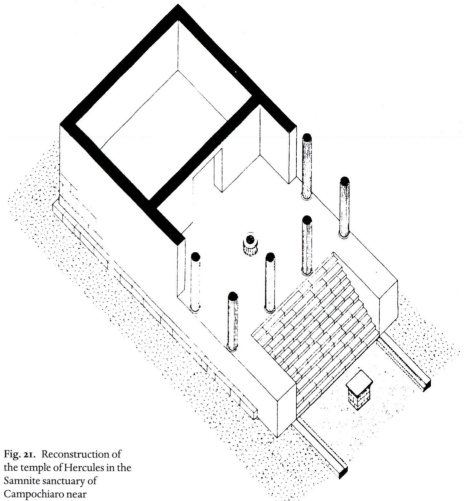

Fig. 21. Reconstruction of the temple of Hercules in the Samnite sanctuary of Campochiaro near Campobasso (after Capini).

the Italic aristocracies. I am here interested in showing that among the Italic peoples too Hercules had, among other functions, that of divine dispenser of the precious product. The best possible proof is offered by the name of a *statio* known from the *Tabula Peutingeriana* in the territory of the Pentri, one of the two main branches into which the Samnites *proprie dicti* were divided—*Herculis Rani*, clearly the name in genitive of a sanctuary (subsequently passed on to the *statio*), which has been convincingly identified with the remarkable Samnite sanctuary of Campochiaro (Fig. 21).[175] Although Hercules' epithet has up to now resisted interpretation, it is not difficult to prove that it has to do with *rano*, a term in the Iguvian Tables that A. L. Prosdocimi interprets as designating a particular

quality of salt, possibly ground salt to be used in the *mola salsa*[176] and therefore to be translated as *Salarius*, the same *epiklesis* of the Hercules of Alba Fucens.[177] As a matter of fact, the architecture of the sanctuary at Alba has been shown to be suitable for a *forum pecuarium*, a sheep market[178] and the Via Valeria, which runs right through the town, constituting its main *decumanus*, is also the major track bringing the stream of transhumance from the Marsian territory to Tibur and to the Latin plain. In much the same way the sanctuary (and the *statio*) of Hercules Ranus was placed on the great 'tratturo'—the customary Italian name for a transhumance track—that connected Samnium with Apulia, and particularly with Canusium, where one of

---

[175] A. La Regina, 'Il Sannio', in P. Zanker (ed.), *Hellenismus in Mittelitalien*, Acts of Conference; Göttingen, 1974 (Göttingen, 1976), 219 f.

[176] A. L. Prosdocimi, 'L'umbro', *Popoli e civiltà dell'Italia antica*, 6 (Rome, 1978), 585 f.

[177] Torelli, in Mastrocinque (ed.), *Ercole in occidente*, 116 f.

[178] F. Coarelli has in preparation an important study on the subject.

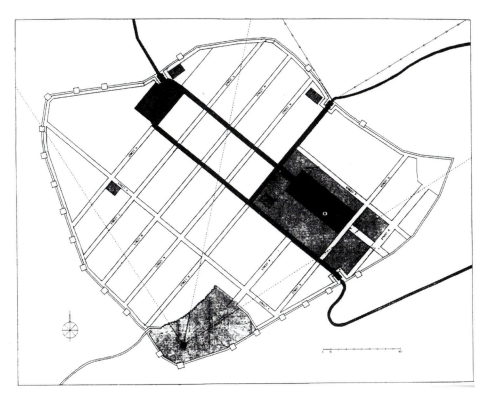

Fig. 22. Plan of the Latin colony of Cosa (after Brown).

the greatest centres of the pre-Roman and Roman wool industry of Italy was located.[179]

The case of the religious and cultural roots of the cult of Hercules Salarius in Alba Fucens is very useful in showing that even in the rather inconspicuous appearance of the local cultic system remarkable care was taken in exploiting Roman and Latin tradition to favour the economic integration between the new foundation and the surrounding indigenous areas, an integration which should be better described in terms of strengthening of the socio-economic domination of the urbanized Latin colonists over their non-urbanized Marsian neighbours. The difference can be perceived by comparing the religious organization of Alba with that of Cosa (Fig. 22), the only other Latin colony sufficiently excavated and published to allow comparison. Again, the cultic situation of this other colony, only a generation later than Alba Fucens, gives us the same picture of a very simple and modest situation. The *arx* (Fig. 23) included, maybe from the very beginning of the life of the colony, a temple identified by F. Brown[180] as belonging to Jupiter and later substituted by a three-cella temple, most likely the Capitolium. Later, at the

beginning of the second century BC, when the temple of Concord in the forum was built, the arx received a second minor cult building, again tentatively attributed by F. Brown[181] to Mater Matuta. It is worthwhile discussing Brown's attempts to give a name to the divinities of the two sacred buildings. As far as the first one is concerned, the proposal of the excavator can be fairly accepted, thanks to the terracotta sculpture part of the decoration of the early or of the later building; the subject of this acroterial group, the abduction of Ganymede, can be understood only if the temple was dedicated to the Father of the gods and author of the mythical deed. There is no stratigraphic evidence for the transformation of the original building into a Capitolium; it is only matter of what chronology is assigned to the architectural terracottas and, eventually, to the podium mouldings. From a historical point of view, the best possible date is after the Fregellan War (125–124 BC), when the magistrates of the Latin cities and colonies acquired Roman citizenship at the end of their term of office, according to a well-documented theory put forward by G. Tibiletti:[182] at that time, the

---

[179] Discussion by F. Grelle, *Canosa romana* (Rome, 1993), *passim*.

[180] Brown, *Cosa: The Making of a Roman Town*, 25 f.

[181] Ibid. 47 f.

[182] G. Tibiletti, 'La politica delle colonie e delle città latine nella guerra sociale', in *RIL* 86 (1953), 45 ff., esp. 55 f.

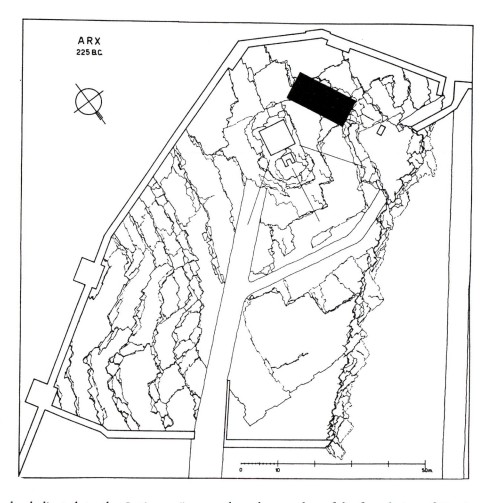

Fig. 23. Plan of the *arx* of Cosa with the *auguraculum* and the conjectured location (in black) of the temple of Jupiter (after Brown).

transformation of a temple dedicated to the Latin Jupiter of the Alban hill, connected with the *auguraculum* and with the augural life of the town, into a copy of the Capitolium of Rome[183] can be understood only if the acquisition of Roman citizenship and therefore of a Roman monumental and religious appearance had become a real issue and an ideological and political goal. For the identification of the second temple we have even less evidence at our disposal: mainly a fragment of the fictile decoration of the pediment showing a man carrying a triumphal *ferculum*, and few anatomic ex-votos, both details pointing to a divinity well established in Latium, with healing qualities and with strong triumphal connections. On those grounds we may think not only of Mater Matuta, as Brown did, but also of the companion goddess of Mater Matuta, Fortuna, and even—but less likely—of Victoria, who received her first temple in Rome on the Palatine in 295 BC

(i.e. at a date close to that of the foundation of Cosa), thanks to the great plebeian general L. Postumius Megellus.[184]

The only other temple known in Cosa is that adjoining the Curia and the *comitium* (Fig. 24). An inscription published by Brown attributes it to Concordia, patently a political cult. We may or may not agree with Brown,[185] who sees in this dedication an attempt to control a possible social unrest due to the arrival of new colonists in 197 BC, at the request of the same town of Cosa, but we cannot deny the strong similarity with the Roman temple credited to have been built by Camillus because of its location near the Senate House. The original emphasis on the *Latinitas* of the colony, though attenuated at least in the course of the second century BC in favour of a stronger Roman colouring, seems to be confirmed by the scanty evidence retrieved from the extensive excavations. Can Cosa then be considered an

[183] Brown, *Cosa: The Making of a Roman Town*, 51 f.

[184] Platner and Ashby, *A Topographical Dictionary of Ancient Rome*, 570.
[185] Brown, *Cosa: The Making of a Roman Town*, 31.

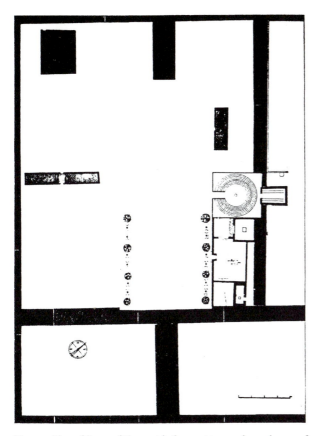

Fig. 24. Plan of *forum* of Cosa with the *comitium* and, south-east of it, the square precinct containing the altar dedicated to Concordia (after Brown).

entirely Latin colony or was there some indigenous, i.e. Etruscan, contribution? The opportunities for onomastic research are minimal, due to the very poor inscriptional material known to have come from the town. The sole Etruscan inscription known to have been found at Cosa, a marble fragment[186] retrieved in the excavations of the *arx*, despite its enigmatic nature both in terms of language and historical significance, would seem to indicate that there was some contribution from the Etruscan side. In this regard, even the name of the colony, derived from the previous Etruscan settlement of *Cusa (to be identified with the nearby site of the modern town of Orbetello, abandoned in

connection with the foundation of the Latin colony),[187] could confirm the circumstance of some strong pressure exerted by the surrounding Etruscan population.

A very important monument of prime ideological significance, however, demonstrates that the situation was much more complex. I am referring to the fragmentary marble group representing a copy of the famous group in the sacred Latin town of Lavinium, the Laurentine Sow, the ominous *Scrofa Laurentina* erected as the symbol of the common origins of the Latin towns and colonies.[188] No stronger sign of the *Latinitas* of the town could be conceived than this sculptural group, possibly dating from the years between the momentous Fregellan War and the Social War, a period when *Latinitas* acquired the new and ominous meaning of main path to the desired Roman citizenship. Cosa, in stressing its Latin origin, was contemporaneously underlining also its particular status as an isolated Latin outpost in a land still widely peopled by Etruscans and close to the old Etruscan metropolis of Vulci. Surrounded by still rich (and possibly hostile) Etruscans, Cosa was not looking to establish with the indigenous people the same ties that Alba was asserting through the emphasis on its Hercules. The most likely answer should be sought in the fact that the socio-economic superiority of Cosa over the old agricultural skills of the Etruscans was not so clearly established as it was in the case of the Alban colonists over the dispersed and weakened Marsi.

5. Conclusions

We may therefore conclude that the evident Roman flexibility in matters of religious practice became a powerful source of ideological pressure or resistance. Many years ago[189] I pointed out the fact that Latin colonization was responsible for propagating, well beyond the original borders of central Etruria, Latium, and Campania, the use of anatomic ex-votos, with all

[186] Brief mention of this inscription by Brown, *Cosa: The Making of a Roman Town*, 45 n. 4, who thinks that this inscription and the name of Tongilii of Cosa's onomastics might allow the hypothesis that Etruscan allies participated in the foundation of the colony: the inscription however, being on marble, has more the flavour of an Augustan antiquarianism (we might in this regard remember that in the list of the Etruscan allies of Aeneas in Virgil's poem we find Cosa: Virg. *Aen.* 10. 168) and the name Tongilius has no discernible Etruscan antecedent.

[187] G. C(iampoltrini), 'Orbetello', in A. Carandini (ed.), *La romanizzazione dell'Etruria: il territorio di Vulci*, Catalogue of the Exhibition; Orbetello, 1985 (Milan, 1985), 91 f.; Brown, *Cosa: The Making of a Roman Town*, 21 believes that the polygonal walls of Orbetello and of Cosa are contemporary.

[188] Brown, *Cosa: The Making of a Roman Town*, 39.

[189] Torelli, 'La colonizzazione romana dalla conquista di Veio alla prima guerra punica', in *Roma medio-repubblicana*, 341 f.

the possible implications of such use—a striking sign of Roman superiority both in the ideological and material sphere. In any event, flexibility was and remained the determining factor of Roman colonial policy in terms of religion, at least until the second century BC. Even in the profound transformation of the political and institutional framework of colonized areas that was brought about by colonies themselves, in most cases the great sanctuaries of the past were preserved and actually made the recipients of special attention, as regards both their maintenance and collective religious fervour. Such an attitude was clear from the very beginning and even during the 'reconquest' of the Latium lost in the fifth century BC, the system of the archaic mercantile sanctuaries along its coast[190] was fully respected, if not actually exploited by the *coloniae maritimae*, even when the old commercial functions of those shrines had become obliterated. The tendency in this direction was already clear in 391 BC, when the earliest Latin coastal colony was founded at Circei,

preserving the archaic mercantile sanctuary of Circe.[191] The same applies to the sanctuaries of Aphrodite and of the Fortunae in the Roman colony of Antium (338 BC), in spite of the long occupation of the country by the Volscians;[192] and to the similar cults of Venus Obsequens and Feronia in the *colonia maritima* of Tarracina, also after an interim Volscian occupation;[193] and even to the Auruncan sanctuary of Marica near the maritime colony of Minturnae,[194] in spite of the fact that the physical elimination of the former inhabitants of the area, the Aurunci, as Livy states,[195] was virtually total. Desire for peace and order and fear of the wrath of alien gods powerfully combined to form this flexible attitude towards local and 'national' religions, to shape a master tool for the early steps of Roman imperialism.

[190]   Torelli, in Mastrocinque (ed.), *Ercole in occidente*.

[191]   R. R(ighi), 'Circei', in *Enea nel Lazio*, Catalogue of the Exhibition; Rome, 1981 (Rome, 1981), 70 f.

[192]   O. J. Brendel, 'Two Fortunae: Antium and Praeneste', *AJA* 64 (1960), 43 f.   [193]   Coarelli, *I santuari*, 113 f.

[194]   On the sanctuary, see P. Mingazzini, 'Il santuario della dea Marica alle foci del Garigliano', *MonAL* 37 (1938), col. 684 f.; F. Trotta, 'Minturnae preromana e il culto di Marica', in F. Coarelli (ed.), *Minturnae* (Rome, 1989), 11 f.   [195]   Liv. 9. 25.

3
ROMAN PAESTUM

1. Reorganization after the Conquest

IN MANY WAYS, THE YEAR 273 BC REPRESENTED A turning point in the Roman policy of conquest. With the foundation of the two twin Latin colonies of Paestum and Cosa, the Romans entered in force (and the Latin colonization really was a forceful 'entry') no longer just into the borders, but into the very heart of the territories of Etruria and Magna Graecia, the two most ancient civilizations of the peninsula. However, as has already been emphasized several times,[1] the Roman policy of establishing the two colonies as 'look-outs' to control the newly acquired extension of conquered territory along the Tyrrhenian coast meant this was much more than a simple episode of agrarian colonization. Both colonies replaced two major centres from which they took their names: thus Cosa supplanted the Etruscan town of *Cusa,[2] one of the coastal strongholds of Vulci on the lagoon of Orbetello,[3] while the Lucanian Paistom,[4] formerly Poseidonia, a Greek city of prime importance, gave rise to Paestum. However, while the colony of Cosa rose ex-nihilo upon the headland of Ansedonia, thus overshadowing its nearby homonymous Etruscan antecedent, Latin

Paestum grew within (and close to) Greek Poseidonia and Lucanian Paestum. This feature which distinguishes the double foundation quite clearly, was undoubtedly accompanied by differences in the parallel urban histories. These I have discussed above[5] and for this reason shall not go into, except to mention that Cosa was characterized by a special insistence on its *Latinitas*, from its entirely Romano-Latin cults[6] to the replica of the Lavinian sow,[7] whereas Paestum, as will soon be more amply demonstrated, shows evident signs of a more marked integration between the colonists and the outside world, a circumstance which shaped its fortunes in a rather special way.

Indeed, while the isolation of Cosa in the heart of an Etruria of *principes*, harshly subdued by defeats suffered between 295 and 280 BC and tied to Rome by an interested *fides*, seems self-evident from its character of an outpost bound to remain isolated for almost a century until the foundation of Saturnia (183 BC), Graviscae (181 BC), and Heba (maybe 151 BC), the birth of Latin Paestum was accompanied by a series of measures which left very little room to doubt the Romans' intentions to capitalize on their conquests made at the expense of the Lucanians and the Samnites, and not only from a military standpoint.

All the coastal territory to the south, well beyond Paestum, shows signs of the conquest: the desertion of the Lucanian site of Roccagloriosa[8]—very close to the ancient Greek colony of Pyxus — stretching out menacingly towards the sea and well defended by nature and by its excellent polygonal walls, is a valuable indication of the hefty confiscation of land carried out by the Romans. In fact in 268 BC, barely five years after

---

[1] E. T. Salmon, *Roman Colonization under the Republic* (London, 1969), 62 f.

[2] The original name of this Etruscan city can be reconstructed from a group of gentilicial names, whose root is precisely this toponym (cf. *mefanate* from Mevania, *sentinate* from Sentinum, etc.), i.e. *cusiθe* (CIE 3360–1; 4099: Perusia), *cusinas* (NRIE 542; SE 34 (1966), 314, no. 11: Volsinii) and *cusine—cusinei* (CIE 604–5; 2061–2062: Clusium; cf. also CIE 5580, female name from Tarquinia, but perhaps of Clusine origins).

[3] On this site, see G. C(iampoltrini), in A. Carandini (ed.), *La romanizzazione dell'Etruria: il territorio di Vulci*, Catalogue of Exhibition; Orbetello, 1985 (Milan, 1985), 91 f.

[4] This toponym seems to be Lucanian or could derive from an indigenous name of the site preceding that of the Greek colony of Posidonia: see G. Pugliese Carratelli, 'Problemi della storia di Paestum', in *La monetazione bronzea di Poseidonia-Paestum*, Atti III Conv. Centr. Int. Num. (Rome, 1973), 6 f.

[5] See above, pp. 39–42.

[6] F. Brown, *The Making of a Roman Town* (Ann Arbor, 1980), 31, 49, 51–6.

[7] Ibid. 39.

[8] M. Gualtieri, in M. Gualtieri (ed.), *Roccagloriosa* (Naples, 1990), 199 f.

the foundation of Paestum, Roman colonial politics underwent an appreciable modification. The new Latin colonies of that year, Ariminum and Beneventum, became holders of a different statute, the much debated *ius Ariminensium* or *ius XII coloniarum* fleetingly mentioned by Cicero,[9] which, as has been proved by E. T. Salmon[10]—and as is maybe concealed by the title of *consul* held by the praetors of the two colonies founded in 268 BC[11]— represented a clear improvement in *status* for the new foundations. On the other hand all these stratagems show a global element, both in legal and political terms, all of whose implications most probably escape us. Indeed in the same year of 268 BC the last grant of *civitas sine suffragio* was made, an institution which just two years previously had aroused serious rebellious controversy with regard to the *legio Campana* of Rhegium and the brutal behaviour of C. Genucius Clepsina[12] towards these *cives sine suffragio*. As we know today,[13] he was responsible for the final *mutatio in deterius* of the formerly glorious *status* of the city heading the lists of the *tabulae Caeritum*[14]—and therefore of the perversion of the statute of the *civitas sine suffragio*, from a favourable institution to a punitive *status*, which therefore presupposes a total dominion over the peninsula, gained in the decade between 280 and 270 BC.[15]

The immediate objective of this new legal and political trend was directed towards the extreme reaches of the two traditional lines of Roman expansion from the late fourth century BC: Campania towards the south and the Sabina and Picenum towards the north-east. In fact the scheme in the north-east included the foundation of Ariminum which took place in 268 BC,[16] the concession—after the grant of the *civitas sine suffragio* in 290 BC—of the *civitas optimo iure* to the Sabini (which

was actually given in 264 BC),[17] and the *civitas sine suffragio* to the loyal Picentes[18]—and the resettlement of the two tribes Quirina and Velina towards the north, scheduled by Dentatus but sanctioned only in 241 BC.[19] The very complex link-up in the south between southern and northern projects to resettle the zone between Campania, Samnium, and Lucania was, however, of chief importance. In effect, if the foundation of Beneventum, which took place in the same year, represented the logical outcome of the foundation of Paestum, the forced transfer of the rebel *Picentes* to the formerly Etruscan territory on the right bank of the river Sele, dated to the same crucial year of 268 BC,[20] seems an equally logical outcome of the same foundation. This deportation did indeed lessen the pressure on newly founded Ariminum, and at the same time freed land for the viritane colonists, whom Dentatus projected to settle in new tribes (originally, as it has been noted, destined for the conquered Sabine land in 290) and who were deprived of vital space not only by the concession of Roman citizenship to the Sabines quartered in the Sabine territory further off, but above all—as E. Gabba has clearly shown[21]—by the sales, under the form of *agri quaestorii*, of the conquered Sabine land closest to Rome, which was particularly coveted by the urban *nobilitas*.

The plan could not have been clearer on a comprehensive political level and the settlement of the southern aspect between 273 and 268 BC appears to be one of the rather few linear moments in the years between 292 and 265 BC, a period which was crucial for the conquest of the peninsula but is also, however, desperately full of gaps owing to the loss of the text by Livy. At this point the political history of Roman Paestum would

---

[9] Cic. *Pro Caec.* 102.

[10] Salmon, *Roman Colonization*, 63.

[11] Cf. *ILLRP* 77 (Ariminum); 169, 553 (Beneventum).

[12] Cfr. Polyb. 1. 7. 11–12, 10. 4; Liv. *Per.* 15; Liv. 28. 28. 3–6; Dion. Hal. 20. 16; Zon. 8. 6. 14–15; Val. Max. 2. 7. 15; Iul. Par. *Epit.* 2. 7. 15; Frontin. *Str.* 4. 1. 38; Oros. 4. 3. 5; *Hist. Misc.* 2. 21.

[13] This important inscription from Caere, not yet fully considered from an historical standpoint, has now been published by M. Cristofani, 'C. Genucius Clevsina pretore a Caere', in *Atti II Congresso Internazionale Etrusco*, i (Rome, 1989), 167 f.

[14] On this institution see the fundamental works by A. Bernardi, 'I "cives sine suffragio"', *Athenaeum*, 16 (1938), 97 f., by M. Sordi, *I rapporti romano-ceriti e l'origine della civitas sine suffragio* (Rome, 1960), and by M. Humbert, *Municipium et civitas sine suffragio* (Rome, 1978).

[15] E. T. Salmon, *The Making of Roman Italy* (London, 1982), 67: 'one can confidently assert that by 268 there was no community south of the Pisa–Ariminum line, apart from Rome herself, that was truly independent'.

[16] Polyb. 3. 90. 8; Liv. *Per.* 15; Vell. 1. 14. 7; Eutrop. 2. 16; Paean. 2. 16; *Hist. Misc.* 2. 22.

[17] Vell. Pat. 1. 14. 6; a slightly different opinion in Humbert, *Municipium*, 234 f.

[18] See lately T. Iwai, 'La concessione della cittadinanza romana nel Piceno', *Studia Picena* 42 (1975), 1 f.; the chronology of the grant of the *civitas optimo iure* to the same Picentes is instead not precisely assessed by Humbert, *Municipium*, 349 (see however p. 237).

[19] Since the name of the tribe Quirina was connected with Cures and that of the Velina with the lacus Velinus and the mons Velinus near Reate, it has been argued that the primitive Sabine location of these tribes underwent radical changes as a consequence of the fact that the original territories considered for land allotment were sold in the form of *agri quaestorii*: see n. 21.

[20] Strab. 5. 251; *Geogr. Gr. Min.* 2. 555; Ptol. 3. 1. 7. 69; Plin. *NH* 3. 38. 70; Sil. It. 8. 580; Mela 2. 69; Steph. Byz. s.v. Πικέντια; Dion. Per. *cum schol.* Eustath. *Paraphr.*; Priscian. *perieg.* 355. On the date see J. Beloch, *Römische Geschichte bis zum Beginn der punischen Kriege* (Berlin and Leipzig, 1926), 474; G. De Sanctis, *Storia dei Romani* (Florence, 1955), ii. 402 n. 97; A. Toynbee, *Hannibal's Legacy* (Oxford, 1965), i. 368 n. 8.

[21] E. Gabba, 'Allora i Romani conobbero per la prima volta la ricchezza', *AIIN* 36 (1989), 9 f. (= *Del buon uso della ricchezza* (Milan, 1988), 19 f.).

have drawn to an unfortunate close, if we had not had the plentiful data of the city's archaeological history to hand, which (thanks to tireless and valuable research, promptly published by E. Greco and D. Theodorescu)[22] have been accumulating from 1980 to the present day. Therefore, not only do I owe an enormous debt to their findings, but I must also add that a large part of this work should be considered as an appendix to their views, and, with their permission, as an integral part both of their existing publications and of their unpublished findings, which they have very kindly kept me abreast of almost right up to the date of this book.

2. The Birth of the Colony

As clearly emerged on the occasion of a recent conference in Acquasparta on colonization in the fourth and third centuries BC,[23] the initial foundation of a Latin colony in the middle years of the Republic necessitated, so to speak, an urban network of streets, the earth-paved *piazza* of the forum with its *saepta* and its *diribitorium*,[24] the main temples, and the walls.

This was illustrated with great clarity by J. Mertens's paper on Alba Fucens.[25] It is also dealt with in F. Brown's publication on Paestum's twin colony, Cosa,[26] and in the paper given in Acquasparta on the same site by R. Scott.[27] Alba and Cosa, the former founded on the site of an extremely modest *oppidum* of the Aequians and the latter *in vacuo*, are two cities which assumed the outline or contours of an urban centre only in the late third century BC. The case of Paestum on the other hand, rising from a structurally Greek city, hardly modified by the Lucanian conquerors, is a very complex event in itself, the reconstruction of which obliges us in fact to look back at aspects of town planning and architecture, at times of extreme antiquity,

and in any case to consider those particular aspects of urban design carried out before the Lucanian occupation.

In spite of the very obvious difference from Cosa and Alba, the essential characteristics of the traces left by the colony on the ancient urban system do not greatly differ from those in Alba and Cosa, with the exception—and an understandable one, independent of the standard of preservation—of the general form of the urban network inherited from its Graeco-Lucanian past. In fact, the structures first established at Cosa or at Alba are present, in forms more than evident, at Paestum as well. Yet in the Paestan case, which, let us remember, is not a foundation *in vacuo*, it is of enormous interest that the whole of the part which roughly coincides with that part of the old city to the east of the State Road no. 18 (Strada Statale n.18)[28] seems to be a Roman addition to the urbanistic structure of Graeco-Lucanian origin, as has been proposed by E. Greco and D. Theodorescu. This apparently banal circumstance, if proved, could be of fundamental importance, in that it demonstrates even on the town-planning level that the foundation of the Latin colony only partly disturbed the arrangement of ownership within the urban area (and we shall soon see, in the rural area as well) and that, therefore, a significant part of the indigenous Lucanian element was enrolled into the new colony. If, on the other hand, we go on to substantiate what has been learnt in recent times as regards the distribution of land to the colonists through the identification of farms dating from the colonial epoch,[29] it seems likely that the *ager centuriatus* should be located in the southern part of the Paestan territory. Besides this circumstance, it can be pointed out that, discounting the denser pattern of farms and very small settlements of the Latin colonial epoch in the territory close to the city,[30] the Roman presence appears sparser than the previous Lucanian one and that, in any case, the elements of continuity in the countryside prevail over those of discontinuity, both in the rustic settlement and above all in the cemeteries. A. Pontrandolfo[31] has produced a few very interesting and revealing examples of the same tenacious continuity between the Lucanian past and the Latin colonial reality (and

[22] E. Greco and D. Theodorescu, *Paestum* (from now on abbreviated as *Paestum*), i (Rome, 1980); ii (Rome, 1982); iii (Rome, 1987); E. Greco, 'La città e il territorio: i problemi di storia topografica', *Atti Taranto* (1987), 471 f.; D. Theodorescu, 'Elements d'urbanisme et de topographie: état actuel et perspectives', ibid. 501 f.

[23] The acts have been published in *DArch* 3rd ser., 6: 2 (1988).

[24] See M. Torelli, 'Il "diribitorium" di Alba Fucens e il campus eroico di Herdonia', in *Comunità indigene e romanizzazione*, Acts of Conference; Rome, 1990 (Rome, 1992), 39 f.

[25] J. Mertens, 'Alba Fucens', in *DArch* 3rd ser., 6: 2 (1988), 87 f.

[26] Brown, *Cosa*.

[27] R. T. Scott, 'The Latin Colony of Cosa', *DArch* 3rd ser., 6: 2 (1988), 73 f.

[28] [P.Gros] and M.Torelli, *Storia dell'urbanistica. Il mondo romano* (Bari and Rome, 1988), 142, fig. 53; cf. above n. 22.

[29] D. G(asparri], in *Paestum, Città e territorio nelle colonie greche d'occidente*, i (Taranto, 1987), 51 f. [30] Ibid. pl. 15.

[31] A. Pontrandolfo, 'Paestum. S. Venera', in *Atti Taranto* (1976), 800 f.

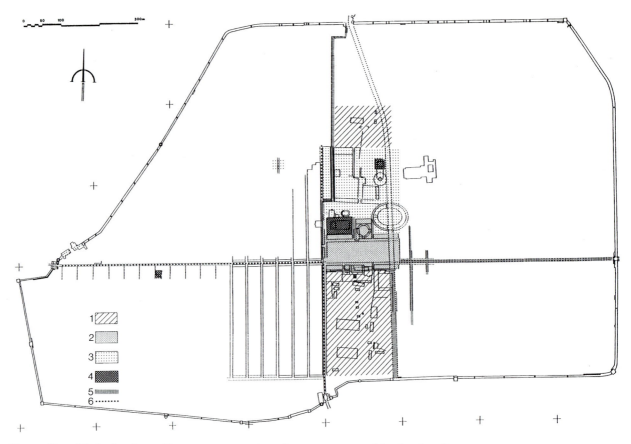

Fig. 25. Plan of the Latin colony of Paestum: 1. sanctuaries; 2. forum area; 3. area of the abandoned Greek agora; 4. piscina publica and sanctuary of Fortuna Virilis; 5. new main streets; 6. main streets preserved (after Theodorescu).

therefore of the enlistment of Lucanians in the Latin city), consisting in funerary enclosures containing cinerary urns from the colonial period (third century BC) placed squarely on top of painted tomb chambers belonging to the Lucanian aristocracy. In as far as we can gather from the archaeological evidence, however, it appears that the Greek element met a different fate, as we shall see later on.

3. Town Planning and Public Buildings

Moving on now to the actual events of the urban history of the colony (Fig. 25), it would seem that an important chapter in the colonial foundation is represented by the city walls. The walls of Paestum are awaiting study with more up-to-date equipment than was previously used and are therefore to be dated pre-

cisely.[32] It is however probable that, as in other colonies, they largely date back to the first years of the new colony. The fact that the large planned Roman addition to the old Lucano-Greek town, corresponding to the quarters in the eastern third of the city, is enclosed by

[32] A project on Paestum walls worked out in the 1960s by a team of the German Archaeological Institute has produced no conclusive results: a totally different approach is instead demonstrated in the preliminary report of a similar project carried out by Greco's team: I. D'Ambrosio, 'Le fortificazioni di Poseidonia-Paestum. Problemi e prospettive di ricerca', *AIONArch* 12 (1990), 71 f. For the German project see however: H. Schläger, *Das Westtor von Paestum* (Munich, 1957); id., 'Zu den Bauperiode der Stadtmauer von Pâestum', in *MDAI(R)* 69 (1962), 21 f.; id., 'Zur Frage der Torverschlüsse von Paestum', *MDAI(R)* 81 (1964), 104 f.; id., ' "Bohrmuscheln" in Paestum', ibid. 245 f.; id., 'Zu paestaner Problemen', in *MDAI(R)* 72 (1965), 182 f.; id., 'Weiteres zu Paestaner Problemen', in *MDAI(R)* 73–4 (1966–7), 270 f.; id., 'Weiteres zum Wallgraben von Paestum', in *MDAI(R)* 76 (1969), 350 f. A general survey of the problems is found in S. Blum, 'Le mura', *Atti Taranto* (1987), 575 f. Most recently, some excavations have been carried out in tha area of Porta Marina: A. Rouveret and R. Robert, in *MEFRA* 104 (1992), 505 f. Such excavations have dated the gate to the last quarter of the 4th cent. BC and brought to light the sacrifice and the ritual burial of a dog: this ritual find has been described at length by R. Robert, 'Rites de protection et de défense. À propos des ossements d'un chien découverts au pied du rempart de Paestum', *AIONArch* 15 (1993), 119 f.

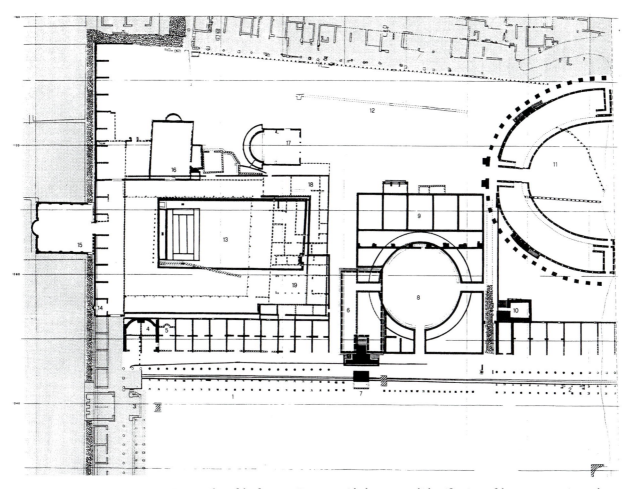

Fig. 26. Plan of the forum at Paestum with the proposed identifications of the extant remains: 1. the double row of sockets for posts marking the area of the *Saepta*; 2. slab-lined pits connected with the *Saepta*; 3. temple of Mercury; 4. temple of Divus Augustus; 5. *schola* of the *collegium* of the *magistri Mentis Bonae*; 6. temple of Mens; 7. balustrade for the exhibition of law proposals; 8. *comitium*; 9. *curia* and *tabularium*; 10. *carcer*; 11. *amphiteatrum*; 12. *xystus*; 13. *piscina publica*; 14. shrine of Fortuna Augusta (?); 15, 16, 19. dynastic *sacraria* of the emperors; 17. *nymphaeum*; 18. *schola* of the *Augustales*.

these walls allows us to suppose that the overall design of the city walls goes back to the foundation years; anyway, in the pre-existing section of the town towards the west it is likely that the new circuit of the Latin colony enclosed parts of the old Graeco-Lucanian walls. The beautiful circular towers of the Porta Marina, showing interesting architectural motifs of late classical times, could be an example of how parts of a more ancient fortification came to be inserted into the new wall enclosing the Latin colony. From another point of view, the well-known inscriptions characterized by the formula *lapis imfosos*,[33] which on palaeographic and

linguistic grounds again date back to the third century BC, must refer to the restoration carried out in view of the Hannibalic threat, when the *scalae* mentioned in one of the texts of the *lapides infossi*[34] were added, to allow for ramps to place siege machines, which the approaching danger of a new army of Hellenistic type, such as Hannibal's, rendered not only useful, but a virtual necessity.

After the walls, the other major section of the new settlement designed in the foundation years must be the forum (Fig. 26). It is evident that the strongest

---

[33] M. Mello and G. Voza, *Le iscrizioni latine di Paestum* (Naples, 1966), henceforth abbreviated as *ILP*, nos. 135–8; on these inscriptions see also

G. Dunst, 'Zu den Inschriften an der Stadtmauern von Paestum', in *MDAI(R)* 73–4 (1966–7), 244 f.

[34] *ILP* 138: *lapis infosus secundo scalas*.

indication of the new Latin presence is given by the relocation of the areas of political life further south of the Graeco-Lucanian agora,[35] still within the vast unitary belt of collective use in the eastern third of the urban area of Poseidonia, but then, in the set-up of Latin Paestum, in the city centre. This belt, dating directly back to the Greek foundation, is characterized by the immense central political space of the *agora* closed in by two huge religious spaces, that of the northern sanctuary, which appears in all likelihood to touch the north limits of the town, and that of the southern sanctuary, which definitely meets the south borderline of the Greek, Lucanian, and Roman city.[36] The piazza of the forum was equipped so as to allow the area to function as *saepta*: in fact, along all the edges of the visible sides of the piazza run two series of small lime-stone blocks with rectangular holes for posts necessary, according to the rite, to define the *templum in terris* constituted by the forum piazza itself. On the occasion of the *comitia* the piazza would be surrounded by linen bands, *cum aliqua loca . . . linteis saepiuntur,* as goes the well-known Festus' entry in referring to these *templa in terris* or *minora templa.*[37] Of the two series (Fig. 26, 1), the older is the one closest to the porticoes and at times is obliterated by them, being previous to the construction of the *porticus* of the forum. Yet that series is very probably later than a third one constituted by the large slab-lined pits, which, as we shall see, must date back to a time fairly close to the date of the foundation. The second series is the more complete and more internal with regard to the piazza and is linked with the creation of the porticoes, since, in front of the most illustrious temple in the forum, the so called 'Temple of Peace', interrupting the series of blocks with post-holes, stands an unusual 'balustrade' (Fig. 26, 7), which I assume to be the exhibition place *in publicum* of the text of newly proposed laws for the ritual *trinundinum,* just as happened in Rome with the temple of Saturn.[38] Finally a fourth series of pits on the short side of the forum, known at Alba Fucens, at Cosa, and now also at

Fregellae and connected with the *diribitorium*, is missing, along with all the evidence of successive developments of the civic body;[39] perhaps these pits at Paestum are still concealed by the modern road, the Strada Statale no. 18, which covers the eastern side of the forum. In recompense, there is an interesting similarity with Cosa to be found in Paestum: two (originally three) large slab-lined pits placed at about two-thirds of the length of the forum (Fig. 26, 2), which, in the light of recent discoveries regarding those in the Latin colony of Fregellae,[40] may perhaps be seen as by far the earliest device for the erection of the temporary structure of the *diribitorium*. With this triple stratification of preparations for installing the *ovile* in the colony of Paestum, as some sources[41] figuratively describe the *saepta*, calling them a sheep enclosure, with its posts and linen bands around the provisional belt, we touch on the complex problem of the development of the structure of the forum after the foundation.

The example of Alba Fucens shows that the first decades of a colony were dedicated mainly to the construction of sacred buildings. As far as the public necessities of the *primordia coloniae* were concerned, the simple definition of the area of the forum to hold the elections for magistrates was more than sufficient. On the other hand, if we pursue F. Coarelli's initial line of thought,[42] I should be inclined to maintain that the transformation of the Roman *comitium,* from rectangular (as it still was after the censorship of C. Maenius in 318 BC)[43] to circular, might be attributed to the 265 BC censorship (the second exceptional censorship of Q. Marcius Rutilus Censorinus, of whose building activity we unfortunately know nothing), two years before the *horologium* from Catana was brought there,[44] proof and *terminus ante quem* for the building's round shape. If this proposal is correct, it follows that the circular 'model' of the *comitium* (Fig. 26, 8) in Rome was soon copied at Cosa, Alba Fucens, and Paestum (and we now know also at Fregellae),[45] in the second half of the third

[35] *Paestum* ii, esp. 70 f., 83 f.

[36] E. Greco and [M. Torelli], *Storia dell'urbanistica. Il mondo greco* (Bari and Rome, 1982), 208 f.

[37] Fest. 146 L. On these *minora templa,* see: M. Torelli, 'Un "templum augurale" d'età repubblicana a Bantia', *RAL* 8th ser., 21 (1966), 293 f.; id., 'Contributi al supplemento del *C.I.L.* IX', *RAL* 8th ser., 24 (1969), 40 f.

[38] On this, see the prescriptions of *lex Cornelia de XX quaestoribus* (*CIL* I², 587): cf. G. Lugli, *Roma antica. Il centro monumentale* (Rome, 1946), 149 f., and F. Coarelli, *Roma,* Guide Archeologiche Laterza, 3rd edn. (Bari and Rome, 1983), 61.

[39] Torelli, 'Il diribitorium'.

[40] F. Coarelli. *Il Campo Marzio: Dalle origini alla fine della Repubblica* (Rome, 1997), 161 ff.

[41] Liv. 26. 22; Cic. *Pro Mil.* 41; Cic. *Pro Rab.* 11; Ov. *Fast.* 1. 53; Auson. *Grat. act.* 3. 13; Serv. *Ecl.* 1. 33; Iuv. 6. 259 *cum schol.*

[42] F. Coarelli, *Il Foro Romano,* i (Rome, 1983), 149 f.; see however id., *Il Foro Romano,* ii (Rome, 1985), 121 n. 115, where he seems inclined to place the circular plan of the Comitium in the years around 300 BC.

[43] Coarelli, *Il Foro Romano,* i. 148, ii. 143 f.; [Gros] and Torelli, *Storia dell'urbanistica,* 94 f.

[44] Plin. *NH* 7. 60.   [45] Cf. n. 24.

century BC when the projects for shops, surely taken into consideration at the time of the foundation, must have been carried out. The Graeco-Lucanian *ekklesiasterion*, which had obviously been used as the *comitium* in the initial phases of the colony, was eliminated at the same time, according to the material found in the refilling of the Greek and Lucanian public-building work, dating from about the middle of the third century BC or soon after.[46] On the other hand, the fact that the chronology of the construction (though certainly not the planning) of the shops cannot be automatically linked with the foundation, appears to be confirmed by the discovery beneath the foundations of one of the shops, the *taberna* no. 10, of a fragment of an ex-voto representing a baby in swaddling clothes, datable without doubt to the first decades of the colonial epoch, as we shall see.[47] Closely linked with the *comitium*, whose eastern side it faces, both on a topographical and a functional level, is the mighty block-built construction of virtually square plan, with many horizontal courses still preserved and abutting upon *taberna* no. 13 (the first to the east of the *comitium*), whose interior was refaced throughout in the early imperial age. Sestieri[48] has proposed identifying it as an *aerarium*, a suggestion taken up by E. Greco with legitimate caution.[49] Considering its very close association with the site for colonial *tribunalia*, and therefore of penal judgements, and the resemblance with the matching *comitium-carcer* in Rome,[50] and moreover in the light of the implications of the impressive analogy between the design of the Paestan structure and the building on the eastern corner of the forum in Cosa, accurately identified as the civic *carcer* by F. Brown,[51] it cannot be ruled out that this building too, acted as the local *carcer*, perhaps ex-

tended in the imperial age to the adjacent *taberna* 13. However, there is insufficient evidence to support either of the explanations outright.

4. The Extramural Sanctuaries

The most revealing aspect of the socio-political climate of the foundation phase is however the religious one. The new colonists, who, as we shall see, undoubtedly blended in with that part of the indigenous population loyal to Rome, to a large extent respected the ancient order of urban cults which was outlined in the two centuries of Greek independence and in the period of little more than a hundred years of Lucanian occupation. Generally, from the little that is known after the frenetic and virtually undocumented excavations of the 1950s and 1960s, all the votive deposits of the classical urban sanctuaries and of the largest suburban ones, including the Heraion at the mouth of the Sele river, contain materials which can be dated with reasonable certainty to the epoch preceding that of the Latin colony, at times with a continuity, as in the case of the sanctuary of S. Venera,[52] which extended from the foundation of Poseidonia right up to the full imperial age. For this reason it is extremely interesting to check, within the somewhat narrow limits of feasibility, just how much was preserved of the city's religious past, noting incidentally what of this past was reutilized or developed, and what instead was the result of a Roman addition.

Starting with the *extra moenia* sanctuaries (Fig. 27), I should mention that Roman material has been found at the Heraion at the mouth of the Sele river, confirming the persistent presence of an ancient and distinguished cult, operating on a lesser scale maybe than in the past, but significant none the less. If the ancient Heraion had a more glorious fate in the Greek and Lucanian phases, it is certain that the sanctuary of Aphrodite of S. Venera on the other hand was the object of special care and attention—as shall be seen later on—between the end of the third and the middle of the second century BC and again between the end of the republican and the beginning of the imperial age.

A little shrine, excavated in 1966 by M. Napoli, is situated 300 m. to the south-west of the walls and was

---

[46] In *Paestum* ii. 83 f., pottery with decoration in superimposed colours, very close to Latin *pocola*, and black-glazed vases inscribed with Latin graffiti (nos. 122 f., pp. 109 f.), found in the fill of the *ekklesiasterion*, have been wrongly dated to the end of the 4th cent. BC; their chronology is instead definitely later—though not much later—than 273 BC and therefore the cancellation of the Greek circular building must be somehow later than the foundation of the Latin colony.

[47] E. Greco, in *Paestum*, i. 18 dates it to pre-Roman times, but unfortunately with no argument; significantly, a second fragment of a similar votive object comes from the fill of the second floor of the area around the so called 'tempio italico' (*Paestum*, i. 20, fig. 36/77), proving that the dispersion of the deposit with the statuettes of babies in swaddling clothes is definitely later than the construction of the 'tempio italico', which belongs to the earliest times of the Latin colony.

[48] P. C. Sestieri, *Paestum*, Itinerari dei Musei, Gallerie e Monumenti d'Italia 84 12th edn. (Rome, 1976) (from now on abbreviated as Sestieri, *Paestum*), 24.

[49] *Paestum*, iii. 66 f.

[50] On this building see Coarelli, *Il Foro Romano*, ii. 64 f.

[51] Brown, *Cosa*, 32. See below.

[52] See below.

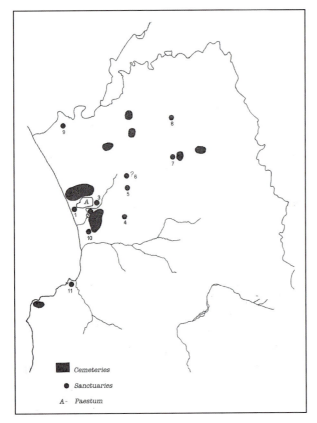

Fig. 27. Map of the Paestan territory with the indication of pre-Roman and Roman sanctuaries: 1. Shrine of Isis in the 'Apollo Camping' area; 2. 'Santa Venera'; 3. 'Stazione di Paestum'; 4. 'Acqua che bolle'; 5. 'Getsemani'; 6. 'Grotta del Granato' (?); 7. 'Fonte'; 8. 'Albanella'; 9. Heraion at the mouth of the Sele river; 10. 'Linora'; 11. 'Agropoli'; 12. 'Capodifiume' (drawing A. Trapassi).

recently partially re-explored by the Soprintendenza Archeologica di Salerno in the area now occupied by the 'Apollo Camping'. The shrine is particularly interesting.[53] The few facts we can reconstruct from the materials in our possession seem to point towards a rather late foundation date, at the end of the third century BC with very few, elusive traces of a previous archaic existence. The plan of the sacellum, shown by a sketch preserved in the Museum storerooms together with the objects of the early excavations (Fig. 28), displays the peculiarity of a pronaos which is wider than the cella. This detail, not without similarities to the set-up of the temples of Isis in Pompeii and in

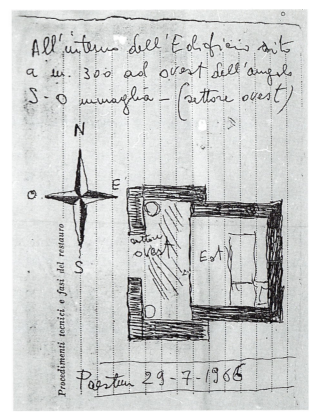

Fig. 28. Plan of the extramural shrine in the area of the 'Apollo Camping' (sketch in the archives of the Paestum Museum).

Dion,[54] together with the abundant presence of lamps and unusual ritual vases, pyxis-cups with a foot,[55] suggests a chapel dedicated to Isis, whose cult in Paestum is epigraphically attested by an inscription commemorating the dedication of a temple by a Laureia Q.f., a member of the ancient republican aristocracy of the city.[56] The identification of the small shrine *extra muros*

---

[53] On this find see: M. Mello, 'Strabone V 4,13 e le origini di Posidonia', *PP* (1967), 402 f.; M. Napoli, in *Atti Taranto* (1966), 246; M. Cipriani, *Il Museo di Paestum* (Agropoli, 1986), 59 f. (henceforth abbreviated as *Museo*); A. Ardovino, *I culti di Paestum* (Naples, 1986), 49 f. (henceforth abbreviated as *Culti*); M. Cipriani, 'I santuari', *Atti Taranto* (1987), 412 f.

[54] On the temple of Isis at Pompeii, whose first phase can be dated still in the 2nd cent. BC, see V. Tran Tam Tinh, *Essai sur le culte d'Isis à Pompéi* (Paris, 1964), together with A.-M. De Vos, *Pompei, Ercolano, Stabia*, Guide Archeologiche Laterza (Bari and Rome, 1982), 72 f.; on the temple at Dion, see D. Pandermalis, in *AA* (1982), 727 f., esp. 732 figs. 5–6.

[55] Four examples of a very similar pyxis-cup have been found in a tomb of the Vittorina necropolis at Gubbio, ancient Iguvium; they had been placed each at one corner of the grave, where lay a man holding a sistrum, possibly an Isis priest. see M. Cipollone, *Iside: il mito, il mistero, la magia*, Catalogue of Exhibition; Milan 1997 (Milan, 1997) 494–8.

[56] *ILP* 160. A *Q. Laur(eius) pr(aetor)* signs an important coin emission (M. Crawford, 'The Form and Function of a Subsidiary Coinage', in *La monetazione di bronzo di Poseidonia-Paestum*, 85 f., no. 25, tav. x, henceforth abbreviated as Crawford, 'Form and Function'), that, were we able to interpret and date it correctly, would provide us with exceptional evidence concerning the history of colonial Paestum. Legends and types, all with mark of value, are as follows: semis: scale and *cornucopia*, Q.LAUR.PR, PAE/ coinage scene, SP.DD.SS, MIL.; triens: heads of the Dioscuri and laurel wreath, Q.LAV/*cornucopia*, LEX. XXXX; sextans: female head, Q.LAV./boar, PAE.

Plate 3. Paestum, Museo. Head of a female statue of alabaster marble from the sanctuary in the area of the 'Apollo Camping' (photo by L. De Masi).

Of the other known suburban and extra-urban sanctuaries,[57] only the one at the source of the Capodifiume (Fig. 27, 4)[58] appears to have definitely continued into the age of the Roman Republic. The best known of all, thanks to M. Cipriani's excellent publication—that of Albanella (Fig. 27, 8)[59]—appears to have already been closed in the late Lucanian age. The same seems to apply to the archaic and classical cult sites of Fonte (Fig. 27, 10),[60] Linora (Fig. 27, 7),[61] Getsemani (Fig. 27, 5)[62] and 'Acqua che bolle' (Fig. 27, 6),[63] whilst the information we have for the sanctuary of Agropoli (Fig. 27, 9),[64] conceivably an Athenaion given the very

with an Isiac cult place is in perfect accord with the iconography and the style of a beautiful head of a female statue, two-thirds lifesize and made of alabaster marble (Pl. 3), discovered in the early excavations; the head is recognizable as Hellenistic work of the first half of the second century BC and has many comparisons among contemporary works from Alexandria or with an Alexandrian flavour. Inside the building was an altar, a decisive characteristic in identifying it as a sanctuary of a mystery cult, and in front of which was a pit containing sacrificial remains. The ex-votos include small female statues, cupids, and doves, which help us to confirm that we are in the presence of a cult of Isis deriving from that of Venus or presented to the Paestans as that of Venus. The closeness of the shrine to the ancient seashore suggests that the cult may have been introduced on the basis of the equivalence between Aphrodite Pontia and Isis Pelagia.

[57] A complete list of all known archaeological finds in the Paestan territory, including cartographical and bibliographical references, can be found in AA.VV., *Paestum* (Città e territorio nelle colonie greche d'Occidente, i). A complete list of the urban and extraurban sanctuaries has been given by G. Tocco Sciarelli *et al.*, 'I santuari', *Atti Taranto* (1987), 361 f. (map at fig. 7). Besides the few examples of continuity between the Graeco-Lucanian period and Roman times, the list of suburban sanctuaries known to be active from the foundation of Posidonia *c.*600 BC up to the Roman conquest is as follows: a sanctuary near Porta Marina, where a 4th-cent. BC votive deposit, including loom-weights, miniature hydriai and amphorae, and lamps speaks for a cult of a feminine goddess, possibly Demeter and Kore, (Cipriani, *Museo*, 58; G. Avagliano and M. Cipriani, in *Paestum* (Città e territorio nelle colonie greche d'Occidente, i), 55; M. Cipriani, in *Atti Taranto* (1987), 401 f.); a 5th-cent. BC sanctuary of Demeter and Kore, discovered last century south-west of the city walls, at the site called Torre di Paestum (thence very near to the above mentioned sanctuary in the area of the 'Camping Apollo' I have proposed to identify as belonging to Aphrodite–Isis), which yielded a huge votive deposit, whose material, now dispersed, included statuettes of individuals offering piglets (E. Gerhard, in *Bullettino dell'Instituto* (1829), 189; Cipriani, *Museo*, 58 f.; Ardovino, *Culti*, 99 f.; Avagliano and Cipriani, in *Paestum* (Città e territorio nelle colonie greche d'Occidente, i), 55; Cipriani, in *Atti Taranto* (1987), 412 f.); a sanctuary at the site of Caggiano, therefore very close to that of S. Venera, of which it could be merely an extension (Cipriani, *Museo*, 59 ff.; Avagliano, in *Paestum* (Città e territorio nelle colonie greche d'Occidente, i), 45); a sanctuary near the Paestum railway station (Cipriani, *Museo*, 60; ead., in *Paestum* (Città e territorio nelle colonie greche d'Occidente, i). 38).

[58] This excavation, which has a remarkable historical importance, is still unpublished: only few lines on it are to be found in *Paestum* (Città e territorio nelle colonie greche d'Occidente, i), 33, and a brief sketch of the finds by G. Greco, in *Atti Taranto* (1987), 419 f.

[59] M. Cipriani, *S. Nicola di Albanella*, Corpus Stipi Votive Italiane, iii. 1 (Rome, 1989).

[60] G. Voza, in *BA* (1964), 366; id., in *Atti Taranto* (1964), 193 f.; G. Avagliano, *Museo*, 65 f.; Ardovino, *Culti*, 131; Cipriani, in *Paestum* (Città e territorio nelle colonie greche d'Occidente, i), 30 f.; Avagliano, in *Atti Taranto* (1987), 428 f.

[61] Voza, in *BA* (1964), 363 f.; M. Napoli, in *Atti Taranto* (1966), 110 f.; G. Voza, ibid. 192 f.; Cipriani, *Museo*, 61 f.; Ardovino, *Culti*, 131; G. Avagliano, in *Paestum* (Città e territorio nelle colonie greche d'Occidente, i), 41; id., in *Atti Taranto* (1987), 414 f.

[62] Avagliano, *Museo*, 63 f.; id., in *Paestum* (Città e territorio nelle colonie greche d'Occidente, i), 32 f.; id., in *Atti Taranto* (1987), 416 f.

[63] A. Ardovino, 'Nuovi oggetti sacri con iscrizione in alfabeto acheo', *ArchClass* 32, (1980), 51 f.; id., *Culti*, 92, 130; M. Cipriani, in *Paestum* (Città e territorio nelle colonie greche d'Occidente, i), 39; ead., in *Atti Taranto* (1987), 415 f.

[64] A. Fiammenghi, 'Agropoli: primi saggi scavo nell'area del Castello', in *AIONArch* 7 (1985), 53 f.; ead., *Museo*, 75 f.; ead., in *Paestum* (Città e territorio nelle colonie greche d'Occidente, i), 47 f.; ead., in *Atti Taranto* (1987), 396 f.

few votive materials discovered, is insufficient to express an opinion regarding a possible continuity, even though the probabilities are rather against it. At Paestum, as in other Latin colonies, the inversion of the trends of a Greek past, so rich in attention to the religiousness of the *chora*, is evident and points to the clear hegemony of the city over the countryside, now merely a productive appendix of the urban system, deprived of its own religiousness, and also indicates a fierce and definitive eradication from the land of the Greek element which had continued to a large extent to occupy the territory even under Lucanian domination.

The sanctuaries *extra moenia* preserved by the Roman colonists are therefore very few and address very specific religious needs: on one hand the presence of Venus in her double guise as Venus Erycina of S. Venera (Fig. 27, 1) and Venus Marina-Isis Pelagia in the small sacellum in the area of the 'Camping Apollo' (Fig. 27, 2), and on the other the very ancient cult of Hera at the mouth of the Sele river (Fig. 27, 3), strongly rooted in the popular culture of the place (to the point of being transplanted during the Middle Ages to the Christian sanctuary of the Madonna del Granato at Capaccio),[65] but almost 'forgotten' in view of the Latin colony's building activity. This old and celebrated sanctuary of Hera could even be the place where the gloomy ceremonies took place commemorating the lost identity of the ancient Greek race which was preserved with difficulty in republican Paestum, a fact indicated by the much-discussed fragment attributed to Aristoxenus, to be dealt with further on.

5. The Northern Sanctuary: The 'Arx' of the Colony

The most significant situation, however, is the one presented by the sanctuaries inside the walls. The clear example of Cosa, but also true of other Latin colonies of the fourth and third centuries BC proves that the ritual of colonial foundations could not be separated from selection of an *arx* for the procedures of the *augurium* and the *auspicium*, practical rituals necessary for the act of the *deductio* itself and for the normal

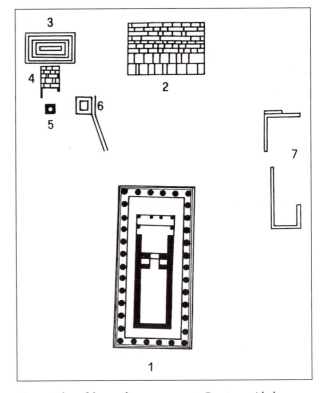

Fig. 29. Plan of the northern sanctuary at Paestum with the proposed identifications of temples and buildings: 1. Athenaion; 2. Greek altar of the Athenaion with Roman restauration; 3. Greek altar of Zeus; 4. Roman altar of Iuppiter; 5–6. votive columns; 7. archaic Greek temple (drawing A. Trapassi).

political running of the city. There is no doubt that the northern sacred area (Fig. 29) was chosen with this aim in mind. Formerly, in the Greek phase, it must once have acted as a symbolic acropolis, with the imposing presence of the late archaic Athenaion (Fig. 29, 1) and with its slightly higher altitude, as opposed to the larger sacred area in the south, which was conceived of as an urban sanctuary of the 'political' city. In the northern sanctuary, in fact reused in the Byzantine village which grew around the 'Temple of Ceres', two monumental twin inscriptions on monolithic blocks have come to light, which, due to their size, are unlikely to have come from far; the blocks perhaps belonged to altars and bore the following dedications:

Iovei [66]

[M]enervae[67]

[65] P. Zancani Montuoro and U. Zanotti Bianco, *Heraion alla Foce del Sele* i (Rome, 1951), 18 f.; on the same subject, most recently, see Ardovino, *Culti*, 189 f. and G. Tocco Sciarelli, J. de la Genière, and G. Greco, in *Atti Taranto* (1987), 385 f.

[66] *ILP* 5 = CIL I², 3147; cf. P. Zancani Montuoro, 'Il Poseidonion di Poseidonia', *Archivio Storico per la Calabria e la Lucania*, 23 (1954), 166 and n. 2.
[67] *ILP* 6 = CIL I², 3148.

Plate 4. Paestum, Museo. Terracotta dolium with a dedication to Minerva, from the Roman votive deposit near the Athenaion (photo by L. De Masi).

Plate 5. Paestum, Museo. Bronze lamina with a dedication to Jupiter (photo by L. De Masi).

The inscriptions are very important for the sacred topography of the city, in that they signal the presence of the great formal cult of Jupiter of pan-Latin character and its pairing in the area—even if this was part of the Greek inheritance, which is highly likely—together with the other local city goddess, Athena-Minerva, who was certainly inherited from the very ancient past and venerated in the splendid late-archaic building known as the 'Temple of Ceres'.[68] We are clearly dealing with a coupling which dates back, if not to the Greek epoch, at least to the phase of the foundation of the Latin colony, since the Hellenistic votive deposit of the Athenaion,[69] full of statuettes of the goddess, contains an archaic Latin inscription[70] from the middle of the third century BC (Pl. 4) with the name of the divinity:

[M]enerv[ae].

Furthermore, a bronze lamina, which is said to come from the 'excavations of the forum' in 1931 and has remained unpublished up to now, of the type well known from the famous Lavinian dedication to the Dioscuri, i.e. to be nailed to an altar in order to commemorate a dedication or to transcribe a *lex sacra*, brings us a dedicatory inscription from the early Latin colonial period (mid-third century BC) with the following text (Pl. 5):[71]

Ive

[68] Cf. Ardovino, *Culti*, 75 f. and G. Avagliano, in *Atti Taranto* (1987), 375 f.; see also the inscription *IG* XIV 664, a dedication of a bronze statuette representing a *canephora*; the cult in the period of the Latin colony is documented also by coins: cf. Crawford, 'Form and Function', 91, no. 31 / 1, tav. XI, pp. 91 f., no. 32, tav. XI.

[69] V. P. C. Sestieri, 'Ricerche poseidoniati', in *MEFR* 67 (1955), 39 f.

[70] *ILP* 7.

[71] A simple paper tag with few register data (n.d'ord.726, n.rif.581) gives to the bronze inscription only a vague provenance from the 'Forum area'; the lamina is 3.6 cm. high, 12.5 cm. long, and 0.2 cm. thick, and the letters, deeply carved into the metal surface, are 2.9 cm. high.

In spite of the provenance given in the Museum inventory to the lamina (we know how little reliance can be placed on the recorded provenance of minor objects from the excavations carried out by Marzullo), it would be tempting to attribute it to the altar immediately to the north of the one belonging to the temple of Athena-Minerva and so to identify it as a cult site of Jupiter. A new Roman altar close to the old Greek one is visible in both cases (Fig. 29, 2–3, 4–5). Although the reassembly made by Sestieri near the altars, of an archaic doric column on top of a triple-stepped base, seems completely hypothetical, there is no doubt that the archaic Athenaion was surrounded by other shrines and cult places, among which M. Cipriani has pointed out one dedicated to Artemis,[72] revealed by a votive deposit. One such cult, to the north of the 'Temple of Ceres' (Fig. 29, 6), could have been sacred to Zeus and later to Jupiter, since it was usual for this god to have a simple cult *sub divo*.

The archaic rectangular shrine (Fig. 29, 7) immediately to the south of the 'Temple of Ceres', dating back to the first half of the sixth century BC, whose roof has been reconstructed by P. Moreno[73] and which does not appear to have had a classical or a Hellenistic successor, could instead have been the first Athenaion of Poseidonia, later substituted by the late archaic 'Temple of Ceres'. The presence of another cult to the north of the Athenaion is revealed in this same area by Sestieri's discovery[74] of a rich and important Hellenistic votive deposit, which Sestieri wished to attribute to Aphrodite, but which should in fact be better identified with the cult of Dionysus-Iacchos, in the *interpretatio latina Liber*, which was very popular in the mintage of colonial Paestum.[75] This idea is supported, apart from the absence of images of Aphrodite, by the many statu-

Plate 6. Paestum, Museo. Statuette of the young Dionysus, seated on a rock, from a Roman votive deposit near the Athenaion (photo by L. De Masi).

ettes of the young Dionysus, crowned and seated on a rock (Pl. 6) and by the figures of young satyrs (Pl. 7) or of ithyphallic youths (Pl. 8), whilst the statuettes of cupids (Pl. 9) and of young girls engaged in the *ephedrismos* (Pl. 10) relate to the erotic initiatory atmosphere traditionally associated with the god, here not by chance present in his youthful guise. Judging by the chronology of the ex-votos, the cult appears to be a very early Roman addition and its location next to the cult of Minerva cannot but lead us to place these sacred traditions of Latin Paestum in the realm of the archaic system of youth initiations, *Liberalia-Quinquatrus*, which, as far as can be deduced from both the Lavinian and Roman testimonies of the period, were still flourishing in the first half of the third century BC.[76] The conscious duplication on the Paestan *arx* of the topography of the Aventine in Rome is striking as regards the location of the two sanctuaries of Minerva and

[72] The cult of Diana is witnessed by coin types of the Latin colony: see Crawford, 'Form and Function', 63, no. 5/5, pl. VII.

[73] P. Moreno, 'Numerazione di elementi architettonici in un edificio arcaico di Posidonia', *RAL* 18 (1963), 201 f.

[74] Sestieri, *MEFR* 67 (1995), 40 f.

[75] The richest and most 'normal' group of emissions of the Latin colony, based on the sextantal reduction and sometimes showing a special mark (ear of corn, caduceus, club, name of the magistrate Q.VA, moon crescent, branch), shows the head of Liber on the triens (and the head of Neptune on the quadrans, of Ceres on the sescuncia or the sextans, of Diana on the uncia); Crawford ('Form and Function', 49 s.) has included these emissions in his second series and has dated them in the late years of the Second Punic War: see Crawford, 'Form and Function', p. 60, no. 5/1, pl. VII; p. 64 f., no. 6/1, pl. VII; p. 67, no. 7/1, pl. VIII; p. 69, no. 8/1, pl. VIII; p. 71, no. 9/1, pl. VIII; pp. 73 f., no. 10/1, pl. VIII; a different emission (again consisting of trientes), though not including all other values, is that on pp. 74 f., no. 11/1, pl. IX; pp. 79 f., no. 18, pl. IX.

[76] M. Torelli, *Lavinio e Roma. Riti iniziatici e matrimonio tra archeologia e storia* (Rome, 1984).

Plate 8. Paestum, Museo. Statuette of ithyphallic youth, from a Roman votive deposit near the Athenaion (photo by L. De Masi).

Plate 7. Paestum, Museo. Statuette of young satyr, from a Roman votive deposit near the Athenaion (photo by L. De Masi).

Liber (not to mention that of Diana).[77] On the Aventine in 236 BC, yet again endorsing the plebeian character of that hill (and its duplicate in Paestum), also stood the temple of Jupiter Libertas,[78] a cult foundation whose

origins are specifically bound to the enlistment of the *volones*, something which, as we shall see, is of remarkable importance in the history of Paestum. The *arx* in Paestum appears to be meant to duplicate not the *arx* of Rome or of other Latin cities,[79] despite the expected and inevitable worship of the pan-Latin Jupiter of the *Latiar*, but to refer symbolically to the Aventine with

[77] For the sanctuary of Minerva Aventina in Rome see S. B. Platner and T. Ashby, *A Topographical Dictionary of Ancient Rome* (Oxford, 1929), 296 f.; discussion on the date of the temple foundation (241 BC, as a consequence of an *evocatio* from Falerii?) in Torelli, *Lavinio*, 53.

[78] See Platner and Ashby, *Topographical Dictionary*, 342.

[79] M. Torelli, 'Topografia sacra di una città latina—Praeneste', in B. Coari (ed.), *Urbanistica ed architettura dell'antica Praeneste*, Acts of Conference; Palestrina, 1988 (Palestrina, 1989), 15 f.

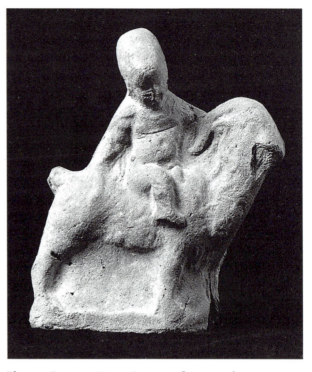

Plate 10.   Paestum, Museo. Statuette of eros seated on a goat (photo by L. De Masi).

Plate 9.   Paestum, Museo. Statuette of eros carrying an amphora of Rhodian type, from a Roman votive deposit near the Athenaion (photo by L. De Masi).

clear and specific allusions to its character as a plebeian stronghold.

The 'Aventine' *arx* in Latin colonial Paestum did not have a temple of Jupiter Capitolinus (sought in vain by archaeologists in a Latin colony, where a Capitolium would not be *de rigueur* at least until the war of Fregellae), but certainly had three sanctuaries (four, if we include the one to Artemis-Diana which probably did in fact exist), dedicated to Jupiter, Minerva, and Liber. The one to Jupiter[80] was associated with the

traditional *Latinitas* of the foundation by means of an explicit reference[81] to the *Latiar* of the Mons Albanus. The other two sanctuaries, those of Minerva and Liber, were drawn together to reproduce the pan-Latin festival of the *Liberalia* in the new colony (we know about the feasts of Liber in Lavinium), whose socio-political importance is particularly highlighted in the case of Paestum, for reasons which we shall see further on. In any event it is certain that the cult of Athena, of definite Greek origin, was put to a different use in order to meet new social needs, just as might have happened to the cult of Zeus at the time of its transformation into that of Jupiter. Thus, apart from determining the plebeian 'tone' of the area, we acquire an interesting insight into the more general issue under discussion.

[80] The possibility should be verified that the Paestan Jupiter, more than the god of the Mons Albanus, could be a Jupiter Liber, a 'child' Jupiter

(cf. *Fortuna Iovis mater* at Praeneste: F. Coarelli, *I santuari del Lazio in età repubblicana* (Rome, 1987), 74 f.), whose juvenile aspect seems to be emphasized by the votive materials found in the above mentioned deposit; it is obvious that in such case the god of Paestum would preserve intact the chance of being understood also as a Jupiter Libertas.

[81] See also the oldest temple on the *arx* of Cosa, later replaced by the so-called Capitolium, which Brown, *Cosa*, 25 f. rightly considers to be a temple dedicated to Jupiter.

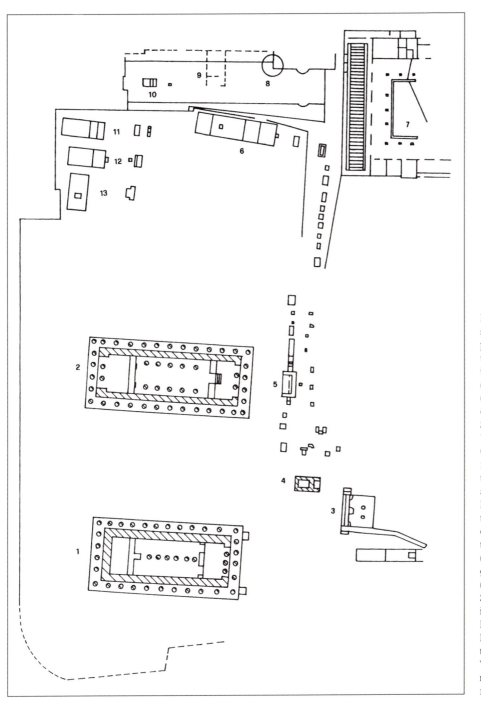

Fig. 30. Plan of the southern sanctuary at Paestum with the proposed identifications of temples and buildings: 1. temple of Hera–Juno ('Basilica'); 2. temple of Apollo ('temple of Neptune'); 3. *lesche* of the Poseidoniate Medical School (the so-called 'waterclock'); 4. temple of Chiron (Sestieri's temple no. 10); 5. Roman altar of the temple 'of Neptune'; 6. the amphiprostyle temple of Herakles–Hercules (Sestieri's temple no. 17); 7. the sanctuary of Aesculapius; 8. the round temple of Herakles–Hercules (?) in the 'giardino romano'; 9. the temple of Mater Matuta (the so-called 'Italic temple', Sestieri's temple no. 19); 10. the imperial phase of the temple of Mater Matuta; 11. temple of Magna Mater (?) (Sestieri's temple no. 14); 12. temple of Victoria (?) (Sestieri's temple no. 15); 13. Sestieri's temple no. 18 (drawing A. Trapassi).

6. The Southern Sanctuary: Between the Forum Holitorium and the Forum Boarium

The facts in our possession relating to the southern sanctuary (Fig. 30) are also very limited and conflict with the complexity of the sacred topography of the place. Before tackling the situation in the Roman period I think it would be opportune to analyse further two features of the pre-existing Greek period. In the first place it is necessary to understand the form—and hence the function and the cult—of the enneastyle building known as the 'Basilica' (Fig. 30, 1). It has long been suggested that this should be identified as the great urban Heraion,[82] which still existed, albeit it in a modest form, in the Roman colonial era,[83] undoubtedly in the guise of a Latin Juno, whose nature and possible epithet we shall consider later. The characteristic 'double' temple form of the Basilica, with central columns and an *adyton* at the back, cannot in fact have been unintentional, and was most probably meant to reflect the original double character of Poseidonia's Argive Hera, an armed virginal goddess and at the same time a *kourotrophos* and mother-like divinity, according to F. Coarelli's reconstruction.[84] Indeed it is no accident that the same architectural details and even the same unusual plan were duplicated in temple B in Metapontum,[85] an Achaean colony like Poseidonia, with an intentional and allusive repetition of the plan (Figs. 31–2), obviously derived from the same proto-type, which we might conjecture to be that at Sybaris, mother-city of Poseidonia and the leading settlement of the Achaean colonists in the west.

Metapontum's topographical situation may provide a valuable clue in reconstructing the cult of the other great Doric temple in Poseidonia, the so-called 'Temple of Neptune'. At Metapontum (Fig. 31), in the sacred area of the agora, beside temple B (which by virtue of its unusual plan of a cella divided in two is identified with the Heraion, whose archaic vine wood columns are recorded by Pliny)[86] stands temple A, confidently identified as being dedicated to Apollo Lykaios.[87] Similarly, at Paestum the so-called 'Temple of Neptune'

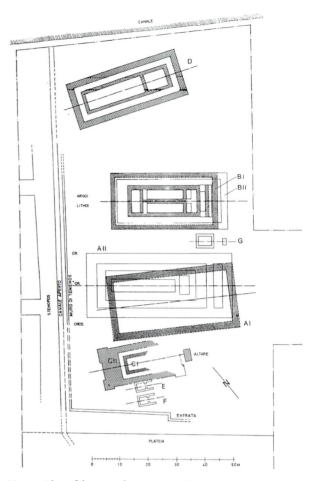

Fig. 31. Plan of the central sanctuary at Metapontum: 1. Athenaion (temple C); 2. Apollonion (temple A); 3. Heraion (temple B); 4. Aphrodision (temple D) (drawing A. Trapassi).

(Fig. 30, 2) stands next to the 'Basilica', which was dedic-ated to Hera, as the materials from the votive deposits discovered all around the temple also demonstrate, showing the same types of ex-votos as those from the Heraion at the mouth of the Sele river.[88] For the sake of brevity I should say straightaway that the best can-didate for the dedication of the so-called 'Temple of Neptune', a well-known masterpiece of early Classical Doric architecture, is Apollo. In fact, it is not simply that the Hera–Apollo pairing imitates the sequence of the temples at Metapontum; there are other pieces of archaeological evidence as well which help to corrobor-ate this theory: a group of terracotta votive offerings from the fourth–third centuries BC was found in the

[82] On the temple, see now G. Gullini, 'Urbanistica e architettura', in G. Pugliese Carratelli (ed.) *Megale Hellas* (Milan, 1983), 232 f.

[83] We have only vague information about the roofing of these temples in the Roman colonial period: but some architectural terracottas in the storerooms of the Museo Nazionale at Paestum attributable to Roman republican times are indicated as coming from the 'Basilica'. Arch. D. Mertens of the German Archaeological Institute in Rome is preparing a complete publication of these terracottas.

[84] F. Coarelli, *Il Foro Boario* (Rome, 1988), 328. Thousands of statuettes of the *kourotrophos* goddess prove (if proof is needed) the matronal character of Hera at Poseidonia, whilst the warlike aspect of the same divinity is witnessed by armed statuettes of this goddess (Sestieri, *MEFR* 67 (1955), 156, fig. 13) and by a well-known silver disc with inscription (M. Guarducci, 'Dedica arcaica alla Hera di Poseidonia', *ArchClass* 16 (1952), 145 f.): the double cult of the Basilica was already discussed, though though a different point of view, by H. Riemann, 'Zur Grundrissinterpretation des Enneastylos von Poseidonia', in *MDAI(R)* 72 (1965), 198 f., F. Krauss, *Paestum. Die griechische Tempel*, 3rd edn. (Berlin, 1976), 66 f., E. M. Stern, 'Zeus und die tempel von Paestum', *MNIR* 42 (1980), 43 f. and now, correctly, Ardovino, *Culti*, 113 f.

[85] The comparison with the first phase of the temple B at Metapontum is made by D. Mertens, 'L'architettura', *Atti Taranto* (1973), 202 f.

[86] Plin. *NH* 14. 9.

[87] Gullini, 'Urbanistica e architettura', Pugliese Carratelli (ed.), *Megale Hellas*, 239 f.; on the cult see F. Graf, 'Culti e credenze religiose della Magna Grecia', *Atti Taranto* (1981), 172 f.

[88] We lack a reliable account of the tumultuary excavations done in this century around and inside the two Doric temples at Posidonia: the sole documented dig is that carried out by A. M. Ardovino, who discusses it in *Culti*, 115.

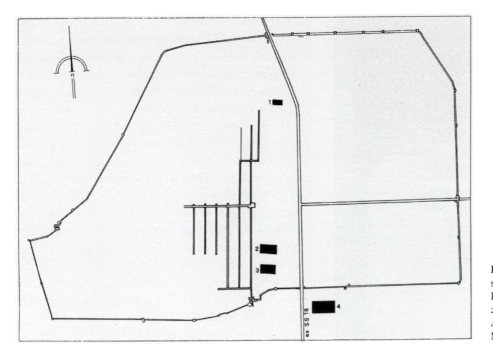

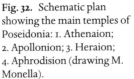

Fig. 32. Schematic plan showing the main temples of Poseidonia: 1. Athenaion; 2. Apollonion; 3. Heraion; 4. Aphrodision (drawing M. Monella).

area between the 'Basilica' and the 'Temple of Neptune', which presents a type of crowned Apollo with lyre (Pl. 11) and also includes examples of very refined workmanship and of larger dimensions than the norm.[89] These pieces not only provide a clue for the identification of the cult performed in connection with the 'Temple of Neptune', but also give a more precise cultic background to the precious silver statuette discovered in Poseidonia and now in the Louvre, which P. Zancani Montuoro, correctly in my opinion, identified as Apollo.[90]

If we broaden our scope to include the urban whole, the analogies between the layout of the great sacred foundations of Poseidonia and those of Metapontum are impressive. At Metapontum (Fig. 31) the temples of the sacred area of the agora appear to be, in succession from south to north, an Athenaion (temple C), an Apollonion (temple A), a Heraion (temple B), and an Aphrodision (the Ionic temple D), a succession that is found again, albeit inverted, (from north to south) and stretched out the whole length of the settlement in Poseidonia (Fig. 32) with the temples of 'Ceres' (Athenaion), of 'Neptune' (Apollonion?), 'Basilica' (Heraion), and the sanctuary of Santa Venera

(Aphrodision). However, the probable character behind the sequence linking the temples of the great urban sanctuaries in Metapontum with those in Paestum (which serves merely to augment a series of very strong cultural analogies between the two Achaean colonies, highlighted primarily in unusual architectural features)[91] has other even more important revelations in store. The particulars of the topography of the great urban sanctuaries in Paestum do in fact demonstrate a further, extraordinary similarity with the situation in Metapontum, which is worth examining in detail. Between the monumental classical altar (Fig. 30, 3) and the one with *cyma reversa* mouldings from the Roman era (Fig. 30, 4) both belonging to the 'Temple of Neptune', i.e. the temple I maintain is the Apollonion, Sestieri's excavations have brought to light 'some stones fixed in the earth in the form of stelae; then another to the south among the roses',[92] essentially the same ἄργοι λίθοι as those in the sanctuary of Apollo Lykaios in Metapontum. To this series of ἄργοι λίθοι in Paestum, which are unfortunately of an unknown number, the excavations carried out in 1982 by A. Ardovino have added another undeniably archaic

[89] The provenance was shown by a tag kept in the same tray where I found these and other statuettes, apparently representing the same god. All this material is unpublished.

[90] P. Zancani Montuoro, 'Il Poseidonion di Poseidonia', *Archivio Storico per la Calabria e la Lucania*, 23 (1954), 172 n. 1.

[91] These features have been elucidated by D. Mertens in two exhaustive studies, *Zur archaischen Architektur der achäischen Kolonien in Unteritalien*, in *Neue Forschungen in griechischen Heiligtümer* (Tübingen, 1976), 167 f., and 'Parallelismi strutturali nell'architettura della Magna Grecia e dell'Italia Centrale in età arcaica', in *Scritti in onore di D. Adamesteanu* (Matera, 1980), 37 f.

[92] Sestieri, *Paestum*, 18.

Plate 11. Paestum, Museo. Statuette of crowned Apollo with lyre, from a votive deposit in the area between the 'Basilica' and the 'Temple of Neptune' (photo by L. De Masi).

Chiron's strong links with Apollo, and in particular with Apollo Maleatas, the Apollo *hiatros* and *alexikakos* par excellence, of whose cult the world-renowned healing sanctuary at Epidaurus was a direct offshoot.[95]

This reclassification of the Greek evidence is a valuable aid in assessing the topography of the sanctuary in the Roman period, considering that the cult persisted at least until the late first century BC, as is confirmed both by the reconstruction of the altar and by the statuettes referred to above. To these we may perhaps link an important remnant of the classical period, a marble torso of an 'ephebe' excavated by Sestieri between the two altars of the 'Temple of Neptune' and dated by him without question to the second century BC.[96] Given his undoubted continuity during the Lucanian period, the Poseidonian Apollo was quite rightly understood by the Latin colonists to be the Apollo *medicus* of Rome, to judge by the evidence of anatomical ex-votos in the votive deposit from the third to second centuries BC discovered by Sestieri beneath the late republican Roman altar of the 'Temple of Neptune'. To quote Sestieri again,

this altar was supported by another pre-existing construction, in the form of a rectangular chest built of large thin slabs of limestone which must have been a votive deposit. In fact in 1947 fragments of female masks made of clay, lifesize votive hands and feet of terracotta, and some extremely simple bronze armlets made of thin strips folded into circular sections were found[97]

a votive deposit of Italic type which we can readily attribute to the mid-republican age.[98]

Thus whilst the southernmost part of the *temenos* was dominated by the great figure of Hera-Juno, the central part, starting from the southern limits of the area between the Basilica and the 'Temple of Neptune', was under the protection of Apollo *hiatros-medicus*

example of τετράγονος λίθος, still *in situ* in front of the so-called 'water clock' (Fig. 30, 5). The same Ardovino, in his recent book on the cults of Paestum,[93] was correct in linking his discoveries to the ἄργοι λίθοι at Metapontum and to the well-known Poseidonian cippus of Chiron, and in the wake of M. Guarducci's convictions,[94] he has expediently laid emphasis on

[93] *Culti*, 18 f.

[94] M. Guarducci, 'Paestum. Cippo arcaico con il nome di Chirone', *NSA* (1948), 185 f.; cf. ead., 'Appunti di epigrafia greca arcaica', *ArchClass* 16 (1964), 138 n. 7.

[95] Paus. 2. 27. 7, with the commentary by [D. Musti] and M. Torelli, *Pausania. Guida della Grecia*, ii (Milan, 1986), 300 f., esp. 306; on the Kynortion sanctuary of Apollo Maleatas at Epidaurus see R. A. Tomlinson, *Epidauros* (Austin, Tex., 1983), 92 f.

[96] This piece seems to correspond with a torso without inventory number (mentioned in Sestieri, *Paestum*, 18) that I have been able find in the Museum storerooms. A closer analysis could perhaps corroborate a 5th-cent. date.

[97] Sestieri, *Paestum*, 18; on these votive finds in the southern sanctuary, see now M. Cipriani, in *Atti Taranto* (1987), 382 f.

[98] On these votive deposits see A. M. Comella, 'Tipologia e diffusione dei complessi votivi in Italia in età medio- e tardo-repubblicana', *MEFRA* 93 (1981), 717 f.; this study emphasizes the fact that Paestum is the southernmost find place of this kind of south Etruscan and Latino-Campanian deposits, in full agreement with its character of southernmost Latin colony on the coasts of the Tyrrhenian Sea.

with his group of monuments: the 'Temple of Neptune', as the seat of the god, and the other little temple of classical period (Fig. 30, 6), Sestieri's no. 10, furnished with its own altar[99] and linked with a monumental *lesche*—the so-called 'orologio ad acqua' (water-clock)[100]—to which a complex system of canals carried water from the south-east. It seems natural to connect the former (the little temple and the altar) to the healing cult of Chiron and the latter (the *lesche*) with a school of medicine, which in the light of the certain presence of the cult of Chiron in the area, must have existed in Greek Poseidonia as it did in nearby Elea,[101] but without managing to earn the reputation and the prestige of the latter, owing to the premature end of Poseidonia's autonomy and of the ruling Greek classes whom that autonomy embodied—in other words of those who would have been able to run the possible local medical school.

We do not know if the Romans took up this cult, something I hold to be highly improbable. It is, however, quite feasible that the Latin colonists were well aware of the healing atmosphere of the eastern-central area of the *temenos* (owing to the probable presence of a spring no longer active today), as clearly evidenced by all the unusual hydraulic fittings of the so-called 'water clock'. The same impression of a cult site of healing waters is evoked by similar fittings in the monumental building which E. Greco[102] has recently returned to explore (Fig. 30, 7) adjacent to the north side of the group of buildings associated with the cult of Chiron, between the north-eastern corner of the *temenos* and the forum. It consists of a large paved area furnished with fountains and gutters, preceded by a courtyard surrounded on three sides by rooms of apparently equal dimensions. Greco has underlined the close connection between it and the forum and therefore its wholly Roman character, and was surely correct when he suggested classifying it as a sanctuary for the cult of a divinity linked with healing waters, either Aesculapius

or Mefitis.[103] In the light of these observations and taking into account the close similarity of its plan to that of a so-called *katagogion*, a characteristic building of the Asklepieia,[104] we can eliminate any element of doubt in choosing between the two proposals and without hesitation attribute the dedication of the sanctuary to Aesculapius. It would then match the one in Fregellae[105] in being a reproduction of the temple erected in Rome amidst great popular expectations and spurred on by the plebeians, led by the well-known Ogulnii brothers in 289 BC, i.e. a few years before the foundation of Paestum.[106] It is noteworthy that the connection between the temple of Apollo and the Asklepieion at Paestum and between the temple of Apollo *medicus* or rather the archaic *Apollinar*, later temple of Apollo Sosianus,[107] and the sanctuary of Aesculapius *in insula* in Rome is substantially the same, a close physical proximity (and an obvious 'theological' similarity)[108] but not an immediate proximity.

This reconstruction enables us to advance, in an anti-clockwise direction, to the so-called 'Italic temple' (Sestieri's no. 19) and the 'giardino romano' (Roman garden)[109] (Fig. 30, 8). This sanctuary is unusual from the point of view both of its topography and its cults. The 'Italic temple' is joined to the forum, together with which it was surely erected, right in the initial stage of the foundation, and is excluded from the great *temenos*, whose wall was rebuilt in the first half of the first century BC.[110] to run close by the amphiprostyle temple (Sestieri's no. 17) (Fig. 30, 9),[111] then 'regularized' at the end of the same century in such a way as to make room for a garden (the so-called 'Roman garden')

---

[99] Sestieri, *Paestum*, 18.

[100] H. Lauter, 'Ein archaischer Hallenbau in Poseidonia/Paestum', *MDAI(R)* 91 (1984), 23 f., the only scholar to have dealt with this unique monument, has very implausibly identified it with a *bouleuterion*.

[101] The building that housed the medical school of Elea-Velia, a gymnasium connected with a spring (exploited for the adjacent baths in Roman times), likely has Hellenistic origins, but has been completely reconstructed in Augustan times: see M. Fabbri and A. Trotta, *Una scuola-collegio di età augustea. L'insula II di Velia* (Rome, 1989).

[102] E. Greco, 'Archeologia della colonia latina di Paestum', *DArch* 3rd ser., 6: 2 (1988), 85.

[103] Ibid.; Greco seems to opt eventually for a sanctuary of Mefitis and to date it to the Lucanian occupation. However, this hypothesis appears contradicted by the perfect alignment with the Roman forum, a notorious innovation in the town urban introduced by the Latin colony.

[104] The examples of this type of building, derived from banquet halls, are very well known in some of the most famous sanctuaries of Asklepios in 4th–3rd-cent. BC Greece, at Epidaurus (Tomlinson, *Epidauros*, 84 f.), Corinth (*Corinth*, 14 (1941), 8 f.; cf. M. Lang, *Cure and Cult in Ancient Corinth* (Princeton, 1977)) and Troezen (G. Welter, *Troizen und Kalaureia* (Berlin, 1941), 31 f.).

[105] F. Coarelli (ed.), *Fregellae, ii, Il santuario di Esculapio* (Rome, 1986).

[106] Sources in M. R. Torelli, *Rerum Romanarum Fontes ab anno CCXCII ad annum CCLXV a.Chr.n.* (Pisa, 1978), 27 f.; see also D. Degrassi, 'Il culto di Esculapio in Italia centrale durante il periodo repubblicano', in Coarelli (ed.), *Fregellae*, ii. 145 f.

[107] On this temple, see E. La Rocca, in W.-D. Heilmeyer (ed.), *Kaiser Augustus und die verlorene Republik*, Catalogue of Exhibition; Berlin, 1988 (Mainz, 1988), 121 f. [108] On this subject see Torelli, *Lavinio*, 177 f.

[109] Sestieri, *Paestum*, 19.

[110] As is shown by the dedicatory inscription *ILP* 142.

[111] Sestieri, *Paestum*, 18 f.

ornamented with an exedra. Characteristically it faces south and seems to be one of the oldest buildings of the colony, sign of a popular cult, whose nature is testified to by the numerous votive deposits discovered in the 'Roman garden', full of statuettes of babies in swaddling clothes.[112] These deposits, which are still unfortunately unpublished, are obsessively concerned with reproduction and fertility (and as far as it appears, only marginally with *sanatio*), for which reason the number of possible candidates for the deity of the place is limited. For additional reasons which we shall soon explain we are led to think that an identification with Mater Matuta is the most likely. She was the specific divinity of birth and very popular in the Latin world, even in the colonies,[113] besides being so in her place of origin in Satricum[114]—and above all in the offshoot of the Satricum sanctuary in the Forum Boarium in Rome,[115] where significantly her temple has an orientation to the south like the building in Paestum. Neither this sanctuary nor the nearby one of Aesculapius is part of the ancient Greek *temenos*, but each has its own enclosure adjacent to it, thereby revealing their origins as cults added to the ancient city plan inherited from the preceding Graeco-Lucanian town. Mater Matuta, even though she is herself of antique Greek

origin as shown by her most archaic cult forms,[116] is felt to be an 'intruder' in the same way as Aesculapius, and could not be equated with the local divinities. Accordingly, she is collocated alongside (not within) the old Graeco-Lucanian street grid, thus further underlining her real character of 'Latin' goddess, well rooted in the religiousness of the new arrivals.

With the decline and the modifications of this religiousness, the 'Italic temple' was suppressed on the occasion of the rebuilding of the forum basilica, i.e. in the course of the early Augustan period,[117] the two having coexisted during the whole of the first basilica's phase, which began at the end of the second century. A natural substitute for the 'Italic temple' would be the tiny little temple (Fig. 30, 10), still completely unpublished, with its modest altar facing east built in the same technique as the basilica, inside the large garden with an exedra—the 'Roman garden' referred to above and which must in fact be of contemporary construction, evidently the *virecta* with the relative *maceries* erected by the *duoviri* L. Caesius L. f. M[acer (?)] and M. Valerius M. f. Ruf[us],[118] at the very beginning of the imperial age. The little temple thus appears to have been erected in the Augustan age, in consequence of the enlargement of the basilica through the addition of a vast *deambulatorium*, when together with the 'Italic temple' another small circular building (Fig. 30, 15), perhaps a temple, aligned to the preceding sacred building and contemporary with it, was also eliminated. As we shall see later, this circular building could be identified as a shrine of Hercules, in view of its round plan.

The construction of the garden, on the other hand, required repairs to the primitive wall of the *temenos* north of the southern sacred area and the programme of repairs to this area as a whole helps to clarify a design consistent with Roman politico-religious ideology, which wished the colonies to be fashioned as *effigies simulacraque parva urbis*.[119] This whole central southern part of the *temenos* and its surroundings was in fact remodelled and adapted in the image of the area of the city of Rome between the Forum Holitorium, the Tiber Island, and the Forum Boarium, in the sequence Apollo *medicus*—Aesculapius—Mater Matuta.

---

[112] Ibid.: 'anche questo, come gli altri, aveva una ricca stipe, contenente una grandissima quantità di terrecotte. Alcune, ancora greche, rappresentano la dea madre seduta, che allatta il figlio, e si riferiscono ancora evidentemente ad Hera Argiva. In seguito il culto è rimasto lo stesso, in onore della dea della fecondità, ma per l'influsso italico ha assunto caratteri di maggiore realismo. Si sono trovati, infatti, oltre a numerosissime statuine di bambini in fasce, un gran numero di uteri in terracotta, e alcune rappresentazioni della fecondità, estrinsecate per mezzo di curiose sculture fittili: sono parti inferiori di figure femminili, il cui ventre è chiaramente ingrossato' (this deposit too, like the other ones, contained a lot of terracotta material. Some of the clay statuettes, still of Greek type, represent the mother goddess feeding her child and clearly still refer to Hera Argiva. Later the cult remained identical, in honour of the fecundity goddess, but under Italic influence acquired a greater realism. In fact, besides a great deal of statuettes representing babies in swaddling clothes, the excavations have brought to light many terracotta uteri and some representations of fecundity, expressed by strange fictile sculptures: these represent lower parts of female bodies, with the belly clearly swollen for child-bearing). Up to now this is the most complete report on that votive deposit (see also *Fasti Archaeologici* (1952), 126 f., no. 1553); the finds, that Sestieri believed to be 'Greek', are fictile statuettes of a *kourotrophos* goddess deriving from 4th-cent. BC moulds, apparently still used in the first decades of the life of Roman Paestum by Latin colonists, who only gradually replaced these relics of the Graeco-Lucanian worship.

[113] At Pisaurum her cult is attested by two of the famous *cippi Pisaurenses*, the inscriptions *ILLRP* 17 and 24.

[114] On the Satricum cult see: C. M. Stibbe (ed.), *Lapis Satricanus. Archaeological, Epigraphical, Linguistic and Historical Aspects of the New Inscription from Satricum* (The Hague, 1980); C. M. Stibbe (ed.), *Satricum, una città latina*, Catalogue of Exhibition; Cisterna, 1982 (Florence, 1982); G. Colonna, 'I templi nel Lazio fino al V secolo compreso', *Archeologia Laziale* 6 (Rome, 1984), 396 f.   [115] Coarelli, *Il Foro Boario*, 205 f.

[116] Ibid. esp. 244 f.

[117] *Paestum* i. 18 f., 32 f.; on the chronology of the basilica, see further.

[118] *ILP* 143 = *CIL* I², 3159.

[119] [Gros] and Torelli, *Storia dell'urbanistica. Il mondo romano*, 132 f.; see also M. Torelli, 'Il modello urbano e l'immagine di città', in S. Settis (ed.), *Civiltà dei Romani* (Milano, 1990), 43 f.

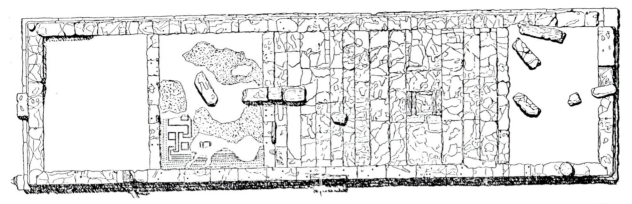

Fig. 33. Plan of the amphiprostyle temple (Sestieri's no. 17) showing the *signinum* mosaic of the cella and a *bothros* in the centre of the pronaos (after Sestieri).

If this is right, we can also suggest the identity of the gods worshipped in the two nearby temples. The first of them, the round sacellum just referred to (Fig. 30, 15), is located in the same peribolos as the 'Italic temple'. The other one, however, is enclosed within the *temenos* of the southern sanctuary, the amphiprostyle temple (Sestieri's no. 17) (Fig. 30, 9) mentioned above. For both temples the best candidate is Hercules, who in the Paestan 'reproduction' of the sacred topography of Rome would logically have occupied such a place: perhaps even the temple morphology was inspired by the great Roman sanctuary of Hercules in the Forum Boarium, mythically and topographically closely linked with Mater Matuta.[120] The round temple reproduces the canonical shape of no less than two temples of Hercules at the *Ara Maxima* in Rome, the *aedes Aemiliana Herculis*, discovered in the fifteenth century and immediately destroyed, and a still surviving building, the so-called Temple of Vesta, convincingly identified with the temple of Hercules *Victor ad portam Trigeminam*.[121] The amphiprostyle temple might be an imitation of the temple of Hercules *Invictus*, which we know was in the Tuscan style and which was reconstructed by Pompey and accordingly called *Hercules Pompeianus*.[122]

The amphiprostyle temple in its current state is a construction on a low podium dating back to the Roman colony; this replaced a previous building which antedated the colony,[123] a fact that, if the temple was dedicated to Hercules as all the evidence appears to show, seems somehow to be expected, both because of the undisputed relevance of the cult of the god among the Lucanian conquerors[124] and because of the mythical presence of Hercules in Greek Poseidonia, echoed on the Latin colonial coinage.[125] The floor of the cella[126] was redone in an elegant *signinum* mosaic of the second century BC (Fig. 33), while in the centre of the extremely deep pronaos, a sort of *bothros*, composed of rectangular slabs, bears close comparison with the *puteal* in the centre of the pronaos of the temple of Hercules in the Samnite sanctuary of Campochiaro near Saepinum.[127] The attribution of the temple to the deified hero is also supported by other data: in fact a small bronze club originating from the southern sanctuary adds to the evidence, gathered by Zancani, of statuettes of Hercules of the 'Italic' type known of from the city.[128]

---

[120] We might think of the tradition connecting Hercules to the Carmentae, who foretell Hercules' immortality and persuade him to found the *Ara Maxima Herculis* (*Orig. gent. Rom.* 6. 5–7; Solin. 1. 10); we might also here recall the very old rite of linking the temple of Mater Matuta and the Forum Boarium through the *pontes* mentioned by Ovid on the occasion of the *Matralia* (*Fast.* 6. 477 f.: 'Pontibus et magno iuncta [*scil.* the *aedes Matris Matutae*] est celeberrima Circo | area, quae posito de bove nomen habet') and the well-known 6th-cent. terracotta acroterion of the 'Servian' temple of Mater Matuta representing the apotheosis of Hercules (A. M. Sommella Mura, 'Il gruppo di Eracle e Atena', *PP* (1981), 59 f.). On the various, possible connections among the archaic cults of the Forum Boarium, cf. Coarelli, *Il Foro Boario*, 127 f.

[121] On these temples see Coarelli, *Il Foro Boario*, 84 f., 164 f.

[122] Ibid. 77 f.

[123] M. Cipriani, in *Atti Taranto* (1987), 381.

[124] As demonstrated by the Lucanian sanctuary at Serra Lustrante near Armento: see C. Masseria, 'I santuari indigeni della Basilicata', Ph.D. diss. (Perugia, 1988), 35 ff. See also H. Dilthey, 'Sorgenti, acque, luoghi sacri in Basilicata', in *Scritti in onore di D. Adamesteanu*, 539 f.

[125] Sources referring the presence of Hercules in Poseidonia: Parthax, *FHG* iii. 641 n. 21 (*ap.* Herodian. περ, μον.λεξ. 19. 9); Diod. Sic. 4. 22. 3; cf. G. Giannelli, *Culti e miti della Magna Grecia*, 2nd edn. (Florence, 1963), 132 f., and in particular Ardovino, *Culti*, 33 f., who rightly mentions in this connection the Attic black-figured amphora with the representation of Herakles' apotheosis, found in the late archaic heroon of the Poseidonian agora (see ibid. the long bibliography). The Paestan bronze coin with the head of Hercules is considered by Crawford, 'Form and Function', 89 f., no. 28, pl. x.

[126] Virtually unpublished, the mosaic is reproduced by Sestieri, *Paestum*, 8 f.

[127] Cf. S. Capini, in S. Capini and A. Di Niro, *Samnium. Archeologia del Molise*, Catalogue of Exhibition; Milan, 1991 (Rome, 1991), 117 f.

[128] P. Zancani, in *Arch. St. Calabria e Lucania*, 23 (1954), 171 n. 1.

Plate 12. Paestum, Museo. Inscribed base with an early Latin dedication to Hercules (photo by L. De Masi).

As for the Roman cult, in addition to an inscription from the second half of the first century BC with a dedication from a freedman to Hercules Victor,[129] we can cite an inscription (Pl. 12) from the so-called 'stipe della Basilica' ('votive deposit of the Basilica'). Incorrectly considered to be Oscan by the excavator (but recognized as archaic Latin by Dr C. Franciosi), it is carved on a small limestone base,[130] which still contains the feet of a bronze statuette of Hercules of the so-called Italic type:

C.Folius.T.f.
H(e)rcolei merit(o)

We have no excavated material concerning the small prostyle tetrastyle republican temple (Sestieri's no. 16) next to the amphiprostyle (Fig. 30, 11). As a pure hypothesis, the Dioscuri come to mind. They were previously venerated in Graeco-Lucanian Paestum and, judging by the coins,[131] by the Latin colonists too, and were often coupled with Heracles in the Italic areas, as

in the great sanctuary of Hercules *Ranus-Salarius* at Campochiaro just mentioned.[132]

Thus we come to the north-west corner of the *temenos*, where there are two small temples (Fig. 30, 12–13) dating from the second century BC (Sestieri's nos. 14 and 15).[133] The more northerly one (no. 14), in view of its double vestibule and the typical arrangement of the cella with large partitioned side-benches and the raised base of a cult statue can with relative certainty be identified with the cult of the Magna Mater, constituting a duplicate of the sanctuary in Rome of 204–191 BC with which it shares also the ritual open side-benches.[134] Ardovino has already conjectured[135] the presence of the Magna Mater among the cults of Roman Paestum, by means of a series of pertinent observations based on the terracotta votive offerings, in particular on statuettes of Attis and of a female figure with tympana and a peacock.[136] We are yet again faced with a transplantation, led by the *exemplum urbis*, of a cult with strongly popular features. Since the location of the sanctuary of the Magna Mater in Rome is well known to be on the Palatine, beside the temple of Victory,[137] founded in its turn in 295 BC by the plebeian leader Postumius Megellus, it would be tempting to recognize in temple no. 15 the Paestan duplicate of the same *aedes Victoriae*, a possibility also suggested by the appearance of the goddess on the city's coins.[138] Furthermore, the two altars of the small temples nos. 14 and 15 in Paestum are placed side by side, a deliberate positioning, which may recall the close relationship between the two cults of Cybele and Victory, demonstrated by the fact that when the *baetilus* was brought from

---

[129] *ILP* 4.

[130] A tag gives the provenance 'SBa', i.e. 'Stipe Basilica' or 'Votive Deposit of the Basilica'. This indication however seems to be a generic and comprehensive way to designate all the objects coming from Sestieri excavations in the area of the southern sanctuary (kind information of Dr M. Cipriani). The little base has an inventory number (3343) and measures 5.8 cm. high, 9.2 cm. long, 7.9 cm. deep. Height of lines: l.1: 7 mm.; l.2: 6.8 mm.

[131] The Dioscuri are missing in the first series of coins minted in the years of the foundation of the Latin colony, but later they appear in two different types, most likely witnessing an increasing importance of the local equestrian class: see Crawford, 'Form and Function', 60, no. 4/4, pl. VII (rare quartuncia in Crawford's second series), p. 86, no. 25/2, pl. VII.

[132] On the identification of the site of Hercules Ranus in the Tabula Peutingeriana and the sanctuary of Campochiaro, uncovered after a 20-year excavation by the Soprintendenza di Campobasso, see M. Torelli, 'Gli aromi e il sale. Afrodite ed Eracle nell'emporia arcaica dell'Italia', in A. Mastrocinque (ed.), *Ercole in occidente*, Acts of Conference; Trento, 1990 (Trento, 1993), 91 f. The Campochiaro sanctuary is no doubt dedicated to Hercules, as proved by the discovery of a marble bust of this god (M. Cappelletti, in Capini and Di Niro (eds.), *Samnium*, 285, e43); furthermore, the excavations have also brought to light an important ex-voto, a silver lamina with the representation of the Dioscuri (M. Cappelletti, in Capini and Di Niro (eds.), *Samnium*, 162 f., d38).

[133] Sestieri, *Paestum*, 19.

[134] P. Pensabene has been excavating this and the adjoining Victoria temple since 1977 and has produced yearly reports of the finds in *Archeologia Laziale*, from vol. I, 1978 up to vol. II, 1990; for a first comprehensive, but still preliminary report, producing data up to the year 1984, see P. Pensabene, 'Area sud-occidentale del Palatino', in *Roma. Archeologia nel centro*, i. Lavori e studi pubblicati dalla Soprintendenza Archeologica di Roma, 6: 1 (Rome, 1985), 179 f.   [135] *Culti*, 57 ff.

[136] P. C. Sestieri, *MEFR* 67 (1955), 40; id., 'Iconographie et culte de Héra à Paestum', *Revue des Arts* (1955), 153.   [137] See n. 134.

[138] See Crawford, 'Form and Function', 94, no. 34, tav. x.

Pessinus it was housed in the temple of Victory during the ten years and more that it took to build the temple of the Magna Mater. Assuming that such hypothetical identifications are correct, the two small temples are thus not only placed in a sort of 'Palatine perspective' with respect to the 'Forum Holitorium–Forum Boarium' arrangement just examined, i.e. in relation to the other temples adjoining Apollo *medicus*, Aesculapius, Magna Mater, and Hercules, but also that the hypothetical Paestan temple of Victory would be situated behind, and in some way linked, as in Rome, with the temple of Hercules Victor. However, rather than a deliberate attempt to imitate the capital city's topography of sacred buildings, it could equally well be interpreted (at least in case of the presumed *aedes Matris Magnae*) as a reference to the *origo Troiana* of the Latins and of Rome.

Whatever the value of this conjecture, we are not in a position to put forward hypotheses of any kind with regard to the small temple no. 18,[139] built in the immediate vicinity of the two preceding temples (Fig. 30, 14). We are dealing with a monumental enclosure without an external altar, but furnished with a central *eschara*, and hence dedicated to a subterranean cult. Its alignment marks it out as of certain Roman origin and possibly later than the two preceding ones, whilst the presence of the chthonic internal altar might designate it as the urban duplicate of the cult of Ceres,[140] which we have to suppose somehow established within a colony of such strong plebeian associations.

7. The Temples in the Area of the Forum: Paestum's 'Aventine Slopes'

We can now pass on to the temples in the forum area, to which incidentally the *temenos* of the so-called 'Italic temple' belongs *de iure* and *de facto*. Recently E. Greco[141] has suggested very convincingly that the huge basin, considered hitherto to be simply the *natatio* of a gymnasium (Fig. 26, 13), should be identified as a

piscina publica linked with the cult of Fortuna Virilis –Venus Verticordia (and I would add of Venus Murcia),[142] the latter to be placed in the projection on the southeast corner of the basin, containing a distyle shrine on an elegantly shaped podium (Fig. 34). This identification opens up the field to a whole series of consequences for the political, social, and architectural history of the city. Above all it lends support to the hypothetical identification put forward by me some years ago of the so-called 'Temple of Peace' with the temple of Mens,[143] the most important 'political' cult of the city, with its own *collegium* headed by *magistri*. The epigraphic evidence connected with this *collegium* and whose provenance is at least vaguely known seems to be concentrated in the forum and on the north side of it,[144] a connection which seems parallel and correspondent to the later one of the *Augustales*, as proved by two dedications[145] and by the name of *Augusta* assumed by the goddess in the Julio-Claudian age.[146] In Rome the temple of Mens was consecrated in 217 BC by order of the Sibylline books on the Capitol (which explains the prominent situation on the forum of the Paestan replica) and dedicated in 215 BC together with and next to (*uno canali discretae*, Livy tells us)[147] that of Venus Erycina.[148] The latter is essentially the same divine

[139] Sestieri, *Paestum*, 19.

[140] A cult building dedicated to Demeter, apparently in use only in Greek and Lucanian times, was located in the area now occupied by the Museum, originally outside the city limits before the Latin colony; the sanctuary has been detected by the fortuitous discovery of a votive deposit (again still unpublished) containing statuettes of men bringing a piglet as an offering: cf. P. Zancani Montuoro, 'Piccole cose pestane', *MDAI(R)* 70 (1963), 27. There is no need to share the doubts put forward by Ardovino, *Culti*, 97, concerning the votive character of the find.

[141] E. Greco, 'Un santuario di età repubblicana presso il foro di Paestum', *PP* (1985), 223 f.; *Paestum* iii. 60 f.

[142] Torelli, *Lavinio*, 78 f.

[143] M. Torelli, 'C. Cocceius Flaccus, senatore di Paestum, Mineia M.f. e Bona Mens', *Annali della Facoltà di Lettere e Filosofia di Perugia—Studi Classici*, NS 18 (1980/1), 105 f.; on this temple see F. Krauss and R. Herbig, *Der korinthisch-dorische Tempel am Forum von Paestum* (Munich, 1939), and D. Theodorescu, 'Le forum et le temple "dorique-corinthien" de Paestum', in *Munus non ingratum*, Proc. Intern. Symp. on Vitruvius' de Architectura and the Hellenistic and Republican Architecture; Leiden, 1987 (Leiden, 1989), 117 f.

[144] *ILP* 8–19; from the area come also *ILP* 10, 11, 14.

[145] *ILP* 19, 21. [146] *ILP* 12, 13.

[147] Liv. 23. 31. 9; cf. Serv. *Georg.* 4. 265; other sources for the foundation: Liv. 22. 9. 10, 10. 10; 23. 32. 20; Ov. *Fast.* 6. 241 f. The *dies natalis* of the temple is 8 June: *Inscr. It.* XIII, 2, p. 467; a restoration is documented (c.107 BC) by M. Aemilius Scaurus *cos.* 115 BC: Cic. *De nat. deor.* 2. 61; Plut. *De Fort. Rom.* 5 (cf.10). This circumstance possibly contributes to localize the temple and the other twin shrine dedicated to Venus Erycina in the same area where the temple of Fides was, a building also restored by the same Scaurus in 115 BC (Cic. *De nat. deor.* 2. 61). From these facts we can conclude that the goddesses Fides, Mens, and Venus Erycina created a true ideological 'system' aimed at representing in a symbolic form the whole complex of Roman class relationships (i.e. those concerning *clientes*, *liberti*, and *libertae*), significantly guaranteed by these goddesses in the most sacred area of the town, the Capitolium.

[148] About this temple we are less informed than about the adjoining building dedicated to Mens: this may be the consequence of the fact that, though the sources concerning the *votum* and the *dedicatio* are identical for both temples (see the preceding note), unfortunately we do not know its *dies natalis*. Normally this calendar date is supposed to have been the same as the one of the *aedes Veneris Erucinae extra Portam Collinam*, 23 April, day of the festival of the *Vinalia Rustica*, but the Fasti give no clue (cf. *Inscr. It.* XIII, 2, p. 447).

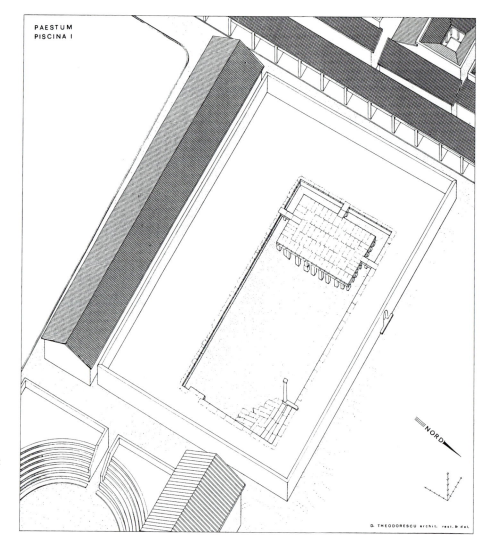

PAESTUM
PISCINA I

D. THEODORESCU archit. rest. & del.

Fig. 34. Reconstruction of Phase I (third century BC) of the area of the *piscina publica*: note the *aedicula* of Venus Verticordia near the south-east corner of the basin and the trilithic structure (here reconstructed as a platform) at its west end (after Theodorescu).

figure of Fortuna Virilis-Venus Verticordia,[149] at Paestum already attested by the cult performed in the nearby *piscina publica* mentioned above, and at the same time may be considered as the divinity of a sort of *intra muros* duplicate of the sanctuary of S. Venera, seat of a very ancient cult of the goddess in her Sicilian–Punic guise.[150] The importance and the significance of this 'replica' in Paestum will be discussed further on.

In this context it may perhaps be added that the largest part of the complex is occupied by the *piscina publica*, similar to its Roman prototype of course, which, situated where the temples of Venus Murcia,

Venus Verticordia–Fortuna Virilis, and Venus Obsequens stood, on the borders between the Aventine and the Circus Maximus, was presumably the original arrival point of the *Aqua Appia*.[151] Its dual function as a large communal cistern and at the same time as a place for the female *balneum* on the occasion of the celebrations for Venus Verticordia–Fortuna Virilis on the calends of

---

[149] Torelli, *Lavinio*, 162 f.

[150] M. Torelli and J. G. Pedley (eds.), *The Sanctuary of S. Venera at Paestum*, i (Rome, 1993); meanwhile, on the cult see R. Ammerman Miller, 'The Naked Standing Goddess: A Group of Archaic Terracotta Figurines from Paestum', *AJA* 95 (1991), 203 f.

[151] Fest. 232 L (see below); Liv. 23. 32. 4; Cic. *ad Q.fr.* 3. 7. 1. The building, which has given its name to a wide area between the Caelian and Aventine hills (cf. Hippolyt. *Philos.* 9. 12, p. 552) and thence to the Augustan XII *regio* of Rome, was bordered (as in Paestum!) by a *vicus* (*CIL* VI, 975; Amm. Marc. 17. 4. 14) and was the seat of *lanii*, called for this reason *piscinenses* (*CIL* VI, 167; cf. Plaut. *Pseud.* 326 f.). H. Jordan (*Topographie der Stadt Rom im Alterthum*, I. i (Berlin, 1871), 447, 458) rightly attributed its construction to Appius Claudius, who would have drawn inspiration from the famous *kolymbetra* in Agrigentum; *contra*, giving no reason and implicitly trivializing, R. Lanciani, 'I commentari di Frontino intorno agli acquedotti', *MemLinc* ser., 3a, 4 (1879–80), 234 f.

Plate 13. Paestum. Stucco decoration of the façade of the baths west of the *piscina publica* (photo M. Torelli).

April,[152] seems to be well illustrated at Paestum by the unusual trilithic structure, placed within the original expanse of water on the west side of the *piscina*, which presents the perfect plan of a peripteral temple, with a pronaos, a cella divided into naves, and an opisthodomos. We can conjecture that perhaps this space, so carefully planned to coincide with the surface of the water (and otherwise inexplicable), situated in a prominent position, opposite the unusual distyle shrine in the south-eastern corner of the large *piscina*, might have acted as the footing of a temporary enclosure built at water-level with large sheets of cloth intended for 'secret' washing operations, first of the statue of the cult of Venus Murcia and, after that, of the washers themselves, that is the patrician and plebeian *matronae* (and not therefore the *ancillae* and the *libertae, humiliores* of rank) accompanied by their respective *nurus*, a rite described by Ovid[153] and symbolized in the festival's *aiton* of Hellenistic flavour related by the same poet.[154]

Another building adjoins west of the *piscina publica*; we do not know whether chronologically later, and if so by how much, but dated by the excavators to the third century BC,[155] and greatly altered by subsequent constructions. The building and the *piscina* were

nevertheless separated by a paved lane, which later on in the imperial age was completely effaced by a large *sacellum* with an apse placed in the area to the west of the *piscina*, and by the small temple situated further to the south of the forum, on the eastern side of the square, which will be dealt with later. The building opened onto the lane and therefore onto the *piscina* with a large podium (which we can imagine surmounted by a colonnade), with splendid stucco decoration from the beginning of the second century BC (Pl. 13). The presence in the north-east corner of the aforementioned podium of a room of circular plan coated by *opus signinum*, without doubt a *laconicum*, shows that this building was actually a very early bath, whose monumental eastern front, with podium and colonnade, conferred a sort of sacral solemnity. Such solemnity may have served a specific purpose, in that in the second century BC the ancient *piscina publica* standing in front appears to have been intended for the *balneum* of the *humiliores*, whilst the later bath complex might have functioned as the *balneum* of the *honestiores*.

In spite of the physical separation caused by the paved lane, the archaic bath, the even older *piscina*, and a more prosaic series of small rooms continuing the sequence of the *tabernae* of the forum (compare the Roman *lanii piscinenses* recorded by our sources)[156] situated to the east, must have functioned in the course

---

[152] *Fast. Praen. ad d. kal. Apr.* (*Inscr. It.* 13. 2, p. 434); Lyd. *De mens.* 4. 65 (cf. 4. 29).

[153] Ov. *Fast.* 4. 133–40.   [154] Ibid. 141–4.   [155] *Paestum*, iii. 43 f.   [156] See n. 151.

of the second and maybe already by the third century BC as a real gymnasium, as evidenced by the *piscina* and the long portico to the north of it, dating from Graeco-Lucanian times,[157] but still in existence in the republican period. In front of this portico runs a long low wall in *opus cementicium*, differing in orientation from the rest of the city plan. Thanks to this wall and the nearby portico we can identify this sector of the area as a *xystus*,[158] obviously part of a gymnasium. The imitation of the *piscina publica* in Rome, a *natatio* and a *ludus* near a sanctuary of Venus, is perfect up to this point, as documented by a passage of Festus: 'piscinae publicae hodieque nomen manet, ipsa non extat, ad quam et natatum et exercitationis alioqui causa veniebat populus, unde Lucilius ait (fr. 1266 M): "pro obtuso ore pugil, piscinensis reses" '.[159] The close correlation between a gymnasium and a cult place, a commonplace in the Greek world, is well documented for the Italic world at Pompeii,[160] where the Samnite Palaestra (actually a gymnasium) with the adjoining *xystus* stands next to the Doric temple in the Triangular Forum. Moreover, there we can detect a subsequent functional development, with the addition of a building which constitutes one of the first exhibitions of the imperial cult in the west, the *heroon* of Augustus' nephew Marcellus. In fact Greco and Theodorescu have noted[161] that, as a parallel to this in the Augustan era or at the latest in the Tiberian era, the complex in Paestum was transformed into an important sanctuary of the imperial cult, by virtue of the obvious connection between the Julian dynasty and the oriental Venus, the Erycina-Verticordia, a 'Trojan' goddess traditionally venerated in that very place, as well as the widespread association between gymnasia and the imperial cult.[162]

The huge space at the back of the forum, where, in chronological order, stood the *piscina publica*, the *balneum* (both built using the ashlar masonry technique) and the *xystus*, thus very soon came to qualify as *campus ubei ludunt*.[163] It was not by chance therefore, that at the beginning of the first century BC,[164] at the eastern end of the aforementioned large space, which had presumably remained free up until that moment for the development of the *ludi*, an amphitheatre was built using the technique of recycled blocks typical of the Roman republican era (the building was later enlarged in brick, at the time of the foundation of the Flavian colony of *classiarii*),[165] giving a monumental look to the traditional place of the *ludus* for the new tastes of the age. This coupling of a *campus* and an amphitheatre is known elsewhere, from Pompeii to Carsulae, and accounts for the Paestan amphitheatre's unusual central position.

The identification of the older complex of *piscina publica* and gymnasium with its adjoining structure of baths as one of the focuses of the imperial cult enables us perhaps to fill in some other details of the topography of the north-west corner of the forum. At the northern extremity of the west side of the forum, that is in the angle between the west and north sides of the square, is a shrine, which was inserted into and partly interrupts the forum colonnade, but was furnished with its own late republican podium and paved with *signinum*. The rear wall of the cella displays an architectural arrangement interpretable as a sequence of three bases for cult statues, or, perhaps even better, as the base of a cult statue between two plinths which supports an *aedicula* framing the statue. The pronaos was once enclosed by *cancella*, as documented by the surviving holes, whilst in front of the *sacellum* the altar

---

[157] *Paestum*, ii. 51 f.

[158] As is shown by the oblique direction of the wall, following that of the portico to the N., by the short wall that closes it to the W. and by the little basin placed at the intersection between this last wall and the columnade, a clear and unmistakable definition of the area as a *xystus*.

[159] Fest. 232 L.

[160] See now P. Zanker, *Pompeji. Stadtbilder als Spiegel von Gesellschaft und Herrschaftsformen*, 9. Trier. Winckelmannspr. 1987 (Mainz, 1987), 12 f.

[161] *Paestum*, iii. 57 f.

[162] See the already mentioned case of Velia (Fabbri and Trotta, *Una scuola-collegio di età augustea*), where we find the association, typical of the Hellenistic world, of a gymnasium, a medical school, and an imperial cult place. On the other hand, a similar association of a *campus* (i.e. a gymnasium) and a heroic cult is now attested by several examples in late republican Italy, at Alba Fucens, at Herdonia (Torelli, 'Il diribitorium') and, in the early imperial age, at Asisium. In this last town of Umbria the late republican *circus* (ILLRP 550) was transformed into a gymnasium-*campus*, possibly by P. Petronius *cos. suff.* 19 d.C., by the insertion of a heroic tomb, which might belong to Petronius' father. Later a Petro[nia] (CIL II. 5406;

G. L. Gregori, 'Amphiteatralia I', in *MEFRA* 96 (1984), 969 f.), most likely the daughter of the *cos.* 19, added an amphitheatre (and may be a theatre) to this heroic gymnasium—an interesting analogy with the Paestan complex, where an original *campus* with *piscina* was converted, part into an amphitheatre and part into an area devoted to the heroic, imperial cult. F. Coarelli is preparing a study of the monumental complex of *circus*, heroic *campus* and amphitheatre in Asisium.

[163] The expression is found in the well-known inscription of L. Betilienus Varus in Aletrium, to be dated in the last quarter of the 2nd cent. BC (ILLRP 528). On *campus* from the archaeological and historical perspective, see H. Devijer and A. Van Wontherghem, 'Il "campus' nell'impianto urbanistico delle città romane: testimonianze epigrafiche e resti archeologici', *Acta Archaeologica Lovanensia*, 20 (1981), 33 f.; idd., 'Ancora sul "campus" delle città romane', ibid. 21 (1982), 93 f.; idd., 'Der "Campus" der römischen Städte in Italien und im Westen', *ZPE* 54 (1984), 195 f.; idd., 'Neue Belege zum "Campus" der römischen Städte in Italien und im Westen', *ZPE* 60 (1985), 147 f.

[164] *Paestum* iii. 65 f.

[165] Ibid. 67; on the Flavian colony see ILP, pp. 323 f.; see also M. Mello, *Paestum romana. Ricerche storiche* (Rome, 1974), 155 f.

Plate 14. Paestum, Museo. Marble base dedicated by P. Avianus P.l. [- - -], *magister Aug[ustalis et] Mercurialis* (photo by L. De Masi).

is easily recognizable (Fig. 26, 3). I am inclined to identify the small temple as a temple of Mercury, since the earliest organization of the Paestan *Augustalitas* was that of the *magistri Augustales Mercuriales*.[166] Proof of

this lies in the beautiful marble altar of urban manufacture already known from the description contained in the *Corpus Inscriptionum Latinarum*[167] and at present in the storerooms of the Paestum Museum (Pl. 14) which was dedicated to Mercury (the god is represented in a reclining pose in the top left-hand corner) by a P. Avianus P.l. [—], *magister Aug[ustalis et] Mercurialis*, portrayed in the act of sacrificing (in the bottom

[166] On the *Augustales et Mercuriales*, later simply *Augustales*, cf. A. Degrassi, 'I magistri Mercuriales di Lucca e la dea Anzotica di Aenona', *Athenaeum*, 15 (1937), 284 f. (= *Scritti vari di antichità*, i (Rome, 1962), 495 f.). The cult of Mercurius is already attested by coin types in the age of the *municipium*, as documented by a Paestan triens with the legend M.OCI.III.VIR: see Crawford, 'Form and Function', 91, no. 31/2, pl. x.

[167] *CIL* X, 485 = *ILP* 30.

right-hand corner). On these grounds, the little temple in the north-west corner of the forum, built in the late republican era, is perhaps attributable to Mercury, the god initially associated with Augustus:[168] it is note-worthy that the marble altar just mentioned dates back to the last years of the first century BC. Topographic-ally the temple functions as a sort of 'hinge' between the forum and the complex of *piscina publica* and gymnasium.

As on the Aventine in Rome[169] the temple of the god stood not far from the cult place of Fortuna Virilis –Venus Verticordia. However in the specific case of Paestum the shrine represented the earliest form of the imperial cult, the first step in a sort of dynastic *climax*, a janitor of the great goddess of the Julii venerated in the area of the *piscina publica*.[170] The imperial cult itself was placed next to the temple, in an apsidal vast hall (Fig. 26, 4) at the western extremity of the northern side of the forum, which occupied the space of two of the old shops of the forum square and might be the local sanctuary of the Lares Publici, on the basis of its resemblance to the temple to the same Lares in the north-east side of the forum at Pompeii. However, a closer scrutiny of the situation both in Pompeii and in Paestum makes an identification with the earliest shrine of the local cult of the founder of the empire more likely: a local *sacrarium divi Augusti* designed according to the example set in Rome by Livia *ad capita Bubula*.[171] Since the bases with dedications of the *magistri Mentis Bonae* whose findspot is known[172] seem to come from the area, the adjacent apsidal hall (Fig. 26, 5), which was inserted within the former third shop to the west of the northern side of the forum and communicated by a small door with the hall we pro-

posed identifying with the *sacrarium divi Augusti*, must be interpreted as the seat of the college. This powerful association, conveniently housed in close contact with the *sacrarium divi Augusti*, with the temple of the god of the *mercatura*, the Augustan Mercury, and the temple of Bona Mens Augusta, organized the freedmen attached to the cult of the nearby monumental temple of Bona Mens, the great goddess of the Paestan *fides*, naturally honoured in the local coinage.[173] For some time the *Augustales* (as beforehand the *Mercuriales*) too may have had their seat there, before they had a sumptuous *curia* of their own (possibly the *Curia Caesarea* of several inscriptions)[174] built later, in the Julio-Claudian age, and appropriately situated in the enclosure of Venus Verticordia as is also proved by the discovery in the area of the piscina of various fragments of their rosters (Fig. 26, 10).[175]

Greco and Theodorescu[176] have reconstructed the plan of this ill-fated building (Fig. 26, 18–19) situated on the eastern side of the *piscina* and barbarically destroyed by the reckless investigation undertaken in the 1950s and 1960s to bring to light monuments of the Greek period. The earliest phase (Fig. 35) consisted of a rectangular hall in the south-eastern corner of the ancient area centred on the *piscina*.[177] Later on in the Flavian era (or perhaps still in the Julio-Claudian age?) this modest construction was substituted by a large complex within the eastern side of the enclosure of the *piscina*, which included (to the south) a building of similar structure to the seat of the *Augustales* at Herculaneum (Fig. 26, 18)[178] and (to the north) a large *schola*, constructed around a rectangular peristyle fac-ing north–south, preceded by a deep vestibule and surrounded by rooms (Fig. 26, 19). In the Hadrianic or Antonine age (Fig. 36)[179] a large hall with an apse was added on the western side,[180] probably intended for the imperial cult of the Antonine dynasty (to which

[168] Hor. *Carm.* 1. 2. 41 f.: cf. K. Scott, 'Merkur-Augustus und Horaz, c.I,2', *Hermes*, 68 (1928), 15 f.; id., 'Mercury on the Bologna Altar', *MDAI(R)* 50 (1935), 225 f.; O. Brendel, 'Novus Mercurius', ibid. 231 f.

[169] Known only through written sources (Liv. 2. 21. 7, 27. 5–6; Val. Max. 9. 3. 6; Ov. *Fast.* 5. 669; Apul. *Met.* 6. 8; Not. *Reg.* XI), the temple is to be located at the SE end of the Circus Maximus, onto which it faced (Platner and Ashby, *A Topographical Dictionary*, 339).

[170] The shrine is placed at the entrance of the *piscina publica* complex, that in the Julio-Claudian age became the seat of the *Augustales* (see below). Notice that at the same entrance on the forum side, after Mercurius' shrine, there is another small chapel, created by adding a little apse to the first of the mid-republican shops that bordered the piazza of the *piscina publica*: a *sacellum* of Fortuna Augusta?

[171] The identification of the Pompeian building VII, 9, 3 as the temple of the Lares Publici is proposed by A. Mau (*MDAI(R)* 11 (1896), 285 f.) and, apart from a ridiculous attempt made by L. Richardson jr., 'The Libraries of Pompeii', *Archaeology* 30 (1977), 400 f. (repeated in his more recent book, *Pompeii: An Architectural History* (Baltimore and London, 1988), 273 f.), to interpret it as a public library, has remained unchallenged.

[172] *ILP* 10, 11; cf. also *ILP* 9 = *CIL* I², 3149.

[173] Crawford, 'Form and Function', 93 f., no. 33, tav. XI.

[174] *ILP* 106–7.   [175] *ILP* 111.

[176] *Paestum*, iii. 56 f., fig. 2.   [177] Ibid. fig. 2 (buildings in red).

[178] Ibid. fig. 2 (buildings hatched in green). For the building of the *Augustales* at Herculaneum see: G. Cerulli Irelli, 'La casa "del colonnato tuscanico" ad Ercolano', *Memorie dell'Accademia di Archeologia, Lettere e Belle Arti di Napoli*, 45 (1974), 11 f.; M. Manni, *Le pitture della casa del colonnato tuscanico*, Monumenti della Pittura Antica scoperti in Italia, III, Ercolano II (Rome, 1974). The inscriptions have been published by G. Guadagno, 'Frammenti inediti degli Albi degli Augustali', in *Cronache Ercolanesi* 7 (1977), 114 f.; id., 'Supplemento epigrafico ercolanese', in *Cronache Ercolanesi* 8 (1978), 132 f.

[179] *Paestum*, iii. 46, the find of a Hadrianic coin in a level below the floor of the hall makes us sure about the chronology of this building.

[180] Ibid. 58 f.

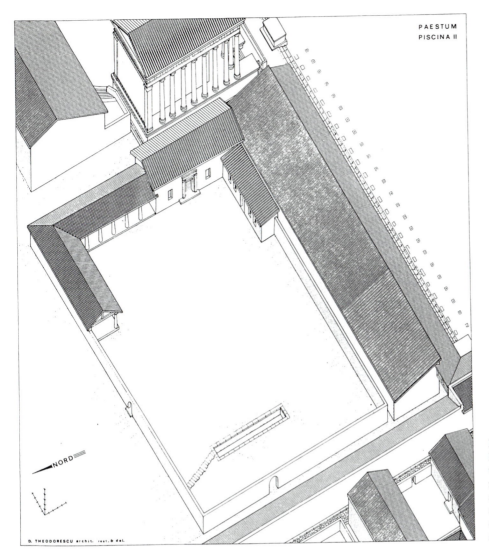

PAESTUM
PISCINA II

D. THEODORESCU archit. rest. & del.

Fig. 35. Reconstruction of Phase II (Augustan period) of the area of the *piscina publica*: note the little rectanguar hall at the south-east corner of the area and the almost complete elimination of the trilithic structure (after Theodorescu).

dedications to Hadrian, to Faustina minor and Lucius Verus might refer),[181] whilst on the northern side, maybe at the beginning of the third century AD,[182] rose two other halls, one facing east–west, possibly a nymphaeum, and another, also with an apse, which might have housed the inscriptions found in the excavations of 1930 and 1954 in the area of the '*gymnasium*' with dedications to members of the family of the emperor Maximinus.[183]

[181] *ILP* 39–41.
[182] *Paestum*, iii. 51, with a rather generic proposal to date it to the 2nd cent. AD.
[183] *ILP* 47 (Maximinus), 48 (deified Paulina), 50 (Maximus Caesar). It is worthwhile mentioning in this connection the series of dedications to the Severan family *ILP* 42–4, 46, perhaps a document of the dynastic cult of the Severi.

8. Sacred Topography and Origins of the Colonists

The sacred topography of Roman Paestum now enables us to consider certain historical and social characteristics of some interest. Even if future research proves some of the conjectures made regarding the titular deities of the various temples to be wrong, the general picture which emerges from the reconstruction of the broad profile of cults practised in the sanctuaries, supported by inscriptional and numismatic evidence, indicates decisively that this aspect of the colonial *sacra* was without doubt very carefully planned. The ancient sanctuaries were in fact 'reused' in very skilful ways, as we have seen starting from the northern sanctuary,

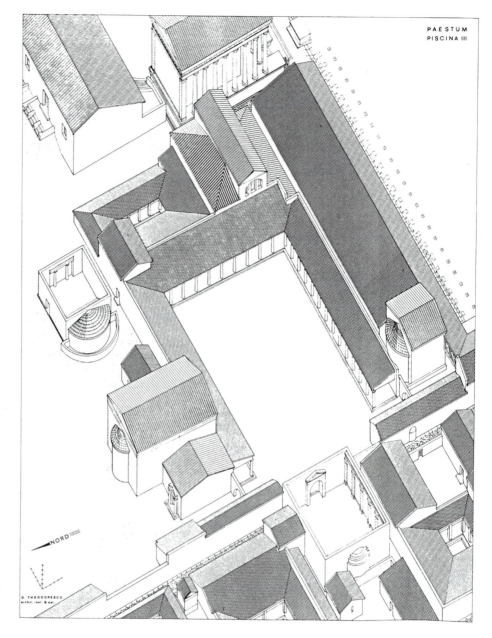

PAESTUM
PISCINA III

Fig. 36. Reconstruction of Phase III (Antonine period) of the area of the *piscina publica*, with nymphaea and shrines of the imperial cult (after Theodorescu).

replanned as the colony's formal, almost stately, religious centre, but with the aim of turning it into a little Paestan 'Aventine' for the by then plebeian youthful rites of passage, according to the rooted popular consciousness of the social value of this formal religious recognition.

Almost at the foot of this symbolic 'Aventine' and in an imaginary continuation of it, those who shaped the new colony, evidently outstanding exponents of the patricio-plebeian culture of the time, placed the *piscina publica* (similar to the *piscina publica* in Rome

positioned at the foot of the Aventine), intended for celebrations of Fortuna Virilis–Venus Verticordia in the colony's truly important 'new' sanctuary, a choice of exceptional socio-political significance, as we shall soon see. In this context the temple of Mens, however much it might appear to be a later and brutal insertion into the urban scene, in reality represented a harmonious continuation of the same theme on an ideological plane, with emphasis perhaps laid on the central place of politics in the forum area, almost 'Capitoline' in flavour, skilfully evoked by means of the dedication of the temple of Mens formulated in the dramatic period of the Hannibalic war. The 'Aventine' connotation of this coherent project is further accentuated (if the cult goes back to the era of the foundation) by the presence of Mercury, which underlines the mercantile nature of the forum area and of the whole colony, in harmony with the picture of strong insistence on the plebeian values of the foundation.

In the southern sanctuary, the ancient and prestigious temple of Hera, still a goddess of a 'plebeian' nature, was probably claimed by the Latin pantheon for the cult of Juno Regina, though it seems to have been of secondary importance in the overall context of the sanctuary. The apparent decline of the sanctuary on the Sele river from the time of the foundation of the Latin colony would seem to confirm this. Also the comprehensive study (which we hope is near at hand) of the votives from Paestum may confirm that the construction, almost to the point of clearing away the zone of the numerous votive deposits connected with the Hera cult of Classical Greek and late Classical Lucanian times, dates back to the period of the foundation of the colony of Paestum. It is evident on the other hand, however, that at the same time the pre-existing temples of Apollo and Hercules moved to become the centre of the great new religiosity of the city, prompting a 'Roman' interpretation of the *temenos* as a 'Tiber' area, with Apollo *medicus inter Forum Holitorium et circum Flaminium* and Hercules Invictus. The same significance and ideological flavour is shared by the other temples built in the area at the time of the Latin foundation, new insertions in the context of the old southern *temenos*, but not by chance separated from it by means of the *temenos'* own walls. The cults of Mater Matuta *in Foro Boario*, of Hercules Victor *extra portam Trigeminam* and of Aesculapius *in Insula*, form a perfect blend, on the urbanistic and ideological plane, between the new area of the forum and the ancient Greek *temenos*: they stress the new values of the Latin colonists and at the same time revive old Greek cults, such as that of Hercules and the prestigious medical (and possibly hiatromantic) connotations of the ancient sacred presence of Chiron.

This rigorous and studied reorganization of the sacred topography, aimed at a specific *imago urbis*, rests nevertheless on a miscellaneous and perhaps unsettled social base, on which it would be limiting to impose the obvious label of 'plebeian', though this has repeatedly

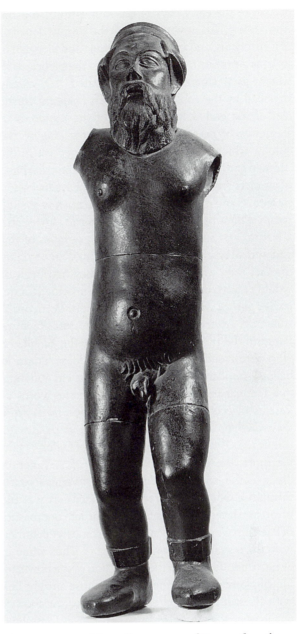

Plate 15. Paestum, Museo. Bronze statue of Marsyas, from the forum area (photo by L. De Masi).

arisen in my discourse, starting with the 'Aventine' nature of the *arx*. Signs and messages come across loud and clear from the archaeological evidence. The well-known statue of Marsyas (Pl. 15),[184] copied in

184 Published by A. Marzullo immediately after discovery (A. Marzullo, 'La statua di Marsyas e la Colonia latina di Paestum', *Atti della Società Italiana per il Progresso delle Scienze*, 5 (1932), 1 f.), the statue has never received detailed study, but attracted attention only among historians, such as A. Piganiol, 'Le Marsyas de Paestum et le roi Faunus', *RA* (1944), 118 f., and G. Tibiletti, 'Marsyas, die Sklaven und die Marser', *Studi Betti* 4 (Milan, 1962), 351 f.

bronze in the early days of the foundation from the Roman original known to us from the famous denarius of Censorinus, and unmistakably Italic and plebeian in style, is a precise *indicium libertatis* of the plebeians,[185] which, as F. Coarelli has corroborated,[186] is clearly signalled by the conspicuously open *compedes* on the feet of the god. Likewise, most of the hundreds of statuettes of *pueri exoptati*, future new *cives* of the colony, which were found in a votive deposit in the 'Roman garden', show the *lorum* (Pl. 16), the cross band of amulets copied from those worn by *hierodouloi* and by *servi*,[187] and only rarely the *bulla* (Pl. 17); however all wear on their heads the unmistakable *pileum libertatis*, a feature rare in other, non-Paestan examples of this widespread type of Etrusco-Italic ex-voto,[188] underlining the fact that, unlike their parents, they had been or would be born *ingenui*. Thus the space provided for the *piscina publica* with the sacellum of Venus Verticordia, was not arbitrary, but intended to introduce to Paestum the rite practised in Rome by the *humiliores*, who performed *supplicatio* to the goddess 'etiam in balineis, quod in iis ea parte corpis utique viri nudantur qua feminarum gratia desideratur', in the words of Verrius Flaccus or αἱ δὲ τοῦ πλήθους γυναῖκες ἐν τοῖς τῶν ἀνδρῶν βαλανείοις ἐλούοντο πρὸς θεραπείαν αὐτῆς (i.e. Ἀφροδίτης), in the words of Lydus.[189] Furthermore, the extra-urban sanctuary of S. Venera[190] discloses the existence of *hierodouloi* of Venus Erycina through a *collegium* of *Venerii* organized—as was the norm for slaves —in *centuriae*; from the late onomastics of Paestum we also happen to know some freedwomen with the revealing *nomen* of Veneria.[191] Thus when in 217 BC (undoubtedly on the suggestion of the powerful Otacilii family from Beneventum, whose ancient link with Paestum I have already referred to on another

[185] M. Torelli, *Typology and Structure of the Roman Historical Reliefs* (Ann Arbor, 1982), 102 f.   [186] Coarelli, *Il Foro Romano*, ii. 95 f.
[187] Pliny the Elder (*NH* 33. 4. 10: '. . . unde mos bullae duravit, ut eorum qui equo meruissent filii insigne id haberent, ceteri lorum') and Juvenal (5. 163 f.: 'quis enim tam nudus, ut illum | bis ferat, Etruscum puero si contigit aurum | vel nodus tantum et signum de paupere loro?') are explicit in this regard (but see also Macrob. *Sat.* 1. 6. 8 f., and Paul. Fest. 32 L); the *lorum* is then a distinctive attribute of *servi* and *hierodouloi*. On the amulets hanging from the *lorum*—mostly crescent-shaped *lunulae* (Plaut. *Ep.* 5. 1. 33; Isid. *Orig.* 19. 31. 17; Tert. *De cult. fem.* 2. 10), and *crepundia* (Apul. *De mag.* 310. 19), almost invariably among the pendants of the *lora* of Paestan terracotta children—see C. Bonner, *Studies in Magic Amulets* (Ann Arbor, 1950).
[188] On this type of ex-voto see now M. C. D'Ercole, *La stipe votiva del Belvedere a Lucera* (Rome, 1990), 125 f. (with previous bibliography).
[189] *Fast. Praen. ad d. kal. Apr.* (*Inscr. It.* XIII, 2, p. 434); Lyd. *De mens.* 4. 65 (cf. 4. 29); see above.
[190] See Epilogue.   [191] *ILP* 180, 208.

Plate 16. Paestum, Museo. Statuette of a newborn child showing the *lorum*, the cross band of amulets, from a votive deposit in the 'Roman garden' (photo by L. De Masi).

expectation for a *libertas* much more precious than the plebeian one. G. Fabre[193] has demonstrated that Mens was the great divinity of freedmen, who on the side of the former slave was meant to be the great sponsor of his enfranchisement and on the side of the former master the guarantor of the *mens*, of the good disposition of the mind and of the *memoria* of the ancient *servi* towards the *patroni*, or, more explicitly, of the recollection of the obligations contracted with the ancient *dominus*. The Roman vote of Fabius Maximus and Otacilius is also to be understood in this sense. In this 'servile' version of the *libertas*, the female part is embodied by Erycina, the male part by Mens, both of them divinities who liberated slaves from *servitus*. The former freed women from their traditional *servitium* of the temple *meretricium* as *Veneriae*, the latter freed men from their *servitium* as slaves.

In fact, after the battle of Lake Trasimene in the same year of 217 BC, faced with the overwhelming need for military manpower to combat the numerous and devastating *clades Hannibalicae*, the Roman ruling classes were forced, at the suggestion of Ti. Sempronius Gracchus, to resort to the compulsory acquisition at state expense of a good 24,000 *servi* bound for the army.[194] Immediately afterwards, in 215 BC, there was a conscription of further 8,000 *volones*, i.e. a massive enlistment of *servi*: 'octo milia iuvenum validorum ex servitiis, prius sciscitantes singulos vellentne militare, empto publico armaverunt'.[195] Not by chance such a revolutionary action was only ratified by the senate in 214,[196] yet again due to Ti. Sempronius Gracchus *cos.* 215, an individual who constantly crops up in the context of the freedom of the *volones* and of the temple *par excellence* of the slave *libertas*, the temple of Jupiter Libertas, founded *pecunia multaticia* by his father *cos.* 238 BC.[197] The same ruling classes, again in the year of 217 BC,[198] propitiously (and with a degree of consistency) conceded to the *libertini pueri*, rather than the coveted *bulla aurea*, privilege of the *ingenui*, the right to exhibit

Plate 17. Paestum, Museo. Statuette of a newborn child showing *bullae*, from a votive deposit in the 'Roman garden' (photo by L. De Masi).

occasion)[192] the cult of Mens was introduced into the colony, side by side with the one already in existence of Venus Verticordia-Erycina, the arrival of the new goddess was fostered by the same local climate of

[192] Torelli, in *Annali della Facoltà di Lettere e Filosofia di Perugia—Studi Classici*, NS 18 (1980/1).

[193] G. Fabre, *Libertus. Patrons et affranchis à Rome* (Rome, 1981), 87 f.; cf. K. Latte, *Römische Religionsgeschichte* (Munich, 1960), 239 f.

[194] Val. Max. 7. 6. 1; cf. N. Rouland, *Les esclaves romains en temps de guerre* (Bruxelles, 1973), 48 f.   [195] Liv. 22. 57. 11; cf. Macrob. *Sat.* 1. 11. 30 f.

[196] Liv. 24. 14. 4 ss.; cf. 18. 12.

[197] The construction of the temple (Liv. 24. 16. 19) should be placed in 246 BC (or slightly later), when the future *cos.* 238 BC was aedile, a position which could give him the opportunity of collecting the *pecunia multaticia* necessary for the building; his son, *cos.* 215 BC, dedicated in that temple a painting representing the banquet of the *volones* after the victory at Beneventum (Liv. ibid.). These family stories certainly contributed to creating the 'subversive aura' of Gracchus' great-grandsons Tiberius and Gaius Gracchi.   [198] Ascon. *ad* Cic. *Verr.* 2. 1. 152.

a *bulla scortea* in place of the traditional *lorum*, thus providing us with a rational explanation for the same change, from the *lorum* to the *bulla*, to be found in the statuettes of children from the votive deposits of the 'Italic' temple in Paestum.

In this sense, the evidence from Paestum so clear and I would say pressing, is proof of the enlistment carried out among the lowest strata of Roman society of freedmen and slaves to populate the 'city of roses'. The words of a great contemporary, Philip V of Macedonia, confirm that this reading of the facts is not the product of a distorted modern interpretation. In 214 BC in his famous letter to the Larisseans,[199] he wrote: 'and they [the Romans], having liberated the slaves, granted them citizenship and offered them the opportunity of holding magistracies; in this way not only did they increase their own fatherland, but they also founded colonies in nearly seventy places.' We may therefore conclude that the foundation of Paestum involved very low strata of Roman society and maybe even the local Lucanian *servitus*, as a series of other circumstances leads us to suppose. However, let us look at some other data relating to the social aspects of this unusual colonial foundation.

Recently F. Arcuri[200] investigated the onomastics of the well-known Latin republican inscriptions relating to the activity of the local *quaestores* and correctly deduced that among the initial population there was a strong local Oscan–Lucanian contingent. Besides the cases she examined, it should be noted that the onomastics of the later local ruling class, up until the beginnings of the empire, contained a high percentage of Oscan–Lucanian *nomina*, such as the Ceppii, the Digitii, the Egnii, the Mineii, the Vennei (or Bennii),[201] almost in the same numbers as the Latin *nomina*, the Claudii, the Coccei, the Flaccei, the Ligustii, the Plaetorii, the Sextilii, the Valerii.[202] However, among the lists of colonists it is also possible to come across some more or less patent cases of *nomina Tusca*. The clearest example is that of Numonii, *numna/numnas*[203]

in Etruscan, a senatorial Paestan *gens* from the late republican period, to which Numonius Vala belonged, a celebrated character from Horace, twice honoured at Paestum as a patron.[204] This throws up a series of onomastic Paestan comparisons,[205] of which the most significant is the one provided by two pieces of graffiti from the Roman fill of the *ekklesiasterion*, a P. Nuom-(onius) and a M. Nu(monius) on bowls of the 'Atelier des Petites Estampilles' not later than the mid-third century BC.[206] Two other highly probable Etruscan *nomina* of an early age are the very rare Galonius, *calune/ calunei* in Etruscan,[207] witnessed at least twice in inscriptions, one from the republican era[208] and one from the early Empire,[209] to be read as Ol(us) Galonius (and not Olgalonius as in *ILP*), and the equally rare Lautinius,[210] the same as Etruscan *lautne/lautnei*.[211] Without ruling out the possibility of enlistment of colonists in Etruria itself, it seems to me much more likely that the *ultima origo* of these people should be sought in the isolated Etruscan ethnic group on the right bank of the Sele, remnants of which we know still survived between Pontecagnano and Fratte up until the eve of the foundation of the Latin colony.[212] The situation seems to have a direct correspondence with the events of 269 BC mentioned above (p. 44), which presupposes an almost total desertion of the Etruscan centres around Salerno and of their *chora*,[213] then occupied by the deported Picentes,[214] and therefore in all likelihood a transfer of these last Tyrrhenians from southern Campania to within the walls of Paestum, a fact to which, as we shall see, I believe the renowned and much-discussed Aristoxenus' fragment alludes.[215] Moreover the entry of aristocrats from Lucanian Paestum into the ranks of the colony is not only attested by the onomastics, but also by archaeology. The cremation enclosures of the

---

[199] *SIG* II4, 543, ll. 32 f.

[200] F. Arcuri, 'In margine ad alcune epigrafi romane di Paestum', *Bollettino Storico di Salerno e Principato di Citra*, 4: 1 (1986), 5 f.

[201] Ceppii: *ILP* 196, 202; Digitii: *ILP* 65, 89, 97, 99, 102, 107, 111, 114, 203, 204; Egnii: *ILP* 91, 111, 116; Mineii: *ILP* 18, 81–5; Bennii/Vennei: *ILP* 100, 102, 113, 198.

[202] Claudii: *ILP* 139, 144–53; Coccei: *ILP* 81; Flaccei: *ILP* 122, 123, 157, 163; Ligustii: *ILP* 118; Plaetorii: *ILP* 90; Sextilii: *ILP* 144–53; Valerii: *ILP* 12, 76, 143, 156, 157, 158, 159, 176, 181.

[203] Cf. the well-known pottery stamp *numnal/vel numnal* (list in *SE* 35 (1967), 560); for *numnas/numni*, attested in the area of Perugia, see *CIE* 3352, 4530, *TLE* 622.

[204] *ILP* 70–1; G. Camodeca, in *Epigrafia e ordine senatorio*, Acts of Conference; Rome, 1981 (Rome, 1982), ii. 150 f., rightly thinks that the Numonii Valae should have Paestan origins.

[205] *ILP* 180.   [206] *Paestum*, ii. 109 f., n.122, fig. 62; 110 n. 123, fig. 77.

[207] *Nomen* almost certainly from Clusium (*CIE* 1462, 1511, 2144–5: Clusium). *CIE* 4282 and *NRIE* 521, respectively from Perusia and Proceno (*ager Volsiniensis*), refer to women.

[208] *ILP* 154.   [209] *ILP* 19.   [210] *ILP* 155.

[211] Cf. *larti lautnei* (*CIE* 159: Volaterrae).

[212] Our information depends entirely on inscriptional evidence: G. Colonna, *Nuovi dati epigrafici sulla protostoria della Campania*, in *Atti Istituto Italiano di Preistoria e Protostoria—Campania* (Florence, 1976), 151 f.; id., *Le iscrizioni etrusche di Fratte*, in *Fratte. Un insediamento etrusco-campano*, Catalogue of Exhibition; Salerno 1990 (Modena, 1990), 301 f.

[213] For Fratte see G. Greco and A. Pontrandolfo, 'L'abitato', in *Fratte*, 29 f.; for Pontecagnano we have no precise evidence, apart from a large imperial necropolis near the port, in the site called Magazzeno, where we find the inscription of a *classiarius* (*NSA* (1880), 67, 187).

[214] See, n. 20.   [215] See further n. 224.

colonial period found in the necropolis of S. Venera, already referred to (Ch. 1), were intentionally laid on top of painted Lucanian aristocratic tombs, thereby demonstrating that, despite the modified funerary custom (probably imposed by Latin colonial laws), a continuity in lineage between the pre-colonial phase and the colonial phase was both sought-after and influential among the descendants of the Lucanian nobility.

I believe the ethnic and cultural element which most succumbed to this intense remingling of linguistic–cultural groups and social strata to have been without doubt the Greek one. From the early Lucanian period on, probably right to the Roman conquest, the dominant classes of the Lucanian *principes* slavishly imitated and drew on Greek culture for their political practices (the use of the Greek *ekklesiasterion* in the Lucanian period sheds the brightest light on this),[216] for their religious displays (the documentation on the continuity of the cult forms in all the sanctuaries of the Greek city is impressive),[217] and for their decorative arts (one remarkable instance is the work of Assteas and Python, the two leading Paestan vase painters, both of Greek origin and language).[218] Not only did the Greeks continue to embody culture in the city, but the Greek language is virtually the only one found in the *instrumentum*.[219] With the Roman foundation, the Greek element disappeared without trace and even artisan production, which traditionally in non-Greek Italy was entrusted to the Greeks, passed into Roman hands or at least under Roman control. The most commonly found pottery in the Paestum of the early colonial

phase is a local imitation of Roman pottery, the black-glazed ceramics of the 'Atelier des Petites Estampilles'.[220]

This combination of circumstances seems to be mirrored almost perfectly in the fragment belonging to a lost Σύμμικτα συμποτικά attributed to Aristoxenus from Tarentum:[221] οἷς (scil. Ποσειδωνιάταις) συνέβη τὰ μέν ἐξ ἀρχῆς Ἕλλησιν οὖσιν ἐκβεβαρβαρῶσθαι Τυρρηνοῖς ἢ Ῥωμαίοις γεγονόσι, καὶ τήν τε φωνὴν μεταβεβληκέναι τά τε λοιπὰ τῶν ἐπιτηδευμάτων, ἄγειν δὲ μίαν τινὰ αὐτοὺς τῶν ἑορτῶν τῶν Ἑλληνικῶν ἔτι καὶ νῦν, ἐν ᾗ συνιόντες ἀναμιμνήσκονται τῶν ἀρχαίων ἐκείνων ὀνομάτων τε καὶ νομίμων καὶ ἀπολοφυράμενοι πρὸς ἀλλήλους καὶ ἀποδακρύσαντες ἀπέρχονται. The fragment has been discussed on various occasions and has given rise to several explanations,[222] none of which seems satisfactory. However, I think I can safely say that the 'barbarization of the Poseidonians' due to the 'Tyrrhenians and Romans' can only be interpreted as a description of the cultural consequences of the foundation of the colony, which revolutionized the social and proprietary relations on which the fortunes of the city's Greek element relied and which to a large degree involved two new *ethne*, the Latin one ('the Romans') and the Etruscan one ('the Tyrrhenians'). This Greek element had been used to the supremacy of the Lucanians for more than a century (hence the passage's silence about them) and had substantially preserved their own language, regular religious festivals, and customs (the written language was widespread, the cults continued) under the domination of an ethnic group which, small in numbers and organized in the socio-economic forms characteristic of archaic Sabellian societies,[223] had simply replaced —and maybe not even totally—the city's dominant Greek class. The 'loss of the language' which the fragment refers to is demonstrated by the disappearance of the Greek vase inscriptions after the foundation of the Latin colony, a phenomenon mentioned above, whilst the decline of Greek language, used only on the occasion of religious ceremonies, represents one of the consequences of the aforementioned continuity of one part of the Greek cults, through the Lucanian 'parentheses',

---

[216] *Paestum*, ii. 81 f.

[217] The Greek cults, with a few exceptions in the *chora*, all continued during the Lucanian occupation of Poseidonia. Paradoxically had we not the few literary sources, the sole Lucanian inscription from the town, significantly a dedication to Zeus—*Zoves* in the *ekklesiasterion* (*Paestum*, ii. 137 f.), and the painted tombs (on these see A. Greco Pontrandolfo, 'Su alcune tombe pestane: proposte di una lettura', *MEFRA* 89 (1977), 31 f.; ead., 'Segni di trasformazioni sociali a Poseidonia tra la fine del V e gli inizi del III sec.a.C.', *DArch* NS 1: 2 (1979), 27 f.; A. Greco Pontrandolfo and A. Rouveret, 'Ideologia funeraria e società a Poseidonia nel IV secolo a.C.', in G. Gnoli and J. P. Vernant (eds.), *La Mort, les morts dans les sociétés anciennes* (Cambridge, 1982), 299 f.; A. Rouveret and A. Greco Pontrandolfo, 'Pittura funeraria in Lucania e Campania. Puntualizzazioni cronologiche e proposte di lettura', (*DArch* n.s. 1: 2 (1983), 91 f.), we could maintain that there was never a Lucanian domination over Poseidonia.

[218] On these two vase painters working at Paestum in the 4th cent. BC and more generally on the Paestan red-figured pottery of these times, mostly connected with the activity of Assteas and Python, see A. D. Trendall, *Paestan Pottery* (London, 1936), E. Greco, *Il pittore di Afrodite* (Benevento, 1970), and A. D. Trendall, *The Red-Figured Vases of Paestum* (Oxford, 1987).

[219] E. Greco, 'Opsophoros', *AIONArch* 2 (1980), 63 ss.; see also e.g. the fragments of a 4th-cent. BC mould with the (abbreviated) name of the craftsman in Greek: *Paestum*, ii. 124, 132 f., nos. 231, 232, 234, 236, fig. 81 f. (see esp. fr. no. 234, where we can read [—]δειδος).

[220] V. *Paestum*, iii. 143, no. 298, fig. 67.

[221] *Ap.* Athen. 14. 632a (= *FHG* II, fr. 90, p. 291).

[222] See now A. Fraschetti, 'Aristosseno, i Romani e la "barbarizzazione" di Poseidonia', *AIONArch* 3 (1981), 97 ss. (with previous bibliography); a different perspective is given by A. Mele, in *Storia del Mezzogiorno* (Salerno, 1991), 278 f.

[223] Cf. A. Pontrandolfo Greco, *I Lucani. Etnografia e archeologia di una regione antica* (Milan, 1982), 127 f.

but in the forms imposed by the religiousness of the Roman colony. The only problem posed by this interpretation arises from the chronology of Aristoxenus, whose death is generally accepted to have definitely preceded the Latin colonisation of Paestum.[224] I favour the interpretation which considers the Σύμμικτα συμποτικά, the work from which the fragment is an extract, to be different from the better known and often quoted Περὶ μουσικῆς or de musica and, unlike the latter, to be an apocryphal product of neo-Pythagorean circles (hence the reference to Aristoxenus), originating within a cultivated milieu,[225] either of the Greeks of Poseidonia–Paestum after the arrival of the colonists or perhaps better of Tarentum itself, in the wake of the Roman conquest of 272 BC, an event virtually contemporary with the foundation of Paestum, dated to the year before.

At this stage we should clear up some other aspects of this somewhat unusual Latin colonial foundation. All the data of a religious and cultural nature, which characterize the social standing of the first colonists, point towards the lowest layers of society. This is borne on by the choice of politico-religious symbols spread around the sanctuaries arranged around the forum to underline the social level and the cultural bias of the majority, if not of the whole of the civic body. On the north side there is the *piscina publica* for the *balneum* of the *humiliores* in the festival of Venus Verticordia–Fortuna Virilis, which because of its proclaimed promiscuity reveals the servile or ex-servile rank of the participants; the 'political' temple at the centre of the principal side of the forum, next to the *comitium*, dedicated to Mens Bona, the supreme virtue of former slaves, the Memory of the benefits received from the old *dominus* and now *patronus*. Here, as in Rome after the *votum* of 217 BC, that cult was linked with the sanctuary of Venus of female slaves, the Venus Verticordia–

Erycina of the *piscina*. On the south side there is first the Mater Matuta of the so-called 'Italic' temple, thanks to whom the colonists could procreate in quantity children 'born' already with the *pileum libertatis*, but still with the *lorum*, already free born of ex-slaves; then immediately after comes the Aesculapius of the political and physical *salus* of the colonists, more than one of whom was drawn from the *turba plebeia* which had enthusiastically welcomed the arrival of the god from Epidaurus in Rome under the political impetus of the Ogulnii brothers, champions of the *libertas plebeia*. On the west side we find Mercury, protector of the *mercatura honesta*, in which the freedman class was already starting to find vital room for its own social ascent and to see the main focuses of its fortune in the port and in the forum of the colony; and Marsyas, who, like the one in Rome, was the symbol of the *libertas* acquired by the new emerging classes, of the political freedom shown by his broken shackles, and of the freedom from want witnessed by his raised hand.

The message could not have been clearer in revealing the ideological bias and the original status of the colonists, who included not only plebeians but also slaves and freedmen. The extremely humble origins of the colonists enable us to identify the specifically naval character of the settlement: Paestum was a Latin colony with a special *foedus* to provide Rome with a supply of battleships fitted out for naval warfare against the great Carthaginian enemy, which already in 273 BC was seen to be approaching, in fact less than ten years before the outbreak of the First Punic War. The mention of a *foedus* of this type in 210 BC between Paestum and Rome and the presence of a Paestan citizen among the *socii navales* of Scipio Africanus' army, a circumstance which I will return to later, are implicit confirmation of the special status of *colonia latina*, that is to say, 'navalis' of Paestum. In fact, the case of Paestum constitutes the clearest precedent for the understanding of the other equally unusual case of the colony *civium Latinorum et libertinorum* (i.e. populated by sons of Roman soldiers and Iberian women) founded at Carteia in Spain in 177 BC,[226] which not by chance stood *ad Oceanum*, thus like Paestum it was a maritime city (a feature impressed strongly upon us

---

[224] His biographical data, mostly deriving from Suida, s.v., and from internal references in his works, are aptly summarized by C. Müller, *FHG*, 269 f. (cf. *RE* II 1 (1895), cols. 1057 f., no. 7) and disclose a chronology between 343 BC, when Aristoxenus, presumably very young, is in Mantinea to learn Arcadian music, and the beginning of the 3rd cent. BC; Suida and Cicero (*Tusc.* I. 41) however positively assert that he was a contemporary of Dicearchus from Messene, largely active in the first quarter of the 3rd cent. BC.

[225] Aristoxenus' aristocratic traits visibly surface in his definite preference for chord and percussion instruments *vis-à-vis* wind instruments, considered too 'easy' to the point that even shepherds can play them with no instruction whatsoever (*ap.* Athen. 4. 174e); typical of the same esoteric attitude appears the xenophobia shown in another fragment (*ap.* Athen. 4. 182 f), where many instruments, long since at home in Greece, such as the enneachordos, are considered as ἔκφυλα, 'stranger'.

[226] Liv. 43. 3. 1–4. The obscure legal circumstances that led to the foundation of the colony of Carteia have been several times discussed: cf. M. A. Marin Diaz, *Emigracion, colonizacion y munipalizacion en la Hispania republicana* (Granada, 1988), 126 f. (with previous bibliography).

by the local coinage).[227] Such too was the other *colonia libertinorum* known to us, the Colonia Julia Laus Corinthus founded by Caesar.[228] Similarly, it is strikingly obvious how the specifically naval character of the Latin colony provides the motivation for which, three centuries later, the Flavian colony founded at Paestum was composed of *classiarii*.

9. The Transformation of the Social Structures

It is unknown whether or not this unusual Latin colony had a decisive part to play in the great naval battles of the First Punic War. The real moment of truth came for certain in the terrible conflict with Hannibal. In the fatal year of 216 BC Paestum offered the gold from its temples,[229] a *iusta pollicitatio* from a *libertus* to a *patronus*, which accounts perfectly for the local duplication of the Roman *votum* in the temple of Mens. In 210 BC the city *ex foedere* sent its own ships to join D. Quinctius' fleet.[230] In 209 BC Paestum was numbered among the eighteen Latin colonies which declared they would continue to send troops to Rome.[231] Finally, in the year 209 BC in Scipio's camp one of the contingent of *socii navales* was Sex. Digitius,[232] most probably of Paestan origin,[233] to whom, for his act of valour in

being the first to climb the walls of Cartago Nova in Spain, C. Laelius in his capacity as *praefectus classis* granted the *corona navalis* and (we may imagine along with Münzer) the *civitas optimo iure* as well.

The fortunes of this individual and his family are crucial for our understanding of many aspects of the social and even architectural history of Paestum in the second century BC. A namesake of his, Sex. Digitius (more likely to have been the man himself rather than his son as Münzer thought),[234] was already a senator in Rome and a praetor in 194 BC, an obvious indication of a rapid political and social ascent which was not alien to the Scipio family either, as we shall shortly see. This Sex. Digitius, as a member of Cato's *comitatus*, obtained Hispania Citerior as a *provincia*, an assignment which ended in a somewhat inglorious manner.[235] In 190 BC he acted for Scipio Asiaticus as *legatus* in Asia, once again with the aforementioned C. Laelius and with M. Valerius Messalla,[236] while in 174 BC he was *legatus* to Macedonia.[237] In 172 he finally obtained a commission to seek grain in Apulia and Calabria.[238] The last we hear of this highly successful Paestan family concerns the latter's son, yet again named Sex. Digitius, who as a *tribunus militum* in 170 BC in Macedonia, reported to the senate the bad conduct of the campaign perhaps in a self-interested way.[239]

As F. Cassola quite rightly observed,[240] it is evident that, through the key-figure of the *praefectus classis* C. Laelius, future *cos.* 190 BC (but at the time of the siege of Cartago Nova only just granted citizenship and not yet embarked on a regular senatorial *cursus honorum*), Digitius with other *socii*, mostly *nominis Latini*, gained the protection of Scipio Africanus and was able to start a successful career in Hispania Citerior, where he was awarded the *corona navalis* and where he worked as a *praetor* in 194 BC.

In the light of these facts let us now turn to examine an unusual Paestan coin (Pl. 18) bearing the image of a portico (and not, as has been maintained, a temple, since the roof is shown as oblique and has no gable) and the inscription CN.CORN. | M. TUC. | PATR., i.e. *Cn. Corn(elius), M. Tuc(cius) patr(oni)*, within a laurel

---

[227] Compare the insistence on maritime themes (such as the head of Neptune, the dolphin, the trident, the rudder, the anchor, the prow, etc.) in Paestan coin types at all periods: see Crawford, 'Form and Function', *passim*.

[228] On the freedmen colony of Corinth, the most recent account (but with no real understanding of the model adopted by the founder) is that of D. Engels, *Roman Corinth: An Alternative Model for the Classical City* (Chicago, 1990), 16 f.

[229] Liv. 22. 36. 9: 'legati a Paesto pateras aureas Romam attulerunt. Iis, sicut Neapolitanis, gratiae actae, aurum non acceptum'.

[230] Id. 26. 39. 5: 'postremo ipse [*scil*. D. Quinctius] a sociis Reginisque et a Velia et a Paesto debitas ex foedere exigendo classem viginti navium, sicut ante dictum est, efficit'.

[231] Id. 27. 10. 8: 'Signini fuere et Norbani Saticulanique et Fregellani et Lucerini et Venusini et Brundisini et Hadriani et Firmani et Ariminenses, et ab altero mare Pontiani et Paestani et Cosani, et mediterranei Beneventani et Aesernini et Spoletini et Placentini et Cremonenses.' To such events Crawford, 'Form and Function', 50, refers the second phase of Paestan bronze coinage.

[232] Liv. 26. 48. 6–13; on this person, see F. Münzer, in *RE* V (1903), col. 544 n. 1.

[233] The diffusion of this *nomen* in Paestum, where we meet 10 Digitii (*ILP* 65, 89, 97, 99, 102, 107, 111, 114, 203, 204), finds no comparison in the entire Roman world and gives a very strong argument in favour of a local, possibly Lucanian, origin of the Digitii (a name to be connected with the oscan *Dekitiis*). The attribution to Paestum of the *socius navalis* of 209 BC was first made by F. Münzer, *Römische Adelsparteien und Adelsfamilien* (Stuttgart, 1920), 92 f., followed by J. Suolahti, *The Junior Officers of the Roman Army in the Republican Period: A Study on Social Structure* (Helsinki, 1955), 158, 359.

[234] Münzer, in *RE* V (1903); *contra*, F. Cassola, *I gruppi politici romani nel III secolo a.C.* (Trieste, 1962), 383 s., who believes the *socius navalis* of 209 BC to be identical to the *pr.* 194 BC and *legatus* to king Perseus in 174 BC.

[235] Liv. 34. 42. 4–43. 7; 35. 1. 1 f.; Oros. 4. 20. 16.

[236] Liv. 37. 4. 2.   [237] Liv. 41. 22. 3, and 42. 2. 1.

[238] Liv. 42. 27. 8.   [239] Liv. 43. 11. 1.

[240] Cassola, *I gruppi politici*, 382 f.

(a)   (b)

Plate 18. Paestan coin bearing on the obverse (a) the image of a porticoed building and on the reverse (b) the inscription CN.CORN. | M.TUC. | PATR. within a laurel wreath (courtesy of the Istituto Italiano di Numismatica).

wreath.[241] Up until now the coin has been for the most part neglected by students of republican Paestum, although the singularity of the inscription, which records a *patronatus* of the city in such an early period, and the unusual representations on both sides ought to have attracted the attention of numismatists, historians, archaeologists, and prosopographers alike. It is difficult not to identify the two *patroni* of Paestum with two well-known historical figures who are readily connected with the Scipios' protection and the Hispanic fortunes of the Digitii—Cn. Cornelius Blasio *pr.* 194 BC and M. Tuccius *pr.* 190 BC. Let us take a more detailed look. Having discarded other Cn. Cornelii of the period for various reasons, the Hispani-Hispalli (who in career terms might have been linked to our Digitius, but for chronological and prosopographic reasons are unlikely to be the Cn. Cornelius of the coin) and the more obscure Merendae, all of whom were somehow politically connected to the Scipios, i.e. the Cornelii branch at the height of its fortunes at the close of the third century BC,[242] the Cn. Corn(elius) of the coin cannot be other than Cn. Cornelius Blasio, *pr.* 194 BC for the *provincia* of Sicily.[243] In fact he appears in Hispania Citerior once before (in 200 BC) in possession of a special *imperium* acquired through *plebiscitum*, whence he returns in 196 BC with the remarkable concession of an *ovatio*. The other *patronus* is identifiable as M. Tuccius, *aed. cur.* 192 BC, *pr.* 190 BC, active in Apulia and Bruttium,

and *III vir col. ded.* of Sipontum and of Buxentum in 186 BC.[244]

I believe the coin speaks quite clearly for itself and permits us to equate the beginning of Sex. Digitius' political career with the grant, thanks to Scipio's and Laelius' favour, of the *corona navalis* and the *civitas optimo iure*, after which he became a follower of Blasio in Spain, where this general was in charge of the exceptional military office entrusted to him directly by the plebs. The laurel, which frames the names of Blasio and Tuccius, must refer to the *ovatio* of 196 BC, which was awarded to Blasio, but to which Tuccius and Digitius himself must have taken part, presumably as Blasio's *legati* (even if Livy, our only source for the events, seems very vague in this regard). The building portrayed on the face of the coin, perhaps the *macellum* (Fig. 37) of the forum (we know that in Rome the *macellum* near the forum was already in existence in 210 BC),[245] must be interpreted as a building constructed just after 196 BC with the *manubiae* due to the *socii Latini*, and points naturally to the appointment of Digitius. Nor is it impossible that the issue of the coin also commemorated Digitius' appointment (in 195 BC) to the praetorship, a rank he held again in the crucial year 194 BC, when, significantly, Africanus was a consul and Blasio a praetor too, and when our *novus homo* full of hopes returned to the lands of Spain where he had made his own fortune, first with Cornelius Scipio and then with Cornelius Blasio, hopes which were then bitterly disappointed, perhaps not helped by the burden of his immediate superior Cato's hostility. This pause in his career was brief and in 190 BC yet again another Scipio, the Asiatic, summoned him to his side in Asia with the rank of *legatus*, this time with equal honours as those conferred on C. Laelius, the ancient commander of our Paestan friend. From this moment the theatre of war for any remaining military and political action of Digitius was no longer Spain, but the Orient, first Asia and then Macedonia. Paestan coins once more give us an important insight into this transfer of interests. I am alluding to a *triens*, which shows on the obverse a Macedonian shield and on the reverse a horn

[241] The coin has been published by Crawford, 'Form and Function', 84 f., no. 24, pl. x.

[242] See however the necessary cautiousness expressed by Cassola, *I gruppi politici*, 20 f. on the extension of the aristocratic solidarity to all branches of the *gens* in this epoch.

[243] On this man see F. Münzer, in *RE* IV 1 (1900), col. 1272, no. 74. Sources on his career: Liv. 31. 50. 11 (*imperium extra ordinem in Hispania Citerior*); 33. 27. 1 (*ovatio*, cf. *Fast. Triumph.*); 34. 42. 4, 43. 7 (*praetura and Sicilian provincia*).

[244] On this man see F. Münzer, in *RE* VIIA 1 (1939), col. 766, no. 5. Sources on his career: Liv. 35. 7. 25, 41. 9 f. (*aed. cur.* 192 BC together with M. Iunius Brutus and construction *aere multatico* of the *porticus inter lignarios extra portam Trigeminam*); 36. 45. 9; 37. 2. 1; 6 (*pr.* 190 BC and *sortitio* of the *provincia* of Bruttium and Apulia); 38. 36. 1 (*prorogatio*); 39. 23. 4 (*III vir col. deduc.* 186 BC).   [245] Liv. 27. 11. 16.

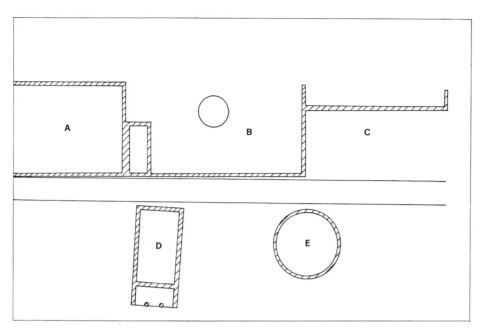

Fig. 37. Plan of Phase I of the area of the 'Italic temple' (early second century BC): A forum shops; B *macellum*; C area of a Lucanian temple (?); D 'Italic temple'; E round building, possibly a temple of Hercules (drawing M. Monella).

(a)   (b)

Plate 19. Paestan coin bearing on the obverse (a) a Macedonian shield and on the reverse (b) a horn of plenty and a bolt of lightning (courtesy of the Istituto Italiano di Numismatica).

of plenty and a bolt of lightning (Pl. 19),[246] an allusion to the Asiatic or Macedonian campaigns in which both senatorial Digitii are seen to be active. However let us reconsider at this point what took place between 194, the year of the praetorship of Sex. Digitius, and 190 BC, the year of the latter's Asiatic *legatio*, in the light of what we have learnt from the coins and in particular of the patronage of Blasio and Tuccius. Digitius' praetorship was not only conferred, anything but coincidentally, in the same year as the parallel appointment of Blasio and Scipio's consulship (evidence of the special political protection conceded to the old *socius navalis* who had distinguished himself at Cartago Nova); it was also the year of the foundation, together with another

seven *coloniae maritimae civium Romanorum* wanted by the Scipios,[247] of the colony of Salernum. This foundation was made necessary because of the rebellion of the Picentes, but it also represented a brilliant piece of clientelary 'bravura': to transform into *cives Romani* one part of the military contingents of *socii* returning from Hannibal's campaigns, among whom it is not hard to imagine there were not a few Paestans, attracted by the closeness of the two cities. The case cited above, of the Horatian character Numonius Vala, originally from Paestum but with a villa in Salernum, may perhaps be a product of these events.

In any case, there is no doubt that this alliance suggested by the coins of *patronatus* must have been a success. Otherwise we would be unable to account for Digitius' appointment in 172 BC to search for grain supplies in Apulia, in the same region where for some years, from 190 to 187 BC, the *patronus* M. Tuccius had operated. Tuccius himself was responsible not only for the foundation in 186 BC of one of the eight *coloniae maritimae* of the Scipios in Apulia itself (Sipontum), but also of another colony of the same type of even greater importance because of its close proximity to Paestum (Buxentum). In the view of the founders and of those who might have supported the foundations, the two *coloniae maritimae civium Romanorum* of Salernum and

---

[246] Crawford, 'Form and Function', 80 f., no. 19, pl. IX.

[247] Liv. 34. 45. 2; Vell. 1. 15. 3; Strab. 5. 251; cf. Salmon, *Roman Colonization*, 96 f., and Cassola, *I gruppi politici*, 375 f.

Buxentum had two main aims: on one hand the new foundations were intended to be good outposts for a Paestum perhaps increasingly less interested in the sea (also because of the profound changes which had taken place in the social body); at the same time Salernum and Buxentum could be two exceptionally good routes whereby other *socii nominis Latini* of Paestan origin could get easy access to the *civitas optimo iure*, an aim which must have had a hand in making these little post-Hannibalic foundations, so hankered after by the Scipios, particularly weak and short-lived. This second aim is confirmed by Livy, who expressly says that the Latins were denied enrolment in the colonies of Puteoli, Salernum, and Buxentum in 195 BC, 'since they were not Roman citizens'.[248]

It is certain, however, that the Digitii, probably of Lucanian origin and we can suppose only too pleased to assume a bogus pedigree of nobility from Praeneste (the role of the Digitii/Digidii in the myth of the origins of Praeneste is sufficiently well known),[249] must have contributed a lot to the development of the city in the course of the second century BC. An almost tacit confirmation of this contribution, freely given on the battlefields of Rome's great imperialistic conquest of the Mediterranean, comes in the shape of an extra-ordinary monument from Paestum, unfortunately from an unknown context (its provenance may only approx-imately be guessed at as the area of the Porta Sirena), today housed in the storerooms of the Paestum Museum. It consists of several blocks of local limestone covered in very fine stucco,[250] decorated with a victori-ous portrayal of arms, Hellenistic armour (Pl. 20), alternating with circular shields (Pl. 21) and oval ones with *umbo* (of Spanish type?) (Pl. 22), which may be compared with the frieze of arms from a Hellenistic monument in the ancient Macedonian capital of Dion.[251]

In fact this period, although among those less well documented from an archaeological standpoint, was

certainly the most brilliant in the colony's history. Important new building innovations can be credited to that time, or more generically to the second century. The beautiful mosaics in *signinum*, more accurately dated now than previously,[252] are an excellent fossil-guide. This brilliant 'novelty' makes its appearance not only in the gleaming remaking of cellae and pronaoi of temples, like the particularly intricate pavement mentioned before in the cella of the amphiprostyle temple that I have attributed to Hercules, but buildings constructed *ex novo* were also paved with this technique, like the one with the inscription *L. Ligus[tius]*, in the southern sanctuary,[253] perhaps a sacellum. Also paved in this style is the great podium-based temple not far from Porta Marina, still unpublished, a building which I would date to the beginning of the second century BC and which, due to its location, might be a sanctuary of Neptune, the ancient eponymous divinity of the city so celebrated by the coinage both of the Greek and the Latin colonies. The temple may have been erected in memory of the city's naval contribution to the Punic war, possibly celebrated also in a series of coins, struck by an Auf(idius) or Auf(eius), including a semis with head of Neptune carrying the trident on the shoulder /prow, legend AVF. PAES. (Pl. 23) and a triens with ele-phant, PAES./*cornucopiae*, legend AVF. (Pl. 24).[254] Thus we can include in the triumphal climate of the victory over Hannibal and the aversion of the Picentine revolt the building of these new temples paved in *signinum* as well as Sestieri's temples nos. 14 and 15 which I have attributed to Magna Mater and with less certainty to Victory.

The paradigmatic family history of the Digitii bears out that at the beginning of the second century BC, after the first three or four generations, the plebeian enthusiasm of the foundation went into decline and in the process we witness the emergence of a local aris-tocracy (in part perhaps descendants of ancient noble Lucanian families), which is responsible for remark-able changes in the urban and social setting. This class left their mark not only on the public building activity of this era, but also (and principally we might add) in the private sector. Several houses amply demonstrate the achievements of this new class. For example, the house adjacent to the western side of the forum and

---

[248] Liv. 34. 8. 9.

[249] Solin. 2. 9; Schol. Veron. *Aen.* 7. 681; Serv. *Aen.* 7. 678. Digitius would be a forged translation of the Greek δάκτυλος; for a different interpretation cf. G. Radke, *Die Götter Altitaliens* (Münster, 1965), 108.

[250] The interesting monument has received no attention and is unpub-lished; the fragments, all without inventory number, have the following dimensions: fr. with more complete cuirass: 0.85 m. high, 0.90 m. long; fr. with less complete cuirass: 0.85 m. high, 0.68 m. long; fr. with hoplite shield (diameter 0.68 m.): 0.77 m. high, 0.60 m. long; fr. with shield of Gallic type: 0.77 m. high, 0.42 m. long.

[251] Brief mention of this monument in *The Princeton Encyclopedia of Classical Sites* (Princeton, 1976), 276, s.v. Dion (P. A. Mackay).

[252] M. L. Morricone, *Scutulata pavimenta* (Rome, 1980), 9 f.

[253] *ILP* 118.

[254] Cf. Crawford, 'Form and Function', 81 f., no. 21/1–2, pls. IX–X.

Plate 20. Paestum, Museo. Part of a monument of stuccoed local limestone, decorated with a Hellenistic armour (photo by L. De Masi).

immediately to the north of the main street, the so-called *decumanus maximus*, has a surface of 1,600 square metres; its luxury displayed by the *signinum* mosaic floors, peristyles, *oeci,* and *triclinia* and the double atrium. All this is a good illustration of the arrival in Paestum of the *luxuria asiatica* for the private use of the aristocracy of the first half of the second century BC. The arrival of the *luxuria asiatica* witnessed also the beginnings of sepulchral *monumenta* built above ground, as documented by the very early *heroa* of the second century, discovered in the cemeteries of the Licinella and the Gaudo.[255]

No differently from what happened at Cosa, at Alba Fucens, and in the big Latin and Campanian cities,

where the first half of the second century BC gave rise mostly to great sacred buildings (but perhaps, as we have seen, also to the monumental *macellum*), the second half was instead the time for a massive public building campaign, of which we have already been given a taste in the monument with the frieze of arms. Diverging at this point from the chronologies suggested by E. Greco and D. Theodorescu,[256] I would ascribe their fourth phase of the area of the so-called Curia to the second half of the second century BC, which is consistent with the destruction of the old *macellum* (Fig. 37), a building furnished with a circular central basin of *signinum* (a *vivarium* for molluscs judging by the many oyster shells found in it), and with the creation of the first judicial basilica in Paestum (Fig. 38).

---

[255] P. C. Sestieri, in *NSA* (1948), 158 f.; now see the exhaustive treatment by H. von Hesberg, *Römische Grabbauten* (Darmstadt, 1992), 68 f., fig. 69.

[256] *Paestum*, i. 30 f.

Plate 21. Paestum, Museo. Part of a monument of stuccoed local limestone, decorated with a circular shield (photo by L. De Masi).

Plate 22. Paestum, Museo. Part of a monument of stuccoed local limestone, decorated with an oval shield, possibly of Spanish type (photo by L. De Masi).

(a)   (b)

Plate 23. Paestan *semis* bearing on the obverse (a) the head of Neptune carrying the trident on the shoulder and on the reverse (b) a prow with legend AVF. PAES. (courtesy of the Istituto Italiano di Numismatica).

(a)   (b)

Plate 24. Paestan *triens* bearing on the obverse (a) an elephant with legend PAES. and on the reverse (b) *cornucopiae* with legend AVF. (courtesy of the Istituto Italiano di Numismatica).

Not only would the 'open' type of basilica have been unthinkable a century later, but also the limestone corinthian capitals in two pieces match perfectly those in temple B of Largo Argentina, dating back to 101 BC.[257] Some support for this chronology is offered by the extraordinary find of 50,000 pieces of clay shots on the floor of this phase of the basilica,[258] which is reasonably explained as part of the organization of an emergency defence in 73 BC in view of Spartacus' sudden and unexpected appearance on the horizon. In the words of Sallust,[259] Spartacus 'propere nactus idoneum ex captivis ducem Picentinis, deinde Eburinis iugis occultus ad Naris Lucanas atque inde prima luce pervenit ad Anni Forum.' The Curia, so-called by the first excavators, should be better called the basilica of Mineia, and belongs in reality to the fifth phase of Greco and Theodorescu (Fig. 39), which dates back not to the third–fourth centuries AD but rather to the years around 15 BC as we shall now see.

[257] F. Coarelli, 'Topografia e storia', in I. Kaianto (ed.), *L'area sacra di Largo Argentina* (Rome, 1981), 16 f.
[258] *Paestum*, i. 17.   [259] *Hist.* 3, fr. 98.

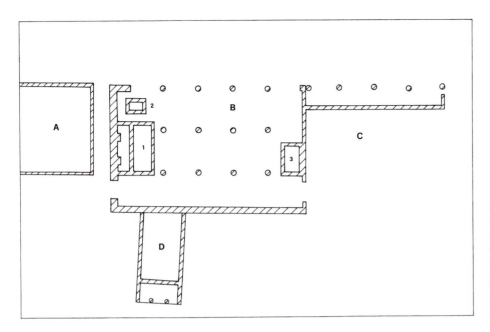

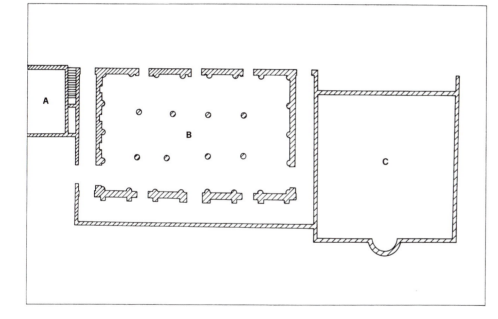

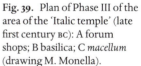

Fig. 38. Plan of Phase II of the area of the 'Italic temple' (late second century BC): A forum shops; B basilica (1. *tribunal*; 2. *horologium* or donarium base; 3. donarium base); C area of a Lucanian temple (?); D 'Italic temple' (drawing M. Monella).

Fig. 39. Plan of Phase III of the area of the 'Italic temple' (late first century BC): A forum shops; B basilica; C *macellum* (drawing M. Monella).

Judging by our texts of the *quaestores*,[260] a programme of works directed towards an early monument-alization of the forum should perhaps be attributed to the late second century BC, from the hesitant work done on the two-floored shops to the partial erection of the colonnades, even though the definitive monumental aspect of the city's central area is a first-century BC affair and of the early imperial period, above all of the epoch between Social War and the age of Augustus. The colossal undertaking of the *duoviri* C. Sextilius L.f. and P. Claudius C.f. to endow the city with at least ten fountains[261] in fact dates back to the first half of the first century BC, and also comprised the rebuilding of the wall of the *temenos* of the southern sanctuary and the construction of the primitive amphitheatre. In the middle of the first century BC Caesar's *lectio senatus*

---

[260] *ILP* 139–41 = *CIL* I², 3151–3; cf. A. Degrassi, 'Il collegio di cinque questori della colonia latina di Paestum', *RAAN* n.s. 41 (1966), 71 f. (=, *Scritti vari di antichità*, iv (Rome, 1971), 65 f.).

[261] *ILP* 144–53 = *CIL* I², 3157 *a–l*.

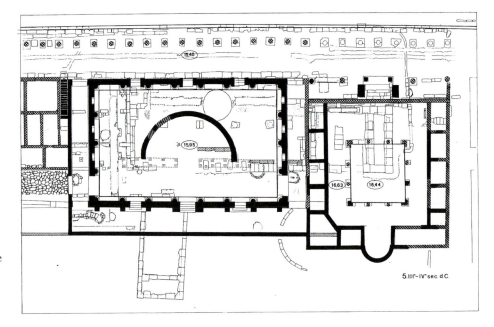

Fig. 40. Plan of the basilica showing in the centre the semicircular late-antique *tribunal* with post-holes for *velaria* and the six niches in the east and west walls to accommodate the statues of Mineia's family (after Greco and Theodorescu).

gave Paestum a new senatorial family, that of Cocceius Flaccus, which bound itself to the equestrian *gens* of the Mineii:[262] I return to this personage and his family's memorable deeds, only because at this juncture it seems useful to underline how the basilica's history fits in with the overall picture of the forum. Both the building technique, an *opus vittatum* rich in comparisons in Pompeii at the end of the Republic and the beginning of the Empire,[263] and the frescoes preserved in the so-called Curia with vast surfaces of undisturbed colour, prevalently red or black, attributable to the Third Style, fits in perfectly with the proto-Augustan chronology: the only addition to the building is the large central hemicycle, i.e. the late-antique *tribunal* (Fig. 40) surrounded by fittings for poles intended to hold up the *vela* for the *secretarium*. An inscription from the fourth century AD commemorates the rebuilding of the *tribunal*, which substituted the more ancient *tribunal* attached to the west wall of the basilica.[264] One of the characteristics of the building is the six niches in the

two side walls with six bases for statues, niches thoroughly suitable for receiving the inscriptions which I have reconstructed as showing the family group of the three Coccei and the three Mineii (Fig. 41): the late C. Cocceius Flaccus, his son C. Cocceius Iustus, and his grandson C. Cocceius Aequus in the three niches on one side, and the powerful Mineia M.f., widow of Flaccus and responsible for the entire programme of public benefactions, with her brothers L. and M. Mineius Flaccus in the niches on the other side. Spinazzola found an almost complete example of one of these six statues (Pl. 25), which provides valuable art-historical criteria to support the dating to the final years of the first century BC of Mineia's public benefactions suggested on epigraphic and archaeological

[262] Torelli, in *Annali della Facoltà di Lettere e Filosofia di Perugia—Studi Classici*, NS 18 (1980/1).

[263] First attested in Pompeii in the Herculaneum Gate of the early years of the colony: J.-P. Adam, *La Construction romaine. Materiaux et techniques* (Paris, 1984), 151 f.

[264] *ILP* 168: 'ex indul[gentia d(omini) n(ostri) —]/ basilicam et [tribunal a fund]amentis pe[cunia publica]/ reformavit C[— curat]ore rei p[ublicae]'. The post-holes in the floor for the late Roman *tribunal* (D. Theodorescu, in *Paestum*, i. 37, fig. 24) were filled with Augustan architectural terracottas, the best possible archaeological proof for the chronology of the *tribunal* and for the extent of the late Roman restorations carried out in the basilica.

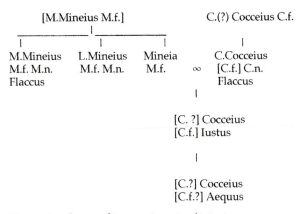

Fig. 41. Family tree of Paestan Coccei and Minei.

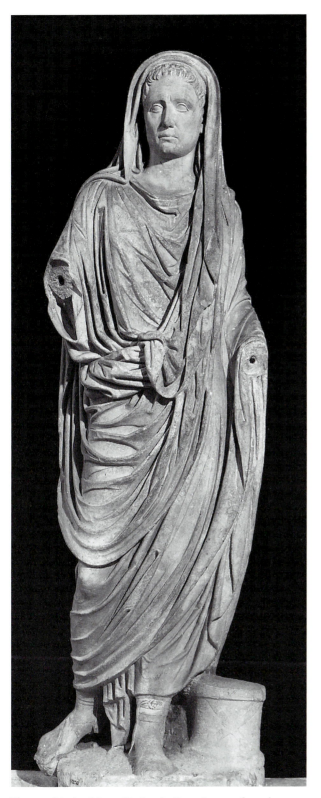

Plate 25. Naples, Museo Nazionale. Portrait statue from the Paestan basilica, belonging to one of the members of Mineia's family (courtesy of the Museo Nazionale di Napoli).

(a)   (b)

Plate 26. Paestan coin showing on the obverse (a) the head of a divinity, possibly Bona Mens and the legend MINEIA M.F. and on the reverse (b) the two-storey building of the basilica (courtesy of the Istituto Italiano di Numismatica).

grounds.[265] The erection of the Augustan basilica destroyed the primitive so-called 'Italic' temple, which was rebuilt, as we have seen, altering its form to that of a little shrine (Fig. 39) within *virecta*, a small building in *opus vittatum*, and then contemporary with the basilica in terms of building technique. It is probable that this unusual transgression of the *religio* all took place under the powerful influence of Mineia, in whose rare honour the local senate minted a coin showing the basilica and the head of a divinity who we may possibly recognize as Bona Mens[266] (Pl. 26). It is also maybe to her interest that we can attribute the restoration of the great sacred building placed on the same axis with her basilica, the temple of Mens in the forum, of whose history unfortunately we know nothing, but whose podium according to D. Theodorescu underwent a major reconstruction (and, we might add also, the construction of the balustrade in front) in the early imperial age.[267]

In the meantime in the north-west corner of the forum the bases for the successive developments of the imperial cult were laid, making redundant the first series of blocks with post-holes going back to the organization of the forum as *Saepta* and substituting them with a second series. The temple of Bona Mens was undoubtedly integrated into the new politico-religious reorganization of the urban spaces in the service of the imperial cult—the divinity perhaps being perceived as a specific hypostasis of Livia. This might account for

[265] S. Aurigemma and V. Spinazzola, 'I primi scavi di Paestum (1907–1922)', in E. Greco (ed.), *I primi scavi di Paestum (1907–1939)*, Ente per le antichità e i monumenti per la provincia di Salerno, Pubblicazioni XII e XIII, (s.l. [but Salerno] 1986), 33 f., fig. on p. 34. Both Aurigemma and Spinazzola wrongly interpret the portrait as belonging to the emperor Claudius.

[266] Crawford, 'Form and Function', 97 f., no. 38, pl. XI.

[267] *Paestum*, iii. 36; id., in *Munus non ingratum*.

the two colossal seated statues of Livia and Tiberius discovered in the area of Paestum in eighteenth century and today in the Archaeological Museum in Madrid,[268] which ideologically can be placed on a different level from the cycle of Julio-Claudian statues with a Tiberius, a Livia, a Nero Gemellus, and maybe a Germanicus,[269] and which should instead be linked to the great building of the *Augustales* previously mentioned. The attention paid to Livia–Concordia can be justified perfectly well in the context of an exploitation of the restoration by Mineia, almost a parallel initiative to that of Eumachia in Pompeii.[270] On the other hand the, by now, scanty local aristocracy seems strongly characterized by a close endogamy, as amply demonstrated by the widespread *cognomen* Flaccus, among Coccei, Mineii, and Flaccei.[271] The impressive benefactions of Mineia are matched by the contemporary activity of two priestesses in the sanctuary of Santa Venera, which we shall discuss later:[272] female philanthropy in these two cases, as in that, also contemporary, of the noble Laureia Q.f.Polla, builder of an urban Isaeum,[273] seems to close the glorious history of six centuries of public constructions in a city that was Greek, Lucanian, and finally Roman.

[268] For the portrait of Tiberius cf. L. Polacco, *Il volto di Tiberio* (Padua, 1955), 136 f., pl. 31, and H. G. Niemeyer, *Studien zur statuarischen Darstellung der römischen Kaiser* (Berlin, 1968), no. 84, pl. 29,2; for the portrait of Livia cf. W. H. Gross, *Julia Augusta*, AGAW, 3. Folge, no. 52 (Göttingen, 1962), 114 f., pl. 23,2, and 25. The discovery was made in 1860 and has been published by W. Helbig, in *Bullettino dell'Instituto* (1865), 95; A. Maiuri, *BA* (1930–1), 15, identifies the find place as a villa (?).

[269] M. Denti is preparing a comprehensive study of these portraits, all virtually unpublished (but see e.g. the portrait of Livia presented in *Fasti Archaeologici* (1956), no. 4731, pls. 38, 101; cf. *AJA* 61 (1957), 378, pls. 109, 18).

[270] On the building see: G. Spano, 'L'edificio di Eumachia in Pompei', RAAN, 36 (1961), 5 f.; W. Moeller, 'The Building of Eumachia: A Reconsideration', *AJA* 76 (1972), 323 f.; id., 'The Date of Dedication of the Building of Eumachia', *Cronache Pompeiane*, I (1975), 232 f.; L. Richardson jr., 'Concordia and Concordia Augusta: Roma and Pompeii', *PP* (1978), 260 f.

[271] Torelli, in *Annali della Facoltà di Lettere e Filosofia di Perugia—Studi Classici*, NS 18 (1980/1); id., in Pedley and Torelli (eds.), *The Sanctuary of Santa Venera*, 204 f.; cf. also *ILP* 77.

[272] See Epilogue.   [273] *ILP* 160.

4

THE ROMANIZATION OF DAUNIA

1. Introduction

THE ROMAN CONQUEST OF THE ITALIAN PENINSULA between the fourth and third centuries BC presented an ideal opportunity for political, social, economic, and cultural experimentation on a grand scale, the results of which would then be put to use in the conquest of the entire Mediterranean world in the following two centuries. The Italian peninsula in this period was a veritable laboratory in which the Roman political class was able to study all the possible variations on the basic model of subjection and 'assimilation' which was developed immediately after the first annexations of cities and peoples outside Latium. Put simply, this basic model consisted of a substantial confiscation of the enemy territory, in general coinciding with the arable land belonging to the leaders of the local anti-Roman faction, and an alliance with the pro-Roman faction, very often the oligarchic party of the defeated city, to whom they then rented, on very advantageous terms, a large part of the confiscated lands that had not been distributed to Latin or Roman colonists.

These extreme measures had numerous and lasting consequences for the economy and the social structure of the indigenous peoples. On the one hand, the victorious aristocratic–oligarchic indigenous groups enjoyed both enviable economic advantages and the guarantee of Roman military protection against external as well as internal foes, while, on the other hand, the losing parties, which is to say the aristocratic anti-Roman faction and, where it existed, the emerging middle class, were either eliminated or rendered harmless. The consequences of this alteration in the social order are clearly visible in the archaeological record, which is characterized by a decrease in the size of both settlements and cemeteries, by the disappearance of products that had been used by the classes now penalized by the Roman conquest, by a general decrease in consumption, and, sometimes, by a sudden increase of wealth among very restricted groups.

These profound economic and social transformations imposed on subjugated peoples by the Romans were obviously accompanied by no less profound changes in the customs and life-style of the privileged classes, in religious ideology, and in political organization, a process generally defined by historians as 'Romanization'. According to most historians and archaeologists, however, this phenomenon is detectable only in its terminal stages, when productive, cultural, and political integration appears to be complete. If we accept this definition, then the Romanization of the Italian peninsula occurred during the period between the final decades of the second and the middle of the first century BC, or, as some would claim, during the half-century following 90 BC, the year Roman citizenship was granted to the *socii Italici*, when the effects of integration, long evident among the local ruling classes, were clearly visible on a large scale.

In reality, of course the process of Romanization was a phenomenon of much longer duration and began at the moment of conquest, and in some cases, such as Daunia, even earlier. Such 'premature' onset of Romanization was often the result of the political, military, economic, and social weakness of the indigenous ruling classes in the face of the Roman model, which was well known to them through political and sometimes military contacts, often facilitated by long-standing 'private' relationships between Roman and local families; or it was the result of the material and ideological pressure exerted by Rome, directly through the export of luxury goods earmarked for the local ruling classes, and indirectly through the political and social prestige associated with the life-style of the Roman aristocracy.

But often the process of Romanization was accelerated either by the threatened collapse of the local ruling classes in the face of internal upheavals which undermined the established social order (as was the case with the Etruscan *principes* threatened by the revolt of the *servi*, beginning with the civil disturbances in Arezzo in 302 BC),[1] or by external threats such as foreign invasion or infiltration that put the stability and even the survival of the established social order at risk, which, as we will immediately have occasion to see, was the case in Daunia between 326 and 314 BC.

2. The Samnite Infiltration of Daunia

A well-known passage from Livy[2] perfectly sums up the situation in Daunia prior to the Roman intervention:

Samnites, ea tempestate in montibus vicatim habitantes, campestria et maritima loca contempto cultu molliore atque, ut fere evenit, locis simili genere ipsi montani atque agrestes depopulabantur.

(The Samnites, who at that time lived in mountain villages, began to pillage the countryside and the coastline [of Apulia], and, in as much as they were peasants and mountain dwellers, they held refined cultures in contempt and, as often happens, also places of this type.)

The contrast could not be more marked: the Samnites, *montani atque agrestes* and settled *vicatim*, in small villages, against the Daunians, inhabitants *maritima et campestria loca*, a social reality that, although not explicitly stated as such (an interesting detail in itself), appears to be strongly urban. The basis of the conflict, then, can be clearly viewed as a conflict between city and countryside, and between the rural pastoralism of the hills and the more developed agricultural economy of the plain (*cultu molliore*), although it assumes the overtones of an ethnic conflict. In any event, the Samnite threat was the pretext which the Daunian *principes* of Arpi used to call on the Romans for help. Little does it matter that Livy presents this alliance,

which was in reality a *foedus*, as a *deditio in fidem*, a concept which was dear to Roman historiography, which took advantage of every opportunity to project Rome's imperialistic 'mission' into the most remote past.[3]

Recent discoveries in archaeology have only now enabled us fully to understand that such economic conflicts in an ethnic guise[4] between the Apennine/pre-Apennine regions and the great plains of Apulia had been in progress from a very early date.[5] They were probably endemic in this, as in other regions, since the early Iron Age, or in any case since agriculture and pastoralism, hitherto economic activities integrated in the same socioeconomic context, became activities dominating the economy of separate areas and carried out by distinct social and ethnic groups. The net result was the overall subordination, both economically and socially, of the mountain regions to the more prosperous plains.[6]

A. Bottini, with his extremely important discoveries,[7] has been able to detect in the archaeological evidence, from at least the middle of the fourth century BC, early Samnite penetration of the region between Melfi and Lavello, a strategic Daunian territory connecting Apulia and Samnium, the obligatory point of passage from the north and west along the Ofanto (ancient Aufidus) valley towards the fertile lands of pasture in Apulia. In fact, the isolated mid-fourth-century tomb of a warrior discovered near the large settlement of Lavello[8] (identified by an inscription[9] as the important Daunian

---

[1] Liv. 10. 1. 4–6: cf. W. V. Harris, *Rome in Etruria and Umbria* (Oxford, 1971), 115; M. Torelli, *Elogia Tarquiniensia* (Florence, 1975), 80 f.; A. Maggiani, ' "Cilnium genus". La documentazione epigrafica etrusca', *SE* 54 (1986), 171 f.

[2] Liv. 10. 13. 6–7: see also M. Torelli, 'Aspetti storico-archeologici della romanizzazione della Daunia', in *La civiltà dei Dauni nel quadro del mondo italico*, Acts of Conference; Manfredonia, 1980 (Florence, 1984), 325 f.

[3] On this and other aspects of Livy's historiography, besides the classic work by W. Soltau, *Livius' Geschichtswerk. Seine Composition und seine Quellen* (Leipzig, 1897), see the commentaries by R. M. Ogilvie, *A Commentary to Livy: Books 1–5* (Oxford, 1965), and by J. Bayet, *Tite-Live, ll. I–VII* (Paris, 1954–68), and the book by P. G. Walsh, *Livy, His Historical Methods and Aims* (Cambridge, 1981).

[4] See now the contributions and discussions in F.-H. Massa Pairault (ed.), *Crise et transformation des sociétés archaïques de l'Italie antique au vᵉ siècle av. J.-C.*, Acts of Conference; Rome, 1987 (Rome, 1990).

[5] In general, on this civilization, see the various contributions in *La civiltà dei Dauni* (above, n. 2), and especially the invaluable synthesis of the archaeological evidence of early Daunia by A. Bottini, in *Popoli e civiltà dell'Italia antica*, viii, 2nd edn. (Rome, 1988), 171 f.

[6] Cf. M. Torelli, 'Le popolazioni dell'Italia antica: società e forme del potere', in A. Momigliano and A. Schiavone (eds.), *Storia di Roma*, i (Turin, 1988), 53 f.

[7] Excellent summary of his discoveries by A. Bottini, M. P. Fresa, and M. Tagliente, 'L'evoluzione di un centro daunio fra VII e III sec.: l'esempio di Forentum', in M. Tagliente (ed.), *Italici in Magna Grecia. Lingua, insediamenti culture* (Venosa, 1990), 233 f. (with previous bibliography), and A. Bottini, 'L'area lucana', in R. Cassano (ed.), *Principi, imperatori, vescovi. Duemila anni di storia a Canosa*, Catalogue of the Exhibition (Bari, 1992), 110 f.

[8] A. Bottini, 'Uno straniero e la sua sepoltura: la tomba 505 di Lavello', *DArch* NS 3 (1985), 59 f.

[9] M. Torelli, 'Contributi al supplemento del C.l.L. IX', *RAL* 8th ser., 24 (1969), 16 = *AE* 1969–70, 148.

city of Forentum, in 317 BC in Samnite hands)[10] is in all likelihood that of a Samnite mercenary. This conclusion is based on the funerary rite, emphasizing in the Samnite style the bronze belt and the cup-skyphos, and on the position of the corpse, which, instead of being contracted, as dictated by Daunian custom, was in a supine position in accordance with the funerary practice of central Italy.[11]

Still more significant, however, are the tombs discovered on the 'acropolis' of Lavello, located in the area of the Cimitero.[12] This site has been found to contain one of the highest concentrations of aristocratic tombs at Lavello from the late fifth and fourth centuries (continuing until approximately 330 BC), a fact most likely reflecting the dominant position of the Cimitero area in relation to the rest of the settlement. Among the individuals buried around the family's progenitor (whose semi-cremated remains, probably transferred from another tomb, were surrounded by objects of great wealth) is a female in supine position, perhaps a Samnite woman who had been fully accepted into the family.

Next to these tombs, Bottini was able to recognize two or perhaps even three exceptional rectangular structures perfectly oriented and evidently used for religious purposes (Fig. 42).[13] The more ancient of these structures were wooden enclosures; the most recent, however, was built of durable materials and had pits positioned in the middle and the corners of the four sides of the structure, filled with extremely fine Apulian pottery which we can easily assume was used in the sacrificial ceremony performed to inaugurate the structure. With these two or three buildings we are almost certainly dealing with *templa in terris* for the *auspicia*. The first two were temporary structures (perhaps used for royal inaugurations, as in Livy's well-known description of the inauguration of Numa),[14] whereas the third, the most recent, was permanent. On the evidence of the Apulian pottery found in the sacrificial pits it can be dated to shortly after the middle of the fourth century BC. To the same complex belongs a small, square *naiskos*; situated at the north-west corner

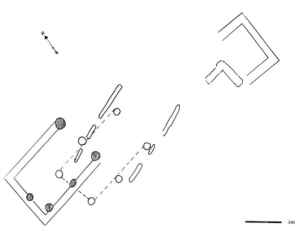

Fig. 42. The three phases of the augural temple at Lavello, Cimitero area: the earliest phase showing only traces of wooden fences; the second phase with provisional walls and votive pits (found empty); the third phase with rubble walls and (hachured) votive pits; east of it, the two phases of the little square shrine decorated with plaster cover and terracotta antefixes (drawing C. Masseria).

of the *templum* and lavishly decorated with antefixes and with classical moulded motifs on the clay walls, it is also contemporary with the *templum*.

Thanks to this archaeological evidence, we can draw a number of conclusions of an historical, political, and institutional nature regarding Forentum in its last century as an independent city. Clearly the Samnite penetration of Daunian society occurred on two levels: that of the lower classes through the recruitment of Samnite military manpower (the isolated mid-fourth-century tomb we have previously discussed), and that of the upper classes by means of matrimonial alliances with Daunians *principes*, as illustrated by the rich tombs of the acropolis. Meanwhile, the Samnitic pressure from the mountains surrounding the vast Apulian plain, at least according to tradition, continued unabated in the form of raids and even open warfare.

At the same time, the transformation of the augural *templum* from a temporary structure into a permanent one seems to have had its basis in the transition from a royal regime, still common in Apulia—as we know from Thucydides[15]—at the end of the fifth century BC, to a republican one toward the middle of the fourth, though the princely tombs of the acropolis prove that the power still remained in the hands of the old aristocracy, albeit weakened to the point of being forced to marry females of the Samnite intruders. Lavello—

[10] Liv. 9. 20. 9.

[11] Publication of the extensive Lavello cemetery in the Casino area by M. Giorgi, S. Martinelli, M. Osanna, and A. Russo, *Forentum, i. Le necropoli di Lavello* (Venosa, 1988).

[12] A. Bottini, M. P. Fresa, and M. Tagliente, *Forentum, ii. L'acropoli in età classica* (Venosa, 1992).

[13] Ibid. 18 f.   [14] Liv. 1. 18. 6–10.

[15] Thuc. 7. 33. 4.

Forentum traditionally had always had the appearance of a 'federation' characterized by six or seven distinct groups of dwellings, each conglomeration dominated by a sort of *anaktoron*,[16] dispersed over the vast plateau of more than 200 hectares. It is certainly not a matter of chance that shortly before the conquest by the Romans new habitations were being erected in different areas of the city. It has recently been shown[17] that this relocation of habitations, often toward the foot of the hills, was accompanied by a change in their structure. From their complex network of hydraulic installations, we can hypothesize that the manufacture and dyeing of wool had taken on an important role. This suggests a radical change in the economy of the city, quite likely the product of Samnite influence. Forentum, which never had defensive walls, was easily conquered by the Romans in 314 BC during the Second Samnite war[18].

3.   The Roman Intervention

This, then, is the context in which the Daunian *principes*, in 326 BC, called on Rome to help them resist the increasing Samnite pressure. Quite certainly the request was given added weight by the usual politics of aristocratic alliances formed through marriage, a practice used by the Apulian principes also on the opposite, Samnite front, as the previously mentioned female corpse buried in supine position in the princely tomb uncovered at Cimitero in Lavello may easily remind to us. The first known official Roman presence in Daunian territory was in 325 BC when a Roman garrison was dispatched to Luceria,[19] a city described in 321 as inhabited by *socii boni ac fideles*,[20] who, nevertheless, handed the Roman *praesidium* over to the Samnites in 319. The actual conquest of Luceria, the first Apulian territory to fall into Roman hands, did not take place however until 315–314 BC,[21] with the subsequent introduction of a Latin colony 2,500 strong.

It is only at this point that we can truly begin to speak of the Romanization of Daunia, a process started between Luceria and Forentum, in this border zone of mixed ethnic composition, where Daunian and Lucano-Samnite groups coexisted. The presence of the latter, as I have already stated elsewhere,[22] must be conceived of primarily in terms of class relationships, rather than simply in terms of ethnic conflict, as sources from the classical world typically do. In reality, there had been extensive mixing between the Daunians, who controlled the principal means of production, and the Sabellian element, still in a subordinate position, but already in the fourth century BC aiming to overturn the prevailing class order.

The epigraphic and archaeological record of the colony at Luceria demonstrates the quintessentially Latin and central Italian character of the colonists, very few of whom must have been drawn from the indigenous population. The archaeological data from this earliest Roman presence in Luceria are extremely clear on this score. The rich votive deposit composed of anatomical parts and veiled heads, found immediately prior to the Second World War[23] on the hill of Belvedere (on which stand the church and the convent of S. Salvatore), appears to be a real *hapax legomenon* in southern Daunian–Samnite territory, where votive offerings of this kind were unknown, being instead typical of the religious practices of the Etruscan–Latin and Campanian koine.[24] These finds constitute an exceptional archaeological document (to whose ideological, historical and religious significance we will have occasion to return) not only of a typological nature, but also for the history of craftmanship, considering that some votive heads found in Luceria derive from moulds previously been known only in Latium.[25]

The epigraphic documentation on the Lucerian cults also points in the same direction. The well-known *lex Lucerina de luco sacro*,[26] dated to the early years of the colony on the basis of the amount of the fine provided for infractions (lower than in the slightly later and analogous *lex Spoletina*[27]), is of considerable help in recreating the cultural and religious atmosphere of the colony's foundation. This has been further confirmed

---

[16] For this *anaktora*, see M. Tagliente, 'I signori dei cavalli nella Daunia antica', *Annali della Facoltà di Lettere e Filosofia di Perugia—Studi Classici*, 9 (1985–6), 303 f.; Bottini, Fresa, and Tagliente, in Tagliente (ed.), *Italici in Magna Grecia*, 238 f.; A. Russo, *Edilizia domestica in Apulia e Lucania. Ellenizzazione e società nella tipologia indigena tra VIII e III secolo a.C.* (Lecce, 1992), 102 f.

[17] Russo, *Edilizia*, 153 f.   [18] Liv. 9. 20. 9; Diod. Sic. 19. 65. 7.

[19] Velleius, 1. 14, who speaks of a colony in this regard, is certainly wrong.

[20] Liv. 9. 2. 5.   [21] Liv. 9. 26. 1–5; Diod. Sic. 19. 72. 8–9.

[22] Torelli, in *La civiltà dei Dauni*, 325 f.

[23] Now fully published by M. C. D'Ercole, *La stipe votiva del Belvedere di Lucera* (Rome, 1990).

[24] This phenomenon, first pointed out by M. Torelli, 'La colonizzazione romana dalla conquista di Veio alla prima guerra punica', in F. Coarelli (ed.), *Roma medio-repubblicana*, Catalogue of the Exhibition (Rome, 1973), 341 f., has been fully explored by A. M. Comella, 'Complessi votivi in Italia in epoca medio- e tardo-repubblicana', *MEFRA* 93 (1981), 717 f.

[25] Comella, *MEFRA* 93 (1981); M. C. D'Ercole, *La stipe votiva*.

[26] *ILLRP* 504.   [27] *ILLRP* 505–6.

by other dedications, as for example that to Fides, the ancient Latin divinity which presided over the ancient relationships of dependence.[28] The dedication to Juno Populona[29] should instead be related to the presence, very understandable in the light of recent evidence, of groups of Samnites in the position of *incolae*[30] within the Lucerian colony.[31]

The foundation of the Latin colony at Luceria, the most distant from Rome in those years, was followed approximately 25 years later by the settlement of the Latin colony of Venusia in 291 BC, just before the end of the last Samnite war. Judging from the scanty materials dating prior to the late fourth century BC which were unearthed in excavations,[32] it appears that this colony in all likelihood was not constructed on the site of the earlier Samnite Venusia, a *polyanthropon* city conquered by the well-known plebeian leader L. Postumius Megellus. The Daunio-Samnite Venusia should instead be identified with a substantial ancient site in the area of medieval and modern Melfi. Here, some 15 miles (24 km.) west of Roman Venusia, archaeological excavations have discovered two large cemeteries of the fourth century BC with supine, i.e. Samnitic burials (again, we have to remember that the Daunians buried their dead in a contracted position, lying on their side) apparently abandoned around the years of the foundation of the Latin colony.[33]

The political circumstances of the foundation of the colony are of a great deal of interest. Tradition, which reaches us in a very fragmentary manner,[34] states that in the year before the founding of the colony a bitter conflict broke out between the consul Megellus and his patrician colleague, Q. Fabius Gurges, who succeeded not only in depriving Megellus of the honour and the right (coveted for the clientele that such an undertaking would bring) of acting as *triumvir coloniae deducendae* in the colony's foundation, but also dragged him into court, where he received a harsh sentence.

4. The Ideological Context of the Conquest and the Politics of Alliance

These aspects of political history[35] are not in any case extraneous to the ideological climate in force at the founding of the new colony, nor to the practical choices made, beginning with that of its name. According to tradition, the original Venusia was founded by Diomedes, the hero-symbol of Daunia (thereby confirming that the Samnite influence on the city was not particularly ancient), who had bestowed that name on the city in order to 'appease Venus, whose wrath had prevented the hero from finding his ancestral home'.[36] But the preservation of the Daunian–Samnite city name by the Latin colony also has other interesting implications. In 295 BC,[37] a few years before the foundation of Roman Venusia, Q. Fabius Gurges dedicated at Rome the *aedes Veneris Obsequentis ad Circum Maximum*, built with the fines paid by adulterous noblewomen, who were then obliged to prostitute themselves near the new sanctuary: the new temple was also conceived with an eye to the celebration at Rome of the great pan-Latin and 'Trojan' festival of the *Vinalia*, which originated in Lavinium in connection with Aeneas.[38]

This, then, is the first real historic shrine dedicated to Venus in the *urbs* under her own name[39] and proves that the Fabii had a specific interest both in the 'Trojan' aspect of the goddess, destined to have enormous success in the following centuries, and in the Samnite

---

[28] *AE* 1969–70, 159. [29] *AE* 1969–70, 154.

[30] As at Aesernia, attested by *CIL* I², 3201.

[31] This conclusion is in contrast to my previous opinions on the subject. An article by D. Izzo, 'Nuove testimonianze sul culto di Pupluna a Teanum Sidicinum' *Ostraka* 3 (1994), 157 ff., shows that the large shrine to the same goddess at Teanum Sidicinum (witnessed by an important group of Latin inscriptions: *CIL* X, 4789–91) has Oscan antecedents proved by Oscan graffiti with dedications to Pupluna; this shrine also has a counterpart—analogous to that of Luceria—in the relatively close Latin colony of Aesernia, as shown again by inscriptional evidence (*CIL* IX, 2630).

[32] Evidence collected by M. L. Marchi, G. Sabbatini, and M. Salvatore, 'Venosa: nuove acquisizioni archeologiche', in M. Salvatore (ed.), *Basilicata. L'espansionismo romano nel sud-est dell'Italia. Il quadro archeologico*, Acts of Conference; Venosa, 1987 (Venosa, 1990), 11 f., esp. 17 f. Since the alleged find of 5th–4th-cent. BC pottery in the area of Roman Venusia (*BA* 1967, 49 f.) is apparently unverified and isolated, probably we cannot place the *polyanthropon* pre-Roman Venusia on the same site as the Latin colony.

[33] Summary of the archaeological evidence of this area by A. Bottini, 'L'area melfese fino alla conquista romana', in A. Giardina and A. Schiavone (eds.), *Società romana e produzione schiavistica*, Acts of Conference; Pisa, 1979, i (Rome and Bari, 1981), 151 f.; on this identification and on the connected topographical problems, cf. M. Torelli, 'La romanizzazione della Lucania', in L. de Lachenal (ed.), *Da Leukania a Lucania*, Exhibition Catalogue; Venosa, 1992 (Rome, 1992), 3 f. [34] Dion. Hal. 17–18. 5.

[35] Liv. *Per.* 11; Dion. Hal. 17–18. 4. 1–3, 5. 1–4; Cass. Dio, fr. 36. 32; Suid. 4. 180 n. 2118; for the new fragment belonging to Livy's Book 11 and containing his account of the story, see B. Bravo and M. Griffin, 'Un frammento del libro XI di Livio?', *Athenaeum*, 76 (1988), 447 f.; G. Liberman, 'À propos d'un fragment presumé de Tite Live', *Athenaeum*, 80 (1992), 192 f.

[36] Serv. *Aen.* 11. 246. [37] Liv. 10. 31. 9.

[38] Serv. *Aen.* 1. 720; cf. M. Torelli, *Lavinio e Roma. Riti iniziatici e matrimonio tra archeologia e storia* (Rome, 1984), 162 f.

[39] Previous names under which the goddess had been known in the Roman cult are Libitina, Murcia, Cloacina, Fortuna: on this see F. Coarelli, *Il Foro Boario* (Rome, 1988), 253 f.

version of the deity. This last fact is confirmed by the singular anecdote narrated by the obscure historian Dositheos and related by the Pseudo-Plutarchian *Parallela Minora*.[40] According to this source, a certain 'Fabius Fabricianus, relative of the great Fabius, took part in the sack of Touxion, metropolis of the Samnites. At the conclusion of this military campaign, he returned to Rome in possession of the Aphrodite Nikephoros, an object much venerated by the Samnites.' The grim and dramatic tale proceeds to relate how, shortly after his return, Fabius Fabricianus was murdered—almost as if in retaliation for his sacrilegious theft—by his wife and her lover. As in Orestes' myth, this crime was subsequently avenged by the victim's son, also named Fabius Fabricianus, who murdered the two lovers.

It is striking that Fabius Fabricianus, referred to as 'relative of the great Fabius', and otherwise unmentioned in the meagre prosopography of the years between 292 and 265 BC,[41] being an adopted should bear *nomen* that of the Fabii and as *agnaticium* that of the greatest general, after Rullianus, of the war against Samnium and Lucania, C. Fabricius Luscinus, *cos.* 282, II 278 BC, whose political connection with the Fabii and with M' Curius Dentatus have been quite rightly emphasized by Cassola,[42] although on different grounds. Everything, from the religious–ideological choices of the great clan of the Fabii to their family politics, conducted by means of politically well-constructed adoptions, seems to point to their special interest in this corner of the peninsula, which would go a long way toward explaining the extraordinary number of colonists at Venusia: 20,000. If this figure, handed down to us from our only source on the subject, Dionysius of Halicarnassus, is correct,[43] then it must necessarily have also included all of the native inhabitants left in the vast settlement, whether enlisted among the colonists, or, and this is the more likely case, whether classified as *adtributi*[44]—rather than as *incolae*—of the Latin colony, following the well-known local pattern of *vicatim* settlement.

It is not difficult to imagine that behind this particular structure of the colony, result either of the extensive granting of Latin citizenship, or of an equally extensive use of the institution of *adtributio*,[45] or of both, was the precise desire of the Fabii to establish, or to strengthen their own Daunian *clientelae*, which had been originally established by the *princeps senatus* Rullianus (the 'great Fabius' of the Pseudo-Plutarch?) during his brilliant campaigns in Apulia in 326[46] and 297 BC.[47] Rullianus was clearly very concerned with maintaining his Daunian clientele, considering that he attempted, through subterfuge, to prevent his son Gurges from being appointed to the consulate in 292 BC,[48] evidently unconvinced—and rightly so—of the latter's military skills. As a sort of confirmation of this Fabian interest in Apulia, we can cite the fact that, as E. Curti has shown, Megellus' colleague in the consulate of 291 BC, C. Iunius Bubulcus Brutus, was also to secure Daunian clientele for himself too.[49]

The indigenous clients of the Fabii in Apulia, whose descent can perhaps be traced to Cunctator (in light of the legendary loyalty of Canusium during the war against Hannibal), must have found in the cult of the 'Trojan' Venus the common bond between themselves and the *gentes Troianae* of Rome, a *syngeneia* or kinship that could be invoked in moments of collective need, as is commonly the case between related aristocratic groups. Further evidence of the presence of a cult of Aphrodite in Daunia, beyond the fact that Venusia bears the goddess's name, which was also known in the nearby Lucanian area,[50] is perhaps revealed in the popular etymology of the name Canusium[51] from *canis*, the dog, an animal usually associated with the Eastern Greek Aphrodite *en kepois*,[52] and not by chance among the sacred animals kept in the Lucerian temple of Athena Ilias.

[40] Pseudo-Plut. *Par. Min.* 37 B.

[41] The sources on this period are conveniently collected in M. R. Torelli, *Rerum Romanarum Fontes ab anno CCXCII ad annum CCLXV a.Ch.n.* (Pisa, 1978).

[42] F. Cassola, *I gruppi politici romani nel III sec.a.C.* (Trieste, 1962), 161 f., 193 f.

[43] Dion. Hal. 17–18. 5. 2. Discussion on this figure in M. R.Torelli, *Rerum Romanarum*, 50 f.; however, see also Torelli, in *La civiltà dei Dauni*, 333 f.

[44] The juridical and historical position of *adtributi* has been discussed by U. Laffi, *Adtributio e contributio* (Pisa, 1966).

[45] The institution is already known in republican times: Laffi, *Adtributio*, 19 f.   [46] Liv. 8. 39. 16.

[47] Liv. 10. 15. 1–2.   [48] Val. Max. 4. 1. 5; Jul. *Par. Epit.* 4. 1–5.

[49] On this see E. Curti, *La romanizzazione della Daunia*, Ph.D. Dissertation (Perugia, 1991).

[50] Cf. the inscription Vetter 182 = Poccetti 158 from the great Lucanian sanctuary of Macchia di Rossano di Vaglio, close to Roman (and modern) Potenza, a dedication made to *Fenzei Mef[itanei]*, i.e. to a Mefitic Venus: see M. R. Torelli, 'I culti di Rossano di Vaglio', in Salvatore (ed.), *Basilicata*, 83 f.

[51] Serv. *Aen.* 11. 246.

[52] On the sacrifice of dogs to Aphrodite, see M. Torelli, 'I culti di Locri', *Atti Taranto* (1976), 149.

5. From Aphrodite to Athena 'Ilias'

The choice of Venus as the 'Trojan' goddess, capable of reinforcing the alliance between Daunians and Romans, had had an important, if not decisive precedent in the great Daunian cult (also of 'Trojan' origin) of Minerva-Athena Ilias, the Iliac Athena embodied in the Palladium of Troy, which the Greek hero Diomedes, *oikistes* of all the Daunian cities, had brought with him to his final destination in the west, which is to say Daunia.

This Diomedean tradition,[53] widely diffused along the Adriatic coast,[54] has had deep roots in Daunia from a very early date,[55] as the long and celebrated account by Strabo[56] documents, and was quite naturally and logically wedded to the great Daunian *hippotrophia*.[57] At this point, the cult of Athena Ilias assumed a nationalistic character of such striking force and social efficiency that it is well worth our briefly retracing its development.

The 'Trojan' goddess appears almost everywhere in Daunia and is often the only cult attested in the smaller municipalities, as in the case of Bantia, where we find just one epigraphical mention of a god, a late-republican dedication to Minerva.[58] The extremely meagre inscriptional evidence from Lavello–Forentum refers to a public work, also late republican, financed by an anonymous local magistrate and built in the vicinity of two temples: one dedicated to Minerva and the other to the Lares.[59] Thanks to the survival of a few remnants of a votive deposit of the fourth–second centuries BC including—among other votive objects—heads of statuettes representing the goddess Minerva,[60] we now know that the magnificent temple

under the church of S. Leucio at Canosa, to which we will return shortly, was also dedicated to this Trojan divinity.

The cult extended throughout ancient Daunia from the south-easternmost part of the territory at Canusium, to the west and north-west at Bantia and Forentum, which were subject to Samnite influence at the time of the Roman conquest, but certainly had Daunian origins. The geographic distribution of the cult perfectly reflects the tradition regarding Diomedes' activity as *oikistes*, which is documented in Arpi, Canusium, Sipontum, Salapia, Luceria, and Venusia, his mythic presence even extending as far as the Latin colonies of Beneventum and Brundisium.[61] In these latter cities, only marginally part of the protohistoric and archaic 'greater Daunia',[62] we also find traces of Diomedean cults. The temple of Artemis at Brundisium (no longer in a Daunian context!), like other shrines in Apulia, contained gifts from the founder Diomedes;[63] at Beneventum instead, according to numerous inscriptions of a relatively late date,[64] the shrine of Minerva Berecynthia—an 'Asiatic' and 'Trojan' Athena according to a late *interpretatio romana*[65]—dominated the spectacular entrance to the city from the Appian way with its colossal terraced shrine of Santi Quaranta.[66]

However, the shrine to Athena Ilias most often mentioned by classical sources is that of Luceria. Strabo speaks of it,[67] and, as I was able to demonstrate some years ago, so does Lykophron.[68] The shrine in Luceria must also be the same temple that both Pseudo-Aristotle[69] and Aelianus[70] mention as existing somewhere in Daunia and purported to have contained the weapons of Diomedes' companions. Further evidence

---

[53] E. Lepore, 'Diomede', *Atti Taranto* (1979), 113 f.

[54] L. Braccesi, *Grecità adriatica*, 2nd edn. (Bologna, 1977).

[55] It should be noted that the Italian myth of Diomedes is already present in Mimnermus, fr. 22 B.   [56] Strab. 6. 284.

[57] Summary of the evidence by M. Tagliente, in *Annali della Facoltà di Lettere e Filosofia di Perugia—Studi Classici* 9, (1985–86), 303–321.

[58] *CIL* IX, 418; cf. M. Torelli, in D. Adamesteanu and M. Torelli, 'Il nuovo frammento della Tabula Bantina', in *ArchClass* 21 (1969), 30 f.

[59] *AE* 1969–70, 149.

[60] I have been able to recover and cite here these votive objects thanks to the kindness of Dr M. P. Fresa, to whom I express my profound gratitude. A 1st–2nd-cent. AD inscription, found in the excavations of the temple, could record the same cult too, but the evidence does not appear totally secure. The little marble plaque, discovered long ago, perhaps in the 1950s (F. Tinè Bertocchi, in *EAA Suppl.* (1970), 179) and mentioned (without a photograph) in M. Chelotti, R. Gaeta, V. Morizio, and M. Silvestrini, *Le epigrafi romane di Canosa*, i (Bari, 1985), Add. 12, pp. 280 f., has been published by Morizio, in *Principi*, 797: the text, interpreted by the editor as 'C. Vibius | Octavius | Min(ervae) | d(ono) d(edit)', should instead be read as 'C. Vibius | Octavius min(ister) | d(ono) d(edit)'.

[61] On the activity of Diomedes as a hero-founder (long list in Serv. *Aen.* 11. 246 *cum schol.*) of Apulian towns (above all, Arpi: Polemon *ap.*Schol. Pind. *Nem.* 10. 12; Virg. *Aen.* 11. 246; Serv. *Aen.* 8. 9; 11. 246; Plin. *NH* 3. 104; Solin. 2. 10; App. *Hann.* 31; Justin. 20. 1. 10; Auson. *Epit.* 6; Steph. Byz. s.v. Ἀργύριππα) and on the diffusion of his legend, excellent summary by D. Musti, 'Il processo di formazione e diffusione delle tradizioni greche sui Daunii e su Diomede', in *La civiltà dei Dauni*, 93 f.

[62] As reconstructed by Musti, in *La civiltà dei Dauni*.

[63] Pseudo-Aristot. *De mir. ausc.* 110; Steph. Byz. s.v. Διομήδεια; Vitruv. 1. 4. 12.   [64] *CIL* IX, 1538–42.

[65] On this Minerva, R. Duthoy, 'La Minerva Bercynthia des inscriptions tauroboliques de Bénevent (*CIL* IX, 1538–42)', *AC* 35 (1966), 548 f.

[66] The site has been recently explored by Dr D. Giampaola of the Soprintendenza Archeologica di Salerno, who has made interesting discoveries—a *cryptoporticus*, possibly connected with the sanctuary, and an adjoining amphitheatre. The *substructiones* were published by A. Meomartini, *I monumenti e le opere d'arte della città di Benevento* (Benevento, 1889), 307 f.

[67] Strab. 6. 264.

[68] Lycophr. 1126–40; cf. M. Torelli, in *La civiltà dei Dauni*, 329 f.

[69] Pseudo-Aristot. *De mir.ausc.* 109.   [70] Aelian. *Nat. anim.* 11. 3.

is provided by the *aition* (significant that it was transposed from the Palladium of the goddess to the *bretas* of Cassandra) described by Lykophron[71] and relevant to the tradition of the black garments worn by Daunian women who had taken refuge in the shrine of Luceria in order to avoid an unwanted marriage. Judging by the number of classical references to this shrine, we can only assume that it was of extreme importance to Daunian culture.

We now know with absolute certainty that the rich votive deposit found on the slopes of the Belvedere hill on which the church and convent of S. Salvatore stand[72] belonged to the temple of Athena Ilias, a fact clearly demonstrated by the presence of heads and statuettes of the armed goddess. This proves that the Roman colonists in Luceria, far from dismantling the city's main religious centre, actually appropriated it and adapted it to their own religious needs, making it the object of rituals quintessentially Roman, as for example the deposition of votive offerings of anatomical parts or of statuettes of a winged genius holding a *diptychon* (Pl. 27), in which it is possible to recognize the *genius* protecting the land division, symbolized either by the diptych or by the *pugillaria* containing the grant of public land.[73]

The founding of the colony at Luceria, then, was accompanied by a skilful strategy of ideological recomposition based on the assimilation of the two 'Trojan' cults of Athena: that of the Ilias of Lavinium, the centre of the *sacra principiorum populi Romani*, and that of Luceria and Daunia, perhaps first known by the epithet Achaia, as the author of the *De mirabilibus auscultationibus* recalls.[74] This latter identity of the goddess seems to be quite ancient, in as much as it was already accepted by Timaeus, who in all likelihood was Strabo's source[75] for his well-known passage in which the shrines of Siris, Luceria, and Lavinium are all explicitly mentioned as dedicated to the same Athena Ilias and as connected to one another.[76] As the late E. Lepore recognized[77] the identity was still operative in the late third century BC on the occasion of the establishment of relations between Rome and the Aetolians.

Plate 27. Lucera, Museo. Statuette of a winged genius holding a *diptychon*, from the votive deposit of the Belvedere Hill (courtesy of M. Mazzei).

While the colony at Luceria had all the characteristics of an outpost far from the growing power of Rome and predominantly populated by colonists of Latin origin, the colony of Venusia, founded a quarter of a century later under totally different historical conditions, appears, on the other hand, to have been a stronghold in which different cultures and ethnic groups were integrated and subjected to a much stricter Roman control. Because of these differing circumstances, the two versions of the 'Trojan' goddess, which were developed by the ruling Roman class in order to qualify the two colonies as centres of ideological integration with the Daunian world, differ notably.

At Luceria, this identification of the local Athena of Achaean origin with the Roman Athena Ilias did not proceed without both pressure and adjustments. First and foremost among these is the obvious removal of the figure of Diomedes, so apparent in the skilled

[71] Lykophr. 1130 f.   [72] D'Ercole, *La stipe.*
[73] Ibid. 178, figs. 63e, 64a.   [74] Pseudo-Aristot. *De mir. ausc.* 109.
[75] *Contra*, but without giving reasons, F. Castagnoli, *Lavinium i. Topografia generale, fonti e storia delle ricerche* (Rome, 1972), 106.
[76] Strab. 5. 232; cf. Virg. *Aen.* 11. 477.
[77] Lepore, *Atti Taranto* (1979).

evocation of the *aition* of the foundation of the temple proposed by Lykophron, and the powerful emergence of the tradition of Cassandra in connection with the Palladium. This process of assimilation of cults seems to have proceeded quite differently in Venusia. As we have already seen from the anecdote concerning Fabius Fabricianus, the eponymous goddess of Venusia, equipped with the significant epithet Nikephoros, seems even to have been the object of theft, if not of true *evocatio* (above all if one accepts, as do some scholars,[78] 291 BC as the date of the temple of Venus Obsequens). One could almost call it the fruit of a happy, though chance agreement between the 'Trojan' politics of the *troiugenae* Fabii, inaugurated in these same years with the dedication of the temple of the Circus Maximus, and the conquest, followed by triumph, of an important centre like Venusia, situated on the uncertain cultural and ethnic border between Daunians, Lucanians, and Samnites, but definitely belonging to the last.

In any case, one or other of these deities played a fundamental role in forming collective and family alliances, gaining clientele and of course furthering the process of Romanization. With the Venus of Venusia, the Romans had undoubtedly concluded the ideological 'surrounding' of Daunia that had begun with the Minerva of Luceria, a feature which recalls the polarity of the two august cult places in Lavinium—the Aphrodision of the Madonnella and the shrine of Minerva-Athena Ilias.[79] This strategy of ideological encirclement not only rationalizes in a 'Trojan' sense the politics of conquest in this part of the peninsula, but also introduces the all-important theme of Rome as a second Troy, a theme employed by the *urbs* to justify the politics of expansion ever since the conquest of Veii at the beginning of the fourth century BC. Such a Hellenizing tradition had been deeply rooted in this area since the arrival in Siris of Colophonian colonists, who, unlike the Achaeans,[80] seem to have made use of the Trojan Athena as an instrument to form alliances with indigenous groups and to protect their own economic interests, connected with stock raising, sheep farming and, above all, with the production of wool.[81]

This Hellenic influence spread along the cattle-tracks of the immense Apulian plain until it reached the heart of Samnium, where we are reminded very clearly of its power by the extraordinary clay statue of Athena from the late fifth century BC, found at Roccaspromonte, near Castropignano in the province of Campobasso and now in Vienna (Pl. 28).[82]

Wool, however, was not Siris' only interest in Apulia and Samnium, given that, as again Lepore[83] clearly saw, the establishment of Diomedes in Daunia as the great Graeco-Apulian hero of equestrian activities, a subject dear to the aristocracy of Siris' homeland, has Colophonian roots. But if we were to end our investigation with these ideological aspects, though they undoubtedly influence both the collective psychology and the social structure, we would not be fully understanding a phenomenon as complex as that of Romanization, which is rooted above all in precise political, economic and material contexts.

6. The Effects of the Conquest in the Third Century BC

The most evident effect of the first century of Roman rule, which is to say up until the end of the Hannibalic war, was the profound modification of the local socio-political structure accomplished through policies of land confiscation, the elimination of the middle class, and the selection of the local ruling class, policies imposed either directly or indirectly by Rome.

The Roman confiscation of lands in the northern part of Daunia appears to have been quite extensive at the time of the settlement of the colony at Luceria, as is proved by the traces of centuriation,[84] executed according to the ancient method *per strigas*. These land distributions may even have been carried out more than once in the course of the third century, most likely in order to accomodate reinforcements to the original colony of 314 BC. Much more mysterious, however, is the situation at Venusia, where there is still no definite

---

[78] Cf. M. R. Torelli, *Rerum Romanarum*, 46.

[79] M. Torelli, *Lavinio e Roma*, 157 f.

[80] M. Osanna, *Le 'chorai' delle colonie greche sul versante ionico della Magna Grecia* (Rome, 1992).

[81] On the enormous importance of transhumance and of wool production in this area from very early times (Strab. 6. 284; cf. Plin. *N.H.* 8. 190 f., 25. 45; Juv. 6. 149 f.), see E. Gabba and M. Pasquinucci, *Strutture agrarie*

e allevamento transumante nell'Italia romana (III–I sec.a.C.) (Pisa, 1979); A. Giardina, 'Gli spazi aperti, gli uomini', in Momigliano and Schiavone (eds.), *Storia di Roma* (Turin, 1989), 91 ff.; G. Volpe, *La Daunia nell'età della romanizzazione. Paesaggio agrario, produzione, scambi* (Bari, 1990), 72 f.

[82] G. Colonna, 'I Dauni nel contesto storico e culturale dell'Italia antica', in *La civiltà dei Dauni*, 266, pl. XLIIIb, who rightly explains this exceptional sculpture by the Greek colonial connections of the inland Samnite tribes.

[83] Lepore, *Atti Taranto* (1979), 129 f.

[84] Volpe, *La Daunia*, 46 (with previous bibliography).

evidence of land divisions,[85] although at least three such divisions must have occurred on the occasions, respectively, of the foundation of 291, the reinforcement of 200, and the triumviral colony of 43 BC.[86] Whatever the case, it seems none the less certain that the expansion of Venusian territory was from the very beginning (not only after the confiscations of 43 BC) extensive enough to warrant the extremely high number of 'colonists' (20,000) attributed to it by Dionysius.

The land confiscations effected between 314 and 291 BC, occurring above all during wars in which the Daunians were often allied with Rome's enemies, were without doubt of major consequence and affected even territories in which there had been no colonies or agricultural divisions; it was enough that these territories belonged to cities which had rebelled during the wars of conquest. The consequences of this severe policy of confiscations, as well as of other political and social factors both within and outside the indigenous environment, are seen most clearly in the transformation of the towns and the disappearance of certain social classes. Although both of these phenomena are most clearly discernible in the smaller settlements, they are also visible in the major cities of the vast Daunian territory.

Better documented are the transformations of settlements in the wake of the Roman conquest. The best-known case, as we have already seen, is that of Lavello–Forentum, where, in the second half of the fourth century BC, there are clear signs of a succession of phases, in part already discussed, which indicate the course of events both before and after the Roman conquest of 314 BC. Judging from the findspots of antefixes from the fifth and fourth centuries BC (a type of find, we shall see soon, revealing the presence of princely houses), the vast archaic and classical settlement[87] was organized around a number of inhabited nuclei, six or seven according to excavations and explorations of the surface. Each of these nuclei had its own cemetery and was characterized by *anaktora*, princely houses built in 'egalitarian' forms, which is to say of the same design and size (Fig. 43), and uniformly decorated by antefixes

[85] Despite the hypothesis of A. Catizzone, G. Giusteschi, and M. Coppa, 'L'assegnazione di Venosa attraverso l'analisi delle struttura ambientale, produttiva e storica', in M. Coppa (ed.), *Fotografia aerea e storia urbanistica* (Rome, 1979), 87 f.
[86] Discussion of these events by M. Torelli, 'Venosa romana', in A. Vaccaro (ed.), *Venosa* (Venosa, 1992), 35 f.
[87] See Bottini, Fresa, and Tagliente, in Tagliente (ed.), *Italici in Magna Grecia*.

Plate 28. Vienna, Kunsthistorisches Museum. Terracotta statue of Athena (late fifth century BC), found at Roccaspromonte, near Castropignano in the province of Campobasso (after *Italia omnium gentium parens*).

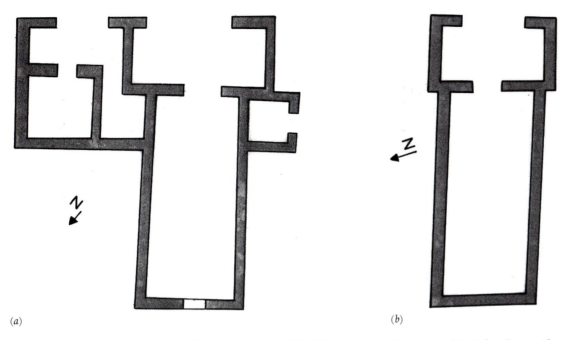

Fig. 43. Lavello: princely houses of the fifth century BC in Casino (*a*) and San Felice (*b*) areas (drawing A. Trapassi).

adorned with gorgon masks and acroteria with the allusive image of the 'Master of the Horses'.[88] Such *anaktora* suggest that each nucleus was controlled by a noble family whose dependants lived nearby in much more modest habitations. In the first half of the fourth century BC, according to very cautious calculations, the total population of the town seems to have reached 2,000. Dominating the entire settlement most likely was the noble family settled in the area close to the modern cemetery (Cimitero area), and it is in this context that, as we have seen, the transition from a regal to a republican form of government perhaps first occurred, although both were firmly based on oligarchic principles. The first notable change in the town's organization occurred shortly after the middle of the fourth century, when, as we have already seen, the Cimitero area was abandoned and the old princely *anaktora* were replaced by houses very different in plan and function, probably as a result of Samnitic influence on the settlement.

After the Roman conquest—318 BC according to Livy,[89] 315 BC according to Diodorus[90]—the picture changed radically. The immense old settlement made up of a series of separate villages gave way to a single settlement concentrated on one of the narrow strips of land already included in the area of pre-Roman Forentum: the plateau of Gravetta. This, because of its high position beside the precipitous coastline, was much more easily defended than the older settlement nearby, the *humile Forentum*,[91] which, according to Diodorus, was captured by the Romans not after a siege, but after an assault, meaning that the city was undoubtedly without walls, *aggeres* or other defensive fortifications. It was here on the heights of Gravetta, a position with limited possibilities for expansion, that the life of Forentum continued, and where recent excavations have uncovered a very interesting shrine dedicated to a divine couple, dating from the second century BC, as well as an inscription which confirms the presence in the same area of a cult of Hercules.[92] It is also here that, beginning in 90 BC, the Roman *municipium* of Forentum pursued its modest existence.[93] Another case of 'induced' urban transformation of an original Daunian settlement, although less easily reconstructed because of the ruins of a great Roman city superimposed on top, is that of Ordona–Herdonia,

[88] Published by M. Tagliente, in *Annali della Facoltà di Lettere e Filosofia di Perugia—Studi classici* 9, (1985–86), 303–321.

[89] Liv. 9. 20. 9.   [90] Diod. Sic. 19. 65. 7.

[91] Hor. *Carm.* 3. 4. 16.

[92] M. Torelli, *RAL* 8th ser., 24 (1969), 17 (inscription to Hercules); Bottini, Fresa, and Guzzo, 'Il santuario di Gravetta', in de Lachenal (ed.), *Da Leukania*, p. 17–20 (new sanctuary of Gravetta).

[93] Plin. *NH* 3. 105; cf. Hor. *Carm.* 3. 4. 16 *cum schol.*

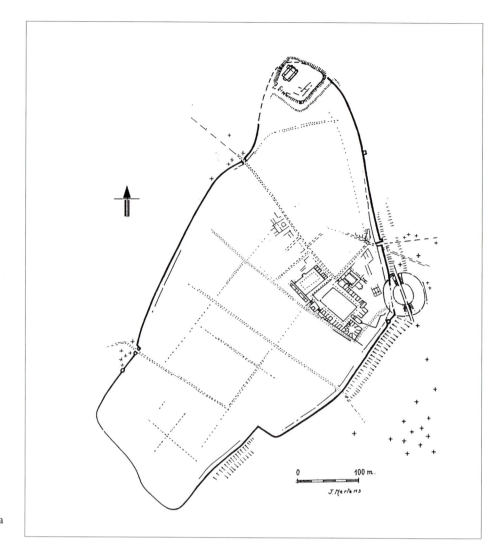

Fig. 44. Plan of the Daunian and Roman town of Herdonia (after Mertens).

which has been energetically explored by the Belgian missions directed by J. Mertens for more than two decades. The chronology, the subdivision and the interpretation of the various phases prior to the Trajanic period is a matter of some discussion. My reading of these phases, although based on the same data, differs slightly from that of my Belgian colleagues,[94] in particular regarding the chronology of the Roman phases.

As investigations conducted outside the city walls indicate,[95] the earliest pre-Roman settlement (Fig. 44), with its huts and tombs dating back to the ninth century BC, extended, with notable density, over a much wider area (4 km. in diameter, more than 1,150 hectares)

than that of the Roman settlement (730 × 300 m., equal to about 20 hectares). Further evidence of the size of the original settlement is provided by the *agger*, which, as we can infer from the large circular holes made at regular intervals in the top of the *agger*, was surmounted by a palisade.[96] This fortification, the first clearly defensive work of the settlement and the first real indication of its urbanization, cuts through Daunian tombs and structures of the sixth and fifth centuries BC, but unfortunately, has proved extremely difficult to date more precisely. Mertens is far from certain;[97] originally proposing an early date, between the fifth and fourth centuries BC,[98] he later retreated to less definite estimations.[99]

[94] J. Mertens, 'Ordona (Apulia), abitato daunio e città romana. Risultati dei recenti scavi belgi', in *La civiltà dei Dauni*, 19 f., and, more recently, 'Ordona 1978–86', in *Ordona*, 8 (Brussels and Rome, 1988), 11 f.

[95] J. Mertens, 'Rapport sommaire sur les campagnes de 1975, 1976 et 1977', *Ordona*, 6 (Brussels and Rome, 1979), 10 f.

[96] Mertens, *Ordona*, 8 (1988), 12, pl. IIb.
[97] Mertens, *Ordona*, 6 (1979), 17.
[98] Mertens, in *La civiltà dei Dauni*, 22.
[99] Mertens, in *Ordona*, 8 (1988), 11.

The subsequent fortifications, consisting of an *agger*, moat, and walls constructed of mud bricks on a foundation of stones, were evidently erected in great haste. The wall, since the Belgian archaeologists discovered the remains of a siege mine inside, probably dates back to shortly before the Hannibalic conflict, which was most likely the reason for its construction. On this occasion the city was subjected to a particularly bitter siege (hence the traces of the mine), which is recounted in great detail, particularly by Livy.[100] The following city wall in *opus incertum*, which Mertens[101] dates to the middle of the first century BC, would seem rather to have been built no later than the middle of the second, thereby coinciding with the urban reorganization of the city centre in the Roman manner and with the palaeography of an inscription inserted in the wall, which perhaps indicated the commitment of a city official to provide for that section of the work.[102]

A fact which, in my opinion, has not been sufficiently emphasized is that the Daunian tombs brought to light within the settlement do not date beyond the first part of the third century BC.[103] This is the date which marks the event of urbanization, and which unequivocally forms the boundary between the end of the pre-existing social order, that *kata komas*, and the birth of the new order, that of urban type, which is to say that directly determined by the process of Romanization. At this time the traditional Daunian funeral rites (corpse in contracted position accompanied by traditional Daunian pottery) give way slowly to different religious and symbolic influences.[104]

At Lavello–Forentum, the concentration of the settlement on the small hill of Gravetta, accurately dated to the end of the fourth century BC, was also accompanied by a significant modification to funerary custom. The new tombs, underground chambers with long *dromoi* located outside the town, were, as far as we know, reserved for the burial of persons of high social rank, as is the case with the extraordinary tomb 669[105]

dating from the end of the fourth century BC, with its rich equestrian panoply and its Roman helmet of a well-known middle-republican type (Pl. 29). Here is direct evidence, as Bottini observed, not quite of the birth, but of the hegemonic role of the cavalry in the formation of an aristocratic class of oligarchic stamp, 'created', so to speak, by the Roman intervention. Having followed Hellenistic fashion between the middle and the end of the fourth century BC (in this

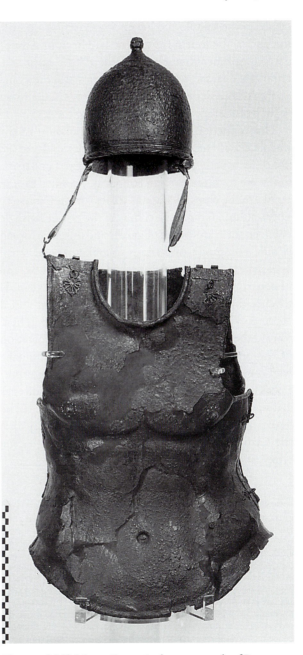

Plate 29. Melfi, Museo. Equestrian bronze panoply of Roman type from a tomb of the Gravetta necropolis at Lavello (courtesy of the Soprintendenza Archeologica della Basilicata).

[100] Liv. 25. 21. 1–10; 27. 1. 3–15.   [101] Mertens, *Ordona*, 8 (1988), 14.
[102] F. Van Wontherghem, 'Les inscriptions (1962–1966)', *Ordona*, 2 (Brussels and Rome, 1967), 138, no. 11 = *CIL* I², 3187.
[103] R. Iker, 'Tombes dauniennes à Herdonia', *Ordona*, 2 (1967), 31 f.; id., 'La tombe LX', *Ordona*, 3 (Brussels and Rome, 1971), 39 f.; K. Van Wontherghem Maes, 'Une tombe à chambre et son materiel funeraire', Ibid. 83 f.; R. Iker, 'Les tombes dauniennes—II', *Ordona*, 7: 2 (Brussels and Rome, 1986).
[104] Iker, *Ordona*, 7 (1986), 727 f.; E. De Juliis, 'Alcuni aspetti del rituale funerario', in Cassano (ed.), *Principi*, 149 f. (for the abandonment in the 3rd cent. of the customary contracted deposition of dead in Daunian tombs).
[105] Only sketchily published by Bottini, Russo, and Tagliente, 'La Daunia interna', in Tagliente (ed.), *Italici in Magna Grecia*, 81 f.

connection we may cite the well-known panoplies from the monumental tombs of Canusium),[106] the cavalry then began to look to Rome for its political models, while preserving, even if, as we have seen, for only a short time, ancient Daunian burial rituals. This is the clearest existing evidence we have so far of how rapidly the process of Romanization could affect the local élites. Equally striking, however, is the disappearance from the cemeteries, by now all outside the city (in contrast to the traditional Apulian custom), of the tombs of the middle and lower classes, which up until the end of the fourth century BC had been of a much greater number than those of the élite classes and, although characterized by an inferior quantity and quality of grave contents, had certainly been consistent with the funerary ideology of the ruling classes.

This reduction, if not outright elimination of the middle classes seems to have been quite rapid and did not differ greatly from that which occurred in Etruria in the wake of the Roman conquest. Another case in point are the cities of Magna Graecia, from Croton to Locri, although there the climax of the power struggle between the pro-Roman oligarchs and the anti-Roman *plethos*, composed of artisans, merchants, and small landowners, occurred during the Hannibalic war, and its consequences were consistent with Rome's attitude toward these cities between the fourth and third centuries BC, an attitude quite different from that held toward the Italic populations.[107] The mass deportation of the population of Herdonia after the Hannibalic war can be seen in the same light if we interpret Livy's text,[108] in which he describes the deportation as *multitudine omni Metapontum ac Thurios traducta*, to the letter, and if we understand, as Livy certainly did, the term *multitudo* to have the same meaning as the Greek *plethos*.

Moreover, the continuous use of the great hypogea of Canusium throughout the entire third and second centuries, and even at times until the middle of the first century BC — as evidenced by the hypogeum Lagrasta I—[109] shows that the local oligarchies, already in the making during the fourth century (as we can see from the luxurious houses surrounded by colonnades from this period, such as that of great beauty located in the centre of Arpi, with elegant late classical—not Hellenistic—pebble mosaics; Fig. 45),[110] took full advantage of Rome's growing power and profited both economically and socially.[111] This is not to suggest, however, that the conflicts between rival aristocratic groups had subsided; on the contrary, these had perhaps even intensified, certainly exploding in moments of international tension, as we can clearly see not only from the contrasting positions of loyalty or defection taken by individual Daunian centres immediately following Cannae, but also from the internal feuds between rival aristocratic groups, such as that which erupted at Salapia in 213 BC between the pro-Roman Blattius and the pro-Carthaginian Dasius.[112]

It should in any case be underlined that by favouring certain social classes, and groups within these, the Roman intervention somehow 'rationalized' a trend that had been developing, with greater or lesser force, throughout the Italic world since the heart of the fourth century BC: the rapid emergence of local ruling classes that were characterized by ever increasing wealth. The net effect of this trend was not only an increased hierarchization of social structures, but also the progressive preference shown (this too resulting in increased hierarchization) to certain more economically fortunate areas. It should be added, however, that this latter practice did not provoke the demographic crisis often attributed to this period, as the Apulian contribution to Rome's military forces in 225 BC, 16,000 cavalry and 50,000 soldiers, would seem to indicate. One important consequence, whether direct or indirect, of this process of greater social hierarchization promoted by Rome was the creation (or strengthening) of cities, a process typical of the period between the end of the fourth century and the beginning of the third century BC and which was quite naturally the first

---

[106] See e.g. the panoply of the Scocchera tomb, in Cassano (ed.), *Principi*, 228 f., nos. 33–40 (E. M. De Juliis), and the helmets, from dispersed grave groups, collected by E. De Juliis, 'Gli elmi', ibid. 547 f.

[107] Fundamental for the study of Roman attitudes towards local élites are A. Toynbee, *Hannibal's Legacy* (Oxford, 1965), and, from a different perspective, A. Momigliano, 'Polibio, Posidonio e l'imperialismo romano', in *Atti dell'Accademia delle Scienze di Torino*, 107 (1972–3), 693 f. (= *Sesto contributo alla storia degli studi classici e del mondo antico* (Rome, 1980), 184 f.); see, however, the very effective synthesis by W. V. Harris, 'The Italians and the Empire', *PMAAR* 29 (1984), 89 f., who correctly states (p. 100) that 'the economic history of allied Italy in the 3rd and 2nd centuries is still waiting to be written', and the well-known passage by Livy (24. 2. 8), who comments upon the effects of the arrival of the 'liberator' Hannibal 'unus velut morbus invaserat omnes Italiae civitates ut plebes ab optimatibus dissentirent, senatus Romanis faverent, plebs ad Poenos rem traheret'.

[108] Liv. 27. 1. 14.

[109] R. Cassano, 'L'ipogeo Lagrasta', in Cassano (ed.), *Principi*, 203 f., esp. 207 f.

[110] M. Mazzei, 'Il IV e III sec.a.C.: il panorama storico-archeologico', in E. Lippolis and M. Mazzei (eds.), *La Daunia antica* (Milan, 1984), 204 f.

[111] M. Torelli, in de Lachenal (ed.), *Da Leukania*, p. xix.

[112] Liv. 26. 38. 6–14.

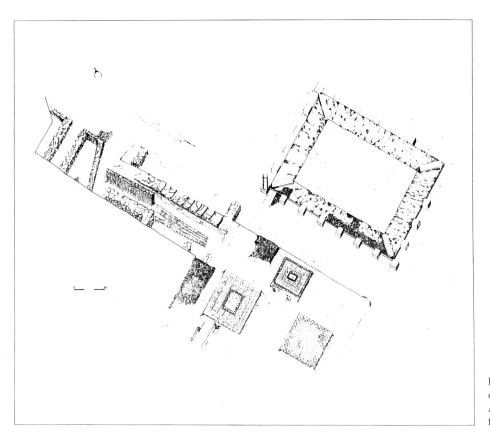

Fig. 45. Plan of a late fourth century BC aristocratic house at Arpi with peristyle and mosaic floors (after Mazzei).

step toward establishing a hierarchy between city and countryside. The following century, until after the Social War, would instead be characterized by an ever greater 'natural' tendency to develop the more advanced Roman and Italic economies according to the dominant forms at the expense of the more archaic local economic forms,[113] which were progressively impoverished and then 'naturally' integrated or subordinated as residual modes of production.[114]

It is for this reason that the whole of the third and the early decades of the second century BC are characterized, both in Daunia and elsewhere in the Italian peninsula, by a modification in the forms of production: a shift which reflected changes in the structure of settlements; changes in the nature, both quantitative and qualitative, of the social forces in play; and changes in the amount of *surplus* withdrawn from various productive spheres. It would be pointless, however, to search for macroscopic signs of this change in the material culture, as for example in artisan production

(and particularly in that part of it best documented by archaeology, i.e. pottery), which would only point to a rapid and evident deterioration, certainly a direct result of the situation described above, first in quantity of production and then also in quality. While certain traditional black glazed or overpainted pots continue to be produced, they definitely decline in quality during the course of the third century and finally disappear altogether in the second century BC.[115] This clearly indicates that in the third century the Roman influence, in contrast to what would occur in the next century, was not yet strong enough to affect local artisan production (a subject, in any case, obscured in part by insufficient microanalysis of local production and distribution), although it certainly had a profound effect on customs and ideology.

Although funerary customs, as we have seen, were progressively modified during the third century, some local traditions were preserved despite external pressures for at least part of the century. These traditions were of course accompanied by the production of

[113] E. Gabba, 'Considerazioni sulla decadenza della piccola proprietà contadina nell'Italia centromeridionale nel II sec.a.C.' *Ktema*, 2 (1977), 280 f.
[114] E. Lepore, 'Geografia del modo di produzione schiavistico e modi residui in Italia meridionale', in Giardina and Schiavone (eds.), *Società romana*, i. 79 f.

[115] E. Lippolis, 'I processi di trasformazione nell'età tardo-repubblicana. La cultura insediativa e le manifestazioni artistiche tra il II e il I sec.a.C.', in Lippolis and Mazzei (eds.), *La Daunia antica*, 216.

Plate 30. Melfi, Museo. Canusine *askos*, known as Catarinella *askos*, from Lavello cemetery (courtesy of the Soprintendenza Archeologica della Basilicata).

objects essential to their preservation—mainly Canusine pottery—which, although of declining quality, were certainly destined for funerary purposes.[116] It should be noted, however, that the decoration applied to this pottery was often influenced by the ideological pressure which Rome exerted on the peninsula's indigenous populations. I am thinking now of the Canusine *askos* from Lavello commonly referred to as the Catarinella *askos* (Pl. 30). As M. Tagliente[117] has recognized, its representation of a funeral is strongly influenced by rituals of a Roman origin. Seemingly the extraordinary polychrome vases found in Arpi (Pl. 31)[118] are another example of how Roman iconography (the panoplies of the warriors) and style (not unconnected with the

pocola, a well-known Roman class of polychrome pottery) influenced Daunian funerary productions in the course of the third century BC.

7. Change and Conflict in the Second Century BC

Although the importance of the Hannibalic war has often been minimized in recent times, largely in reaction to Toynbee's somewhat apocalyptic *Hannibal's Legacy*, there is no doubt that it left lasting scars on Apulia, which was the theatre of the *Cannensis clades*, and of a long series of other bloody conflicts for nearly a decade. But the war and its destruction made a less dramatic impact on the political and social conditions of the region than did the drastic, often bloody reprisals carried out by the Roman victors against those populations guilty of collaborating with the

[116] On this class, see now F. van der Wielen, 'La ceramica a decorazione policroma e plastica', in Cassano (ed.), *Principi*, 520 f.

[117] [A. Bottini] and M. Tagliente, 'Due casi di acculturazione del mondo indigeno della Basilicata', *PP* (1990), 206 f., esp. 220 f.

[118] M. Mazzei, 'Nota su un gruppo di vasi policromi decorati con scene di combattimento da Arpi (Fg)', in *AIONArch* 9 (1987), 167 f.

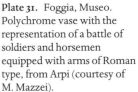

Plate 31. Foggia, Museo. Polychrome vase with the representation of a battle of soldiers and horsemen equipped with arms of Roman type, from Arpi (courtesy of M. Mazzei).

Carthaginians:[119] mass deportations, as was the case with Herdonia; entire populations sold into slavery, as was perhaps the case with the mysterious Acuca, near Herdonia;[120] and the extensive confiscation of the rebels' lands, as the traces of vast centuriations in the territories of Herdonia, Aecae, and Arpi, along with the perhaps dependent Salapia, demonstrate.[121] It appears, however, that this practice was most often employed in the area between Luceria and Herdonia, where we find more than 80 per cent of the Roman land divisions in Daunia. We also know that in 201 BC a commission of ten senators was formed[122] *agro Samniti Apuloque . . . metiendo dividendo* to carry out the promised redistribution of land to Scipio's veterans, an act which led to the foundation of a *colonia civium Romanorum* at Sipontum, carried out in 194 BC in the former territory of Arpi. This colony replaced the large Daunian town in the area of Masseria Cupola, most likely to be identified with the not-too-distant Daunian Sipes–Sipontum,[123] and was one of the *coloniae maritimae* founded in southern Italy during this period.[124]

It is highly probable that, at least in this phase, a large portion of the confiscated lands remained undistributed.[125] This hypothesis is given added weight by the fact that in this same area, a few years later, as we significantly happen to know in connection with the Bacchanalian question of 185 BC, we hear of *pascua publica*.[126] No less significant is the case of the brothers L. and A. Hostili Catones (187 BC), of whom we will soon speak at greater length. Certainly belonging to the Scipionic party, and at that time L. Cornelius Scipio's envoys in Asia, these two members of the aforementioned agrarian reform commission came to strike at or more simply to disrupt powerful Roman interests; no wonder that they were soon after put on trial accused of being corrupted by king Antioch, though the trial resulted in the acquittal of one brother and the condemnation of the other.[127]

If the confiscated lands remained in large part undivided, it is certainly not surprising that a small part of the Apulian aristocracy, that part which had maintained a pro-Roman stance during the recent

[119] Toynbee, *Hannibal's Legacy*, ii. 115 f.   [120] Liv. 24. 20. 8.
[121] Volpe, *La Daunia*, 40 f.   [122] Liv. 30. 27. 1–4.
[123] Strab. 6. 284.
[124] On the meaning of these foundations see Toynbee, *Hannibal's Legacy*, ii. 201 f.

[125] Still valuable for this problem are the classical works by G. Tibiletti: 'Il possesso dell' "ager publicus" e le norme "de modo agrorum" sino ai Gracchi', *Athenaeum* 36 (1948), 173 f.; 'Ricerche di storia agraria romana', *Athenaeum*, 38 (1950), 183 f.; 'Ancora sulle norme "de modo agrorum" ', ibid. 245 f.
[126] Liv. 39. 29.   [127] Liv. 38. 55. 4 ss.; 58. 1.

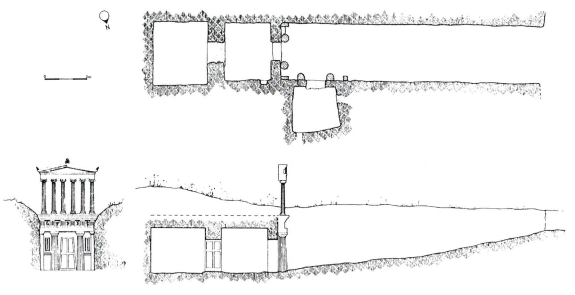

Fig. 46. Plan, cross-section and view of the Lagrasta II tomb of Canosa (after Mazzei).

conflicts (in the same manner in which the pro-Roman Tarentines were rewarded after the sack of their city in 209 BC), took full advantage of the circumstance; beside them, in this prosperous area of Apulia, we now meet the earliest wave of Roman speculators, who, in this era of the first intensive exploitation of the peninsula's resources, were looking to Italy's economic nerve centres. The situation was similar to that of the previous century, but the potential for exploitation was much greater, and the number of oligarchs sharing the spoils much smaller. The result of such a favourable convergence of circumstances for this exiguous and extremely rich class of aristocrats, who were to be found throughout Daunia and Apulia, is the extraordinary wealth of their tombs, which E. Lippolis[128] correctly identifies as dating to the end of the third and the first quarter of the second century BC, rather than a century earlier, as was somewhat uncritically proposed more than fifty years ago. The wealth of this 'new class' of indigenous oligarchs and *possessores* found expression in the fabulous contents of tombs like the 'tombe degli Ori' at Canosa and Teanum Apulum, and tomb No. 6 from the locality 'Serpente' at Ascoli Satriano, all products of a formal culture and craftsmanship comparable to that evident in the Tarentine Rothschild Treasure, which dates from the same period.[129]

Thanks to the excavations which have been conducted in the cemeteries of this region in the last twenty years, we now know that the model for this strongly élitist culture was the Macedonian aristocracy, a model which represented a point of reference necessary for such a life-style, and not, as many have insisted on arguing, even in the absence of any historical evidence, simply an easy (and unproved) market for the exports of Magna Graecia.[130] The proof of this is in the gradual adoption in Apulia of cultural models and modes of behaviour consistent with the complex system of ethical and formal values of the world of the Diadochs, an influence which is clearly evident in this corner of the Hellenistic world during the third century. This adoption of a Macedonian model by the Apulian élites of the early Hellenistic period seems quite natural, given their taste for the refined and opulent culture of early Hellenism, and is quite evident in their adoption of tomb models based on elaborate naomorphic façades (Fig. 46), as well as in their choice, in the second century BC, of tombs whose interiors were modelled after the Macedonian type, covered with a semi-cylindrical vault, such as the one discovered at Arpi.[131]

It is in fact from this period that we find the first epigraphic record of Apulian individuals in Greece: *Blattos*

[128] E. Lippolis, 'Toreutica', in E. Lippolis (ed.), *Gli ori di Taranto*, Catalogue of the Exhibition; Taranto, 1984 (Milan, 1984), 33 f.

[129] On these tombs, see the new chronologies convincingly proposed in Lippolis (ed.), *Gli ori*.

[130] Discussion of these fanciful theories by M. Torelli, 'Macedonia, Epiro e Magna Grecia. La pittura di età classica e protoellenistica', *Atti Taranto* (1984), 379 f.

[131] E. De Juliis, 'Ricerche ad Arpi e a Salapia', *Atti Taranto* (1972), 392 f.

Matourou and *Salsius Tagyllios* of Arpi were *proxenoi* at Delphi in 195–194 and 192–191 BC,[132] as a certain *Dazos Dazou* was at Epidaurus[133] in the first half of the second century. It is surely no accident that this development of *luxuria* in the Italian provinces coincides with the sudden diffusion of *leges sumptuariae* by Rome.[134] The first of these measures was the *lex Oppia* of 215 BC, approved under the pressure of the Hannibalic conflict and, after a first attempt at its abrogation in 195 BC, abolished shortly afterwards. In the following years, however, the enormous quantity of riches flowing into Rome and the concomitant spread of *luxuria* led, under the pressure of Cato's moral crusade, to the proliferation of a series of such laws: the *lex Orchia* of 182 BC, the *lex Fannia* of 161, the *lex Didia* of 143, and the *lex Licinia* of 140.

In the cities that had remained loyal to Rome and were therefore spared from reprisals, first among these Canusium, the existing social structure underwent only partial modification, as we have seen in the continued use of the great hypogea of the nobility of the third century. The socio-political, as well as emotional climate in Canusium at this time was conditioned by both immense relief that the danger had passed and the general situation in Apulia after the Hannibalic war, a situation which favoured the flourishing of the pro-Roman aristocracy. This, then, represents the potent psychological base on which the most complex and enigmatic structure of pre-Roman Canusium seems to have been built: the colossal temple of Minerva-Athena Ilias found under San Leucio (Figs. 16 and 17). Current opinion,[135] evidently choosing the earliest possible chronology—as P. Pensabene[136] has recently done in the most complete and intelligent presentation of the evidence—maintains that the temple was constructed at the end of the fourth or the beginning of the third century BC. This evaluation appears highly suspect, however, when the building is compared in plan and style to other, clearly datable structures of almost a century later. The most significant case in point is the so-called 'temple of Peace' at Paestum,[137] which was certainly constructed after the *comitium* which was built after (and most likely not immediately after) the foundation of the Latin colony in 273 BC, and thus belonging to a date towards the end of the third century BC. As we have seen, this objective circumstance would seem to corroborate the hypothesis that identifies the Paestan temple as the temple of Mens,[138] erected to commemorate the loyalty shown to Rome by this *colonia libertinorum* during the difficult times of the Second Punic War.

Furthermore, similar architectural features are found for example in the temple of Feronia in Lucus Feroniae,[139] erected after the city was sacked by Hannibal[140] (most likely between 180 and 170 BC), possibly by a Cn. Egnatius C.f. Stell., identical with the builder of the Via Egnatia and certainly of Capenate origin, as we learn from a monumental inscription, still not adequately studied, found re-employed in the basilica floor at Lucus Feroniae.[141] Some architectural elements are conceivable only in terms of the architecture of the second century BC. I am thinking specifically of the telamones which, although their position in the structure is unclear, are comparable either in style or in function to those found in the neighbouring zones of Montescaglioso[142] and, though different in scale, of Rossano di Vaglio,[143] hardly to be dated earlier than the mid-second century BC. In terms of its design, elevation and conception as a temple built on a high podium, following the Etrusco-Italic canonical forms, the colossal structure of S. Leucio represents a novelty without precedent in the Daunian world, which had, up until this time, never erected a formal temple with cella and peristyle, preferring instead to adhere to (and also this quite rare) the extremely simple formula of the *naiskos* of Lavello described earlier or of the various little square shrines, typical of the adjoining Lucanian area.[144]

---

[132] Dittenberger, *Syll.*[3], 585, l. 13, and l. 65. [133] *IG* IV, I. 225.

[134] On these *leges* see now G. Clemente, 'Le leggi sul lusso e la società romana tra III e II sec.a.C.', in Giardina and Schiavone (eds.), *Società romana*, i. 1 f.

[135] Conveniently summarized by M. Mazzei, in Lippolis and M. Mazzei (eds.), *La Daunia antica*, 207.

[136] P. Pensabene, 'Il tempio ellenistico di S. Leucio a Canosa', in Tagliente (ed.), *Italici in Magna Grecia*, 269 f.; see also a more synthetic entry on this temple by the same author, in Cassano (ed.), *Principi*, 620 f.

[137] See Ch. 3.

[138] Ibid.; cf. M. Torelli, 'C. Cocceius Flaccus, senatore di Paestum, Mineia M.f. e Bona Mens', *Annali della Facoltà di Lettere e Filosofia di Perugia—Studi Classici*, NS 18 (1980/1), 105 f.

[139] The remains of this monumental temple are virtually unpublished: short description and bibliography by M. Torelli, in *EAA* Suppl. (1970), 442 f., and M. Torelli, *Etruria* (Rome and Bari, 1985), 34.

[140] Liv. 26. 11. 8–9; Sil. It. 13. 84 ff.

[141] M. Torelli, 'Ascesa al Senato e rapporti con i territori d'origine. Italia: Regio VII (Etruria)', in S. Panciera (ed.), *Epigrafia e ordine senatorio*, ii (Rome, 1982), 297.

[142] Only sketchily mentioned in *AA* (1927), c. 136.

[143] D. Adamesteanu and H. Dilthey, *Macchia di Rossano. Rapporto preliminare* (Lecce, 1992), 77, fig. 25, pl. LIII.

[144] On such cult places see C. Masseria, *I santuari indigeni della Basilicata*, Ph.D. Dissertation (Perugia, 1988).

Plate 32. Present location unknown. Statuette of Athena from the excavation of the temple of S. Leucio at Canosa (courtesy of the Soprintendenza ai Beni Artistici e Storici della Puglia).

To sum up, the Canusine temple of S. Leucio, another *hapax legomenon* in Apulian territory and constructed according to the tenets of Etrusco-Italic sacral architecture of early republican ascendancy, is the first clear example of the local acceptance of exclusively Roman cultural models (and therefore not imported into this region, as well as into Rome, from the Hellenistic world of the eastern Mediterranean, i.e. from the common source of many cultural borrowings made by Apulia in the third century BC). The discovery during the temple's excavation of a series of votive objects and of two statuettes of Athena (Pl. 32),[145] goes to prove that the sanctuary belonged to that divinity, the same Athena Ilias of nearby Luceria. It was certainly not by chance that this temple was dedicated to Minerva-Athena Ilias, the deity on which Rome

had based its first proposal of alliance/*syngeneia* more than a hundred years earlier at Luceria.

We also find striking evidence of ample urban and cultural change during the second century BC in the more unfortunate town of Herdonia. During this period the city's centre was reorganized on the Roman model. The previously mentioned city wall in *opus incertum* was erected, as was the forum square (Fig. 47), with its shops and temple B,[146] dedicated to the otherwise unknown indigenous deity *Dafes*.[147] One has the impression that the forced exodus of the population—or that part of it which was politically undesirable—had an only temporary effect. The city appears to be repopulated by means either of an almost immediate return of a part of the banished inhabitants or of a very quick replacement of the old population. This was followed by the rapid reorganization of the city, an important site because of its favourable position in the centre of the Apulian plain, from where it could control both the trade routes coming from the land of the Frentani and from Samnium and those connecting the hinterland and the sea, source of ever greater overseas trade and of the precious salt collected in the great salt pans of the lagoon of Salapia.[148]

This Roman influence on urban planning was of course strongest in the principal centres of Daunia, such as Canusium and Herdonia, for the greater part of the second century BC. Unfortunately, our knowledge of the process in the smaller towns and in the countryside is very limited. Even recent excavations of the oldest strata at the colony of Sipontum have yielded very little information regarding pre-imperial times. This lack of archaeological evidence confirms not only the short life-span of this colony,[149] found deserted only a decade after its foundation,[150] but also its marginal character from an economic point of view, proof that the growth of urban centres was not an exclusively 'political' phenomenon. This fact seems quite clear when we consider that both towns of privileged *socii*,

---

[145] I am grateful to M. P. Fresa, who pointed out to me the existence of photographs of the votive objects in the archives of the Soprintendenza ai Beni Artistici e Storici della Puglia.

[146] F. Van Wontherghem, 'Un tempio di età repubblicana sul foro di Herdonia', *Ordona*, 6 (1979), 27 f.

[147] J. Smeesters, 'Les inscriptions 1966–1975', *Ordona*, 6 (1979), 129 f.

[148] Good summary of these resources by Volpe, *La Daunia*, 13 f. and 60 f.; detailed accounts of the Daunian environment in pre-Roman and Roman times, by C. Delano Smith, 'The Buried Lagoon and Lost Port of Sipontum (Foggia, Italy)', *IJNA* 3: 2 (1974), 275 f.; ead., 'Sfruttamento dei terreni agricoli e fattori socio-economici in Capitanata', *Rassegna di Studi Dauni* 3: 4 (1976), 5 f.; ead., 'Coastal Sedimentation, Lagoons and Ports in Italy', in H. M. K. Blake and D. B. Whitehouse (eds.), *Papers in Italian Archaeology. I*, BAR Suppl. Series, 41 (Oxford, 1977), 25 f.; ead., *Daunia vetus. Terra, vita e mutamenti sulle coste del Tavoliere* (Foggia, 1978).

[149] Cf. Cic. *Leg. agr.* 2. 71.   [150] Liv. 34. 45. 3; 39. 23. 3.

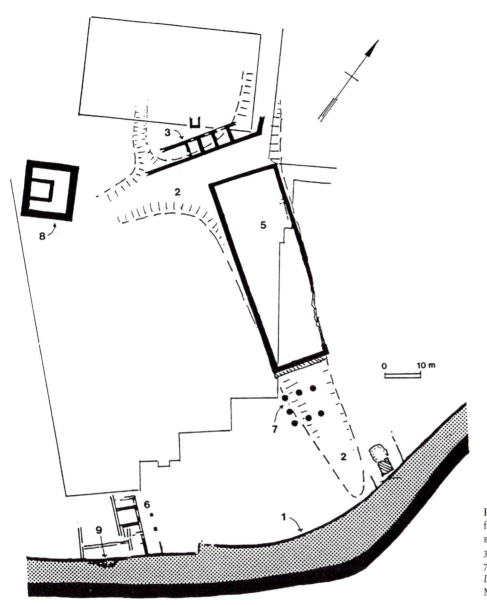

Fig. 47. Herdonia, plan of the forum area in the third century BC: 1. city wall; 2. large ditch; 3. shops; 5. *horreum*; 6. shops; 7. portico (?); 8. temple of *Dafes*; 9. *heroon* (?) (after Mertens).

such as Canusium, and harshly punished *socii*, such as Herdonia, flourished, while politically privileged Roman colonies, such as Sipontum, did not. In other words, the Roman policy of 'rational' exploitation, which favoured certain 'selected' classes and settlements, continued inexorably.

It is understandable that the situation in the country-side could only deteriorate, resulting finally in the defini-tive destruction of traditional Daunian society, which has been justly defined as cantonal and 'archaic'.[151] At this time the system of the 'Catonian' villa was still unknown, and would not be introduced

until the Gracchan period, as we shall shortly see. The immense Apulian countryside appears to have been marked by the decline of minor settlements, of *vici* and of the few rural centres that had animated it. The fate of its inhabitants was certainly no brighter. The indigenous subordinate classes, reduced to pauperism and transformed into farm labourers,[152] were by now of no higher status than the ever more numerous slaves working in the fields and watching over the now huge flocks. Despite these dramatic changes in the lot of the local population, the land continued to be the same fertile granary and pasture—and of increasing

---

[151] Lippolis, in Lippolis and Mazzei (eds.), *La Daunia antica*, 211 f.

[152] Cf. Varr. *RR* I. 29. 2.

importance in the production of wine by the second century BC[153]—that the natural disposition of the *siticulosi* soils and the techniques of pastoral and agricultural exploitation, practised for at least a milennium, had created. The Romans rapidly reactivated this productive capacity, beginning at least as early as 172 BC,[154] and used the ports of Sipontum and Salapia for the grain trade, which the growing needs of the corn supply for the Roman poor rendered of utmost importance. However, among other major differences from the past, the profits were now distributed among an ever smaller group, many of whom were foreigners.

Given the situation, it comes as no surprise that Apulia was the scene of a violent revolt in 187 BC, which Rome put down with the well-known *senatus consultum de Bacchanalibus* and the consequent repressive action. The uprising was engineered by a conspiracy in which the Apulian shepherds, acting in the context of a *jacquerie* based on Dionysiac mystery rites,[155] played a major role. They brought about an alliance between the urban masses of Rome and other large Italic cities, their numbers swollen by migration from the countryside, and the subordinate classes of Etruria and Apulia, the areas most deeply affected by the profound social upheaval. This upheaval which marked the end of social classes based on the archaic dependence of the *clientela–servitus* relationship that was deeply rooted in these lands dominated by ancient *principes*.

One consequence of the revolt was the suppression of the above mentioned Dionysiac cult. The private Dionysus sacellum at Volsinii, deconsecrated and completely destroyed,[156] is a clear example of this suppression, as may well be a similar case in Lavello–Forentum, where, according to A. Bottini *et al.*,[157] an analogous deconsecration of a public Dionysiac shrine at Gravetta took place. This was marked by the last expiatory sacrifice of a deer, concealed near an altar on the bottom of a large pool with a mosaic floor, which was evidently carried out immediately before the final abandonment and filling of the pool, presumably in compliance with Roman provisions intended to suppress the conspiracy.

The economic and social consequences of this revolt are not expressly documented in the written tradition, which treats them only in a desultory manner, and is therefore of little use in forming a clear picture of the regional history.[158] Livy's account[159] maintains that 7,000 *pastores* were condemned to death in Apulia in 185 BC and that the praetors were assigned numerous cases until at least 180 BC, when there was a renewal of repression. Whatever the details, one can safely conclude that the consequences were not light, accelerating the increase both in poverty and in the number of gaps in the social structure which our sources define as the *Italiae solitudo*. The 'scorched earth' of which A. Toynbee[160] repeatedly speaks, evidently influenced by the experience of modern wars of conquest, and especially those of a colonial nature, can be, in this context, more aptly applied to the effects on the social structure than to those on economic resources. The former resulting from the intensive exploitation of the lower classes rather than from the devastation produced by a ten-year war, as Toynbee documents in his discussion of new economic developments and class struggle in post-Hannibalic Italy.[161] In any case, we can only conclude that the repression was effective, given that the archaeological record shows the area continuing to develop until the Gracchan age, and always more rapidly as the years progressed, along the same lines fixed at the beginning of the century.

8. Between the Gracchan Period and the Civil Wars: Total Assimilation

The definitive transformation of Daunia took place at the time of the Gracchan colonization,[162] when, as the *Liber Coloniarum*[163] states, land divisions ordered by the

---

[153] Volpe, *La Daunia*, 64 f.; needless to mention in this connection the celebrated passage by Varro, *RR* I. 8. 2, where two out of the four techniques of marrying high vine trees to other plants are attributed to Daunia, one to Canusium (binding with fig trees) and another to Arpi (binding to reeds).

[154] Lippolis, in Lippolis and Mazzei (eds.), *La Daunia antica*, 221.

[155] C. Gallini, *Protesta e integrazione nella Roma antica* (Rome and Bari, 1970), and J.-M. Pailler, *Bacchanalia. La répression de 186 av. J.-C. à Rome et en Italie* (Rome, 1988).

[156] F.-H. Massa Pairault, 'La maison aux salles souterraines. 1. Les terres cuites sous la peristyle', in *Bolsena*, 5 (Rome, 1983), 1 f.

[157] Bottini, Fresa, and Guzzo, in de Lachenal (ed.), *Da Leukania*.

[158] Extremely useful is however the work by M. Pani, 'Economia e società in età romana', in *Storia della Puglia*, i (Bari, 1979), 99 f.

[159] Liv. 39. 17–19; 41; 40. 19.

[160] Toynbee, *Hannibal's Legacy*, ii. 12 f., 100 f., 247 f.

[161] Ibid. ii. 155 f., 313 f., 395 f.

[162] A useful bibliography on the Gracchan colonization is that of E. Badian, 'Tiberius Gracchus and the Beginning of the Roman Revolution', in *ANRW* I: 1 (1972), 668 f.; see however, besides the articles of Tibiletti (see n. 125), U. Kahrstedt, 'Ager Publicus und Selbstverwaltung in Lucania und Bruttium', *Historia*, 8 (1959), 174 f.; D. C. Earl, *Tiberius Gracchus. A Study in Politics*, Coll. Latomus, 66 (Brussels, 1963); J. Carcopino, *Autour des Gracques*, 2nd edn. (Paris, 1967); H. C. Boren, *The Gracchi* (New York, 1968); E. T. Salmon, *Roman Colonization under the Republic* (London, 1969); C. Nicolet, *Les Gracques*, 2nd edn. (Paris, 1971); J. Molthagen, 'Die Durchführung der Agrarreform', *Historia*, 22 (1973), 424 f.

[163] *Lib. Col.* i. 210L.

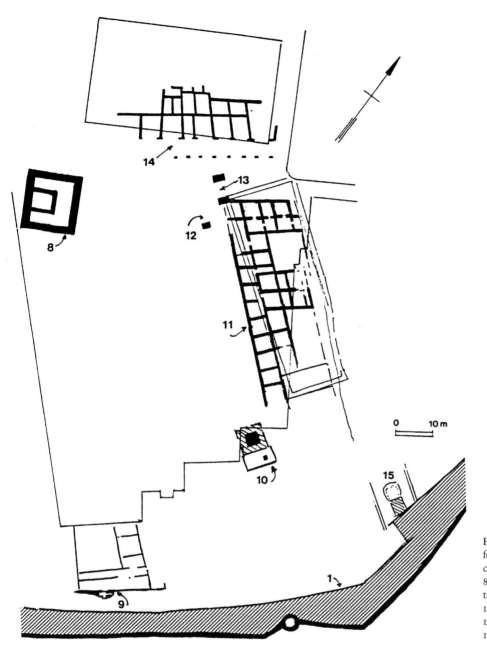

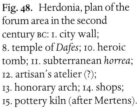

Fig. 48. Herdonia, plan of the forum area in the second century BC: 1. city wall; 8. temple of *Dafes*; 10. heroic tomb; 11. subterranean *horrea*; 12. artisan's atelier (?); 13. honorary arch; 14. shops; 15. pottery kiln (after Mertens).

tribunes occur in Ausculum, Salapia, Herdonia, and Venusia. The discovery in this zone[164] of Gracchan *cippi* and the political decision which left most of the *ager publicus* of Apulia undivided, a policy which Toynbee,[165] with picturesque, but effective exaggeration, describes as 'laisser faire for private enterprise', both underwrite the extensive traces of centuriation in the area between

Luceria, Ausculum, and Herdonia,[166] of which at least those in the Herdonian countryside should be considered beyond doubt of Gracchan origin.

The immediate effect of the Gracchan presence is evident in a number of extremely important archaeological finds from Herdonia and its surrounding countryside. It is, however, quite difficult in the urban context to say whether the construction in *opus incertum* of the large subterranean vaulted storehouses on the north side of the forum (Fig. 48)[167] should be attributed

---

[164] *AE* (1973), 222; see A. Russi and A. Valvo, 'Note sul nuovo termine graccano di Celenza Valfortore', in *Quinta Miscellanea Greca e Romana* (Rome, 1977), 225 f., and M. Pani, 'Su un nuovo cippo graccano dauno', *RIL* 61 (1977), 119 f.   [165] Toynbee, *Hannibal's Legacy*, ii. 239 f.

[166] Volpe, *La Daunia*, 50, 209 f.   [167] Mertens, *Ordona*, 8 (1988), 36 f.

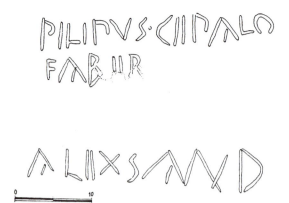

Fig. 49. Drawing of the inscription of Greek *faber* Pilipus Cepalo(nius ?), in the subterranean *horrea* at Herdonia (after Mertens).

to the presence of a Gracchan colony nearby or simply to the growing importance of the city, owing to its lines of communication with the ports of Sipontum and Salapia. Built perhaps on the site of a large, primitive, rectangular *horreum* without dividing partitions (Fig. 47, 6),[168] the structure was clearly modelled after the Roman *porticus Aemilia*,[169] and an inscription certifies that this *horreum* was executed by the Greek *faber* Pilipus Cepalo(nius ?), who, however, signed the work in Latin (Fig. 49).[170]

The most relevant archaeological discovery in the countryside is the modest farm (approximately 400 m²) in the locality of Posta Crusta[171] near Herdonia (Fig. 50). This can be attributed to a Gracchan colonist and is the first known example in Apulia of a villa of the 'Catonian' type. We know of only a few other examples of this farm type, perhaps also belonging to Gracchan colonists: the villas of S. Vito near Salapia,[172] and Masseria Nocelli near Nocera,[173] where, beginning from the middle of the fourth century BC,[174] there was

an explosion of farms, some of them to become great villas of the 'Varronian' type.[175] We know at least thirty-four of these structures, some quite exceptional[176] and almost all of the maritime type. The appearance of the 'Catonian' villas coincides with the diffusion of the Apulian wine amphorae Lamboglia 5, which were increasingly exported after the beginning of the first century BC.[177]

Beginning in the last quarter of the second century BC, the Romanization of Daunia was accelerated by the presence of these new Gracchan colonists alongside the previously existing ones of Luceria, Venusia, and Sipontum, and above all by the economic and social integration of Daunia into the broader context of the Italian peninsula. However, the region, in common with the many other areas of Italy involved in the same process of Romanization, retained its individual microeconomic peculiarities[178] to be reused in the new mechanism of Roman Italy's economy. The archaeological record is quite helpful for our understanding of this phenomenon, and the small town of Banzi–Bantia,[179] on the eastern border of Daunia, is particularly useful in reconstructing Daunia's history immediately prior to the Social War.

At the beginning of the third century Bantia, like Herdonia, fortified itself with a substantial *agger* preceded by a moat, thus reducing the size of the originally extensive and dispersed settlement to a few hectares. In the late second century BC, the northern part of the settlement, which has been explored by M. Tagliente,[180] was the scene of an urban reorganization which, without arriving at a 'hippodamic' regularity or pre-established modules, nevertheless ordered the

[168] Ibid. fig. 12.   [169] Coarelli, *Il Foro Boario*, 75 f.

[170] J. Mertens, 'Ordona (Foggia)—Cacciaguerra', *Taras* 9 (1989), 224. The text—*Pilipus Cepalo faber*, to be interpreted as *Philippur Cepalo(nius) faber* better than *Philippur Cepalō* (i.e. *Cepalū*, son of *Kephalos*) *faber*—has a strong epigraphic connection with the Latin signature of a Greek craftsman on architectural terracottas from the temple of the goddess Cupra at Cupra Maritima in Picenum (*CIL* IX, 6078, 75; *IG* XIV, 2404, 6), in the form *Dionisios | Coloponius | epoi*, and from Rimini, in the form *[Dio]nysios / Coloponius / epoi* (i.e. *Dionysius Coloponius ἐποίει*).

[171] G. De Boe, *NSA* (1975), 516 f.; Volpe, *La Daunia*, 130 f., no. 167.

[172] M. Marin, 'Scavi archeologici nella contrada S.Vito', *Archivio Storico Pugliese*, 17 (1964), 167 f.; Volpe, *La Daunia*, 174 f., no. 390.

[173] G. D. B. Jones, 'Il Tavoliere romano. L'agricoltura romana attraverso l'aerofotografia e lo scavo', *AClass* 32 (1980), 94 f.; Volpe, *La Daunia*, 127 f., no. 153.

[174] For these villas see the fundamental work by Volpe, *La Daunia*, 115 f., with a list of 428 rural sites spread on the Daunian territory, most of which show a phase between the 1st cent. BC and the 1st cent. AD.

[175] On the 'Varronian villa' cf. A. Carandini, 'La villa romana e la piantagione schiavistica', in Momigliano and Schiavone (eds.), *Storia di Roma*, iv (Turin, 1989), 101 f.

[176] Compare the great villas at Agnuli, near Mattinata (Volpe, *La Daunia*, 183, no. 402), at S. Maria di Merino, near Vieste (ibid. 198 f., no. 411), at Casalene, near Bovino (ibid. 140 f., no. 230), at Casa del Diavolo near Lavello (ibid. 150, no. 271), and at Avicenna, near Cagnano Varano (ibid. 202, no. 417), at Santannea, near Sannicandro Garganico (ibid. 207, no. 428), just to mention the excavated or better known examples.

[177] G.Volpe, 'Primi dati sulla circolazione delle anfore repubblicane nella Puglia settentrionale', in *Atti I Convegno di Studi sulla Puglia Romana*, Acts of Conference; Mesagne, 1986 (Galatina, 1988), 77; id., 'La circolazione delle anfore nella Daunia romana: dati preliminari', in *Amphores romaines et histoire économique*, Acts of Conference; Siena; 1986 (Rome, 1989), 629 f.

[178] As clearly shown by F. Grelle, 'Canosa. Le istituzioni, la società', in Giardina and Schiavone (eds.), *Società romana*, i. 181 f.

[179] On this town, little but very important from the point of view of the history of legal and religious institutions, a full account of archaeological discoveries and bibliography up to 1983 by A. Bottini, 'Banzi', in *Bibliografia Topografica della Colonizzazione Greca in Italia*, iii (1984), 390 f.

[180] M. Tagliente, *'Banzi'*, in Salvatore, *Basilicata*, 71 f.

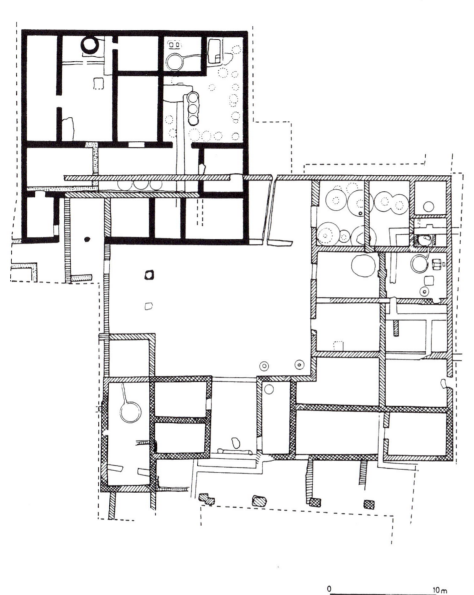

Fig. 50. Plan of the late second century BC farm (in black) in the locality of Posta Crusta near Herdonia (after Mertens).

0   10 m

streets according to orthogonal axes, marking off rectangular blocks of varying sizes (Fig. 51). This fact points unequivocally to the end of the old social relationships on which production was traditionally based and was fairly represented by the dispersed settlement of villages dominated by single families of *principes*, and to a much stronger trend toward urban organization than was present at the beginning of the previous century.

Further proof of the planned character of Bantia's urban reorganization is provided by the recent dis-covery in the same section of the city, but reused in a medieval wall, of a dedication in Latin characters but in Oscan language.[181] The text gives the name of the titular god of the dedication, that of the highest deity—*Zoves*, 'of Jupiter'—and the political authority responsible for the gift, *tr. pl.*, 'the tribune (or "tribunes") of the people'. This text is very important, because it gives flesh and blood to the activity of the *tribuni plebis*

[181] M. Torelli, 'Una nuova epigrafe di Bantia e la cronologia dello statuto municipale bantino', *Athenaeum*, 61 (1983), 252 f.

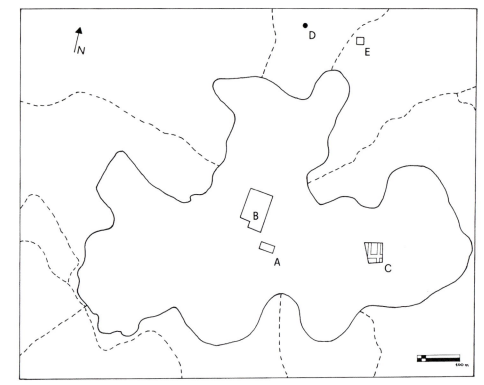

Fig. 51. Plan of the conjectured extension of the late Samnite and Roman Bantia the second century BC: A. the augural temple; B. the medieval abbey; C. second-century BC quarters showing a regular grid of streets; D. suburban shrine in the 'Fontana dei Monaci' area; E. location of the second-century BC farm in the Mancamasone area (drawing C. Masseria).

known from the Oscan Law of Bantia, as we shall see in a moment; such activity, very unusual according to the Roman constitutional standards, derives directly from that of their counterparts in the nearby Latin colony of Venusia, where an inscription commemorates the construction of a road by a *tribunus plebis*, a certain Q. Ovius Ov.f.[182] The exceptional role of these local *tribuni plebis*, undoubtedly the product of local social tensions reflecting those which affected Rome at that time, allows us to relate the inscribed document to another, and much better known, epigraphic text, the *Tabula Bantina Osca*, a constitutional law of the city inscribed on bronze also in Latin characters but in the Oscan language. This document appears to be based on the constitution of a Latin colony, most likely that of the nearby Venusia.[183]

To this series of archaeological and inscriptional documents we can add another important archaeological–epigraphic find, the *templum augurale* of Bantia,[184] which I discovered a number of years ago, and which was meant to create in the little Daunian town a *templum in terris*, to make virtually perfect the Bantine imitation of the Roman juridical models. This *templum* would serve to take the *auspicia* by observing the flight of birds, a necessary religious complement to the assumption of *imperium* by the magistrate (i.e. by the republican political–military power) according to a religious institution that was already present in an indigenous form in the complex of the Cimitero area at Lavello,[185] but that in the inscriptions on the *cippi* of the *templum* appears to be completely changed—except that the names of the deities are still Oscan—in order to adapt it conceptually and linguistically to Roman doctrine. This extraordinary simultaneous emergence of such a wealth of archaeological, urbanistic, epigraphic, and institutional evidence in one small centre like Bantia proves that we are dealing with a concerted effort to remake the face of the city, the patterns of

[182] *ILLRP* 699.

[183] This is the opinion I expressed more than twenty years ago, when publishing the new fragment of the Tabula Bantina (*ArchClass* 21), and nothing of what has been subsequently published (on this subject, mainly H. Galsterer, 'Die "Lex Osca Tabulae Bantinae". Eine Bestandaufnahme', *Chiron*, i (1971), 191 f., a view expressed in a more general perspective in his otherwise excellent book, *Herrschaft und Verwaltung im republikanischen Italien* (Munich, 1976)) has convinced me of a later chronology for the Oscan text, i.e. at the time of the Social War or even after this war. More recently on this *lex*, L. Del Tutto Palma, *La tavola bantina (sezione osca): proposte di rilettura* (Urbino, 1983).

[184] M. Torelli, 'Un "templum augurale" d'età repubblicana a Bantia', *RAL* 8th ser., 21 (1966), 293 f., and 'Contributi al supplemento del C.l.L. IX', *RAL* 8th ser., 24 (1969), 39 f.   [185] See n. 12.

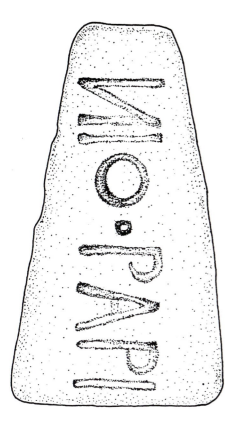

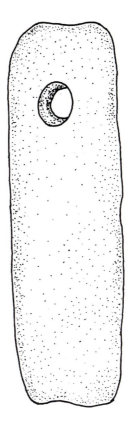

Fig. 52. Oscan inscription mentioning a *Nio(msiís) Papi(ís)*, on a loom-weight from Lavello (drawing M. Monella).

social life, and the entire complex of institutions animating the public sphere, and all of course as much in the image of Rome as possible. We are able to deduce, from the chronology of the *Tabula Bantina Latina* (which, due to the presence of the *iusiurandum in legem*, must be from around 100 BC), that the urban and political reorganization took place between 100 and 90 BC. Its principal inspiration was the nearby Latin centre of Venusia, and its objective was to obtain for the local ruling classes full rights as citizens in Rome's eyes: thence the choice of a statute of *ius Latii*, as was the statute of Venusia, an objective which required it to assume all the trappings—political, religious, urbanistic, and institutional—of a city, or better of the *urbanitas*, the ethical model indispensable for the complete integration of the local élites into the Roman political structure.

Beyond its obvious political power, Rome also wielded ever increasing cultural influence in the thirty years before the Social War. Roman funeral rites and cremation became increasingly common throughout Daunia, where the ancient funerary ideology and ancestral practices such as inhumation in contracted position had been abandoned for quite some time. If

we lack for the moment macroscopic evidence of the local ruling classes' total identification with Roman architectural (and ideological) models, which appear with ever greater frequency in neighbouring Lucania between the second and first centuries BC (as the examples of the Roman plan of the house at Civita di Tricarico[186] and of the farmhouse at Monte Moltone di Tolve[187] in nearby Lucania clearly show), we need only examine a simple loom-weight from Lavello–Forentum inscribed in the Samnite alphabet and language, final evidence from the late second century BC of the continuous Samnite pressure on Daunia. The inscription (Fig. 52) of the proprietor's name, *Nio(msiís) Papi(ís)*, demonstrates Latin's linguistic influence in the area through the introduction of the letter 'o',

[186] Russo, *Edilizia domestica*, 182. This astonishing house of perfect Roman plan, placed on top of a fortified Lucanian *oppidum*, at a height of more than 3,500 feet, was commissioned *c.*100 BC by a local aristocrat, together with an adjacent little temple of Etrusco-Italic type; patently an ostentation of his high status, exerting maybe even the control of the cult performed in the adjoining shrine, possibly his possession of Roman citizenship.

[187] Russo, *Edilizia domestica*, 173 f. The villa has a first phase (late 4th cent. BC) with a plan close to those of the contemporay Greek (e.g. the so-called Dema House in Attica) and Hellenized Italic farmhouses; later (late 3rd cent. BC) it acquires an aspect close to that of a Roman house.

previously unknown in the Oscan alphabet, and the consequent hyper-latinization of the praenomen, *Niomsiis* in place of *Niumsiis*.[188] Nor should it be forgotten that between the two centuries (and certainly much earlier as well) there were Roman citizens of high social rank present in Daunian cities, as the massacre of a number of them during the Social War shows.[189]

The close relationship between Venusia and the surrounding Daunio-Samnite territory, which perhaps originates from its anomalous beginnings as a colony of 20,000 inhabitants, becomes very clear during the Social War. This conflict was provoked by a series of concurrent factors, but perhaps mainly by the socio-economic pressure that Rome exerted on the indigenous ruling classes, who finally responded by demanding total integration, politically too, into the Roman state. In fact, Venusia was the only Latin colony in the peninsula actively to support the revolt, a fact certainly due to the complex political, economic, and social relations that had begun to form at the colony's inception, and that continued to develop over two centuries of close contact with the local population, even if it is quite likely that this choice was also conditioned by the presence of the Italic general C. Vidacilius in the area.[190] Although recorded in an unfortunately fragmentary manner, the conflict, brought to a rapid conclusion in the course of 89 BC with the retaking of Venusia, the burning of Salapia and the probable punishment of the revolt's leaders by Q. Caecilius Metellus Pius and C. Cosconius, resulted, as far as we know, in relatively minor consequences for the local population and in the inscription of the Apulian communities into Roman tribes. This phenomenon, thoroughly examined by Pani,[191] shows that in some way the 'pacification' of the area could be attributed to Marian patronage, without however being involved in Sullan vendettas, if we are not to attribute to Sulla even the foundation of the mysterious colony of Firmum Apulum, in the vicinity of Candela.[192]

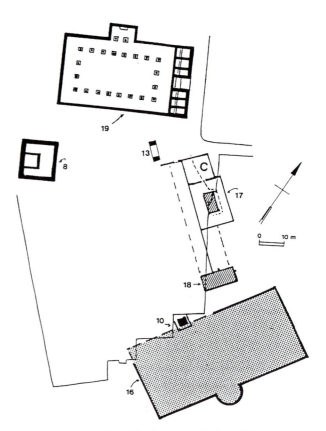

Fig. 53. Herdonia, plan of the forum area in the mid-first century BC: 8. temple of *Dafes*; 10. *heroon*; 13. honorary arch; 16. *palaestra*; 17. bath complex; 18. *piscina*; 19. basilica (after Mertens).

The following half century is characterized by the urbanization of Apulia,[193] which is to say the completion of Daunia's assimilation into what was finally destined to merge into the Augustan *tota Italia*.[194] Another example from Herdonia can perhaps shed more light on the obscure events which befell the country in this tormented period of the Civil Wars. The post-Gracchan and pre-Augustan phase of the local forum contains (Fig. 53), in addition to a basilica built on the shorter side (Fig. 53, 19) of the piazza, an interesting reconstruction of the old *horrea* on the north-east side of the forum. This extremely large and harmoniously planned group of structures included, on the lower level, an honorary arch (Fig. 53, 13) and an axial complex of rooms centred on a vast hall with a pool (Fig. 53, 17–18), and, on the upper level, a large square encircled by a turreted wall. On the long side of

[188] M. Torelli, 'Numerius Papius, sannita di Forentum', in Tagliente (ed.), *Italici*, 265 f.   [189] App. *B. civ.* I. 190.

[190] On these events, see the comments by F. Grelle, in Giardina and Schiavone (eds.), *Società romana*.

[191] M. Pani, 'Sulla distribuzione delle tribù romane in Apulia e Calabria dopo la guerra sociale', *Ricerche e Studi del Museo Provinciale F.Ribezzo, Brindisi*, 9 (1976), 119 f.

[192] This mysterious colony, witnessed by *ILLRP* 592, explains the circumstance, unknown until the discovery of that inscription, that the Latin colony of Firmum on the Adriatic coast received the epithet Picenum, to be distinguished from the (later) colony near Candela in Apulia, purposely called Firmum Apulum.

[193] M. Pani, 'I "municipia" romani', in *Atti I Convegno di Studi sulla Puglia Romana*, 21 f.

[194] M. Torelli, 'Gesellschaft und Wirtschaftsformen der augusteischen Zeit', in H. G. Martin (ed.), *Kaiser Augustus und die verlorene Republik*, Catalogue of the Exhibition; Berlin, 1988 (Mainz, 1988), 23 f.

Plate 33. Foggia, Museo. Fragment of a marble heroic statue from Herdonia (courtesy of M. Mazzei).

the hall containing the pool, a complex of uncertain use, but perhaps recognizable as the meeting-place of the *juvenes* who performed in the palaestra immediately above.

This elaborate monumental setting permits us to formulate a hypothesis concerning the identity of this personage, buried in the *heroon* and honoured with the monumental gymnasium, a man whose *floruit* can be archaeologically dated to the middle years of the first century BC. This date is confirmed by the style of the statue, which is analogous to that of Cartilius Poplicola from Ostia[198] and the heroic statue from the theatre in Cassino (representing Varro?),[199] both dating from no later than the second quarter of the first century. At that time a minor personality in the Roman firmament, a M. Hostilius, was active in the area. Vitruvius[200] remembers this personage for two acts of philanthropy, the reconstruction of Salapia after the fire of 89 BC and the draining of the swamps around the city.[201] Cichorius[202] has long ago identified this man with M. Hostilius M.f.Vel., an *eques* from Picenum who belonged to the *consilium* of Pompeius Strabo in Ausculum,[203] and who was therefore a member of the powerful Pompeian clientele in Picenum, as his tribe confirms.

This philanthropic gesture, which appears to have also indirectly benefited Herdonia because of its links to the great lagoon of Salapia and the granary ports of Sipontum and Salapia, which had become increasingly important for the *frumentationes* of Rome (here we are reminded of the *horrea* of Herdonia mentioned previously), was certainly not a simple act of charity, but rather a political manœuvre aimed at developing urban and Italic clientele, which would in turn lead to further enrichment and the advancement of political careers, in this case tied to the fate of the Pompeian party. It is likewise possible that this M. Hostilius of Picenum had for sometime been associated with Apulian clients through his probable Adriatic interests.

this wall a large *exedra* was built, in order to emphasize a monumental *heroon* 'a dado'(Fig. 53, 16)[195] placed on the opposite side of the same square. As I have had occasion to state elsewhere,[196] this large square must be interpreted as a great gymnasium built to honour a personage of rank, the lower part of whose marble statue (Pl. 33), significantly portrayed in a pose similar to that of Neptune or of the Rondanini Alexander,[197] has fortunately been recovered. Clearly this gymnasium, centred on the *heroon* with the associated tomb, was the ideological focus of a complex which included perhaps also the triumphal arch and the area around

[195] Mertens, *Ordona*, 8 (1988), 40 f.

[196] M. Torelli, 'Il "diribitorium" di Alba Fucens e il "campus" eroico di Herdonia', in J. Mertens (ed.), *Comunità indigene e romanizzazione*, Acts of Conference; Rome, 1990 (Brussels and Rome, 1991), 39 f.

[197] First published by E. Lippolis, 'La cultura locale nella mimesi del modello urbano', in Lippolis and M. Mazzei, *La Daunia antica*, 282, fig. 338.

[198] F. Zevi, 'Monumenti e aspetti culturali di Ostia repubblicana', in P. Zanker (ed.), *Hellenismus in Mittelitalien*, AGAW, n. 90 (Göttingen, 1976), 56 f. (with previous bibliography).

[199] G. Carettoni, 'Statua eroica da Cassino', *MPAA* 6 (1943), 53 f., pls. 1–4; F. Coarelli, 'Il ritratto di Varrone. Un tentativo di paradigma indiziario', in '*Splendida civitas nostra*'. Studi in onore di A. Frona (Rome, 1995), 269–80.

[200] Vitruv. 4. 1. 11–12.

[201] On these events, see the perceptive pages by E. Gabba, 'La rifondazione di Salapia', *Athenaeum*, 61 (1983), 514 f.

[202] F. Cichorius, *Römische Studien* (Leipzig and Berlin, 1922), 166.

[203] *ILLRP* 515.

A very plausible hypothesis if, as many maintain,[204] he was a descendant of the brothers Hostilii Catones, the previously mentioned members of the Scipionic agrarian reform committee who had been tried for corruption in 187 BC. Whatever the historical connection of the Hostilii of Picenum with Daunia may be, there can be no doubt concerning that of the son of M. Hostilius, L. Hostilius Dasianus. Senator, rather than a simple knight like his father, he was also quite likely *tribunus plebis* in 72 BC[205] and governor of Achaea around 70 BC.[206] We know unequivocally that this *inquies animi*[207] was descended from Daunian stock, as the name Dasianus, whether deriving from an adoption or from maternal kinship, reveals.

Probably Pompey's envoy during his victorious war against the pirates in 67 BC, L. Hostilius Dasianus was part of the staff of Cn. Lentulus Clodianus, commander of the vast Adriatic military zone, along with the commander's nephews.[208] In Herdonia, the *heroon*, the gymnasium with the building of the *juvenes*, and (significantly) the arch were all dedicated to this man. So too was the statue, which depicts him as a victorious admiral, in much the same manner as other victors of naval battles, Poplicola and Varro, were portrayed. His is the first certain name of a senator of Daunian origin to emerge from the late republican era, a first small mark on the blank pages of the region's senate album that I tried to investigate more than twenty years ago.[209] But this small discovery has another and perhaps more important significance. It unequivocally reveals the importance, still relevant even after the concession of citizenship to the Italic peoples following the Social War, of marriages and clientele as instruments to form alliances capable of producing immediate advantages for the family and prospects of social advancement for its descendants, longstanding methods practised by the aristocracy to accumulate wealth, prestige and power: a final record, if one wishes, of the culture of the *principes*, perhaps among the less fortunate of the many that Italy saw rise and fall in its long arc of history prior to the Roman empire.

---

[204] T. P. Wiseman, *New Men in the Roman Senate: 139 BC—14 AD* (Oxford, 1971), 55.

[205] As certified by the inscription *ILLRP* 465a, with the comments by A. Degrassi.   [206] Schol. Cic. *Verr. act.* 1. 6.

[207] Sall. *Hist.* fr. 55.   [208] Flor. 1. 41. 9–10.

[209] M. Torelli, 'Contributo dell'archeologia alla storia sociale—L'Etruria e l'Apulia', *DArch* 4–5 (1970–1), 439 f.

5

FICTILES FABULAE

REPRESENTATION AND ROMANIZATION IN THE REPUBLICAN TERRACOTTA FIGURED CYCLES

1. Introduction

Hic templum Iunoni ingens Sidonia Dido
condebat, donis opulentum et numine divae,
aerea cui gradibus surgebant limina nexaeque
aere trabes, foribus cardo stridebat aënis.

. . . .

namque sub ingenti lustrat dum singula templo
reginam opperiens, dum quae fortuna sit urbi
artificumque manus intra se operumque   455
laborem miratur, videt Iliacas ex ordine pugnas
bellaque iam fama totum vulgata per orbem,
Atridas Priamumque et saevum ambobus Achillem.
constitit et lacrimans 'quis iam locus' inquit 'Achate,
quae regio in terra nostri non plena laboris?   460
En Priamus. Sunt hic etiam sua praemia laudi;
sunt lacrimae rerum et mentem mortalia tangunt.
solve metus; feret haec aliquam tibi fama salutem.

THESE FAMOUS VERSES[1] REPRESENT A PERFECT epigraph for this article of mine, reflecting as they do the intense emotional impact aroused by the great figured representations put up to ornament temple buildings. Such depictions, whether carved or painted, were in fact intended for the collective memory, persuasion, and elevation of the ancient onlookers[2] and not for the classificatory pseudo-typological and pseudo-stylistic libido of contemporary archaeologists: the extraordinary Virgilian description of the temple of Juno in the mythical Carthage of Dido proves useful in recalling this fact to all those (and they are not a few) who have ended up by losing track of this very banal reality, which is the substance of our work as scholars of ancient history.

In the harmonious Virgilian verses therefore, Aeneas and the faithful Achates climb the hill of Juno and admire the majestic dimensions of the temple; then, while they wander round the building, they recognize the events of one section of the decoration, which obviously—judging by the movement of the protagonists ('. . . dum lustrat . . .') and by the quantity of the events narrated, almost ten episodes—must have been depicted in a long continuous pictorial frieze (further on in verse 465, Virgil speaks explicitly of *pictura*), a frieze in which the episodes of the Iliad are unravelled one after another, of the Cypria and of Aethiopis, virtually until the outset of the Ilioupersis: it is possible that Virgil had the *bellum Iliacum plurimis tabulis* in mind, a proper pictorial cycle, the work of the late classical painter Theoros,[3] which decorated the early Augustan *porticus Philippi*, just as it is probable that the *Tabulae Iliacae*, which were fairly popular among aristocrats in the poet's day,[4] were not unrelated to the composition of these famous Virgilian images. The psychological impact on the two spectators, directly affected by the depictions, is immense and Virgil works in a very able manner to have them discover in a dramatic sequence the various protagonists in a series of paintings with large figures: the very close link

---

[1] Virg. *Aen.* 1. 446 f.
[2] See the remarks by A. Rouveret, 'Les lieux de la mémoire publique. Quelque remarques sur la fonction des tableaux dans la cité', in *Opus*, 6–8 (1987–9), 101 f.

[3] Plin. *NH* 35. 144.
[4] Cf. the standard work by A. Sadurska, *Les Tables Iliaques* (Warsaw, 1956).

between memory and image, between poetry and illustration, is confirmed by the fact that a little later, in the formal banquet given for him by the Carthaginian queen, the Trojan hero Aeneas, urged on by Dido (the renowned 'infandum, regina, iubes renovare dolorem . . .'),[5] will recount the sequel to the events depicted in the series of large figure paintings in the temple, i.e. the fall of Troy and his own personal adventure within the great tragic scenario of the Ilioupersis. The depiction therefore acts as a prologue to Aeneas' later narration and as a spur to his memory and that of his public.

As for the pictures of the temple of Carthage, however, Virgil's *inventio* is not born of an innovation introduced by the Augustan poet with no traditions behind it, nor it is a mere pretext for allowing the later flashback narration of the earlier adventures of the protagonist hero, thus closely following the Odyssean model which is at the base of the first six books of the Aeneid. The Hellenistic tradition of the *ekphrasis*, to which in some way Virgil refers, does in fact have an undoubted antecedent in Callimachus' *Aitia*, where the antiquarian subject found certain nourishment in the figured decorations of antique monuments or in particularly significant *agalmata*: in the Callimachean poem two examples will suffice, those of the *aitia* of the statue of Hera in Samus and of the anchor of the ship Argo in Cyzicus.[6] Neither, in the light of the content, does the Virgilian *ekphrasis* appear to be used as a pretext. The temple of Dido's Carthage is opportunely decorated with Trojan scenes, since the goddess worshipped in the sanctuary is Hera-Juno, who secured from Zeus the end of the traditionally hostile city of Troy and who, in the guise of Tanit, required by the *interpretatio punica*, protects instead the newly founded city of Carthage:[7] representing the Trojan war is not, therefore, a mere narrative expedient of Virgil's, but a feature characterized by a real ideological similarity. For our purpose it serves to remind us of the relevance that those conceptual systems assumed in the ancient way of thinking, which linked buildings, images, and messages together in a unifying, though polysemic, mechanism.

From this standpoint, therefore, Virgil's text would turn out to be so much the more meaningful if we were certain of the truth of the hypothesis that he had a precedent for this passage in the ancient *Bellum Poenicum*. For it has been authoritatively suggested that Virgil's predecessor, Cn. Naevius, drew inspiration from the pediment of a large temple[8] for his own digression on the Ilioupersis similar to that narrated by Aeneas (we do not know whether to Dido or to King Latinus).[9] Such a temple could be the Olympieion in Agrigentum, in which, according to the famous description of Diodorus,[10] the Ilioupersis featured together with the Gigantomachy: we actually seem to have a fragment of Naevius' description of that Gigantomachy.[11] According to this hypothesis, Naevius would have seen the famous pediments whilst serving in the army in Sicily in the course of the first Punic war.[12] The centuries-old example of the Greek world did in fact assign to the theme of the Gigantomachy the function of evoking the glorious victory of the forces of Good, in this case impersonated by the Romans, over those of Evil, in this case the Carthaginians. As far as the Ilioupersis is concerned, in the Greek propagandistic stereotype this was a subject totally aimed at bringing out Greek heroism; according to a stereotype well known through Lykophron's poem and at home in cultivated Roman circles since early Hellenistic times, the same theme embodied the initial moment of the long providential story of Aeneas destined to lead to the birth of Rome and therefore to the glory of the Roman empire.

If this interpretation of the fragments of the *Bellum Poenicum* concerning Aeneas and his flight from Troy is correct, the saturnian verses of Naevius ought ideally to have presented the two titanic clashes—that of the gods against the giants and that of the Greeks against of

---

[5] Virg. *Aen.* 2. 3.   [6] Call. *Aet.*, frr. 100–1, 108 Pfeiffer.

[7] F. Della Corte, 'La Iuno-Astarte virgiliana', in *Atti I Congresso Internazionale Studi Fenici e Punici* (Rome, 1983), iii. 651 f.

[8] The hypothesis produced by H. Fränkel, 'Griechische Bildung in altrömischen Epen—II', *Hermes* 70 (1935), 60 f., though it can be traced back to an old essay of Bergk, 'Ueber die Sprache der altrömischen Epiker', *Zeitschrift für Altertumswissenschaft*, 9 (1842), 191. Fränkel's conjecture has been widely accepted (among others by H. T. Rowell, 'The Original Form of Naevius' Bellum Poenicum', *AJPh* 68 (1947), 28 f.; for a *recensus* of scholarly opinions, see M. Barchiesi, *Nevio epico* (Padua, 1962), 271 f., though other scholars have proposed alternative solutions, such as e.g. a description of a shield (E. Fränkel, 'The Giants in the Poem of Naevius', *JRS* 44 (1954), 14; *contra* H. T. Rowell, review of S. Mariotti, *Il Bellum Poenicum e l'arte di Nevio* (Rome, 1955), in *AJPh* 78 (1957), 420). The problem of the structure of Naevius' poem should be probably reconsidered in the light of the discovery of the inscriptions of the gymnasium of Tauromenion (G. Manganaro, 'Una biblioteca storica nel Ginnasio di Tauromenion e il P.Oxy.1241', *PP* (1974), 389 f.), where we are told that in Fabius Pictor, generally considered one of Naevius' sources, the arrival of Aeneas was preceded by the coming to Latium of Heracles.

[9] As conjectured by G. Serrao, 'Nevio, Bellum Poenicum, fr. 23 Mo.', *Helikon* 5 (1965), 514 f.   [10] Diod. Sic. 13. 82. 4.

[11] Naev. *bell.Poen.* fr. 19 ap. Priscian. 1, 198 Hertz.

[12] The relevant evidence is collected by F. V. Marmorale, *Naevius poeta*, 2nd edn. (Florence, 1967), 21 f., 26 f.

the Trojans—against the background of the other great battle, also of particular importance for the result of the war of Rome against Carthage—possibly the first of the two terrible sacks of Agrigentum, the capital of the Punic eparchy of Sicily, in 261 BC at the hands of the Romans. Such structural analogies between the three wars would allow a topos dear to the ancient mentality, the cyclical correspondence between *aetates*,[13] the sack of Agrigentum being situated in historical times, i.e. in the *aetas hominum*, while the cycles depicted on the pediments would portray the two previous *aetates*, the *aetas divina* of the Gigantomachy and the *aetas heroica* of the Ilioupersis. In allusively reproposing Naevius' model, Virgil might perhaps also have underlined the 'predestination' of the fall of Carthage (a theme extremely clear in Polybius' well-known description of Scipio Aemilianus contemplating Carthage in flames),[14] by means of an itinerary Troy—Agrigentum—Carthage, somehow reflecting Aeneas' itinerary. Coming back to our theme, such an itinerary seems again to be reflected in the repetition of the 'proleptic' myth of the *Troiae halosis*, first in reality and then in the highly effective *imagerie* of the decorations of the great civic temples.

Unfortunately we have lost virtually all the pictorial representations put up to adorn ancient sacred and public buildings, expressions of ancient painting, which have rightly been defined as the 'art-guide' of antiquity. The three-dimensional equivalents or complements of such paintings, be they relief friezes or pedimental sculptures, however noble and of particular interest for the spectator they may have been (as we know from the not infrequent recurrence of their mention by Pausanias), are considerably less rich in narrative possibility than the painted panels or friezes.[15] Nevertheless, as we learn from the indissoluble connection between 'triumphal painting' and 'Roman historic reliefs',[16] the link between painting and sculpture, be it in the round in pediments, or in high- or low-relief in pediments and friezes, is fundamental for reconstructing the logic of ancient propaganda art.

2. The Diffusion of a Model: Architectural Terracottas and Etrusco-Italic Temples

The conquest of Italy involved, as is well known, a grandiose effort on the part of Rome, not just in the military sense, but also in a political and organizational way, centred on the foundation of colonies of Latin right (and to a lesser extent, on those of Roman right) and on distributions of land done *viritim*. A necessary and important complement to that policy of foundations of colonies and distributions of land was the grant of the *civitas sine suffragio* and to a lesser extent, of the *civitas optimo iure*. The assimilation of Roman culture and ideology on the part of Italic peoples by the end of the second century BC was virtually total, as proved by the well-known case of Bantia,[17] the product of the prestige and of the pressure of the Roman model, which in the eyes of the allies embodied the power of a successful imperial expansion. But such assimilation was also promoted by conscious persuasion, which, as the previous chapters have made clear, have always found particularly fertile ground in the religious sphere—i.e. in the world of myth and rite.

The close link between Roman colonization of the mid-Republican period and the diffusion of anatomic ex-votos was emphasized by A. Comella and by me some time ago,[18] and more evidence has emerged in recent years, thanks also to the publication of the 'Corpus of Votive Deposits in Italy' (I'm thinking here primarily of the important edition of the Belvedere deposit in Lucera),[19] filling in the picture in significant ways, outlining interesting areas of interference in the phenomenon, especially in the contact zones between different religious traditions. In this particular respect and purely by way of example, we might take the manifest differences of behaviour between the area of the Sabines and that of the Aequicoli, in the same

---

[13] See the topical correspondence among the mythological panels of the *Ara Pacis Augustae*, M. Torelli, *Typology and Structure of the Roman Historical Reliefs*, 2nd edn. (Ann Arbor, 1992), 38 f.

[14] Polyb. 38. 21; cf. App. *Lib.* 132 = Polyb. 38. 22; Diod. 32. 24; cf. A. E. Astin, *Scipio Aemilianus* (Oxford, 1967), 282 f.

[15] All this is well analysed by A. Rouveret, *Histoire et imaginaire de la peinture ancienne (ve siècle av. J.-C.—1er siècle ap. J.-C.)* (Rome, 1989), 129 f.

[16] See Torelli, *Typology and Structure*, 119 f.

[17] Cf. M. Torelli, 'Un "templum augurale" d'età repubblicana a Bantia', *RAL* 8th ser., 21 (1966), 293 f.; id., 'Contributi al supplemento del C.I.L. IX', *RAL* 8th ser., 24 (1969), 39 f.; [D. Adamesteanu] and M. Torelli, 'Il nuovo frammento della Tabula Bantina', in *ArchClass.* 21 (1969), 30 f.; M. Torelli, 'Una nuova epigrafe di Bantia e la cronologia dello statuto municipale bantino', *Athenaeum*, 61 (1983), 252 f.; see Ch. 4.

[18] First description of this link by M. Torelli, 'Stipi votive', in F. Coarelli, *Roma medio repubblicana*, Catalogue of the Exhibition; Rome, 1973 (Rome, 1973), 138 f.; full analysis of the evidence by A. M. Comella, 'Complessi votivi in Italia in epoca medio- e tardo-repubblicana', *MEFRA* 93 (1981), 717 f.

[19] M. C. D'Ercole, *La stipe votiva del Belvedere di Lucera* (= 'Corpus delle Stipi Votive in Italia', ii: 2) (Rome, 1990).

compass of territory acquired by Rome on a single occasion through the conquests of M' Curius Dentatus. On one hand we have the votive deposits of Latin type at Sabine Trebula Mutuesca[20] and at Aequicolan Corvaro[21] and on the other hand the votive deposits of Umbrian type at Plestia[22] or strongly influenced by Sabine culture at Nursia.[23] These diversities reflect the difference in treatment of the areas after the Roman conquest and the consequences of different types of population mix. Trebula and Corvaro, with their more distinctly Roman cultural and religious characteristics, suggest that their territories were included in the *agri quaestorii*[24] and were therefore lands primarily, if not exclusively inhabited by Roman citizens, while the votive deposits of Nursia and Plestia, with their mixed character, partly of Latin and partly of Umbro-Sabine flavour, perfectly reflect the situation of the *praefecturae* —and particularly, in the case just cited, the *praefectura Nursina* and the *praefectura Plestina*—where, for some time at least, *cives optimo iure* cohabited with *cives sine suffragio*.[25]

When we move to scrutinize the diffusion of the architectural terracottas of Etrusco-Italic type, we find several elements in common with those we have seen concerning votive customs, but also some significant differences. The fact is, a substantial basic variation exists between the two phenomena, not only on the functional and conceptual level (actually architectural models and ritual traditions are incommensurable), but also in their genesis. Indeed, while the votive deposits with anatomic material originate in a territory which, starting from southern and central Etruria, includes Latium and northern-central Campania, the architectural decorations of the so-called Etrusco-Italic type originate very definitely within the limits of Etruria itself and of Latium, where they have common origins (Fig. 54) and follow a homogeneous development since the archaic period,[26] if we ignore a few slight regional differences and a greater southern Etruscan and Latin precocity compared to northern and central Etruria.

In other words, although, with only a few differences, we find in Campanian territory the same use of anatomic ex-votos of southern Etruscan and Latin type, Campania follows its own very distinct formula in architectural decoration, with a proper, specific tradition of technical knowledge and a well-defined cultural background,[27] on which M. Bonghi has recently produced a book with a series of important observations.[28] This circumstance is of a remarkable interest when it comes to the reconstruction of the various forms of the Romanization process in Italy. If indeed we go on to analyse closely the distribution of the architectural terracottas of Etrusco-Italic type, we note (as a few years ago I was able to do in a very brief form and as M. J. Strazzulla has confirmed with further arguments)[29] that outside the area of primary development constituted by Etruria and Latium, they are not only consistently present in the Latin and Roman colonies or where there are extensive viritane land distributions, but in specific zones they are found only in lands occupied by Roman or Latin citizens. That this assertion corresponds to the truth is proved above all by the situation in the Cisalpine area, where the activity of Roman colonists is in strong contrast to the political, cultural, and artisan traditions of the indigenous Celtic, Ligurian, and Venetic peoples. As a matter of fact, architectural terracottas are known from the following cities of Cisalpine Gaul:

[20] P. Santoro, 'Il deposito votivo di Trebula Mutuesca. Riesame critico alla luce dei nuovi scavi', *Archeologia laziale*, 8 (1987), 352 f.

[21] A. M. Reggiani Massarini, *Santuario degli Equicoli a Corvaro*, Lavori e studi di archeologia pubblicati dalla Soprintendenza Archeologica di Roma, II (Rome, 1988).

[22] D. Manconi and M. C. De Angelis, 'Il santuario di Ancarano di Norcia', *DArch* 3rd ser., 5: I (1987), 17 f.: this short, but valuable account reports that in this important sanctuary abundant materials of Roman origin (*skyphoi* of the Ferrara 585 Group; pottery of the well-known Roman 'Atelier des petites estampilles'; *pocola*; coins) and a few anatomic ex-votos (such as, for instance, a veiled woman's head: ibid. 26, fig. 24; also votive uteri: ibid. figs. 25–6) were found together with little bronze figurines of the typical Umbrian manufacture of various dates (ibid. 23 f., figs. 16–19).

[23] Unsatisfactory, preliminary report by U. Ciotti, in *Atti I Conv.St.Umbri* (Perugia, 1964), 100 f.; see also the inscriptions from the sanctuary, published by A. E. Feruglio, in *Antichità dell'Umbria a Leningrado*, Catalogue of the Exhibition; Leningrad, 1990 (Perugia, 1990), 355 f., which mention the Umbro-Sabine goddess *Cupra* with the epithet *Mater Plestina*.

[24] As proposed by E. Gabba, 'Allora i Romani conobbero per la prima volta la ricchezza', *AIIN* 36 (1989), 9 f. (= *Del buon uso della ricchezza* (Milan, 1988), 19 f.).

[25] On this subject full treatment by M. Humbert, *Municipium et civitas sine suffragio* (Rome, 1978), esp. 356 f. (Nursia), and 400 f. (Plestia).

[26] Half a century after its publication the standard work is still A. Andrén, *Architectural Terracottas from Etrusco-Italic Temples*, Skrifter utgivna av Svenska Institutet i Rom, 4°, vi: 1–2 (Lund and Leipzig, 1940), henceforth abbreviated as Andrén.

[27] Standard work by H. Koch, *Dachterrakotten aus Campanien mit Ausschluss von Pompei* (Berlin, 1912).

[28] M. Bonghi (ed.), *Artigiani e botteghe nell'Italia preromana* (Rome, 1990).

[29] M. Torelli, 'Edilizia pubblica in Italia centrale tra guerra sociale ed età augustea: ideologia e classi sociali', in M. Cébeillac (ed.), *Les 'Bourgeoisies' municipales italiennes aux IIème et Ier siècles av. J.-C.*, Acts of the Colloquium; Naples, 1981 (Rome, 1983), 243 f.; M. J. Strazzulla, 'Le terrecotte architettoniche. Le produzioni dal IV al I sec.a.C.', in A. Giardina and A. Schiavone (eds.), *Società romana e produzione schiavistica* (Rome and Bari 1981), 187 f. (henceforth abbreviated as Strazzulla); ead., *Le terrecotte architettoniche della Venetia romana* (Rome, 1987), 16 f.

Fig. 54. Map of distribution of architectural terracottas of Etrusco-Italic type: hachured the original area; in grey the second-century BC diffusion as a consequence of imitation (Umbrian area) or of the influence of Roman colonization (Picene and Samnite areas) (drawing A. Trapassi).

Placentia, a Latin colony of 218 BC, reinforced in 190 BC, where antefixes showing a Genius with *thymiateria* have turned up, belonging perhaps to a shrine of a *prothyraios* god and dating from the late second century BC, a group of terracottas still awaiting a closer scrutiny (Fig. 54, no. 1).[30]

Cremona, a Latin colony of 218 BC, reinforced in 190 BC, where we know a fragment of pedimental sculpture apparently in the round, dating from the first half of the first century BC (Fig. 54, no. 2).[31]

Aquileia, a Latin colony of 181 BC, where various terracottas pertaining to urban and extra-urban sacred buildings have turned up, starting with the extraordinary figured pediment of Monastero and its related revetment plaques, to which one may add terracottas belonging to a second temple in the same area of Monastero and to a shrine in the suburban area at Strassoldo-Cisis (Fig. 54, no. 3).[32]

Luna, a Roman colony of 177 BC of the 'new' type after the end of the Latin foundations, i.e. characterized by extensive grants of land, whose architectural terracottas with the associated figured pediments

[30] M. Pensa, *La decorazione architettonica in Emilia Romagna: aspetti e problemi*, in *Studi sulla città antica. L'Emilia Romagna* (Rome, 1983), 384 f.; M. Marini Calvani, 'Piacenza in età romana', in *Cremona in età romana*, Acts of the Colloquium; Cremona, 1984 (Cremona, 1985), 268 f.; Strazzulla, 16; M. L. Pagliani, *Placentia*, Città antiche in Italia, 3 (Rome, 1991), 27 n. 26, 99 f.

[31] B. M. Scarfi, 'Recenti rinvenimenti archeologici in Lombardia', *Annali Benacensi*, 3 (1976), 7 f.; ead., 'Testimonianze artistiche dell'antica Cremona: mosaici e resti fittili di statua da via Plasio', in *Cremona in età romana*, 101 f.

[32] Strazzulla, *Le terrecotte architettoniche della Venetia*, 75 f.; F. Fontana, 'Rappresentazione di una vittoria nel frontone fittile di Monastero', *Ostraka*, 3 (1994), 173 f.

belonging to two distinct temples are all too well known (Fig. 54, no. 4).[33]

Bononia, a Latin colony of 189 BC, where we know of the discovery, in 1912, at the corner of Via Indipendenza and Via Manzoni, of fragments of an antefix belonging to the well-known type of the *potnia theron* and dating to the years close to the foundation of the colony (Fig. 54, no. 5).[34]

Ariminum, a Latin colony from 268 BC where some antefixes have turned up,[35] to which we should add a group of high-relief plaques with floral decoration signed by the *officinator* Dionysius Colophonius, who was also active, according to G. Susini,[36] in Picene territory, at Cupra Marittima, though their typology and style, similar to those of the 'Campana' plaques, seem to better agree with the early imperial age (Fig. 54, no. 7).[37]

Ravenna requires a separate discourse. A *civitas foederata* and urban centre of very ancient history (as proved by the traditions about its mythical foundation, said to be either Thessalian, or Umbrian, or Sabine)[38] and frequented quite early by the Etruscans,[39] it became in 132 BC a pivotal town for the reorganization of the territory previously occupied by the Boian Gauls and for its Romanization, by means of the creation of the Via Popilia, which linked it with Atria and Forum Popilii. Actually, Ravenna has produced a fragment of fictile sculpture in the round (Fig. 54, no. 6), which

awaits more attentive study than has been devoted to it up until now.[40]

It is abundantly clear that the arrival in this area of strongly organized urban centres, as Latin colonies were, and of a set of cultural phenomena with a highly political and propagandistic impact, such as the temples of Etrusco-Italic type, built in the course of the first half of the first century BC, is of great historical relevance. In this context we can affirm that the religious forms had undoubtedly changed, for the colonists, though they imported a very traditional typology of sacred buildings (e.g. the two temples in Luni, the best known because of the favourable circumstances of research), did not bring with them the ritual custom of the anatomic ex-voto. We must therefore conclude that this ritual custom represents a religious attitude exclusive to the mid-Republican koine, an attitude which clearly by the second century BC had already lost much of its strength, whereas it had been a prominent religious form in the colonies throughout Italy before and during the first two Punic wars.

The impact that these buildings had in the more general process of Romanization is also evident from the fact that, as again shown by M. J. Strazzulla,[41] architectural terracottas of central Italian inspiration are widespread within the Transpadane region with ever greater frequency since the late second century. Evidence for the creation of new temple buildings of the second century BC in northern Italy comes from the geographical distribution of a typical element of their fictile decoration, the antefix of the *potnia theron* type. 'Invented' in Falerii around the middle of the third century,[42] from the beginning of second century BC onwards, the type enjoyed a particular favour in Italian cities, a fact which ought to be better known than it is. Bearing this in mind, the presence of such antefixes in Padua, Concordia, Vicetia, and Altinum, can be considered clear evidence of intense building activity, virtually all contemporary, carried out in the years close to the date of the grant of the *ius Latii* to the Transpadane people in 89 BC, perhaps immediately before rather than immediately after that momentous

[33] Andrén, 282 f.; A. Minto, in *SE* 22 (1952–3), 38 f.; G. Caputo, in *SE* 24 (1955–6), 221 f.; M. Bonghi Jovino, in A. Frova (ed.), *Scavi di Luni*, i (Rome, 1973), 796 f.; ead., in A. Frova (ed.), *Scavi di Luni*, ii (Rome, 1978), 572 f.; Strazzulla, 201 no. 8; G. Cavalieri Manasse, 'Appendice sulla decorazione architettonica dei monumenti lunensi', in *Studi lunensi e prospettive sull'Occidente romano*, Acts of the Colloquium; Lerici, 1985 (1987), 149 f.; M. Forte, *Le terrecotte ornamentali dei templi lunensi* (Florence, 1991); M. J. Strazzulla, 'Le terrecotte architettoniche frontonali di Luni nel problema della coroplastica templare nelle colonie in territorio etrusco', in G. Maetzke and L. Tamagno Perna (eds.), *La coroplastica templare etrusca tra il IV e il II sec.a.C.*, Acts of the Colloquium; Orbetello, 1988 (Florence, 1992), 161 f.

[34] *NSA* (1913), 199 f.; Andrén, 312; Pensa, in *Studi sulla città antica*, 390.

[35] Pensa, in *Studi sulla città antica*, 384.

[36] G. Susini, in *ArchClass* 17 (1965), 302 f.; Pensa, in *Studi sulla città antica*, 384 f. (with previous bibl.).

[37] Strazzulla, *Le terrecotte architettoniche nella Venetia*, 17 n. 13.

[38] Its foundation is given as Thessalian in Strabo (5. 214) and Zosimus (5. 27), Umbrian again in Strabo (5. 214, 217, 219, 227), Sabine in Pliny (*NH* 3. 115).

[39] As shown by the well-known bronze statuette from Ravenna now in Leiden with Etruscan inscription *TLE*² 709 (see M. Martelli, 'Il Marte di Ravenna', *Xenia*, 6 (1983), 25 f.).

[40] The very fine torso, apparently fully in the round (possibly an acroterion) and of quite early date (3rd cent. BC?), has been published by G. Ghirardini, 'Gli scavi del Palazzo di Teodorico a Ravenna', *MonAL* 24 (1917–18), 807 f., figs. 33 f.

[41] Strazzulla, *Le terrecotte architettoniche della Venetia*, 32.

[42] A. M. Comella, *Le terrecotte architettoniche del santuario dello Scasato a Falerii (Scavi 1886–1887)* (Perugia, 1992), 64 f.

year. The construction of sacred buildings in this style in the leading Transpadane indigenous centres (oddly enough in the same moment in which Rome was abandoning the old tradition of fictile revetments in favour of stone epistyles of Hellenistic taste) is likely to represent a sort of ostentatious exhibition of the full *urbanitas* reached by the local populations in order to justify the request (and the grant) of the more favourable statute of the *Latinitas*, which was immediately after bestowed by Pompeius Strabo. It would not then be by chance that with another equally comprehensible chronological time-lag, the Doric frieze (a 'new' model of architectural decoration for stone and fictile epistyles devised in the late second century BC in Rome from Hellenistic neoclassical models) is taken up and imitated in terracotta in various Transpadane cities in the course of the successive Romanizing wave, that is in the decades around the middle of the first century BC, soon to merge into the cultural effects of the Triumviral and Augustan colonizations. To follow the sense of this new formal choice, we have the sequence, again reconstructed by M. J. Strazzulla,[43] which starts in the second century BC with the architectural terracottas attributed to the temple of Quirinus in Rome and, by way of the terracottas of Vetulonia and Arezzo (third quarter of the second century BC) and the friezes of Lucus Angitiae and Schiavo d'Abruzzo (late second–early first century BC), reaches Aquileia, Parma, and Ariminum in the central years of the first century BC to end with the early Augustan temple of the Dioscuri in Este.

If we look in the opposite direction, the outlines of the phenomenon are drawn more precisely by means of a contrast between the central and the southern areas of the peninsula. In the central area we can distinguish three zones, each with its own fairly well-defined characteristics: the western part of Umbria, the rest of Umbria and Picenum, and the Augustan region of *Sabina et Samnium*.

The finds in western Umbria, i.e. that part in close contact with Etruria, with the mid-Republican architectural terracottas from Iguvium (Fig. 54, no. 10) and Tuder (Fig. 54, no. 15),[44] and the late republican architectural terracottas from Asisium (Fig. 54, no. 11),

Vettona (Fig. 54, no. 12), Urvinum Hortense (Fig. 54, no. 14), Ocriculum (Fig. 54, no. 21), Hispellum (Fig. 54, no. 13), and again Tuder (Fig. 54, no. 15),[45] demonstrate that the Umbrian aristocracies fully accepted the Etrusco-Latin temple architecture, at least from the fourth century BC (if not actually from the sixth century BC, if the fictile figured frieze of the so-called Phase I from Ocriculum[46] is not, as seems at the moment, a completely isolated case). Given the strong Etruscan character possessed by the Umbrian territory bordering on the Etruscan territory, such distribution is, as it were, to be expected; none the less it is highly significant. It represents a further parameter indicative of the process of urbanization which occurred in the fifth and fourth centuries BC in the leading Umbrian cities,[47] such as Tuder and Iguvium (but we can also add Ocriculum), whereas it only took place in the second century BC in the other more peripheral Umbrian areas. It is not by chance that in these more backward areas the architectural terracottas seem to refer primarily to great extramural sanctuaries like those known in Asisium and Hispellum, and that the great public works coincide with the decades immediately prior to the social war and with a massive programme of 'self-Romanization', as demonstrated by the best-known case, that of Asisium, recently investigated by F. Coarelli.[48]

The second area coincides with eastern Umbria and Picenum. Here the massive presence of Latin colonies (Hatria, *c.*283 BC, and Firmum, 264 BC), of Roman colonies (Sena Gallica, 283 BC, and Castrum Novum, *c.*264 BC), and of viritane land distributions carried out on a vast scale reduced the zones populated by *socii Italici* so they were fairly scarce, both in the territory of the Picentes and in the *ager Gallicus*. Only the sanctuary of Colle Guardia near Offida (Fig. 54, no. 17), from the middle years of the first century BC, with revetment plaques and an antefix of the well-known type showing the winged genius,[49] can be considered to belong to

[43] Strazzulla, *Le terrecotte architettoniche della Venetia*, 32 f.

[44] Strazzulla, 196 no. 12 (Iguvium, Guastuglia, unpublished); ibid. no. 15; G. Gualterio, in M. Bergamini and G. Comez (eds.), '*Verso un museo della città*', Catalogue of the Exhibition; Todi, 1982 (Todi, 1982), 125 f.; M. Tascio, *Todi* (Rome, 1989), 66 f., nos. 47 and 49 (Tuder, temples of S. Maria in Camuccia and Porta Catena).

[45] Strazzulla, 203: no. 28, Asisium—S. Maria degli Angeli; no. 29, Vettona; no. 31: Urvinum Hortense; no. 33, Ocriculum; no. 35, Hispellum, extramural sanctuary at Villa Fidelia; no. 36, Tuder.

[46] G. Dareggi, 'Una terracotta architettonica da Otricoli. Qualche considerazione sul centro preromano', *MEFRA* 90 (1978), 627 f.

[47] M. Torelli, 'Le popolazioni dell'Italia antica: società e forme del potere', in A. Momigliano and A. Schiavone (eds.) *Storia di Roma*, i (Turin, 1988), 68 f.

[48] F. Coarelli, 'Assisi repubblicana: riflessioni su un caso di autoromanizzazione', *Atti Accademia Properziana del Subasio—Assisi*, 6th ser., 19 (1991), 5 f.

[49] *NSA* (1876), 144; Strazzulla, 206 no. 67.

the territory of the allies, being placed in the eastern section of the *ager Ausculanus*.[50] Indeed, the famous terracottas from Civitalba (Fig. 54, no. 9),[51] with a remarkable frieze and the no less remarkable pediment, were found in a territory within the *ager publicus p.R.* The same applies not only to the terracottas from Iesi (Fig. 54, no. 8),[52] a city situated in the *ager Gallicus* distributed to Roman colonists, but also to the extraordinary terracotta sculptures decorating the great sanctuary of Monterinaldo (Fig. 54, no. 16),[53] which seems to belong fully to the *pertica* of the colony of Firmum Picenum. In short, it seems to me highly significant that in the territory of both *Umbri* and *Picentes*, there is no comparison to be found with the extension and the quality of the architecture promoted by the Roman colonists in the same zone.

The third area includes the territories of the Augustan *regio IV, Sabina et Samnium*, where the Roman presence is organized in two complementary forms, in the Sabine area with *viritim* land allotments to Roman citizens and early co-optations of loyal indigenous people into the citizenship, whereas in the Samnite territory there was a marked prevalence of large Latin colonies placed both in the centre (Alba Fucens, Carseoli, Aesernia, Beneventum) and on the borders (Cales, Fregellae, Luceria, Interamna, Sora, Venusia) of the lands left to the defeated Samnites. In the Sabine area, our distribution map appears empty, with the sole exception of Villa San Silvestro near Cascia, where we know of an Etrusco-Italic temple in an exceptional state of preservation with associated revetment plaques and antefixes (Fig. 54, no. 18).[54] Such a find is nevertheless only an apparent exception, since the site is set in the compass of the territory of Nursia, notoriously an

object of extensive *viritim* land distributions after the conquests by M' Curius Dentatus.[55] In the Samnite area, in all the Latin colonies which have been subjected to methodical exploration or even only to trial trenches beneath the modern towns which are frequently continuations of the ancient centres, we know of temples of Etrusco-Italic type and/or associated architectural terracottas, as shown by the following list:

Fregellae, a Latin colony of 328 BC, where we know of at least one urban and two extra-urban temples of Etrusco-Italic type and their architectural terracottas (Fig. 54, no. 26).[56]

Luceria, a Latin colony of 314 BC, where Etrusco-Italic architectural terracottas and antefixes of both Campanian and Tarentine types have turned up, as well as fragments of a pedimental decoration in high relief, associated with the votive deposit of Etrusco-Italic type, recently published in a finally complete form (Fig. 54, no. 34).[57]

Interamna Lirenas, a Latin colony of 312 BC, where architectural terracottas seem to have been discovered, as yet unpublished.[58]

Alba Fucens, a Latin colony of 303 BC widely explored by the Belgian archaeologists, where at least two temples of Etrusco-Italic type with related architectural terracottas have turned up, and where plaques and antefixes of the *potnia theron* type belonging to a third sanctuary of unknown location have also been discovered (Fig. 54, no. 24).[59]

Sora, a Latin colony of 303 BC, where we know of a temple of Etrusco-Italic type in an exceptional state of preservation and of the related architectural

[50] G. Conta, *Ausculum*, ii: 1 (Pisa, 1982), 218 f., n. 143; though with no ascertained provenance, an antefix of the *potnia theron* type is preserved in the Museum at Ascoli: M. Bonghi Jovino, in Frova (ed.), *Scavi di Luni*, i. 804.

[51] M. Verzar, 'Archäologische Zeugnisse aus Umbrien', in P. Zanker (ed.), *Hellenismus in Mittelitalien* (Göttingen, 1976), 122 f. (with previous bibliography); F.-H. Massa Pairault, in P. Santoro (ed.) *I Galli e l'Italia*, Catalogue of the Exhibition; Rome, 1978 (Rome, 1978), 197 f.; ead., *Recherches sur l'art et l'artisanat étrusco-italiques à l'époque hellénistique* (Rome, 1985), 143 f.; M. Landolfi, 'Le terrecotte di Civitalba di Sassoferrato', *Ostraka*, 3 (1994), 73 f.

[52] Strazzulla, 206 no. 65; as far as I know, these terracottas (which seem to include also pedimental sculptures) are still unpublished.

[53] L. Mercando, 'L'ellenismo nel Piceno', in Zanker (ed.), *Hellenismus in Mittelitalien*, 172; Strazzulla, 206 no. 66. In a private conversation of more than a quarter of century ago the late A. Degrassi told me that a Latin inscription of republican times had been reported to him to have been found in this same sanctuary, but of this text there is no evidence in the literature.

[54] *NSA* (1938), 141 f.; Andrén, 320 f.; *SE* 34 (1966), 306; Strazzulla, 203 no. 30.

[55] On the personality and work of M' Curius Dentatus still useful is the article by G. Forni, 'Manio Curio Dentato, uomo democratico', *Athenaeum*, 31 (1953), 170 f.

[56] Cf. N. Pagliardi, 'Terrecotte architettoniche da Fregellae', *Archeologia Laziale*, 2 (1979), 209 f.; ead., 'Terrecotte architettoniche da Fregellae', *Archeologia Laziale*, 3 (1980), 183 f.; G. Manca di Mores and N. M. Pagliardi, 'Le terrecotte architettoniche', in F. Coarelli (ed.), *Fregellae, 2. Il santuario di Esculapio* (Rome, 1986), 51 f.; R. Känel, 'Ein neuer Fundkomplex architektonischer Terrakotten aus Fregellae', *Ostraka* 3 (1994), 109 f.

[57] D'Ercole, *La stipe votiva del Belvedere*, 257 f.

[58] Pagliardi, *Archeologia Laziale*, 2 (1979), 209.

[59] The temples have been published by J. Mertens, 'Deux temples italiques à Alba Fucens', in *Alba Fucens*, ii. 6 f. (temples on the Pettorino and San Pietro hilltops); id., 'Alba Fucens', *DArch* 3rd ser., 6: 2 (1988), 89 (plaques and antefixes of an unknown sanctuary); the architectural terracottas are published in *NSA* (1952), 234 f., and *AC* 23 (1954), 364 f.; see also Strazzulla, 206 no. 68.

terracottas, of which we only have preliminary information (Fig. 54, no. 25).[60]

Venusia, a Latin colony of 291 BC, where recent explorations have brought to light revetment plaques and a fragment of a high relief pediment depicting a Satyr, belonging to a sanctuary situated in the area of the amphitheatre, near the northern gate of the ancient city (Fig. 54, no. 28).[61]

Hatria, a Latin colony of 289–263 BC, where both in the past and in recent times architectural terracottas have been found (Fig. 54, no. 22).[62]

Aesernia, a Latin colony of 263 BC, where at least two temples of Etrusco-Italic type have come to light in an excellent state of preservation and, it seems, also architectural terracottas, all materials yet again unpublished (Fig. 54, no. 29).[63]

From such a list we have a clear confirmation of the fact that the Latin colonies very soon became a vehicle of strong Romanization, establishing in these zones (as they did in the Cisalpine region) a socio-economic model, which for brevity's sake we shall call urban, previously unknown to the indigenous peoples and at the same time endowed with an explosive force. The superiority of the model, which implied a more widespread possession of the best of the fundamental means of production—the most productive land and its more efficient exploitation—rendered easy and consequential the exportation of the cultural forms ingrained in that model. Among these cultural forms Etrusco-Italic temple building (which we should actually call Latin) with its related terracotta decoration took first place, not only for all the reasons which I gave at the beginning of this chapter, but also because of the central role which the sacred building held in the structure of the city, the pillar of the new socio-economic

and political system spread by the self-same Latin colonies.[64]

The success of the building type and of its decoration in the Samnite area, already by the third century BC,[65] but above all in the course of the following century, was enormous. We can fairly say that in this area peopled by *socii*, every *pagus* or tribal segment, every *vicus* or village, and every *oppidum* or settlement with proto- or pseudo-urban features has turned up signs of the prestige enjoyed by the model, whose diffusion is attributed primarily to the Latin colonies which studded the zone. Thus, immediately beyond the Hernican territory, politically and culturally Latinized since the archaic period, where we encounter the substantial towns of Aletrium and Anagnia with relatively early temples and architectural terracottas,[66] in the Samnite area of southern Latium conquered quite early by the Romans, we have evidence of architectural terracottas in Aquinum (Fig. 54, no. 27)[67] and in Casinum (Fig. 54, no. 28).[68] However, it is above all in the territories belonging to the tribes of the Praetuttii, the Marrucini, the Samnite Pentri, and the Samnite Caretini, that the Etrusco-Italic temple gains an absolutely extraordinary success: we may quickly recall, among those best known, the finds from Teramo (Fig. 54, no. 20)[69] and Tortoreto (Fig. 54, no. 19)[70] in the Praetuttian territory, of Chieti and Colle San Giorgio in the Marrucine area (Fig. 54, no. 23),[71] at Pietrabbondante,[72] Campochiaro,[73] Ielsi,[74] Gildone in the Samnite area (Fig. 54, nos. 30–3).[75] All demonstrate how effective the cultural pressure of the Latin colonies was on the peoples surrounded by them, how popular and widespread the architectural

[60] A. Zevi Gallina, 'Sora. Scavi alla Cattedrale', *Archeologia Laziale*, 1 (1978), 64 f.; M. Lolli Ghetti and N. Pagliardi, 'Sora: scavo presso la Chiesa cattedrale di Santa Maria Assunta', *Archeologia Laziale*, 3 (1980), 177 f.; mention of the architectural terracottas by Pagliardi, in *Archeologia Laziale*, 2 (1979), 210.

[61] G. Sabbatini, 'Le terrecotte architettoniche', in M. Salvatore (ed.), *Il Museo Archeologico Nazionale di Venosa* (Matera, 1991), 101 f.

[62] *NSA* (1901), 188 f.; G. Iaculli, 'Ancora su Colle S.Giorgio', *Quaderni dell'Istituto di Storia Antica dell'Università di Chieti*, 2 (1981), 61; see also G. Azzena, *Atri*, Città antiche in Italia, 1 (Rome, 1987), 18.

[63] A. Gallina Zevi, 'Isernia. Lo scavo del tempio della colonia latina', in R. Cantilena (ed.), *Sannio, Pentri e Frentani dal VI al I sec.a.C.*, Catalogue of the Exhibition; Naples, 1981 (Naples, 1981), 102 f.; C. Terzani, 'La colonia latina di Aesernia', in S. Capini and A. Di Niro (eds.), *Samnium. Archeologia del Molise*, Catalogue of the Exhibition, Milan, 1991 (Rome, 1991), 112 f.

[64] On this subject, see M. Torelli, 'Il modello urbano e l'immagine della città', in S. Settis, *Civiltà dei Romani, i. La città, il territorio e l'impero* (Milan, 1990), 43 f.

[65] At Pietrabbondante plaques and antefixes of Etrusco-Italic type are known already in the 3rd cent. BC: M. J. Strazzulla, *Il santuario sannitico di Pietrabbondante* (Rome, 1971), 42 f.

[66] Andrén, 390 f.; Strazzulla, 203 no. 37 (Aletrium); Pagliardi, *Archeologia Laziale*, 2 (1979), 209 (Anagnia).

[67] Pagliardi, *Archeologia Laziale*, 2 (1979), 209.

[68] *SE* 14 (1940), 445 f.; Strazzulla, 204 no. 40.

[69] Strazzulla, 206 no. 73.

[70] Ibid. no. 74; the terracottas seem however better refer to the decoration of a private villa.

[71] Strazzulla, 206 nos. 60–70; G. Iaculli, *Il tempio italico di Colle S.Giorgio (Castiglione Messer Raimondo)* (Chieti, [1993]); A. Campanelli, 'Le terrecotte architettoniche della Civitella di Chieti: le lastre a matrice', *Ostraka*, 3 (1994), 123 f.; G. Iaculli, 'Chieti-Civitella. La decorazione a stecca', ibid. 155 f.

[72] Strazzulla, 207 no. 80; in the same area also the finds of Colle Sparanise: see Strazzulla, 206 no. 70.

[73] Ibid. no. 76.   [74] Ibid. no. 78.

[75] A. De Niro, *Gildone*, in *Sannio. Pentri e Frentani dal VI al I sec.a.C.*, Exhibition Catalogue; Isernia, 1980 (Rome, 1980), 264 f.

model was among these *socii*, not by chance the first to join the Italic revolt. I do not think it is necessary to re-assert how valuable the display of this model must have been as 'proof' that the state of *barbaries* and *rusticitas* had been overcome, denial of that negative stereotype, embodied in Roman eyes by the Samnite no less than by the Gaul, both *ethne* marked by the *nota* of *infamia* connected with a kind of gladiator named after them.

Further south the picture changes considerably. At Minturnae, a Roman colony of 296 BC, we can place the boundary line between the two main areas character-ized by specific typological traditions of manufacturing architectural terracottas, that of the Etrusco-Latin type and that of Campanian type (Fig. 54, no. 35). As happens in the archaic period at Satricum, where strongly differing types and styles of architectural terracottas originating from Cerveteri and from Capua meet, so too at Minturnae the architectural terracottas of the city temples follow the Roman models,[76] whilst those of the old extra-urban sanctuary of the Auruncan goddess Marica are deeply influenced by types from Campania.[77] Further south again, still other architec-tural typologies dominate undisputed. In northern Apulia and in Lucania we do not encounter revetment plaques or figured pediments, friezes, and acroteria, but only antefixes of a Metapontine or Campanian type[78] decorating the funerary *naiskoi* and the small square temples typical of the indigenous religious tradition;[79] in the rest of Apulia and in Bruttium only the Graeco-colonial types are found,[80] before the urban models of architectural terracottas and of antefixes with palmettes from the final decades of the Republic and the early Empire supplant these old and resistant local traditions.[81]

In this context the behaviour of the Latin colonies planted in the south of Italy is particularly interesting together with that of the very small and only partially successful Roman colonies in the same area. Whereas fairly little is known about the republican phase of the

Latin colony of Brundisium (244 BC),[82] our information on the other two foundations of the Augustan *regio III*, *Lucania et Bruttium*, i.e. Thurii–Copia, a Latin colony of 193 BC, and Poseidonia–Paestum, a Latin colony of 273 BC, is relatively large. As far as this last city is concerned, a superficial examination of the known data and the ac-cessible museum storerooms indicates that terracottas of Etrusco-Italic type are completely absent and that the innovations in sacred architecture brought by the Latin colonists (basically the 'temple of Peace', the complex of the so-called Italic temple of the 'Roman garden' and of the probable adjoining Asklepieion, and the small temples nos. 14, 15, and 16 according to Sestieri's numbering),[83] when given architectural decoration at all, used terracottas of Campanian type. For example, the only published colonial building with fictile decoration, a portico added in the third century BC to the front of the shrine of Venus in the extra-urban sanctuary of S. Venera, was ornamented with antefixes of the Campanian disc type.[84]

No less significant for our purposes is the other case of Copia, extensively excavated between the end of the 1960s and the end of the 1970s and exemplarily published. The vast areas of the Roman city explored and the numerous trial trenches carried out in depth in search of Graeco-colonial levels have been astonish-ingly poor in finds of our sort. After an accurate exam-ination of the published material, apart from a few fragments of revetment plaques and of antefixes of Tarentine type related to the phase of the Greek colony of Thurii[85] and two fragments of plaques of the con-ventional type of the end of the Republic,[86] I was able to find only one fragment of sima with concave strigils of Etrusco-Italic type,[87] proof that in at least one case the Latin colonists in Copia erected a sacred building of traditional type, though its location unfortunately is

---

[76] Andrén, 480 f.; Strazzulla, 197 no. 30.

[77] Andrén, 491; Strazzulla, 197 no. 30.

[78] E. M. De Juliis, 'L'età del Ferro', in M. Mazzei (ed.), *La Daunia antica* (Milan, 1984), 152, 163; I. Rainini, 'Terrecotte architettoniche dal Melfese', *BA* 62–3 (1990), 57 f.

[79] Now listed and studied by C. Masseria, *I santuari indigeni della Basilicata*, Ph.D.Thesis; (Perugia, 1988).

[80] Strazzulla, 200 nos. 62–71 (with bibliography); P. Guzzo, *I Brettii. Storia e archeologia della Calabria preromana* (Milan, 1989), 35 f. (antefix of Campanian type from Castrovillari).

[81] L. Anselmino, 'Le antefisse dal I a.C. al II d.C.', in Giardina and Schiavone, *Società romana*, i. 209 f.

[82] B. Sciarra, *Brindisi. Il museo archeologico provinciale*, Musei d'Italia. Meraviglie d'Italia (Bologna, 1976), 39 f., nos. 263–77; Strazzulla, 199 no. 51.

[83] See Ch. 3.

[84] C. Masseria, 'Le terrecotte architettoniche', in J. G. Pedley and M. Torelli (eds.), *The Extramural Sanctuary of Santa Venera at Paestum*, i (Rome, 1993), 189 f.

[85] *NSA* (1969), I Suppl., 102 no. 15, fig. 99 (= Strazzulla, 200 no. 68); *NSA* (1970) III Suppl., 137 no. 176, fig. 125; *NSA* (1974) Suppl. 261 no. 243, fig. 256, and 355 no. 153, fig. 335 (cf. ibid. 535 f.).

[86] Ibid. 407 nos. 129–30, fig. 446. We do not mention here the numerous late republican and imperial palmette antefixes, some of which even show the stamp of the still unexplored local *figlinae* (strangely ignored by L. Anselmino, in Giardina and Schiavone, *Società romana*); I think we should include in this type also the enigmatic fragment published as an antefix in *NSA* (1970), III Suppl., 506 no. 727, fig. 446.

[87] *NSA* (1972), Suppl., 324 no. 55, fig. 363.

not known to us. However, luckily for us, in this connection we can refer to another discovery in Copia, that of an elegant Doric epistyle of the fourth century BC, which bears the following monumental Latin inscription:[88]

Aedem de senat[us sententia ref(iciundam) cur(averunt)]
L.Anni(us) V.f., M.Pet[roni(us)—f . . .] vel M.Pet[illi(us)—f - - -].

The epistyle was discovered reused in the 'Casa Bianca' section of the city's walls, a haphazard work to be connected perhaps with the piratical wars.[89] I would be inclined to date the inscription to the time of the foundation of the colony or a little later for both textual, onomastic, and palaeographic reasons, as we can infer from the use of the Italic *praenomen* Vibius and from the form of the open P with straight strokes. This goes to show that, in Copia, as in Paestum, the reuse of old temples of the Greek colony by the Latin colonists must have been deliberate and greatly reduced the scope for building new monumental temples on which the local ruling classes could lavish money and to which they could entrust strong symbolic and political messages.

In no uncertain sense, the lengthy analysis of the distribution of the architectural type conducted so far, with its specific territorial differences, proves that there is a close link between the diffusion of Etrusco-Italic temples in Italy and the Romanizing processes of the peninsula, in which the leading role was performed by the Latin colonies. Together with a few buildings of politically significant type, such as the forum square used as *saepta* for the electoral meetings and the circular *comitium* for the *contiones* and the *iudicia*, the great civic temples represent the most relevant monumental component of the urban model exported by the colonies into territories hitherto completely ignorant of it or exposed to it in only a partial and embryonic form. The model, acknowledged as an instrument of self-affirmation of an acquired *urbanitas* and therefore of the maturity of the conditions for a consequent bestowal of more elevated political rights, possessed an effectiveness measurable by the rapid rate of its diffusion which we have reconstructed as regards Italy

between the Rubico and the Aufidus rivers in the course of the second century BC and the Cisalpine region in the course of the following century.

The great void, which coincides in the south with an imaginary border joining the Liris with the Aufidus, is only in part filled by the prestige enjoyed by the Campanian models. Next to the 'frontier' case of Minturnae, mentioned above, we can cite the case of Pietrabbondante. The mixture of Campanian and Latin features in the Pietrabbondante temple B, in which we find not only podium mouldings closely imitating those of the Fondo Patturelli temple in Capua,[90] but also architectural terracottas of a type widespread in Latium, represents explicit and unequivocal evidence of both the extent and the limitations of the influence exercised by the great Etrusco-Latin architecture in consequence of the expansion of Romanization. Thus, even in the course of the second century BC, when the effects of the Romanization process were becoming more and more evident, the Greek cities of Magna Graecia and the inland areas peopled by indigenous Italic tribes, which had been for centuries subject to powerful Graeco-colonial influence, appear to be immune to the reception of the architectural models characteristic of the power of Rome, a power, let us remember, which already from the third century BC had assumed imperial connotations. For these reasons it is not rash to propose that at the roots of this behaviour we should see the prestige enjoyed by Greek culture, capable even of inducing the Latin colonists of Paestum and of Copia to make use of ancient sacred buildings and, as a consequence, to limit the expression of their autonomous cultural choices, presupposed in the establishment of temple buildings of Etrusco-Italic tradition. The issue appears all the more significant, in that it takes place in circumstances, as in Paestum, where we cannot question the energy of the Latin colonists, who on the contrary seem to have exerted considerable violence towards the surviving culture and the religious traditions of the local Greek element.[91]

It should be remembered that between the late second and the beginning of the first century BC the *socii Italici* appear to be busy with the embellishment or the rebuilding of dozens of large local sanctuaries, which housed ancient and prestigious native cults and important 'national' memorials. These restorations are there

---

[88] Ibid. 247 no. 242, fig. 193 (P. G. Guzzo, in *AMS Magna Grecia* (1972–3), 44, tav. LVI c; *NSA* (1974), Suppl., 453, fig. 436) = *CIL* I², 3163 c.

[89] It is most likely the same work mentioned by the following inscription found in the same area of Casa Bianca and datable to the first half of the 1st cent. BC (*NSA* (1972), Suppl., 213 no. 90, fig. 220): [——]LE [-/— (?) Pertin]ax | [murum, turrei]s, portas | [de sua pecunia] refecit, | [viam stra]vit texitque.

[90] A. La Regina, 'Il Sannio', in Zanker (ed.), *Hellenismus in Mittelitalien*, 229 f., tav. IV.   [91] See Ch. 3.

to testify not only to the relative well-being acquired by those *socii* as a share of Rome's Mediterranean conquests, but rather to the elevated rank of the cultural resistance maturing at local level in the face of unbearable economic, social, political, and cultural Roman pressure. The corollary of this reality is the fact that in the lands of the *socii*, beginning with Samnium and to the north of it, this wave of cultural resistance is dressed up, as is to be expected from the ruled, in the clothes of their rulers, and makes use of traditional Roman architectural models more or less disguised by the Hellenistic *nouvelle vague*, models which are persistently associated with prestige. In contrast, in the areas previously part of the Magna Graecia hinterland, the same resistance of the indigenous peoples ignores the Roman models and allows indigenous building types to rise to monumental dignity. Let us explain all this with two outstanding and parallel examples. On one hand, we have the sanctuary at Pietrabbondante, the political and ethnic foyer of the Samnite Pentri, that in the late second century BC sees the construction of temple B (Fig. 55), a colossal temple of Etrusco-Italic type with related decorative terracottas;[92] on the other hand, there is the great sacred and political centre of the Lucanians, the sanctuary of Rossano di Vaglio (Fig. 56),[93] it too rebuilt in the course of the second century, its design reproducing the traditional structure of the aristocratic Lucanian residences of the fifth–fourth century BC (Fig. 57), made known to us by the excavations of M. Gualtieri in Roccagloriosa.[94] Such differences of choice, made in expressing analogous political and ideological needs by the Samnites Pentri (more exposed to Roman influence) and by the Lucanians (tied to the culture of the old Greek colonial world) cannot escape notice by anyone seeking to evaluate the ways and means which the great sacred buildings and their decoration made an impact in the process of the Romanization of ancient Italy.

This is, therefore, the material and structural context of Etrusco-Italic type temple construction between the third and the first centuries BC, i.e. when Roman Italy was itself being constructed. Within this framework we have to read the messages conveyed by the *fictiles fabulae*, the figured terracotta decorations of

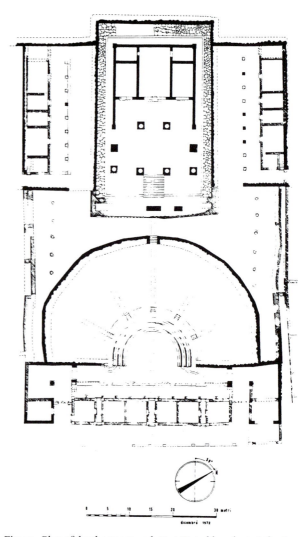

Fig. 55. Plan of the theatre-temple B at Pietrabbondante (after La Regina).

the temples, which were the privilege, as we have seen, mostly of Latin and Roman citizens and only to a small extent and in later times passed to the *socii Italici*. Among the allies, however, the Etruscan *poleis* occupy a particular position that the previous pages, in view of their chosen focus, have necessarily ignored. In the Etruscan cities, the antiquity and the 'national' character of the Etrusco-Italic temple type indeed played a remarkably different function, though northern Etruria fully participated during the second century BC in the programme of renovation of the terracotta revetments of the temples, and their stylistic and cultural forms now clearly derive from those devised by Rome and propagated by means of the numerous peripheral

---

[92] Strazzulla, *Il santuario sannitico di Pietrabbondante*.

[93] D. Adamesteanu and H. Dilthey, *Macchia di Rossano. Rapporto preliminare* (Lecce, 1992).

[94] M. Gualtieri , in M. Gualtieri (ed.), *Roccagloriosa* (Napoli, 1990), 63 f.

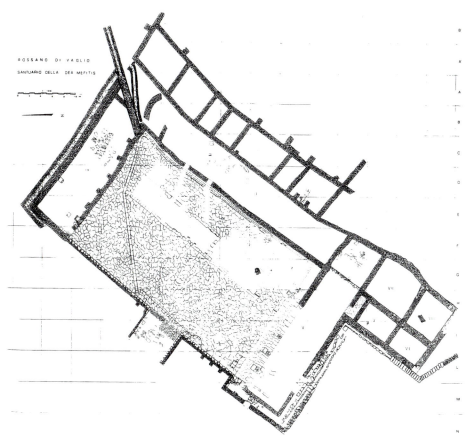

Fig. 56. Plan of the sanctuary at Rossano di Vaglio in Lucania (after Adamesteanu).

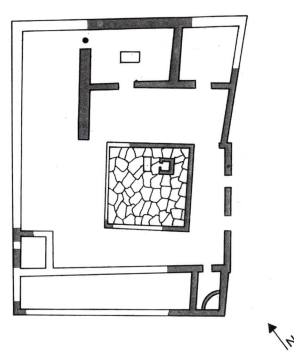

Fig. 57. Plan of an aristocratic Lucanian house at Roccagloriosa; in the paved courtyard a little domestic shrine and its altar (drawing A. Trapassi).

centres scattered throughout the peninsula and radiating Roman culture.

3. Pedimental Sculpture: Statutes, Representation, and Political Conflicts

So far, we have seen how important it was for the local prestige to build temples of Etrusco-Italic type. Within this strongly unified structure, composed of specific and inimitable cultural and craft traditions, of inequalities in urban evolution, of variations in the economic formations of the Italic micro-societies—we must ask ourselves—do figured pediments and friezes of these widespread temples share any common content or common element of a politico-ideological nature? Most recently many discussions have raised such iconological problems and, in the light of what we have seen so far, I maintain it is possible to indicate at least some very general tendencies.

In full awareness of over-simplifying the problems, I would like to divide the evidence into two main

Fig. 58. Reconstruction of the *arx* at Cosa, showing (on the left) the Capitolium with the pediment decorated with a triumphal procession (after Brown).

groups. The first of these is that of the patently political representations, expressed in direct narrative or even symbolic language, but whose features wish to celebrate precise 'historical' events, in other words ethical–political themes historically determined or determinable. These are the scenes of 'historical' character, in the sense commonly attributed to Roman 'historical' representations,[95] whose most well-known and illustrious prototype is the pediment found in the Via S. Gregorio in Rome, a building which recently and independently of one another M. J. Strazzulla and I have identified as the temple of Fortuna Respiciens *in Palatio*.[96] In addition to that, however, there are several other important complexes. I refer to the frieze of a house in Fregellae,[97] to the fragments of the Praenestine frieze republished by P. Pensabene,[98] and to the

pedimental terracottas of the so-called Capitolium at Cosa (Fig. 58),[99] in which we can reconstruct a sacrifice in the presence of a divinity (Jupiter, Mars) celebrated at the end of a *triumphus*, with a *pompa triumphalis* attested to by the presence of a *ferculum*.[100] Indeed, in the light of the terracottas from the Fregellan house these documents discovered at sites other than Rome should now be seen in a new light, as examples of what we could call a Latin 'triumphal art',[101] intended to celebrate *pompae triumphales* of victories gained in the quality of *socii nominis Latini* under Roman command and maybe also *pompae* celebrated locally (rather than the more hypothetical *triumphi Albani*). The Praeneste example, which is reconstructible with relative certainty, is a case in point. In fact, in this city, where we

[95] In the sense I have indicated in my book *Typology and Structure of the Roman Historical Reliefs*, 2nd edn. (Ann Arbor, 1992).

[96] M. J. Strazzulla, 'Fortuna etrusca e Fortuna romana. Due cicli decorativi a confronto (Roma, Via S.Gregorio e Bolsena)', *Ostraka* 2 (1993), 317 f.; M. Torelli, in M. Steinby (ed.), *Lexicon Topographicum Urbis Romae* (Rome, 1993), 337.

[97] F. Coarelli, 'Due fregi da Fregellae: un documento storico della prima guerra Siriaca', *Ostraka* 3 (1994), 93 f.

[98] P. Pensabene, 'Su un fregio fittile e un ritratto marmoreo da Palestrina nel Museo Nazionale Romano', in H. Blanck and S. Steingräber (eds.), *Miscellanea Archaeologica Tobias Dohrn dicata* (Rome, 1982), 73 f.

[99] First edited by E. H. Richardson and L. Richardson Jr., 'Cosa II: The Temples of the Arx', *MAAR* 26 (1960), 98 f., 225 f., 363 f., these important pieces have been analysed several times: M. J. Strazzulla, 'Le terrecotte architettoniche nell'Italia centrale', in M. Cristofani (ed.), *Caratteri dell'ellenismo nelle urne etrusche*, Acts of the Colloquium; Siena, 1976 (Florence, 1977), 41 f.; ead., 'Le terrecotte architettoniche', in A. Carandini (ed.), *La romanizzazione dell'Etruria. Il territorio di Vulci*, Exhibition Catalogue; Orbetello, 1985 (Milan, 1985), 97 f.; R. T. Scott, 'The Decorations in Terra Cotta from the Temples of Cosa', in Maetzke and Tamagno Perna (eds.), *La coroplastica templare*, 91 f.

[100] Richardson, *MAAR* 26 (1960), 336 f., figs. 25–32.

[101] Again in the sense I have proposed in *Typology and Structure*.

have evidence for a local *porta triumphalis*,[102] we know of the existence of *statuae* of triumphal character, like the one *in foro statuta, loricata, amicta toga, velato capite, [et tria signa] cum titulo laminae aeneae inscripto*, of M. Anicius, the Praenestine *praetor* commanding the *Praenestinorum cohors*, who strenuously defended the city of Casilinum from the siege of Hannibal.[103] Though the data are very scarce, the fact that this genre of terracotta sculpture is so far documented only in Rome and among the *Prisci Latini* (Praeneste) and the *socii nominis Latini* (Cosa) to my mind is not accidental: the close connection between *auspicia, manubiae, triumphus*, and great sacred monumental buildings, which we know so well in the case of the colossal achievements of the *viri triumphales* in Rome, together with the *dona* of statues made by the same generals in the Latin and Roman colonies, as we learn from the famous *tituli Mummiani*, actually limits the formal juridical opportunity for the exhibition of the triumphal retinue to the Romans and the Latins alone. As a matter of fact, even after the dissolution of the Latin League in 338 BC, the consul-praetor of Rome, celebrant —let us recall—of the *sacra* of the *feriae Latinae* acted as depositary of *auspicia* common to all the Latins. The latter in short could easily make an exhibition of *pompae triumphales*, since their particularly favourable statute, laid down by the *foedus Cassianum*, allowed them that which none of the other *socii* was not allowed, regardless of the favour of the *foedus*, and that is to proclaim as theirs the victories obtained *ductu auspicioque* of a Roman magistrate. In fact, in the other cities,[104] especially but not only in the Etruscan ones,[105]

the figured 'historical' representations, both painted and sculptured, subsequent to the submission to Rome, are simple scenes of *profectio* of the deceased in magistrate's clothing for the 'great journey' into the hereafter, without any triumphal significance.[106] That things were different prior to the submission is handsomely proved by the François tomb in Vulci, a 'triumphal' monument *par excellence* belonging the age of Etruscan autonomy, despite its character of private monument (or maybe actually because of it), where the extraordinary cyclical conception of the paintings of the so-called 'tablinum' culminates in the unequivocal figure of *Vel Saties* caught in the act of auspicating and dressed in the triumphal *toga picta*.[107]

Apart from these 'historical' depictions, we have the second group to which I alluded earlier, where the representations placed to decorate temples as a rule follow the technique of the allusion, of the symbol, of the allegorical reference, carried out by the instrument of the myth.[108] This technique, put to the test for centuries in Greek culture, had been fully accepted in the Etrusco-Italic world since the early archaic period, though not in a slavish way, since they integrated the Greek mythical inheritance into their own, according to a careful selection, as M. Menichetti has shown,[109] in order to produce a satisfactory expression of their own ideological needs, often of a nature rather different from the contemporary Hellenic ones. In the middle Republic, when the use of mythical allegories is still tied to the models of the classical age, it is at times possible to read very precise and direct political messages.

[102] M. Torelli, 'Topografia sacra di una città latina—Praeneste', in B. Coari (ed.), *Urbanistica ed architettura dell'antica Praeneste*, Acts of the Colloquium; Palestrina, 1988 (Palestrina, 1989), 29 f.; the hypothesis has been accepted by G. Colonna, 'Praeneste arcaica e il mondo etrusco-italico', in B. Coari (ed.), *Le necropoli di Praeneste*, Acts of the Colloquium; Palestrina, 1990 (Palestrina, 1992), 42. See also the well-known Praenestine cista now in Berlin (G. Bordenache Battaglia, *Le ciste prenestine*, i: 1 (Rome, 1979), 56 f., no. 6), where already A. Michaelis (in *Annali dell'Instituto* (1876), 105 f.) wanted to see the representation of an Alban triumph (see H. S. Versnel, *Triumphus: An Inquiry into the Origin, Development and Meaning of the Roman Triumph* (Leiden, 1970), esp. 60 f., with mention of the cista): a more satisfactory interpretation has been given by M. Menichetti, 'Praenestinus Aeneas. Il culto di Iuppiter imperator e il trionfo su Mezenzio quali motivi di propaganda antiromana su una cista prenestina', *Ostraka*, 3 (1994), 7 f.

[103] Liv. 23. 19. 17–18.

[104] Evidence gathered by B. M. Felletti Maj, *La tradizione italica nell'arte romana* (Rome, 1977).

[105] I am thinking, for example, of the rather enigmatic relief with slingers in the Museum at Ascoli Piceno (Felletti Maj, *La tradizione italica*, 256 f., fig. 115), close to the other relief of a cinerary urn in the same museum showing a magistrate sitting on a *sella curulis*, exhaustively studied by H. Gabelmann, *Antike Audienz- und Tribunalszenen* (1984), 163 f., no. 72, tav. 22;

in the light of the peculiar form of the funerary monument (in the last years of the Republic and in the early Empire sepulchral customs appear to be rather uniform) this last relief could still belong to the period of the independence of Ausculum.

[106] The scene on the Volterra cinerary urn, formerly in the Forman Collection and now in the British Museum in London (Felletti Maj, *La tradizione italica*, 98 f., fig. 12 a–b, with previous bibliography), which shows a *processus* of horsemen and lictors, with onlookers agitating *palmae*, cannot be a triumphal representation, since there is also depicted a sacrifice in front of a *naiskos*, most likely a monumental tomb: the association between sacrifices and *palmae* is well known in the Romano-Italic world, as proved by the simple comparison of this scene with the *census* representation on the 'altar of Domitius Ahenobarbus'.

[107] On the subject of the paintings and their programme see F. Coarelli, 'Le pitture della tomba François a Vulci: una proposta di lettura', *DArch* 3rd ser., I: 2 (1983), 43 f.

[108] Extremely important on this subject is the momentous book by F.-H. Massa Pairault, *Iconologia e politica nell'Italia antica. Roma, Lazio, Etruria dal VII al I secolo* (Milan, 1992), where many points of my arguments can find perfect consonance.

[109] M. Menichetti, 'L'oinochoe di Tragliatella: mito e rito tra Grecia ed Etruria', in *Ostraka*, I (1992), 7 f., and *Archeologia del potere* (Milan, 1994).

It is worthwhile recalling here a fundamental piece of Etruscan political and religious history which we owe to F.-H. Massa Pairault and M. J. Strazzulla, thanks to their identification of the subject of the pedimental sculptures of the Belvedere temple in Orvieto,[110] the same as the famous votive offering of the Achaeans at Olympia, a masterpiece by Onatas of Aegina and described to us by Pausanias.[111] In the adoption of the myth of the choice by lot of the Achaean champion for the duel with the Trojan champion, we can read an obvious allusion to the isonomic political values annexed by the ruling oligarchies of the Etruscan *poleis* at the choice of the *praetor Etruriae* made in Volsinii itself, together with an incidental reference to the punishment of Veii, guilty of having broken the federal oligarchic isonomy and therefore conquered by the Romans; the scene of the pediment is also a strong reaffirmation of the Etruscan ethnic identity with the Achaeans repeatedly proclaimed by the *principes Etruriae* since archaic times, as opposed to the Roman one, identified with the Trojans.[112]

In this same perspective it is interesting to consider the extraordinary decoration of the pediment of the 'new' (so to speak, having been discovered in 1924) temple of the Scasato, which G. Colonna and M. Cristofani independently made known at the same conference in Orbetello in 1988.[113] The data so far published allow us to identify the basic outline of the depiction with reasonable clarity. In the *columen* plaque, at the centre of the pediment, we might place the fine standing figure of Minerva (Pl. 34), reconstructed with great competence by G. Colonna;[114] Jupiter (Pl. 35)[115] and Juno (Pl. 36)[116] are seated on either side of the goddess, to compose a sort of Capitoline triad. These gods were probably assisted by other Olympian divinities, among which we can distinguish a diademed goddess

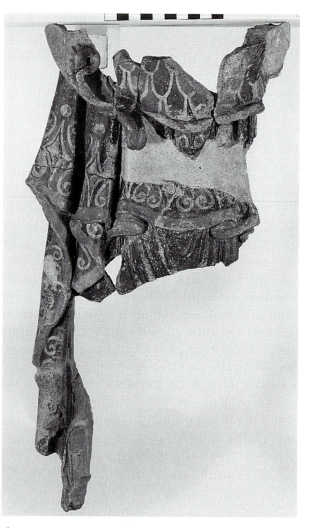

Plate 34. Rome, Museum of the Villa Giulia. Standing figure of Minerva, from the pediment of the temple of Scasato II (courtesy of the Museo di Villa Giulia).

(we might surmise the twin sister of Apollo, Diana),[117] a youthful figure with a delicate torso and folded arms, who we can identify with the hero Ganymede (Pl. 37),[118] well established in Falerii,[119] and perhaps the great Faliscan god Apollo Soranus, recognizable in a very beautiful youthful torso with curly blond hair (Pl. 38).[120] Two other plaques contained each a chariot, both depicted racing, one towards the right and driven by a divine male figure (Pl. 39),[121] the other towards the left

[110] F.-H. Massa Pairault, *Recherches sur l'art et l'artisanat étrusco-italiques à l'époque hellénistique* (Rome, 1985), 41 f.; M. J. Strazzulla, 'La decorazione frontonale del tempio del Belvedere di Orvieto', in G. Maetzke (ed.), *Secondo Congresso Internazionale Etrusco—Atti*, Acts of Congress; Florence, 1985 (Rome, 1989), ii. 971 f.

[111] Paus. 5. 25. 8.   [112] See Ch. 6.

[113] M. Cristofani, 'La decorazione frontonale in Italia centrale fra IV e II sec.a.C.: scelte iconografiche e stile', in Maetzke and Tamagno Perna (eds.), *La coroplastica templare*, 101 f. (henceforth abbreviated as Cristofani); G. Colonna, '*Membra disiecta* di altorilievi frontonali', ibid. 37 f. (henceforth abbreviated as Colonna); for a more recent and fully illustrated publication of these terracottas see M. Cristofani and A. Cohen, 'Terrecotte frontonali del Fondo Belloni in loc. lo Scasato di Civitacastellana', *RIA* 14–15 (1991–2), 73 f.   [114] Colonna, pl. I; Cristofani, pl. V.

[115] Cristofani, pl. II a;.   [116] Colonna, pl. I; Cristofani, pl. VI.

[117] Cristofani and Cohen, *RIA* 14–15 (1991–2), 91 n. 35, fig. 19.

[118] Cristofani, pl. III.

[119] Ganymedes, significantly part of the Dardanian royal family of Troy, appears on the famous eponymous vase of the Faliscan Diespater Painter: for the meaning of this last scene, strongly connected with our pediment, see F.-H. Massa Pairault, 'Stili e committenza nei cicli figurativi fittili di età repubblicana', *Ostraka*, 2 (1993), 244 f.

[120] Cristofani, pl. IV.   [121] Cristofani, pl. VII.

Plate 35. Rome, Museum of the Villa Giulia. Head of Jupiter, from the pediment of the temple of Scasato II (courtesy of the Museo di Villa Giulia).

Plate 36. Rome, Museum of the Villa Giulia. Bust of Juno, from the pediment of the temple of Scasato II (courtesy of the Museo di Villa Giulia).

Plate 37. Rome, Museum of the Villa Giulia. Youthful torso with folded arms, possibly Ganymede, from the pediment of the temple of Scasato II (courtesy of the Museo di Villa Giulia).

Plate 38. Rome, Museum of the Villa Giulia. Youthful torso with blond hair, possibly Apollo, from the pediment of the temple of Scasato II (courtesy of the Museo di Villa Giulia).

Plate 39. Rome, Museum of the Villa Giulia. Chariot driven by a divine male figure, possibly Neptune, from the pediment of the temple of Scasato II (courtesy of the Museo di Villa Giulia).

driven by a goddess (Pl. 40) and possibly escorted by Mercurius (Pl. 41).[122] Since the two plaques are too big and the groups too large to be acroteria placed at the extremity of the roof, as Cristofani would like, we have to interpret them as if they move from the central scene of *concilium deorum*, to reach the human world. Even though placed on separate plaques, the chariots and the divine charioteers by right belong to the assembly of the gods in the centre, according to the principles of composition of the classical Etruscan pediments where unitarian scenes are designed as a series of large, independent panels. Furthermore, the only piece of the pediment published before 1988, a head wrongly claimed to be Zeus (Pl. 42),[123] together with other fragments of several youthful armed and

unarmed figures (Pl. 43),[124] does not seem to belong to the world of gods, but rather to that of heroes. The differences in module of the sculptures pointed out by the editor are not due to a hierarchy of pediments, unproven and without comparisons (the frontal one more important and consequently showing figures of greater scale and the rear one less important and therefore with figures of smaller scale), but merely for reasons of isocephaly: the larger figures, those of Jupiter and Juno, are larger because they are seated, whereas the others are plainly standing. We might, therefore, reconstruct the composition in its outlines as follows:

---

[122] Cristofani, pl. VIII.

[123] Cristofani, pl. I. Cf. also M. Santangelo, 'Una terracotta di Falerii e lo Zeus di Fidia', *BA* (1948), 1 f.; M. Torelli, in R. Bianchi Bandinelli and M. Torelli, *L'arte dell'antichità classica, ii. Etruria e Roma* (Turin, 1976), no. 133; T. Dohrn, *Die etruskische Kunst im Zeitalter der griechischen Klassik* (Mainz, 1982), 34 f.

[124] Cristofani, pl. II b.

Plate 40. Rome, Museum of the Villa Giulia. Chariot driven by a divine female figure, possibly Venus, from the pediment of the temple of Scasato II (courtesy of the Museo di Villa Giulia).

Plate 41. Rome, Museum of the Villa Giulia. Fragment of the flying figure of Mercurius, from the pediment of the temple of Scasato II (courtesy of the Museo di Villa Giulia).

central *columen* plaque occupied by a triad similar to that of the Roman Capitol and by the figures of Ganymede, Diana, and Apollo (?), in a scene similar to that depicted by the great Faliscan master of vase painting, the Diespater Painter, in his eponymous vase;

two intermediate *mutuli* plaques, of which the first on the right shows a chariot driven by Venus and Mercury, and the second on the left a second chariot driven by Neptune;

two terminal *mutuli* plaques, with standing figures of heros, both nude and armed.

The centrality of Minerva in the composition, as G. Colonna has rightly observed,[125] testifies that she is the

god to whom the temple was dedicated, but not only because of this. Minerva is the culminating figure of the big scene, because she is its protagonist. True to her character as oracular divinity particularly developed in the Faliscan and Veientan area,[126] the goddess *fata canit*, 'sings the oracle', in the presence of the supreme divinities, her *consortes*: Jupiter and Juno, not by chance the same as in the supreme temple in Rome, and above all Apollo. This last god, as in the nearby city of Veii, whose fate was similar to that of Falerii, stands at the side—maybe not only in an imaginary way—of the oracular *Menerva* of the Portonaccio temple,[127] maybe as warrant of the Delphic matrix of the prophecy, a guarantee evidently established for its own isonomic ends by the

[125] Colonna, 113.

[126] M. Torelli and [La Regina], 'Due *sortes* preromane', *ArchClass* 20 (1968), 221 f.; see above, Ch. 2.

[127] Extensive treatment of Portonaccio cults by G. Colonna, 'Note preliminari sui culti del santuario di Portonaccio a Veio', *ScAnt* 1 (1987), 419 f.

Plate 42. Rome, Museum of the Villa Giulia. Head of hero, from the pediment of the temple of Scasato II (courtesy of the Museo di Villa Giulia).

Plate 43. Rome, Museum of the Villa Giulia. Head of hero, from the pediment of the temple of Scasato II (courtesy of the Museo di Villa Giulia).

Hellenizing oligarchy in power. The gods driving the two chariots allow us also to propose the occasion for this intervention of Minerva in her aspect of goddess of destiny: the unusual combination of the opposed movement of chariots, that of Venus–Aphrodite, escorted as is customary by Mercury–Hermes,[128] and that of

Neptune-Poseidon, is understandable only in relation on the one hand to Halesus–Alesus, son of the eponymous Poseidon of Falerii and Argive by birth,[129] and on the other to Aeneas, son of Aphrodite, 'father' of the Latins and Trojan by birth. The gods, according to the well-known Homeric model, would be bringing rapid help to their sons, who could be identified with the heroic armed figures I have tentatively placed in the plaques covering the two terminal *mutuli*.

The complex scene, subdivided into possibly five 'vignettes' corresponding to the plaques covering the central *columen* and the four lateral *mutuli*, would be a sort of *psychostasie*[130] carried out by Minerva on the eve of an heroic duel between Halesus and Aeneas, this too a traditional feature in the Greek epic, faithfully

---

[128] On the role of 'escort' of Hermes, see M. P. Nilsson, *Geschichte der griechischen Religion*, 3rd edn. (Munich, 1967), i. 505 f.; on his cultic association with Aphrodite, particularly well established in Samos and in other centres, as in Locri Epizephirii, see E. Buschor, 'Aphrodite und Hermes', *AM* 72 (1957), 77, and H. Prückner, *Die lokrische Tonreliefs* (Mainz, 1968), 15 f.; on the representations of Aphrodite and Hermes on the chariot, cf. E. Simon, *Die Geburt der Aphrodite* (Berlin, 1959), 36 f.

[129] According to one tradition, Halesus is the eponymous hero of Falerii, originating from Argos and son or companion of Agamemnon (Serv. *Aen.* 7. 723, 695; Ov. *Am.* 3. 13. 31 f.; *Fast.* 4. 73; Solin. 2. 7; cf. Cato fr. 68 P; Sil. It. 8. 474 f.); another tradition (Serv. *Aen.* 8. 285) makes him son of Neptune and ancestor of the kings of Veii, whose *carmen saliare* included the name of Halesus; such ambiguity in our sources hides the complex prehistoric ties between the Faliscan and the Veientan areas and the Etruscan colonization of Campania (M. Torelli, *Storia degli Etruschi* (Rome and Bari, 1981), 42 f.); on Halesus, cf. G. Garbugino, 'Aleso', in *Enciclopedia Virgiliana*, i (1984), 90.

[130] Sources and summary of the discussion by E. Wüst, in *RE* XXIII (1939), c.1439 f. It is also worth noting that the Greek tradition makes a metaphoric use of the image of the *psychostasie*: cf. e.g. Aesch. *Sept.* 21; *Ag.* 438.

reflected in the Virgilian poem.[131] Consistent with his Roman perspective, Virgil indeed has Halesus die at the hands of Pallas:[132]

> fata canens silvis genitor celarat Halesus;
> ut senior leto canentia lumina solvit,
> iniecere manum Parcae telique sacrarunt
> Euandri. quem sic Pallas petit ante precatus:
> 'da nunc, Thybri pater, ferro, quod missile libro,
> fortunam atque viam duri per pectus Halesi.
> haec arma exuviasque viri tua quercus habebit.'

We are not well informed as to the origins of the tradition followed by Virgil, who gives Halesus an 'old father', evidently Thybris (that is *Tiberinus pater*)[133] appealed to immediately afterwards by Pallas: it is of interest rather to note the fact that Virgil, we might say understandably, turning the perspective just outlined upside down (and *pour cause*, of the rest), has the father 'sing' the death of Halesus, thus as in our pediment Minerva, poliadic goddess of Falerii, sings the *fata* of the conflict between the two heroes, a conflict which obviously the commissioners, members of the Faliscan aristocracy, will have felt and maybe even celebrated in their *carmina convivalia* as favourable to their founder. Virgil, who elsewhere styles the hero of Falerii 'Agamemnonius, Troiani nominis hostis', seems here to gather elements of traditions about Halesus, which link him to oracles. Furthermore, we should note that in the *precatio* of Pallas the gesture of weighing the lance before the blow is described as an intervention of the *Parcae* when consigning the lance to Pallas and with a sacred language ('da nunc, Thybri pater, ferro, quod missile libro, fortunam atque viam'), not without allusions to the gesture of the *psychostasie*, particularly in the act performed by Pallas, that of 'weighing' the lance before landing the blow.

The pediment has been dated by G. Colonna[134] to the years following the direct conflict between Rome and Falerii after the fall of Veii and close to the traditional chronology of the Faliscan Diespater Painter, whose work shows strong analogies in composition and style with our pediment.[135] As we can readily infer also from the anecdotes in the Roman annalistic tradi-

tion regarding Camillus' siege of the city, the conflict did not terminate with a winner and a loser. The conclusion of the war must have been taken by each of the parties to be a victory. We could not imagine a stronger assertion of the primacy of an aristocratic Falerii, 'a city which found itself all of a sudden sharing with Rome the predominance over the lower valley of the Tiber' (I repeat Colonna's words), than the presentation of the dramatic confrontation between the ancestors of the Argive-Faliscans and of the Trojan-Romans as a fatal event, pronounced by the prophesying song of the same poliadic goddess. There is also possibly an allegorical interplay and a reference of a cyclical nature between protagonists (Halesus and Apollo) and events (*fata* of foundation and *fata* of victory) with the other prophecy of Halesus, which A. Comella has plausibly reconstructed as the subject represented in the tympanum of the temple of Apollo Soranus, as perhaps the Scasato I should be called.[136]

The Greek tradition, since the great pictorial and sculptured cycles of the age of the Severe Style, had set a fashion and the very sudden and dramatic appearance of Rome on the military and political stage of the peninsula could not have been indicated in a more evident way. Had we possessed more information than the too fragmentary pediments of the middle of the fourth century BC of the 'Ara della Regina' of Tarquinia, of Pyrgi and of Vulci,[137] the cases of Volsinii and of Falerii would probably not turn out to be unique in showing us the reactions of the great Etruscan *poleis* to the first dramatic act of the conquest of Etruria at the hands of Rome, the seizing of Veii. I do not believe it is ever excessive to underline the relevance of this event, which, as M. Sordi realized,[138] created enormous shock in the Etruscan world; on the other hand we know that effects of immense importance were also felt in Roman politics during the years immediately subsequent to the conquest of the ancient Etruscan rival.[139]

---

[131] Needless to say that the ζῆλος ὁμηρικός brings Virgil to imagine the *psychostasie* of Turnus and Aeneas: Virg. *Aen.* 12. 725.

[132] Virg. *Aen.* 10. 417–23.

[133] On this exchange of names between Tiber and Thybris in Virgil's poem see J. Carcopino, *Virgile et les origines d'Ostie*, 2nd edn. (Paris, 1968), 505 f.

[134] Colonna, 111 f.

[135] J. D. Beazley, *Etruscan Vase Painters* (Oxford, 1947), 73 f.

[136] A. Comella, 'Apollo Soranus? Il programma figurativo del tempio dello Scasato di Falerii', *Ostraka*, 2 (1993), 301 f.

[137] M. Cataldi Dini, in M. Bonghi Jovino and C. Chiaromonte Trerè (eds.), *Gli Etruschi di Tarquinia*, Catalogue of the Exhibition (Milan, 1986), 357 f. (Tarquinia); G. Colonna, in G. Colonna (ed.), *Santuari d'Etruria*, Catalogue of the Exhibition; Arezzo, 1985 (Milan, 1985), 139 (Pyrgi); ibid. 79 f. (Vulci).

[138] The whole book by M. Sordi, *I rapporti romano-ceriti e l'origine della civitas sine suffragio* (Rome, 1960), is founded on this argument.

[139] V. M. Torelli, 'Il sacco gallico di Roma', in Santoro (ed.), *I Galli e l'Italia*, 226 f.; id., 'Veio e la colonizzazione plebea', in M. Cristofani (ed.), *Civiltà degli Etruschi*, Catalogue of the Exhibition; Florence, 1985 (Milan, 1985), 314 f.; id., 'Aspetti della società romana tra metà del IV e metà del III sec.a.C. La documentazione archeologica', *AIIN* 31 (1989), 19 f.

4. Pediments of the Romanization: The Removal of Policy and the Coming of Dionysus

Figured pediments in areas not subject to direct Roman rule are scarce from the second quarter of the third century down to the beginning of the second century BC, that is for the whole of the century of the great conquest, and with good reasons, in view of the devastating effects of the submission and of the successive Punic wars on the Italic populations. Once again it is only in Falerii that material of importance has turned up. G. Colonna[140] has proposed that the Vignale and

Fabbrica di Roma terracottas are more correctly dated on stylistic grounds to the fourth century BC. The theme of 'victory' of the Fabbrica di Roma pediment (Pl. 44) certainly does not suit the Faliscan perspective of the events of the third century. Accordingly, only the terracottas of the Scasato I pediment, very close to those of the temple of Victory in Rome erected by Postumius Megellus in 295 BC,[141] are left in the third century, possibly to a moment prior to the decade of the great conquest of southern Etruria (282–273 BC), whose subject reflects a more distant and 'antiquarian' atmosphere, that of the origins of Falerii. The same appears to apply to the theme of another figured temple decoration from Falerii, the high relief plaque showing the enchained figure of Andromeda (Pl. 45), correctly considered by Colonna[142] to belong to the first half

Plate 44. Rome, Museum of the Villa Giulia. Figure of victory, from a temple at Fabbrica di Roma (courtesy of the Museo di Villa Giulia).

Plate 45. Rome, Museum of the Villa Giulia. High relief plaque with the figure of Andromeda from Falerii (courtesy of the Museo di Villa Giulia).

[140] Colonna, 112, 122.

[141] New archaeological evidence by P. Pensabene, in *Archeologia Laziale*, 3 (1980), 75 f., pls. 16, 2 and 17, 1.   [142] Colonna, 122.

of the third century BC: the scene is linked as much to Poseidon, father of Andromeda, and therefore to Halesus, the founder of Falerii and also a son of the god, as to the Argive origin of Perseus, the redeemer of Andromeda. The insistence on local traditions is clear, but then political themes gradually drift into the shadows or are rarefied to such an extent, that to our eyes, ignorant of the petty local debates of small provincial towns by now deprived of autonomy (as were also the *poleis* of Italy by the mid-third century BC), they appear to have dissolved into generic allusion or into the simple re-evocation of native virtues and of glories of a distant or mythical past.

It is precisely in this context in which a choice of values begins to stir, promoted by the local culture under the heel of Rome in the real century of Romanization, the second century BC. The Hellenistic reception of the myth, which passed rapidly into Roman, Etruscan, and Italic circles from the great centres of elaboration in the Greek East, favours the evasion and the nostalgic rediscovery of the past. It removes the ethical content which was typical of the spirit of the political thrust of the classical period, and thus becomes a vehicle for fundamentally intellectual values, largely deprived of really polemical bias. In Rome instead, where political clashes rage and where the struggle for power is fought with every possible weapon, the myth, even if intended in general to create a propaganda prevalently within the vertices of society, preserves a relevant part of the original capacity to evoke non-generic meaning is of an ethical-political nature. Even choices of style, as happens in the case of poetic language and judicial and political oratory, bear strong connotations of the various factions in the field. One cannot understand Roman politics of the late Republic if one does not grasp the high-aristocratic significance of the classicist option or the logic of the Asian rhetoric of the *populares*, a fact which has undergone important examination in the history of Roman republican art only in the research of F. Coarelli,[143] of T. Hölscher[144] and of F.-H. Massa

Pairault.[145] Similarly it is not possible to set aside, with regard to the sector which interests us most here, the work of M. J. Strazzulla, who, developing suggestions proposed by F. Coarelli,[146] has shown the existence of a close tie between the formal choices of the pediments at Luni and the stylistic trends in the capital,[147] an element which is undoubtedly of extraordinary importance for our subject.

This cultural climate, which we can only here evoke in a very sketchy form, leads us to declare that actually only the Roman milieu and the ruling classes in the capital (which however include both Latin and Roman citizens in the various colonial foundations) are really productive as regards our aims. To make its own protest Italy could only use a series of Dionysiac themes. The Italic *socii*, though sharing the same Dionysiac soteriology with the Roman lower classes, expressed it in rather dramatic and feverish forms, which do not find real comparisons with the dominant aulic or 'historic' themes in the imagery in the capital. In short, though Rome experienced the phenomenon of Dionysiac protest to a degree that threatened stability between the classes, since it favoured promiscuous relations,[148] Roman figured monuments seldom represented revolutionary themes or even simple allusions to soteric values and hopes, which instead ran through the rarer figured documents of the cities of the *socii*. We might cite here the little *columen* plaque from the Ponte Rotto necropolis at Vulci (Pl. 46),[149] together with the several small tufa pediments in low relief from tomb façades of the same necropolis:[150] this simple pedimental

[143] F. Coarelli, 'L'ara di Domizio Enobarbo e la cultura artistica in Roma nel II sec.a.C.', *DArch* 2 (1968), 302 f.; id., 'Polycles', *Studi Miscellanei*, 15 (1970), 75 f.; id., 'I primi contatti di Roma con l'ellenismo e la formazione dell'arte romana', *DArch* 4–5 (1970–1), 173 f.; id., 'Classe dirigente romana e arti figurative', ibid. 241 f.; id., 'Architettura e arti figurative in Roma: 150–50 a.C.', in Zanker (ed.), *Hellenismus in Mittelitalien*, 21 f.; id., 'Arte ellenistica ed arte romana: la cultura figurativa in Roma tra II e I sec. a.C.', in Cristofani (ed.), *Caratteri dell'ellenismo*, 35 f.

[144] See, above all, T. Hölscher, 'Römische Bildsprache als semantisches System', *AHAW* 2 (1987).

[145] Cf. Massa Pairault, *Recherches sur l'art*; ead., *Recherches sur quelques séries d'urnes de Volterra à représentation mythologiques* (Rome, 1972); ead., 'Un aspect de l'artisanat d'albâtre à Volterra. Quelques visages d'atelier', *DArch* 6 (1972), 11 f.; ead., 'Un nouvel atelier de Volterra. Autour du Maître de Myrtilos', *MEFRA* 85 (1973), 91 f.; ead., 'Ateliers d'urnes et histoire de Volterra', in Cristofani (ed.), *Caratteri dell'ellenismo*, 154 f.; ead., *Iconologia e politica nell'Italia antica*.

[146] Besides the articles mentioned in the previous notes, see F. Coarelli, 'La fondazione di Luni', *Quaderni del Centro di Studi Lunensi*, 10–12 (1985–7), 17 f.

[147] Strazzulla, in Maetzke and Tamagno Perna (eds.), *La coroplastica templare etrusca*.

[148] The immediate perception by the ruling classes of the *Bacchanalia* as a festival disruptive of the Roman class system is very well described by C. Gallini, *Protesta e integrazione nella Roma antica* (Rome and Bari, 1970). Very useful also are both the collective volume *L'Association dionysiaque dans les sociétés anciennes*, Acts of the Colloquium; Rome, 1984 (Rome, 1986), and the standard work on the subject by J.-M. Pailler, *Bacchanalia. La répression de 186 av. J.-C. à Rome et en Italie* (Rome, 1988).

[149] M. Bonamici, 'L'edicola di Ponte Rotto a Vulci', in Maetzke and Tamagno Perna (eds.), *La coroplastica templare etrusca*, 127 f.

[150] We lack a definitive publication of this important group of funerary monuments; in the meantime see T. Dohrn, in Helbig, *Führer*⁴, iii, n. 2502, 481 f. (with previous bibliography); Bonamici, in Maetzke and Tamagno Perna (eds.), *La coroplastica templare etrusca*, 137 no. 54.

Plate 46. Florence, Museo Archeologico. Columen plaque with Dionysus and Ariadne, from the Ponte Rotto necropolis at Vulci (courtesy of the Museo Archeologico Nazionale, Florence).

representation of the Dionysiac couple is closely related to a well-known group of terracottas from a house in Bolsena and in particular the unique terracotta 'throne' for the celebration of the Dionysiac mysteries again from Bolsena.[151] To put it in a very synthetic form, the few Etruscan and Italic monuments of the second century BC belonging to the cult of Dionysus which survived the Roman suppression, reflect a system of values that in general appears to have been hard to integrate with those ingrained in the local tradition, despite the diffusion in late-Hellenistic Etruria of the 'official' cult of *Fufluns*, attested in particular at Vulci with the significant epithet Bacchus, that is as *Fufluns—Paχa*.[152]

[151] F.-H. Massa Pairault and J. M. Pailler, *La Maison aux salles souterraines. i. Les terres cuites sous le péristyle,* Bolsena 5: 2 (Rome, 1978); F.-H. Massa Pairault, 'La Restauration du trône en terre cuite de Bolsena. Confirmations et nouveautés', *MEFRA* 93 (1981), 495 f.

[152] M. Cristofani and M. Martelli, '*Fufluns Paχies* Sugli aspetti del culto di Bacco in Etruria', *SE* 46 (1978), 119 f.; but see also F.-H. Massa Pairault, 'En quel sens parler de la romanisation du culte de Dionysos en Etrurie?', *MEFRA* 99 (1987), 573 f. and G. Colonna, 'Riflessioni sul dionisismo in Etruria', in F. Berti (ed.), *Dionysos. Vita e mistero,* Acts of Colloquium; Comacchio, 1990 (Comacchio, 1991), 117 f.

Plate 47. Bologna, Museo Civico. Fragment of a frieze showing the flight of the Gauls after the sack of Delphi, from Civitalba (courtesy of the Museo Civico, Bologna).

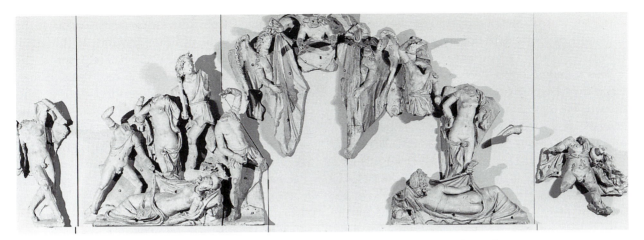

Plate 48. Bologna, Museo Civico. Pediment with the Dionysiac thiasos discovering two women asleep on mount Parnassus, from Civitalba (courtesy of the Museo Civico, Bologna).

On the other hand Roman religious culture offered, as is clearly visible at Paestum,[153] the possibility of integrating the new Dionysiac trend into the popular Dionysiac religion of the traditional festival of the *Liberalia*, a factor which may help us understand otherwise disquieting evidence, such as the dancing Satyr decorating a second-century BC temple of Venusia. However, for the *cives Romani* spread throughout Italy, another way to integration lay in the erudite and hyperhellenized philological culture of Hellenism, in particular Pergamene antiquarianism, which the *nobilitas* of the *urbs* had immediately learnt to appreciate as *instrumentum regni* and therefore held supremely dear. One particularly significant example of this tendency is provided by the terracottas from Civitalba,[154] which occupy an important position in the context of the peninsula's Romanization. I believe the key to their correct interpretation lies in not separating conceptually the frieze with the sacking Gauls fleeing the sanctuary in Delphi in 279 BC (Pl. 47) and the pediment depicting a complex scene of Dionysiac epiphany (Pl. 48). Both refer to the same topographic sphere, which the frieze indicates in an unequivocal manner as the Delphic one. The Dionysiac tradition associated with Delphi is fairly rich and the pediment shows us two apparently distinct scenes, a discovery-awakening of two women by the Dionysiac thiasos, with a quite deliberate revival of the iconography of the sleeping Ariadne, and a central 'discovery' which represents the conceptual climax of the action of the entire pediment. Now the celebration every fourth year at Delphi of

the spring *pannychis* of Dionysus, i.e. of the god whom Plutarch defines as 'the lord of the winter' of the oracle sanctuary,[155] actually culminates in the festival of Dionysus Liknites, a festival which the sources connote as an 'awakening' celebrated on Parnassus.[156] Dionysus Liknites was the Dionysus of the λῖκνον, 'of the basket', symbol of vegetation in the awakening stage,[157] but also of the Dionysiac mystery, and in the pediment of Civitalba a basket, a *cysta mystica*, must have occupied the central space of the *parapetasma* lifted by the Erotes. The scenes at either side must then represent in symbolic form the legend of the foundation of the Dionysiac cult of Delphi,[158] the 'call' of Thyia, daughter of the hero Kastalios, eponymous of the source and high priestess of Dionysus.[159] According to a mythical account firmly established in Delphi, the Bacchic retinue had found Thyia asleep on Parnassus in company with other women from Delphi, ancestors of the Thyades,[160] who we know used to celebrate the awakening of Dionysus Liknites in a festival they shared with the Bacchic *thiasos* of the Athenian Thyades.[161] Alternatively, the scene could be read as another famous 'rediscovery', again made by the Dionysiac *thiasos*, that of the Theban heroine Ino, she too a high priestess of Dionysus 'wandering' on

---

[153] See Ch. 3.   [154] See n. 51.

[155] Plut. *De E apud Delphos*, 9.   [156] Plut. *De Iside et Osiride*, 35.
[157] For a different view on this festival see M. P. Nilsson, *The Dionysiac Mysteries of the Hellenistic and Roman Age* (Lund, 1957), 21 f.
[158] On the origins and the foundation myths of maenadism see H. Jeanmaire, *Dionysos. Histoire du culte de Bacchus* (Paris, 1951), 198 f.
[159] Mentioned by Paus. 10. 6. 4.
[160] On the Thyiades see now M.-C. Villanueva Puig, 'À propos des Thyades de Delphes', in *L'Association dionysiaque*, 31 f. (with previous bibliography).   [161] Paus. 10. 4. 3.

Parnassus, a myth sung of in a tragedy by Euripides and—what is most interesting for us—also in one by Ennius.[162]

This reconstruction allows us not only to establish the wholly Delphic connections between the frieze showing the expulsion of the Gauls from Delphi at the hand of Apollo and Artemis and the pediment which celebrates Dionysus taking possession of Parnassus. The latter myth, already known to Aeschylus,[163] had a central role to play in the construction of the Delphic art of divination,[164] but we can also guess at a complex series of precise soteriological allusions of highly refined Hellenistic stamp. For a long time we have known, as D. Musti[165] has emphasized in recent times, that the dynastic cult of Pergamum exploited the Delphic Dionysus in a very sophisticated way, through the figure of Dionysus Sphaleotas.[166] This Dionysus, though venerated in Delphi, certainly originated in Mysia, and could therefore be matched with Apollo, the central god in the propaganda and in the dynastic cult of the rival Seleucids. Let us not forget that the epithet Liknites, other than in Plutarch, is only found in the Orphic Hymns,[167] whose Pergamene origin is widely recognized.[168]

The same soteric values of the cult, as elaborately nurtured as among the intellectuals of the Attalid court, also provided a precise pretext of a 'cyclical' nature for the tie between the Apollo of Delphi and the Dionysus of Parnassus–Pergamum. The Corycian Cave is the place, where the Thriai are found, 'repliques apolliniennes des Thyades', the alternative and complementary figures to the Thyades, as Villanueva Puig[169] correctly calls them; in the same Cave, as Herodotus informs us,[170] the inhabitants of Delphi would have found refuge when faced with the descent of the Persians. The salvation from the Persians, which was offered by the mountain cave, simultaneously under the protection of Dionysus and Apollo and inhabited by the nymphs and Pan, could be regarded as a prefiguration of the salvation which the same

gods assured Delphi from the Galatian invaders. In the cyclical conception of history so dear to the intellectuals of Hellenism, the Gauls had returned, as the forces of Evil periodically do, in the tracks of their wicked and barbarian predecessors, the Persians. Similarly, the intervention of the Delphic god could also be read as a portent of the more general salvation promised to mortals by the *liknon*, the basket which had saved the infant Dionysus Liknites. There is no doubt that behind this extraordinary series of terracottas in Civitalba lies the influence of a very elaborate Hellenistic culture, only conceivable as a product of intellectual circles in the capital.

4. The Years of Crisis: Integration, Social Issues and Roman Propaganda

The passing of the decades of the second century BC made the distinctions between winners and losers, between conquerors and conquered, ever more slight and uncertain. The economic and social pressure until that time exercised by the capital over the Italian periphery was transformed into an urgent need for integration, experienced by the various peoples and by the various cities in a manner which we can imagine was at times conscious and at times unconscious.[171] It is in this context that a powerful tool for an ideological unification is offered by the culture which I would define as the culture of the *Origines*, from the name of the historical work by Cato, not by chance a man of provincial extraction and unconnected to the old *nobilitas*.[172] It is to such a culture, active in Rome as in the rest of Italy, that the recovery of local traditions is owed, a central feature of Hellenistic historiography and culture, which in Italy becomes the instrument capable of giving voice to the conquered peoples in Italy, for more than a century reduced to silence. According to Cato, Ameria has a foundation date actually even earlier than that of Rome,[173] and Antemnae is considered more ancient than Rome;[174] long heroic genealogies of the cities and of the peoples, the Theban, the Arcadian, and the Argive lineage of Tibur[175] and the Lacedaemonian origins of Sabines,[176] are codified in the *Origines*; Cato's book revives myths and legends of the Faliscans and of the Etruscans, of the Campanians

[162] On Ennius' *Athamas* see H. D. Jocelyn, *The Tragedies of Ennius* (Cambridge, 1967), 267 f.   [163] Aesch. *Eum.* 22 f.

[164] P. Amandry, *La Mantique apollinienne à Delphes* (Paris, 1950), 296 f.

[165] D. Musti, 'Il dionisismo degli Attalidi: antecedenti, modelli, sviluppi', in *L'Association dionysiaque*, 105.

[166] G. Daux and J. Bousquet, 'Agamemnon, Télèphe, Dionysos Sphaleotas et les Attalides', *RA* (1942), 113 f.; (1943), 19 f.

[167] *Hymn. Orph.* 30, 42, 52.

[168] Nilsson, *Geschichte der griechischen Religion*, ii. 364.

[169] Villanueva Puig, in *L'Association dionysiaque*, 44.

[170] Herod. 8. 36. 2.

[171] See Ch. 4.

[172] Good synthesis of Cato's personality by F. Della Corte, *Catone censore. La vita e la fortuna*, 2nd edn. (Florence, 1969).   [173] Cato, fr. 49 P.

[174] Cato, fr. 21 P.   [175] Cato, fr. 56 P.   [176] Cato, frr. 50–1 P.

and of the Veneti, whose mythical heroes now act within a single scenario and within a single chronological framework, a circumstance made even more highly historically significant by the fact that all it was conceived of in the city of the conquerors.

It is in this climate that we can place the intense revival of local cultures which characterizes the whole of Italy in the second half of the second century BC, principally reflected in the frenetic activity in the field of sacred building which I alluded to above. On the temple façades of both the Roman citizens of Italy and the *socii italici* we find, standing side by side with the by now usual Amazonomachies and Celtomachies (as those depicted in the terracottas of the Catona temple at Arretium),[177] myths and legends of the local past and *concilia deorum* of the city, such as in the pedimental groups from Luni[178] and from Tivoli.[179] These dramatic or classicistic representations of local mythical events no longer have the task of celebrating the great civic ethical–political values, the party choices of the struggling aristocratic *partes* or the alliances and the hostilities between more or less nearby *poleis*, but are expressive of artful though remunerative *syngeneiai* with Rome or with ancient cities of Latium, as documented by a famous second-century BC inscription celebrating the *syngeneia* between Centuripe and Lanuvium,[180] or, more simply, the *antiquitas* and the consequent *sanctitas* of the place, which, legitimized by the centre, had now become the main ideological issue in the periphery of Italy.

In our figured temple decorations we can sometimes discover, though concealed by more superficial messages, evidence of the most dramatic events of the times, from the *coniuratio* of the *Bacchanalia* to the dramatic events of Gracchus and beyond. The exceptional success enjoyed by the culminating episode of the Theban saga, the mutual murder of the brothers Eteocles and Polynices, in the late Etruscan urns of Chiusi, Volterra, and Perugia,[181] also touches, as is well

known, the pediment of the temple of Talamonaccio (Pl. 49).[182] This extra-urban temple stands in a territory which, in the light of the extent of the Latin and Roman colonial foundations of Cosa, Heba, and Saturnia, had to belong to the *ager publicus p.R.*, though it is possible that it was occupied by Etruscan tenants.[183] In any case the contiguity with lands directly colonized by Rome and inhabited by Roman colonists leads us to believe that the message conveyed by the pedimental reliefs must have been appreciated as much by Romans as by Etruscans; even if we were to recognize Etruscans as the commissioners of the figured pediment (and I am convinced of the exact contrary), they certainly took account of the overwhelming presence of Roman citizens in the area, if not actually directing a precise discourse at them in the allegorical form of the disaster of the Seven against Thebes and the ruin of the house of Oedipus.

What then is the meaning of this gigantic fresco in terracotta, of this *fictilis fabula*? F.-H. Massa Pairault posed the question pretty well when she said that 'between Rome and Etruria there were open questions . . . those of the colonies, the confiscated land and the coexistence of communities organized according different statutes' and that, nevertheless, 'it is not at all demonstrated that the scene of Eteocles and Polynices reflects conflicts arisen inside of the Roman colonies in Etruria'.[184] The level at which the representation in its most complete sense operates, possesses universal values, even though its thrust is born of very specific circumstances. The great political debate which takes

[177] Massa Pairault, *Recherches sur l'art et l'artisanat*, 160 f.; E. Ducci, 'Le terrecotte architettoniche della Catona', *SE* 55 (1987–8), 131 f.; ead., 'Le terrecotte architettoniche della Catona', in Maetzke and Tamagno Perna (eds.), *La coroplastica templare*, 325 f.

[178] M. J. Strazzulla, 'Le terrecotte frontonali di Luni', in Maetzke and Tamagno Perna (eds.), *La coroplastica templare*, 167 f.

[179] Massa Pairault, *Recherches sur l'art et l'artisanat*, 152 f.

[180] The inscription has been published by G. Manganaro, 'Un *senatus consultum* in greco dei Lanuvini e il rinnovo della *cognatio* con i Centuripini', *RAAN* NS 38 (1963), 23 f., a text giving full confirmation of some well-known assertions by Cicero, *Verr.* 2. 5. 83 f.(cf. ibid. 2. 3. 129 and Plin. *NH* 3. 91).

[181] On these monuments see I. Krauskopf, *Der thebanische Sagenkreis und andere griechische Sagen in der etruskische Kunst* (Mainz, 1974).

[182] O. W. von Vacano and B. von Freytag gen. Löringhoff, *Talamone. Il mito dei Sette a Tebe*, Catalogue of the Exhibition (Florence, 1982); O. W. von Vacano, *Gli Etruschi a Talamone* (Bologna, 1985), 102 f.; B. von Freytag gen. Löringhoff, *Das Giebelrelief von Telamon* (Mainz, 1986), with previous bibliography; L. Sensi, *Gli scavi di G.Sordini sul Poggio di Talamonaccio* (Florence, 1987); B. von Freytag gen. Löringhoff, 'Annotazioni al frontone dei Sette a Tebe', in Maetzke and Tamagno Perna (eds.), *La coroplastica templare*, 69 f.

[183] On this territory see F.-H. Massa Pairault, 'Talamone e l'area costiera', in Carandini (ed.), *La romanizzazione dell'Etruria*, 115 f., who appropriately recalls (p. 116) the discovery of three Etruscan inscriptions in this territory (an Etruscan inscription on marble, still unpublished, but mentioned by F. E. Brown, *Cosa: The Making of a Roman Town* (Ann Arbor, 1980), 45 n. 4, is known also to have been discovered in Cosa), which could refer to Etruscan land tenants of Roman *ager publicus*; finally, it is difficult to share the assertions of B. von Freytag gen. Löringhoff, 'Annotazioni al frontone dei Sette a Tebe', in Maetzke and Tamagno Perna (eds.), *La coroplastica templare*, who mixes up political statutes with the circulation of craftsmen and artisanal models, belonging to different levels, not necessarily identical.

[184] Massa Pairault, *Recherches sur l'art et l'artisanat*, 232: 'entre Rome et l'Étrurie ont joué . . . la question des colonies, de la diminution du territoire et des conséquences qu'entraînait la cœxistence de communautés régies par des droits différents . . . il n'est pas parfaitement prouvé que la scène d'Étéocle et Polynice constitue la transposition de conflits nés à l'intérieur et autour des colonies romaines en Étrurie'.

Plate 49. Florence, Museo Archeologico. Pediment from the Talamone temple (courtesy of the Museo Archeologico Nazionale, Florence).

place in the second century BC in Rome and then is reflected in Etruria, where it becomes associated in particular with the destruction, certainly incomplete, of the ancient serfdom,[185] revolves constantly around the grand theme of the *concordia ordinum* and of the ethical reasons for its maintenance, with all the references to the *paradeigmata* of the myth suggested by the tragedies and by the tragic oratory of the period. However, the meanings are perhaps even more complex and even go beyond the warning concerning the *connubia*: let us consider, for instance, the *exemplum* which the depiction of the end of Amphiaraus was undoubtedly meant to express, an example of the 'good use of the art of divination', one of the strongest areas of cultural and political interference between the Etruscan sphere and the Roman sphere, and one where not infrequent reference is made to the wickedness and the bad faith of the *haruspices*.[186] On the other hand the insistence in the haruspicy on themes of aristocratic

isonomy, the *adfectactio regni* and the *concordia ordinum* is well known: such famous *responsa haruspicum* as 'ne per optimatium discordiam dissensionemque patribus principibusque caedes pericula creentur', 'ne occultis consiliis res publica laedatur', 'ne rei publicae status commutetur',[187] lead us into the same world of second-century conflicts both locally and at large to which nearby Cosa affords us a valuable clue with its forum temple dedicated to none other than Concordia.[188]

Temple decorations in these crucial years of Italian history may provide some indication of further conflicts. F. Buranelli[189] has recently republished, with several novelties, the architectural terracottas of the second century discovered during the excavations carried out in the ancient city of Vulci by the brothers Campanari. These terracottas include antefixes with human figures almost fully in the round, relating to the myth of Orestes, and a continuous frieze, in which we can read the triumph of Semele. The triumph is celebrated

---

[185] M. Torelli, *Storia degli Etruschi* (Rome and Bari, 1981), 257 f.; id., *La società etrusca. Età arcaica e classica* (Rome, 1987), 87 f.; the connection with the theme of *concordia* was recognized by Massa Pairault, *Recherches sur l'art et l'artisanat*, 236 f.

[186] As happens in the *procuratio* of the prodigy connected with the statue of Horatius Cocles: Gell. 4. 5. 1 f.

[187] Cic. *De har.resp.* 40. 55. 60.   [188] Brown, *Cosa*, 31, 38.

[189] F. Buranelli, 'Vulci: appunti sugli scavi della società Vincenzo Campanari-Governo Pontificio (1835–1837)', in *Atti Secondo Congresso Internazionale Etrusco*, 231 f.; id., *Gli scavi a Vulci della società Vincenzo Campanari-Governo Pontificio (1835–1837)* (Rome, 1991), 130 f.; id., 'Divagazioni vulcenti', in Maetzke and Tamagno Perna (eds.), *La coroplastica templare*, 143 f.

Plate 50. Vatican Museum. Fragment of a terracotta frieze with a nereid carrying a shield, from Vulci (courtesy of the Musei Vaticani).

by flying figures in the act of transporting other figures carrying objects and by a marine *thiasos* composed of one or more chariots drawn by *kete*, these, too, bearing figures carrying attributes (Pl. 50). Buranelli has already recognized iconographic similarities with the frieze of the so-called 'altar of Domitius Ahenobarbus'.[190] In particular, the seemingly contemporary presence of these figures in flight and on the surface of the sea, at least two of whom wear a *nebris* and brandish either a *clipeus* or a *volumen*, suggest us the coexistence, or rather the desired contrast between a heavenly 'triumph' in the Dionysiac sphere and a marine 'triumph', between the world of Dionysus and the world of Poseidon. The first frieze, to which at least nine fragments belong, would have celebrated a celestial apotheosis of Semele at the centre of a flying procession of maenads and young Satyrs,[191] while the other, of which there are at least six fragments, would have represented the triumph of Neptune on his chariot with a train of tritons, female tritons, and *kete* ridden by figures in poses which could have been symmetrical to those of the Satyrs and maenads transported by their flying

Plate 51. Vatican Museum. Fragment of a terracotta frieze with a cuirassed figure, from Vulci (courtesy of the Musei Vaticani).

companions.[192] The two events are linked together not only by the similarity of the iconography of the 'transport of human figures', held up by flying persons or by *kete* on the surface of the water, but also by an important detail: from the iconographic point of view there were some extensive overlaps between the two processions; at least one fragment exists showing a flying maenad caught in the act not only of holding up the rudder of a ship, but also of transporting a Satyr wearing a *nebris* and bearing a *clipeus*. This transport of arms in both the friezes cannot end in any way other than in the arms being consigned to Achilles, whose armoured figure may even have been preserved (Pl. 51).[193]

The blending of the two iconographies is not devoid of significance, since it would seem to indicate the matching of a cult of the god of the sea with that of Dionysus, a 'triumphal' apotheosis of Semele to a consignment of arms to Achilles, the latter I would say,

[190] Buranelli, *Gli scavi a Vulci*, 160; id., in Maetzke and Tamagno Perna (eds.), *La coroplastica templare*, 149.

[191] Buranelli, *Gli scavi a Vulci*, 137 no. x (Semele transported by an eagle together with two maenads); 135 f., no. IX, and 147 no. XXI (flying woman bringing a spear or a rudder and transporting a man holding a clipeus); 139 no. XII (man bringing a *volumen*); 143 no. XVII (flying woman transporting a man wearing a *nebris*); 144 no. XVIII, and 149 no. XXV (flying man transporting a woman bringing a spear); 147 no. XXI (woman transporting a man). *Adde* Buranelli, in Maetzke and Tamagno Perna (eds.), *La coroplastica templare*, pl. VIII, fr. with flying woman transporting a man wearing a *nebris*.

[192] Buranelli, *Gli scavi a Vulci*, 135 no. VIII, and 145 no. XIX (feminine monsters with snake coils bringing men); 140 f. nos. XIII–XIV (chariot wheels and coils of *ketos*); 142 no. XV, and 149 no. XXVI (man on *ketos*). The following fragments can belong to either frieze: 146 no. XX, and 151 no. XXVII (seated man); 147 no. XXII (two men); 147 nos. XXIII–XXIV (two women); 151 nos. XXVIII–XXIX (woman).   [193] Buranelli, *Gli scavi a Vulci*, 153 no. XXXI.

however, being done almost syncretistically by characters belonging to both processions. The answer to this unusual hybrid iconography possibly lies in an event which took place in the capital, solemnly celebrated by a monument already cited in comparison with the frieze: the 'altar of Domitius Ahenobarbus'. Many years ago I maintained[194] and, since I have not read any serious arguments contrary to my interpretation put forward by other scholars in the last ten years, I still maintain that this monument, saved miraculously from the lime-kilns of the Campus Martius, should be interpreted as a base (or one of the bases) of the sculptural group depicting the consignment of arms to Achilles by Tethys, the work of Scopas Minor, recorded by Pliny as placed *in delubro Cn. Domiti*, that is in the temple of Neptune *in Circo*.[195] The motivation of this votive offering could most likely be the renewal of the *lex Sempronia militaris* by Cn. Domitius Ahenobarbus *cens.* 115 BC. The *lex Sempronia militaris*, passed by C. Gracchus during his first tribunate in 123 BC, provided for the distribution of arms for military service at the expense of the state to all citizens:[196] the renewal would fall in the same year as the murder of the tribune, 122 BC, when Cn. Domitius Ahenobarbus was consul.

The votive monument by Scopas Minor celebrated that eventual *lex Domitia militaris*[197] in a symbolically allusive form, i.e. by staging the myth of the consignment of arms to Achilles by his mother the goddess, in a blend—so dear to Hellenistic mind—with another version of the same myth, which made the Oceanids the protagonists of the consignment.[198] To paraphrase the famous opening of Virgil's first *Ecloga*, 'deus nobis haec arma dedit' might be the translation of the propagandistic message of Domitius Ahenobarbus, who in this most sophisticated way emphasized his link with Neptune (his propaganda quite openly tends to identify him with the king of the sea), that is the divinity of 'his' temple,[199] the *aedes Neptuni in Circo*, or

delubrum Cn. Domitii, who was meant to be the celestial inspirer of the political operation conducted by means of the law which he had approved. It would take too long here to deal with the complex history of the semantics of this myth, so popular among the early aristocracies of Italy as affirmation, in the face of political pressure from the non-aristocratic classes, of a real 'divine right' to the possession of arms.[200] In archaic Italy this theme had had direct and important repercussions in the monumental scenes on the ceremonial war chariots from Monteleone di Spoleto and Todi,[201] rich in significance as regards the self-representation of their owners. Now, in the turbulent climate of the late Republic, the same myth acquired meanings which, if not radically opposite, were certainly very different, and which previously only show up in the unusual mixture / juxtaposition made in the Vulci frieze of two *thiasoi*, that of Dionysus and that of Poseidon. In a sacred context dominated by Dionysus, the operation must in all likelihood have favoured the introduction of the new political message brought by Neptune–Ahenobarbus, the whole in a double context of triumphal nature, that of the apotheosis of Semele and that of the *pompe* of Poseidon.

But was there any sense in showing this myth in the Vulci of the last decades of the second century BC? The answer comes yet again from the historical context of the city, where, as stated elsewhere,[202] numerous factors suggest the possibility that Vulci was the object of a Gracchan colony, on a par with nearby Tarquinia.[203] This event seems certified by archaeological data, essentially a tomb of the late second-century containing an oil-lamp shaped in the form of the Capitoline she-wolf[204] and the 'House of the Cryptoporticus', so typically

[194] Torelli, *Typology and Structure*, 8, 14 f.

[195] Plin. *NH* 36. 26 with the articles by Coarelli, cited above (n. 142).

[196] Plut. *C. Gracch.* 5. 1; cf. E. Gabba, *Esercito e società nella tarda repubblica romana* (Florence, 1973), 15 f.

[197] G. Rotondi, *Leges publicae populi Romani* (Milan, 1912), 308, calls the Gracchan law *lex Sempronia militaris*.

[198] The lost tragedy by Aeschilus, *Nereides* (cf. H. G. Mette, *Der verlorene Aischylos* (Berlin, 1963), 118), is very important for the constitution of the iconography of this myth, which goes back to the older, Thessalian version of the legend and has the Nereids as protagonists: cf. A. Kossatz-Deissmann, *Dramen des Aischylos auf Westgriechischen Vasen* (Mainz, 1978), 18 f.

[199] The connection between the Ahenobarbi and the temple of Neptune *in Circo* has been explored by Torelli, *Typology and Structure*, 16.

[200] S. C. Miller, 'Eros and the Arms of Achilles', *AJA* 90 (1986), 159 f.

[201] On the chariot from Monteleone di Spoleto see A. Emiliozzi, 'Il Carro di Monteleone: dal rinvenimento al restauro', in F. Roncalli (ed.), *Antichità dell'Umbria a New York*, Catalogue of the Exhibition; New York, 1991 (Perugia, 1991), 103 f. (with previous bibliography); on the chariot from Todi see M. Torelli, 'La società della frontiera', in Bergamini and Comez (eds.), *Verso un Museo della Città*, 57 f.

[202] See Ch. 5.

[203] For the case of Tarquinia we have not only the support of the onomastic data, but also that of the sources, since a colony *lege Sempronia* is mentioned in the *Liber Coloniarum* (p. 219 L): cf. M. Torelli, *Elogia Tarquiniensia* (Florence, 1975), 186 f. The researches and discoveries of the last quarter of century would allow scholars to rewrite the chapter of the Gracchan colonies in southern Etruria, to be identified with the land i ndicated as ἔρημος or peopled by οἰκέτας ἐπεισάκτους καὶ βαρβάρους in the famous passage in Plutarch's life of Ti. Gracchus (*Ti. Gracch.* 8): in the meantime, see W. V. Harris, *Rome in Etruria and Umbria* (Oxford, 1971), 204 f.   [204] Buranelli, *Gli scavi a Vulci*, 168 f.

Roman in plan and ostentatious luxury, from the same period.[205] To the archaeological evidence we might add important epigraphical data, primarily the inscriptions indicating that clients of the Gracchi took possession of the so-called tomb 'of the Inscriptions'—an Etruscan tomb of collective property and in part of seemingly public character or at least not gentilicial, belonging to a female college of *hatrencu*.[206] Further evidence in this direction comes from the onomastics, which, as in Tarquinia, point to an extensive replacement of the leading Etruscan aristocracy with families of Latin origins.[207] The presence of a Gracchan colony in this area would favour the celebration of an event, i.e. the probable lex *Domitia militaris*, which had among its main objectives that of placating the dissatisfaction among the followers of the murdered tribune. The general political interest was linked, in this particular case, to the personal and local interests of Cn. Domitius Ahenobarbus in extending his own clientele in a zone, in particular the coastal area of Etruria and the area formerly of Vulci, in which the economic presence of the Domitii is most marked and well recognized, partly due to the numerous *villae* they owned on these coasts and to the name of *Domitiana positio* attributed to a port on the Mons Argentarius.[208]

Bent once more to fit new needs, in the background of which we can sense the fierce political conflicts of the end of the Republic, the myth shown in these *fictiles fabulae* foreshadows the allegory of the Empire's official art, in which by means of Hellenistic *subtilitas* thousands of allusions are generated for the *laus principis*, though within the rigid frame of a necessary, close correlation between myth and rite, between sacred confirmation of the political act and symbolic representation of the act itself. Unfortunately we have lost the ultimate example of these *fabulae*, the one adorning the *aedes Herculis Pompeiana ad Circum Maximum*, the last exponent in Rome of the tradition of temples built *tuscanico more*. Rome was to lose its fictile apparel, soon replaced, in accordance with Augustus' programme, by marble veneer, whilst Italy, its assemblies reduced to symbols, would very soon seem to have lost its political centrality, cause and effect of so much propaganda spread in the last century of the Republic in the cities of the peninsula. Nevertheless, it is undeniable that the poor clay of pediments and friezes, with their powerful allure of colour and the evocative capacity of their mythical tales, contributed not a little to the creation of the unitarian culture of *tota Italia*, mainstay and might of the 'Roman revolution', responsible for the birth of imperial power.

[205] G. Gazzetti, 'La Casa del Criptoportico', in Carandini (ed.), *La romanizzazione dell'Etruria*, 64 f.

[206] M. T. Falconi Amorelli, in *SE* 31 (1963), 185 f. The property of the tomb is subdivided in this way (being perfectly oriented, the chambers are indicated through the cardinal points): N. chamber, *prus´lnas* family, inscr. no. 3: *vel prus´lnas*; S. chamber, *zimarus* family, inscr. nos. 13 and 14: *vel zimaru ∞ ramθa murai hatrencu*; NW chamber, *prus´lnas* family, inscr. nos. 18–21: *vel prus´lnas ∞ ramθa ceisatru*; NE chamber, property of a certain *prus´lnai ramθa hatrencu* and of a *zimarui r(amθa) hatrencu*, inscr. no. 4; E. chamber, *prus´lnas* family, inscr. nos. 5–10: *arnθ prus´lnas ∞ visnei ramθa h(atrencu)*, maybe parents of *vel*, in his own turn father of another *v(el)* and of *a(rnθ)*, replaced by a L. Sempronius L.f. and by a Gaia Postumia (inscr. nos. 11–12), presumably a couple; W. chamber, property of a *zimarui ramθa hatrencu* (inscr. no. 17), most likely the same person (inscr. no. 4) of the NE chamber, and of a *murai ramθa* (inscr. no. 16), replaced by a Sex. Sempronius L.f., presumably brother of L. Sempronius L.f. mentioned in the inscr. no. 17, and by a woman whose name is illegible (inscr. no. 15), most likely the wife of Sex. Sempronius. From the location of the inscriptions and from the onomastic, it is easy to conclude that the tomb was founded by *vel prus´lnas* (inscr. no. 3), who designated the nearby NW chamber for the burial of his grandson (married to a *ceisatru*) and his great-grandsons; the distribution of the property, however, was settled by a *prus´lnai r(amθa) hatrencu* (inscr. no. 4), not by chance a member of the same *hatrencu* college as *zimarui r(amθa) hatrencu*, who admitted into the tomb (S. chamber) the *zimarus* family not related to the *prus´lnas*, and who had furthermore full use of the W. chamber. We are dealing with an original gentilicial property of the *gens prus´lnas* succeeded by other families, through the intervention of some women belonging to the college of *hatrencu*, possibly a funerary college (if the word *hatrencu* is linked with *hatrs*, this last word being connected with the funerary sphere according to M. Pallottino, ibid. 198). The arrival of the Sempronii (i.e. a family with the same gentilicial name as the Gracchi) is sudden and shows no relation whatsoever with the Etruscan families who had previously had the full use of the tomb.

[207] Cf. also the case of Volsinii which I have recently analysed: M. Torelli, 'Praedia clarissimorum Etruriae', *ArchClass* 43 (1991), 474.

[208] D. Manacorda, 'Produzione agricola, produzione ceramica e proprietari nell'*ager Cosanus* nel I sec.a.C.', in Giardina and Schiavone, *Società romana* ii. 44 f.

6

THE 'CORSINI THRONE'

A MONUMENT TO THE ETRUSCAN GENEALOGY OF A ROMAN *GENS*

1. Discovery and Early Studies

IN 1730 A LONG-COVETED DESIRE OF THE PATRICIAN Corsini family finally came to pass: in that year an offshoot of the old Florentine house became pontiff of the Holy Roman Church, choosing for himself the name of Clement XII. The newly appointed pope was a man of high culture (among other things, he was the founder of the magnificent library still bearing the family name, the Biblioteca Corsiniana)[1] and he nourished a strong belief in the secular role of the Roman pontiffs. No wonder, therefore, that he conceived great building projects for Rome and Roman churches, and summoned two among the brightest architects of his age, Ferdinando Fuga and Alessandro Galilei, to accomplish the reconstruction of the façades of two of the major basilicas of Rome, S. Maria Maggiore and the Lateran.

As it was then the norm, Clement XII also ordered a tomb for himself in one of those basilicas and chose the church which would appear politically most significant in those early days of the age of Enlightenment: his preference thus was for the original cathedral of Rome, donated by Constantine the Great and revered by Charlemagne, the *basilica Salvatoris*, better known as St John Lateran. Clement felt that his personal glory ought to be united with the glory of his lineage, so he commanded the architect Galilei to add to the first bay of the left aisle of the basilica an entire chapel dedicated to the family saint, S. Andrea Corsini, where he decided to place his own coffin, using an object strongly symbolic of the past, a Roman porphyry urn said to come from the Pantheon, to be further adorned by the renowned sculptors Carlo Monaldi and Giovanni Battista Maini.

However, the works, started in 1732, encountered many difficulties, mainly infiltrations of water due to the presence of a great fill—actually several metres high—which had been created between the basilica and the Aurelian wall by the superimposition of the debris of at least four levels of massive buildings: the basilica of the eighteenth century, the Constantinian church, the Severan *castra equitum singularium*, and extensive remains of some early imperial villas. Huge excavations became necessary, causing a number of noteworthy archaeological discoveries, fortunately reported by contemporary chroniclers. Extremely important in this regard are a drawing by P. L. Ghezzi[2] and a diary of the years 1700–42 kept by the humanist Valesio, published by Th. Schreiber.[3] In the diary the dump explored on the site of the Corsini chapel and the façade of the church between March and October 1732, is described as filled with jumbled fragments of ancient marble statues, 'frammenti di statue rotte accatastate insieme'. Needless to say, a great part of those marbles found its way to the Palazzo Riario, just purchased by the Corsini, i.e. by the pope himself and by his nephew cardinal Neri Corsini, and being refurbished in its present form as the Villa or Palazzo Corsini alla Lungara by the other papal architect Ferdinando Fuga. Together with some other marbles from family estates near Rome

---

[1] On the family in Rome and its cultural importance, see P. Orzi Smeriglio, 'I Corsini a Roma e le origini della Biblioteca Corsiniana', *MAL* 8 (1959), 293 f.

[2] Drawing in MS Lanciani 104, fo. 25 (here an incorrect date of the discovery, 1703): cf. L. Guerrini, *Marmi antichi nei disegni di P. L. Ghezzi* (Rome, 1971), 33.

[3] Th. Schreiber, *Unedierte römische Fundberichte aus italienische Archiven und Bibliotheken* (Leipzig, 1885), 9 f. (esp. nn. 10, 16, 17, 21, 22); on the excavations carried out in 1732 during the construction of the Corsini chapel, cf. A. M. Colini, 'Storia e topografia del Celio nell'antichità', *MPAA* 7 (1944), 321 f. (esp. 347 f.).

(the Villa Corsini near Antium should be mentioned),[4] the sculptures found in 1732 became the core of the Corsini collection of antiquities, still intact today and now owned by the Accademia dei Lincei, which has its seat in this magnificent palazzo.[5]

In the first printed report of the excavations by A. M. Lupi,[6] dated 1734, we read a summary list of the finds, containing precious evidence for the discovery of imperial and private portraits, heads of philosophers, and decorative statues. Some of them are easily traceable among the pieces of the Corsini collection, while, as we shall see later, the actual identification of others can be only conjectured. A later report, published in 1757 by the antiquarian F. Ficoroni[7] and a subsequent version of it, given in 1790 by C. Fea,[8] add very few pieces of information to Valesio's and Lupi's texts. Lupi is the first to mention, among the other finds, the object of this essay, a curious marble monument still preserved in the Corsini palace and known to archaeologists as the 'Corsini throne' (Pl. 52). He describes the throne as

[4] A secure provenance from Anzio is given for at least two pieces in the collection: G. De Luca, *I monumenti antichi di Palazzo Corsini* (Rome, 1976), henceforth abbreviated De Luca, 4 f.

[5] On the history of the collection, see De Luca, 1 f.

[6] A. M. Lupi, *Dissertatio et animadversiones ad nuper inventum Severae martyris epitaphium* (Palermo, 1734), 43.

[7] F. Ficoroni, *Gemmae antiquae* (Rome, 1757), 126.

[8] C. Fea, *Miscellanea filologica, critica e antiquaria*, i (Rome, 1790), cxxxii ff., § 43: Fea's chronology of the excavations, 1734, clearly derives from the date of his source, the book by Lupi.

'cathedra marmorea anaglypha, Etrusci (ut putatur) artificii, fabulis sive historiis exculpta' (a marble throne carved with myths or histories, of Etruscan manufacture, as it is thought).

This early attribution to Etruscan workmanship was hardly due to the modest knowledge of Lupi, but must reflect the remarkable erudition of A. F. Gori, who, between five and eleven years years after the discovery of the 'Sedia Corsini', in his monumental work *Musaeum Etruscum* published a drawing of the throne,[9] described as a 'Thronus Mithriacus Etruscus' (an Etruscan throne connected with the religion of Mithras). This rather elaborate and whimsical conclusion embodied a partial truth, as we shall see, but the monopoly held by Florence and Tuscany over early Etruscology (which virtually equated Etruria with modern Tuscany)[10] ensured that the throne, an unparalleled object discovered and preserved in Rome (and not in Tuscany), did not feature in Etruscan studies during the eighteenth and nineteenth centuries.

Thus the Corsini throne excited no further interest after its mention in *Musaeum Etruscum*; Gori's views remained unchallenged until 1879, when the monument finally made a rather awkward entrance in the modern archaeological literature. In this year the famous German scholar W. Helbig, secretary of the Instituto di Corrispondenza Archeologica (by then on the point of being transformed into the Deutsches Archäologisches Institut), presented to one of the Instituto's periodic meetings—and subsequently published in its *Annali dell'Instituto*—an essay aiming to be the *editio princeps* of the throne.[11] Helbig's conclusions are surprising, constituting what we might actually consider to be a regression in the modern understanding of the monument: for him the Corsini throne was a piece of 'Oscan' art, i.e. of pre-Roman workmanship attributable to the Samnite area of central Italy. Although it is not impossible to see why he thought this, Helbig's theory found little support in the scholarly world of the last quarter of the nineteenth century. Only three years later, F. von Duhn, familiar with the most recent Felsinean discoveries near Bologna, correctly returned

the piece to the Etruscan sphere.[12] Despite the rising interest in the Sedia Corsini, however, we have to wait until 1916 for a really modern (and as such unsurpassed) *editio princeps* of this singular object, by P. Ducati, one of the founders of modern Etruscology.[13]

Ducati's observations are on the whole correct, though his explanations of the scenes depicted on the throne appear sometimes unsatisfactory and his ideas on the motives behind its creation are entirely misleading. Let us finally enter into the fascinating world of the reliefs.

2. Decoration and Chronology

On the back, we have two superimposed friezes (Pl. 53). In the upper one a parade of armed men, moving from right to left, consists of alternately five foot-soldiers and three horsemen. In the lower frieze we find instead three scenes of boar-hunting: two virtually identical lateral groups with a bowman and a dog (omitted in the group on the left) assailing the animal, and one in the centre with a hunter armed with a spear and a dog. Much more complex are the scenes on the cylindrical lower part of the throne, constituting the support of the seat. Here the only figured frieze is actually made up of two different, but correlated scenes, one with a funerary sacrifice (Pl. 54) and one with funerary games (Pl. 55). Perhaps under the influence of Helbig's interpretation,[14] nobody up to now has seen that the two scenes, though tightly bound together in terms of ideology, are distinctly separated in terms of composition. The sacrificial procession is divided from the funerary games by means of the simple device of presenting the terminal figures of each scene with opposing backs, in one case the horseman and the wrestlers, in the other the two men seated in front of the games and the two men marching at the end of the sacrificial procession. Only L. Bonfante has correctly pointed out the strong compositional emphasis on the group of the sacrifice (the horseman, the tree, the altar, and the victim guided by the first attendant), though she avoids giving

[9] A. F. Gori, *Musaeum Etruscum* (Florence, 1737–43), 379 f., pls. CLXXXI–CLXXXV.

[10] On this subject, see M. Cristofani, *La scoperta degli Etruschi. Archeologia e antiquaria nel '700* (Rome, 1983).

[11] W. Helbig, *Annali dell'Instituto* (1879), 312 f., and *Monumenti dell'Instituto* 11, pl. 9.

[12] F. von Duhn, in Matz-Duhn, *Antike Bildwerke in Rom*, iii (Leipzig, 1882), 126, n. 3075.

[13] P. Ducati, 'La Sedia Corsini', *MonAL* 24 (1916), 402 f.

[14] Helbig, *Annali dell'Instituto* (1879), 314, considered the horseman an abbreviated representation of a horse-race, part of the funerary games; same view by Ducati, *MonAL* 24 (1916), cols. 442 f. and, more hesitantly, by De Luca, 94.

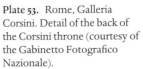

Plate 53. Rome, Galleria Corsini. Detail of the back of the Corsini throne (courtesy of the Gabinetto Fotografico Nazionale).

Plate 54. Rome, Galleria Corsini. Detail of the lower part of the Corsini throne with a funerary sacrifice (courtesy of the Gabinetto Fotografico Nazionale).

Plate 55. Rome, Galleria Corsini. Detail of the lower part of the Corsini throne with funerary games (courtesy of the Gabinetto Fotografico Nazionale).

an explanation of the meaning of the horseman.[15] In other words, the horseman is not performing in athletic games, but is the main character of the funerary sacrifice.

It is, in fact, better to analyse the two scenes separately. The sacrificial scene starts with the figure of a man on horseback who is the recipient of the religious act. He looks at the burning fire of the altar nearby and a tree, placed between him and the altar, with its branches extending in both directions, has the function of both connecting the horseman and the altar and alluding to a non-urban setting of the sacrifice, either in a sacred grove or in the vicinity of the tomb of the horseman. The altar is approached by a sacrificial attendant, who carries an axe on his shoulder and drags the victim, a bull, to the imminent sacrifice. Next is another attendant with a *stimulus*, a whip thought to be used to keep the animal moving, followed by two more

attendants bringing a *simpulum* and a stick to which a large *situla* is appended. That part of the scene and the following—a woman carrying a *kantharos* in her left hand and a large, flat basket on her head—conveys the meaning of the bloodless section of the sacrifice. Two men of rank, dressed as they are (clearly unlike the attendants) with long, perhaps cowled cloaks (signalling perhaps the distance they have covered to go from their town to the suburban area of the funerary sacrifice), conclude the procession. Considering the economy of the narration, they cannot be different from the men in charge of the sacrifice, maybe public officials or more likely close relatives of the dead.

Two other men, seated on a double stool and looking in the opposite direction, start the scene of the funerary games. I am inclined to see in them the same persons shown at the end of the sacrifice. Again their rank is emphasized by their dress and by their seat, very similar to a collegial *sella curulis*: the games are performed under their supervision, as is also emphasized by two upstanding spears, intended to mark the limit of the area for the athletic competitions nearby. Two athletes with *halteres* are competing for a prize, a helmet represented between them. Then a rather obscure scene follows, a giant man (whose scale is probably more the product of the sculptor's rough workmanship than an intentional difference in size), has placed his head in a pit (a basket?; or a pot?), perhaps to play a ludicrous game,[16] although the man rushing towards him of armed with a spear does not suggest any comical or theatrical performance, but something closer to a gladiatorial context. The last group of the sequence is again a sporting event. The explanation proposed here gives, I think, a better insight into the original meaning of the decoration of the throne, which can be compared to all the monuments celebrating the *oikos*-oriented ideals of the archaic aristocracies of Etruria.[17] The coherence of the ideological programme displayed in

---

[15] L. Bonfante, 'The Corsini Throne', *Journal of the Walters Art Gallery*, 36 (1977) (*Essays in Honor of Dorothy Kent Hill*), 111 f.

[16] Ducati, *MonAL* 24 (1916), considered this scene to be an agonistic game, while Helbig (above, n. 14) alluded to a sort of show of individual skilfulness, and De Luca, 94, expresses the view that the subject is instead the representation of a prodigy, according to her connected with the well-known depiction (on late Etruscan urns) of the appearance of the so-called monster Olta. Another attempt to explain the scene is that of L. Bonfante, 'The Corsini Throne and the Man in the Pot', in *Essays in Honor of B. Trell* (Detroit, 1985), 105 f. Bonfante thinks (mostly leaning on the questionable evidence of the *kantharos* held by the woman) of an obscure representation of Hercules. More promising seems to be the analogy noted by the same scholar (p. 108) between our scene and the tondo of Attic red-figured vases showing a satyr plunging in a *pithos* for grotesque reasons.

[17] See on this M. Torelli, *Storia degli Etruschi* (Rome and Bari, 1981), 90 f.

all four scenes is beyond question: all were intended to celebrate the quasi-ceremonial activities the aristocrat was expected to perform. The careful division between the four scenes separates those depicted on the back of the throne, concerning the life and the 'civilian' duties of the aristocrat (his right to command troops and to go hunting), and those on the support, relating instead to his personal religious expectations and to his prerogatives after death.

The wholly archaic conception behind the friezes bring us to the question of the throne's date. Ducati concluded his monograph by connecting the iconography of the scenes with the northern Etruscan art of Bologna and assigned the throne to a period between the mid-fourth and the mid-third centuries. This attempt to give to the throne a purely Etruscan lineage is very weak—contradicted in the first place by the material, marble, extremely rare in Etruscan craftmanship;[18] second by the findplace, Rome and not an Etruscan town; and, last but not least, by the clearly non-Etruscan style of the reliefs.

The chronological issue appears to be rather difficult to resolve. The shape of the throne derives from the familiar Etruscan ceremonial chair of the orientalizing period, used by male and female members of the local princely or royal families as a sign of the very high rank of the owner. Of such thrones[19] we have bronze and even wooden originals from seventh-century tombs of Praeneste, Chiusi,[20] and Verucchio near Rimini,[21] terracotta miniature copies (seventh–sixth century BC) again from Chiusi, full-scale reproductions in the rock-cut tombs of Cerveteri of the seventh and sixth century, and depictions in relief on the Bologna *stelai*. With these last documents[22] we reach the middle of the fourth century BC, when the throne type appears to have become the exclusive possession of women and

therefore to have lost its original meaning as a symbol of public power: its last appearance as insignia of power belonging to a man dates to the late sixth century BC, when we find in Chiusi the so-called Berlin 'Pluto', a well-known monumental cinerary urn sculptured in 'pietra fetida' in the shape of an enthroned man.[23] In its latest, fourth-century appearance in the Bologna *stelai*, the throne eventually possessed a purely 'private' significance being permitted only to women, in their role as absolute mistress of the house; in this respect it might even have been forbidden to men, since it could have had too powerful a connotation as a sign of monarchic rule, though we know that Roman aristocrats used to receive their *clientes* in their role of *patroni* 'seated on a throne', *in solio residentes*.[24] Maybe already in the late sixth century BC, as we learn from the Tarquinian tomb 'of the Jogglers',[25] certainly up to the end of the fifth century on the frieze of the sarcophagus from the Cerveteri tomb 'of the Sarcophagi'[26] or to the beginning of the fourth century BC with the Vulcian sarcophagus from the *Tetnies* tomb,[27] official insignia of 'public' power among male members of the south Etruscan aristocratic society was the Italian version of the Greek *diphros*, the *sella curulis*.[28] As far as central and northern Etruria are concerned, evidence is surprisingly scanty for the fifth century BC, but the above mentioned 'Pluto' from Clusium seems witness to a reluctance on the part of local aristocrats to accept the same isonomic regulations so much earlier in force in the southern republics, suggesting a possible, though marginal survival of monarchic institutions down to a relatively late date. Roman history in the fifth and early fourth centuries BC provides us with more than one example of attempts made by aristocrats and by adventurers to seize power and to exert it in a monarchic form, in reality acting as demagogic tyrants with

---

[18] See n. 34.

[19] On Etruscan thrones and similar pieces of furniture, after the classic work by G. Richter, *The Furniture of the Greeks, Etruscans and Romans* (London, 1966), where our throne is to be found at 86, pls. 428 f.); cf. S. Steingräber, *Etruskische Möbel* (Rome, 1979), esp. 93 ff., 148 ff., our throne is at 198 f. no. 27); and F. Prayon, *Frühetruskisches Grab- und Hausarchitektur* (Heidelberg, 1975), esp. 107 f.

[20] The wooden example of Chiusi seems to be a full-scale throne and not a miniature: see L. Milani, in *Museo Italiano di Antichità Classica*, i (1885), 314.

[21] I allude to the impressive wooden mid-7th cent. BC example, virtually complete, from Verucchio, published by G. V. Gentili, in *La formazione della città in Emilia-Romagna*, Exhibition Catalogue; Bologna, 1987 (Bologna, 1987), 243 f. no. 93, and belonging to a royal tomb of this northern Etruscan peripheral settlement.

[22] Listed in Ducati, *MonAL* 24 (1916), cols. 402 f.

[23] Cf. M. Cristofani, *Statue-cinerario chiusine di età classica* (Rome, 1975), 49 f.

[24] Cf. the attitude of the king as described by Livy, I. 41. 6: 'Servius (*scil.* Tullius) cum trabea et lictoribus prodit ac sede regia sedens decernit, de aliis consulturum se regem esse simulat'; see also Ov. *Fast.* 3. 358 f., and Cic. *De leg.* 1. 3. 10, with E. Wistrand, 'Das altrömische Haus nach den literarischen Quellen', *Eranos*, 68 (1970), 191 f.

[25] Cf. M. Moretti, *Nuovi monumenti della pittura etrusca* (Milan, 1966), fig. p. 23: here a man (either the deceased or a magistrate entrusted with the care of the funerary games), dressed in a purple cloak and holding a long staff or sceptre in his right hand, sits on a *diphros* and watches the games; on *diphroi*, see Steingräber, *Etruskische Möbel*, 110 f., 161 f.

[26] See Helbig, *Führer*, 4th edn., i (1963), no. 612, 474 f. (Th. Dohrn).

[27] See Rh. Herbig, *Die jüngeretruskischen Steinsarkophage* (Berlin, 1952), no. 5, 13 f.

[28] On this subject see now T. Schäfer, *Sella curulis* (Mainz, 1989).

popular support.[29] Since the sculptured friezes of the Corsini throne show that the original clearly belonged to a man entrusted with the highest possible power, we have to date it at the latest between the end of the fifth century, when we last hear of Etruscan kings such as the king of Veii at the moment of the Roman siege in 406–396 BC, and the middle of the fourth century BC, the date of the king (again, most likely a tyrant) of Caere mentioned in the *Elogia Tarquiniensia*.[30]

It is precisely to such a date that other details point, mainly the floral decoration—the two friezes, one with ivy-leaf and one with stylized waves, repeated on the back of the throne and in the centre of the support, the palmette and lotus buds frieze on the lowest section of the support: G. De Luca[31] rightly pointed out that the same motifs consistently appear on the Attic red-figured pottery of the late fifth century. At that same time we know that both Etruscan soldiers[32] and the Roman legions (around 390 BC)[33] adopted the type of armament of Celtic origin which is depicted on the throne. Paradoxically enough, in this way we arrive at a chronology not so different from that proposed by Ducati, a chronology however, which he gave to the Corsini throne itself, not to its original model or proto-type arguing for an original throne of the sixth century, copied and, so to speak, updated in marble between 350 and 250 BC. In fact, Ducati's proposal represents only a one (and rather unsuccessful) attempt at a coherent explanation for the several conflicting elements present on the throne, such as the early popularity of the type of chair, the indisputably later date of the vegetal decoration and the even later chronology suggested by the use of marble[34] and the style of the reliefs.

A definitive argument which demolishes Ducati's ideas is the shape of the helmet appearing in the lower frieze on the back of the throne as a prize offered for the athletical competition. This type of helmet is demonstrably later than the latest possible chronology assigned to the copy of the throne by Ducati; it is a late Hellenistic form, popular in the second–first centuries BC.[35] In other words, we are dealing with an 'updating' of a helmet which presumably appeared on the Etruscan original, an 'updating' carried out at a time when Etruria as a political unit practically did not exist any more. Such a puzzling conclusion is further strengthened if we inspect the general rendering of the style more closely. The best stylistic and iconographic comparisons for our helmet are to be found in the metopes of the Doric friezes on honorary and funerary monuments of central Italy in the second half of the first century BC, a class of monument which I first studied more than thirty years ago[36] and which has proved to be one of the most coherent and characteristic products of the so-called *arte plebea*[37] (plebeian art), as Bianchi Bandinelli has happily defined the art of the municipal élites of central Italy from the middle of the first century BC to the middle of the first century AD. As L. Bonfante has observed,[38] it is in this 'plebeian art' that we find the best overall comparisons of style; I would add that inherent in the 'plebeian style' is the same inorganic, non-naturalistic rendering of our helmet, even its lack of proportion, and, more generally, the flat treatment of the figures and the compositional parataxis of the friezes. All this perhaps helps to explain why Helbig in 1879 attributed the Sedia Corsini to 'Oscan' art: he was actually assigning the marble throne to the area where 'plebeian' art is mostly to be found. However, he gave this art a misleadingly ethnic name, since it is by no means 'Oscan' but simply Roman of the late Republic and the early Empire.

Given the chronological difficulties, we have to work more or less as philologists do with ancient texts and with manuscript tradition, mainly by the reconstruction of archetypes and the identification of interpolations, keeping firmly in mind Pasquali's golden rule, *recentiores non deteriores*. And the final conclusion is relatively easy from what I have shown so far: we are dealing with a lost bronze original of the fifth century BC, probably from the area between Chiusi, Perugia,

[29] Cf. M. Torelli, *La società etrusca—L'età arcaica, l'età classica* (Rome, 1987), 78 f.

[30] Cf. M. Torelli, *Elogia Tarquiniensia* (Florence, 1975), 72 f.

[31] De Luca, 95.

[32] As is shown again by the Bologna *stelai* (P. Ducati, 'Le pietre funerarie felsinee', *MonAL* 20 (1911), cols. 665 ff.); see e.g. the *stelai* no. 160, fig. 76, cols. 667 f.

[33] See E. Gabba, 'Istituzioni militari e colonizzazione in Roma medio-repubblicana', *RFIC* 103 (1975), 144 f.

[34] On early (and extremely rare) use of marble by the Etruscans, see A. Maggiani, in *Artigianato artistico. L'Etruria settentrionale interna in età ellenistica*, Exhibition Catalogue; Volterra, 1985 (Milan, 1985), 123 ff.

[35] On Hellenistic helmets, see P. Dintsis, *Hellenistische Helme* (Rome, 1986), and G. Waurick, *Helme der hellenistischen Zeit und ihre Vorläufer*, in *Griechische Helme: Sammlung Lipperheide und andere Bestände des Antikenmuseums Berlin*, Exhibition Catalogue; Berlin, 1988 (Mainz, 1988), 151 f.

[36] M. Torelli, 'Monumenti funerari con fregio dorico', *DArch*, 2 (1968), 32 f.

[37] R. Bianchi Bandinelli, 'Arte plebea', *DArch*, 1 (1967) 7 f.; extensive exemplification of monuments of 'plebeian art' in *Studi Miscellanei*, 10 (1966).

[38] Bonfante, *Journal of the Walters Art Gallery*, 36 (1977), 121 f.

Arezzo, and Volterra[39] (the archetype), copied (the extant copy, i.e. the Corsini Throne)—in a marble which according to J. B. Ward Perkins could be Pentelic[40]—by a modest artisan (the scribe) from central Italy in the second half of the first century BC, who added his own style (the style of the scribe) and even some probably unconscious updating of the original iconography such as in the helmet (the interpolations).

3. Its Meaning and Owners

This reconstruction helps us to solve another series of even more puzzling questions raised by the Corsini throne: why was a ceremonial seat of Etruscan times so carefully copied? why in the second half of the first century BC? and finally: why was it found in Rome? We have seen the answer given by Ducati: leaving aside the incorrect dating of the copy, his explanation clarified neither the reason for its manufacture nor its Roman provenance. G. De Luca, who published the excellent catalogue of the Corsini collection, thought vaguely of Roman art-collecting,[41] while L. Bonfante, to whom we owe the most penetrating recent study of the throne,[42] also spoke of art-collecting, favoured by the full Romanization of north Italy in the age of Caesar, but used by the family for priestly purposes once it was taken to Rome. To a certain extent both answers could be considered correct, provided that we give the term 'collecting' a very particular meaning: the man who commissioned the copy of the original Etruscan throne did not want it for its 'beauty' nor—as Bonfante proposed—as a real object to be used on religious occasions, but for its strong ideological value, as a symbol.

In actual fact, as we have just seen, the Corsini throne depicts scenes connected only and explicitly with the archaic life of princes and kings—processions of warriors and horsemen, the great aristocratic entertainment of hunting, funerary sacrifices, and games. The exhibition of such a monument in the atrium of a wealthy house of late republican Rome will have had just one meaning: to remind all visitors, clients and friends, i.e. his peers as well as the poor, that the owner, through this marble copy of a fifth-century royal throne of Etruscan origin, claimed a descent from a glorious line of Tyrrhenian kings, to which the original insignia—the *solium regium*, the regal seat—pertained. In a sense, the Corsini throne is the perfect sculptural counterpart of what in the literary world is the well-known address of Horace to Maecenas, 'Maecenas atavis edite regibus' (Maecenas, sprung from royal stock),[43] and in the epigraphic domain, the Tarquinian *elogia* of the Spurinnae.[44] All three phenomena not only belong to the same age and cultural atmosphere, but also have the same function. With his address, Horace wanted to praise in the most solemn way his patron, the Arretine knight C. Maecenas, who on his maternal side could claim descent from the Arretine royal family of the Cilnii. The Spurinnae *elogia*, a genealogy of one of the noblest families of Tarquinia still surviving in the first century AD, displayed in the forum of Tarquinia the glorious deeds of ancestors of that lineage who in 413 BC joined the Athenian army in the ill-fated siege of Syracuse and in 358–351 BC defeated the Romans, liberating the Arretines from a slave revolt and overthrowing the king of Cerveteri. Successful military actions all through Italy and even against Rome presented as family trophies, kings and royal lines meant to dignify personal ancestries, glories reaching into the remote past—here are the ingredients of the same aristocratic pretences behind the flattery of Horace, the boast of the Spurinnae, and the ostentation of the owner of the Corsini throne.[45]

[39] Following Ducati, more recent discussions of the throne have insisted on the connections between the Sedia Corsini and Felsinean and Venetic late orientalizing bronzes (see e.g. De Luca, 93 f., and Bonfante, in *Essays in Honor of B. Trell*, and in *Journal of the Walters Art Gallery* 36 (1977)). I am inclined to think that the unmistakable similarities between these northern bronzes and the Corsini throne can be historically better explained as both deriving from lost Etruscan (and not from the meaningless 'Situlenkunst') prototypes of the area between Chiusi and Arezzo, i.e. the area from which the iconographies and style of the Etruscan Po Valley dominions and of the Venetic and Illyrian countries seem to have originated: on this subject see L. Bonfante, *Out of Etruria*, BAR International Series 103 (Oxford, 1981), and M. Torelli, *Arte degli Etruschi* (Rome and Bari, 1985), 38 f.

[40] Expertise given by J. B. Ward Perkins in a letter to L. Bonfante, in *Journal of the Walters Art Gallery*, 36 (1977), III n. 7 (quoting A. Claridge and D. Michaelides).   [41] De Luca, 98 f.

[42] Bonfante, *Journal of the Walters Art Gallery*, 36 (1977).

[43] Hor. *Carm.* . . , I, I. (trans. C. E. Bennett).

[44] Torelli, *Elogia Tarquiniensia*.

[45] For a reconstruction of Etruscan culture and ideology at the end of the Republic and the beginning of the Empire, see M. Torelli, 'Senatori etruschi della tarda repubblica e dell'impero', *DArch*, 3 (1969), 285 f.; 'Per la storia dell'Etruria in età imperiale', *RFIC* 99 (1971), 498 f.; 'Senatori etruschi della tarda repubblica e dell'impero; qualche addendum', *Arheolosky Vestnik*, 28 (1977), 251 f.; 'Ascesa al senato e rapporti con i territori d'origine. Italia: regio VII', in *Epigrafia e ordine senatorio*, Acts of Conference; Rome, 1981, ii (Rome, 1982), 275 f.; 'I "duodecim populi Etruriae" ', in *Annali della Fondazione per il Museo C. Faina*, 2 (1985), 37 f.; 'Problemi di romanizzazione', in *Atti II Congresso Internazionale Etrusco*, Acts of Conference; Florence, 1985 (Rome, 1989), 393 f.

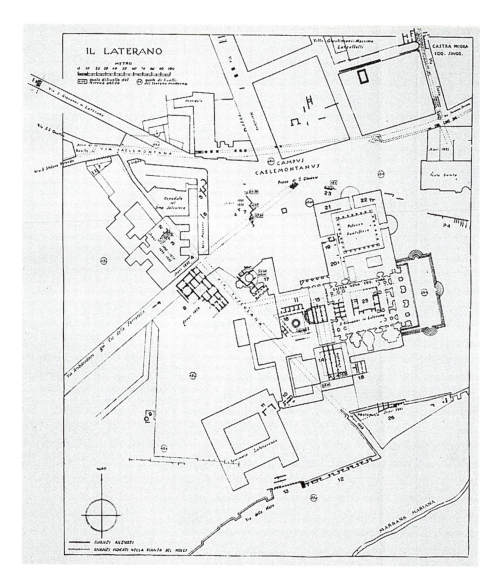

Fig. 59. Plan of the Lateran
area (after Liverani).

All this exhibition of Etruscan pride and ancestry belongs to the same world of the Etruscan *domi nobiles*, the municipal élites promoted after the Social War to share in the government of Rome with the remains of the old Roman *nobilitas*. For them to provide evidence of noble ancestry was a matter of higher social status, of higher offices, of richer provinces, and what survived of the glorious Etruscan aristocracy and entered the Roman Senate in the last days of the Republic had good material indeed to show. As the throne of the Etruscan king Arimnestos added glory and respect to the temple of Hera in Olympia where it was exhibited,[46] so the Corsini throne, placed as a *monumentum triumphale* among the ancestral portraits in the atrium

of an aristocratic house of late republican Rome, was a self-glorification of the gentilicial line of the owners. There in the same atrium a real *stemma*, a genealogical tree, was set up with connecting ribbons to these *imagines maiorum* and in this case the tree went back to Etruscan *reges* and *principes*, in other words to kings and aristocrats of the most prestigious civilization of the emergent *tota Italia*.

Fortunately the circumstances of the find during the reign of Clement XII may permit us to suggest the name of the owners of the house where the Corsini throne was exhibited. Thanks to the careful reconstruction by the late A. M. Colini,[47] the area (Fig. 59) between the façade of the church, the Corsini chapel

---

[46] Paus. 5. 12. 5, to be compared with the throne presented to Apollo at Delphi by the Phrygian King Midas (Herod. 1. 14).

[47] Colini, *MPAA* 7 (1944), 321 f.; see also P. Liverani, 'Le proprietà private nell'area Lateranense fino a Costantino', *MEFRA* 100 (1988), 891 f.

and the Aurelianic wall seems to coincide with the site of the *aedes Laterani*, the magnificent urban villa of the noble family of the Plautii Laterani, whose name is still preserved in that of the Christian basilica and of the adjoining papal palace—the Lateran. Of that villa Juvenal speaks in these terms: 'it was for this that in the dire days Nero ordered Longinus and the great gardens of the over-wealthy Seneca to be put under siege; for this was it that the noble Palace of the Laterani was beset by an entire cohort.'[48] Juvenal is recounting how all these rich men, Seneca, Cassius Longinus, and Plautius Lateranus, fell together in the repression of the Pisonian conspiracy under Nero, as Tacitus too reports,[49] and their luxurious properties were confiscated by the emperor. It might be interesting to recall that the gardens of Longinus were also located in the same area of the Lateran, as is proved by an inscribed water-pipe found nearby,[50] and we know how eager Nero was to merge large and luxurious properties in order to create immense imperial estates close to the centre of the town, such as those included in his Domus Aurea.[51]

We might even have actual remains of the villa of the Plautii Laterani, consisting of extensive reticulate sub-structures found in 1941 on the left side of the Via Tusculana[52] and other reticulate walls under the Lateran basilica.[53] Certainly in the second century AD 'the conspicuous house', the *egregiae aedes* as it is called by Juvenal, extending widely over the area of the basilica and beyond, appears to be safely in imperial hands, since under Septimius Severus[54] the site was occupied by the barracks of the imperial mounted guard, the *equites singulares*. Another Severan intervention in the area is remarkable: as we learn from an inscribed lead water-pipe[55] and even from literary sources,[56] the same emperor donated part of the vast imperial properties to an aristocratic family of high prestige in the second century AD, the Sextii Laterani. He perhaps intended to imbue such philo-senatorial largesse with the aura of a

sort of return of a glorious *gens*, considered in that era to be the same family of a remote past, to a place which popular fame however had already consecrated as the *Lateranum*.[57]

Plautius Lateranus, the victim of Nero, was a descendant of a wealthy family from a small town near Tivoli, Trebula Suffenas, and his family tree has been successfully reconstructed by the great American historian L. Ross Taylor.[58] The family of the Plautii surfaces, as do many other *domi nobiles*, in the days of the Social War, with two senators, an A. Plautius *leg.* 90 and 87 BC and a M. Plautius Silvanus *tr.pl.* 89 BC, most likely brothers. The real head of the line is, however, a son of the first of these two persons, an A. Plautius, who, as *homo novus*, does not proceed any further than the praetorship obtained in 51 BC (his proconsulate in Bithynia 49–48 BC is dubious).[59] From him the family splits into two main branches, one marked by the cognomen of Silvanus and another which, for the sake of brevity, we could call the Plautii Laterani, from the *cognomen* actually possessed only by the last of the line. This second branch is definitely less lucky than the first; one of its members gains the first consulship of the line in 1 BC, a year after the cousin Silvanus, who shows also the higher distinction of the rank of *ordinarius* and the story of the subsequent members of the line is on the whole undistinguished. The two sons of the *cos.* 1 BC get their consulships (the first is *suffectus* in AD 29 and the second is finally *ordinarius* in 36), and then comes the last offspring of the line, the above-mentioned Plautius Lateranus, who was designated as a consul for 65, but died in 64 during the repression of the Pisonian conspiracy just before taking up his office.

The branch of the Silvani appears politically much more successful than the parallel one of the Laterani. It was shown long ago by Ross Taylor[60] that the Silvani fortunes derived from imperial favour, gained through the close friendship established by the empress Livia with a lady of a rather unusual name, Urgulania, the mother of the first consul of the branch, M. Plautius

---

[48] Juv. *Sat.* 10. 15 ff. (trans. G. G. Ramsay); the other Lateranus in Juvenal (8. 146) is instead a Sextius Lateranus, see n. 57.

[49] Tac. *Ann.* 15. 49, 53; cf. also 11. 30, 36; 13. 11.

[50] *CIL* XV, 7513, found during the excavations of the Baths of the Lateran on the right side of the via Tusculana; this might account for the gradual loss of importance of the old consular road which passed through the Aurelianic wall through a mere *posterula* (not a real gate and furthermore even closed up), since it had become virtually a path running inside a property of the imperial *fiscus*.

[51] On the Domus Aurea, in general, see A. Boethius, *The Golden House of Nero: Some Aspects of Roman Architecture* (Ann Arbor, 1960).

[52] Colini, *MPAA* 7 (1944), 343, and 342 fig. 282.

[53] Ibid. 344 f.   [54] Ibid. 353 f.   [55] Ibid. 372.

[56] Aur. Vict. *Epit. de Caes.* 20. 6.

[57] Cf. the inscription *RAC* 22 (1936), 17: 'Quintus Lactearius . . . qui fuit de domum Laterani'.

[58] L. Ross Taylor, 'Trebula Suffenas and the Plautii Silvani', *MAAR* 24 (1956), 7 f. (here also a discussion of earlier bibliography); the discovery of a new inscription (*AE* 1972, 162) has rendered possible an amendment to the *stemma* (U. Vogel-Weidemann, in *ArchClass* 19 (1975–6), 135 f.). See also A. Licordari, 'Ascesa al senato e rapporti con i territori d'origine. Italia: Regio I (Latium)', in *Epigrafia e ordine senatorio*, Acts of Conference ii (Rome, 1982), 45 f.

[59] T. P. Wiseman, *New Men in the Roman Senate: 139 BC–14 AD* (Oxford, 1971), 322 f.   [60] Ross Taylor, *MAAR* 24 (1956), 26.

M.f.A.n. Silvanus, who was *cos. ord.* in 2 BC together with Augustus. This lady was quite a character, as Tacitus informs us, and the friendship she had developed with Augustus' wife Livia set her above the law, 'quam supra leges amicitia Augustae extulerat':[61] but when her grandson, during his praetorship in AD 24, killed his pregnant wife Apronia, a member of a famous and respected family of Rome, by throwing her out of the window of his house, Urgulania offered the young man a sword to commit suicide, which he actually did soon after.[62]

J. Heurgon[63] was first to discover that this terrifying woman had Etruscan ancestry. Subsequently, in the above-mentioned *elogia* of the Tarquinian Spurinnae, I was able to detect a king of Cerveteri, dethroned by Aulus Spurinna by the middle of the fourth century BC, named Orgolnius, a more archaic form of the same family name of Urgulania, both deriving from an Etruscan name which we can reconstruct as *Urclna*. The presence of the same name in the *elogia*, a document published in the age between Tiberius and Claudius, makes us even surer that the real or pretended royal ancestry of Urgulania was a subject of some interest circulating among aristocratic families of Etruscan birth. Following the established practice of the oldest aristocracy of Italy, Urgulania arranged a careful matrimonial policy for both lines of the Plautii, the Silvani and the Laterani: her son, the *cos.* 2 BC, married another Etruscan woman, a Lartia Cn.f., as her name clearly declares,[64] and so did a grandson of hers, an A. Plautius *q.* 31 and *pr.* 36 (?), whose wife, Vibia Marsi f. Laelia nata, daughter of C. Vibius Marsus *cos. suff.* AD 17,[65] even shows, in perfect Etruscan style, her matronymic. But Urgulania's masterpiece was the marriage of her granddaughter, Plautia Urgulanilla, to the future emperor Claudius, who, not by chance, displayed a profound interest in Etruscan studies, proved by no less than twenty books he wrote on *Tyrrheniká* (Etruscan Histories).

In the other line, marriages are less conspicuous, but as noteworthy for our purposes as those in the previous branch. Although we do not know the name of the wife of the consul 1 BC (I am inclined to think she was a Sextia, who gave origin to the *cognomen* Lateranus of her grandson),[66] two of their children, A. Plautius *cos.* AD 29 and Plautia A.f., both took Etrusco-Umbrian spouses. Plautius married the notorious Pomponia Graecina from Iguvium (an Umbrian town about 25 miles (40 km.) east of Perugia, but in the cultural and political sphere of Etruscan Perusia), while Plautia (unknown to L. Ross Taylor)[67] was the wife of P. Petronius *cos. suff.* AD 19, probably from Perugia or from the adjoining Umbrian town of Assisi.

The cluster of matrimonial alliances is interesting: even if Urgulania's home-town is unknown,[68] almost all the attested marriages of both branches of the family imply connections with the areas around Perusia, from Iguvium to Asisium, according to an endogamic policy traceable in Etruscan traditions,[69] very effective in enlarging contiguous family properties and increasing political and social control in the territories of origin. The growth of power of the family, however, emerges from the non-Etruscan marriages of the grandchildren of Urgulania, the above-mentioned wife of Claudius Urgulanilla and her ill-fated brother, who married first Fabia Numantina, offshoot of the glorious patrician family of the Fabii, and then Apronia, descending from a lineage less old, but certainly much better off and closer to the emperor Tiberius than the declining Fabii.[70] It is perhaps the failure of this last marriage of Silvanus that caused the terrible anger of Urgulania

---

[61] Tac. *Ann.* 2. 34.   [62] Ibid. 4. 21 f.

[63] J. Heurgon, *La Vie quotidienne chez les Etrusques* (Paris, 1961), 105 f.

[64] Early examples in Etruria, whence clearly the *nomen* derives (as a 'Vornamengentile' from the Etruscan *praenomen* Lary): CIL XI, 2319, 2369 (Clusium); the arguments for an Umbrian origin have already been produced by Ross Taylor, *MAAR* 24 (1956), 27.

[65] Dubious origins of the man from Larinum (G. Camodeca, 'Ascesa al senato e rapporti con i territori d'origine. Italia: regio I, II, III', in *Epigrafia e ordine senatorio*, 145); we might establish connections with the Vibii from Perusia (Torelli, ibid. 291) or from the neighbouring Asisium (M. Gaggiotti and L. Sensi, ibid. 264). I am inclined to think that all these Vibii from Perusia and Asisium belong to just one single *gens*.

[66] On the family, see *RE* II A, 2 (1923), cols. 2038 f., nos. 14–17, 22, 26–7, 29–30, 40–1; their *origo* is Ostia (cf. besides Juv. *Sat.* 8. 161, the tribe *Voturia* and the Ostian *quinquennalitas* of T. Sextius Africanus in AD 36: *Inscr. It.* 18: 1, 219 f.): the first consulship in the family is however quite late, AD 59, perhaps due to their provenance from a colony of Roman citizens, normally not very productive of *laticlavia*, as we know (cf. T. P. Wiseman, *CQ* 1 (1964), 130 f., and Licordari, 'Ascesa al senato e rapporti con i territori d'origine. Italia: regio I (Latium)', in *Epigrafia e ordine senatorio*, 37) or even because of their humble origin (cf. the *mulio consul* of Juv. *Sat.* 8. 146 ff., referring to the *cos.* AD 94).

[67] Discussed by R. Syme, 'The Early Tiberian Consuls', *Historia*, 30 (1981), 202 (= *Roman Papers*, iii (Oxford, 1984), 1363).

[68] Too hastily perhaps, in *Elogia Tarquiniensia*, 70 f., I accepted a Caeretan origin for the family, on the grounds of the Etrusco-Latin funerary inscription from Cerveteri CIE 6187 (corrected by J. Kaimio, in *SE* 48 (1979), 341 no. 55) = CIL I² 3309, a *[Th]ania Orculnia*, who however, as a woman, may easily not be of Caeretan birth.   [69] See Torelli, *DArch*, 3 (1969).

[70] On these families, see most recently R. Syme, *The Augustan Aristocracy* (Oxford, 1986), 417 f., 427; in the same year Silvanus' former wife Numantina was acquitted of her husband's accusation of sorcery (Tac. *Ann.* 4. 22. 3) and later married Sex. Appuleius *cos.* AD 14, closely related to the Julian family (is this divorce and trial a sign of a more directly pro-Tiberius policy pursued by Urgulania?). L. Apronius *cos.* AD 8 is instead explicitly mentioned by Velleius (116. 3), good evidence for the closeness of the Apronii to Tiberius.

and her manlike gesture of invitation to suicide: maybe she had already experienced or sensed the even more momentous failure of Urgulanilla's wedlock with the future emperor Claudius, a marriage which ended with a divorce and with the death of the fruit of that wedding, a child named Drusus, already betrothed to a daughter of the powerful praetorian prefect, Sejanus.[71]

From this perspective the Corsini throne acquires a fuller historical position and significance. The unusual object is a symbol of the royal ancestry of the most important woman of the *gens*, Urgulania, a sort of *monumentum triumphale* destined to stand in the *tablinum* both of the original and of the acquired family; the original Etruscan throne, model of the Corsini throne, was then copied to be displayed in the bride's new house, that of the Plautian family, which the princely Etruscan woman entered around 40 BC through her marriage with M. Plautius Silvanus, barely a *vir praetorius*, but soon after awarded by the emperor with a high priesthood, the membership in the *collegium* of the *VII viri epulones*. Indeed a date around 40 BC would be perfect for the execution of the marble throne, suitable to the 'plebeian' style of the reliefs and to the atmosphere of the moment, which many aspiring aristocrats (as Plautius was) believed to be favourable to the sudden rise of political fortunes of *domi nobiles* and *novi homines*.[72] Even Urgulania's cluster of further marriage alliances, all located in the area around Perusia, might give a clue to her *ultima origo* and the provenance of the model for the Corsini throne: we know that the Perugian area played an important role in the Etruscan colonization of the Po valley[73] and we have seen that on more than one occasion scholars have linked the iconography of friezes of the Sedia Corsini with the Etruscan art of that remote northern province. As shown beyond any doubt by the inscriptions of the funerary monument belonging to her husband's branch of the Plautii Silvani, the famous marble circular tomb at Ponte Lucano near Tivoli,[74] Urgulania's line ended in AD 59,

when the last member of the line, the still young and undistinguished A. Plautius (the son of Pulcher, who had been *q.* 31, *pr. ad aer. c.*36 and *procos. Siciliae c.*40, promoted to patriciate in 47, but apparently not to consulship), was murdered by Nero because of his closeness to Nero's mother Agrippina. The Tivoli tomb was then inherited by an Aelius Lamia, adopted into the line with the name of Ti. Plautius Silvanus Aelianus, a distinguished patrician member of the family of the Aelii Lamiae, who acquired glory and triumphal insignia in the age of the Flavian emperors.[75] But, as was often the case, the adoption did not involve a great part of the property of the branch,[76] which perhaps passed to the parallel line, the Laterani, and that would explain why the Sedia Corsini, a monument originally belonging to the Silvani branch, was found in a property of the Laterani. In accordance with old Roman practice when a line became extinct, both the throne and the related *imagines maiorum* would have had to be exposed there, in the public part of the house, although in this instance for the short span of only five years between the tragic ends of both branches, the Silvani in AD 59 and the Laterani in 64.

4. The Throne: Its Fate

In this dramatic year of AD 64 the beautiful urban villa was confiscated and all the objects connected with the family were eliminated, as memorials of a treacherous lineage: so the Corsini throne found its final destiny in the dump excavated in 1732. From this dump, rich in portraits and statues, we would like to believe that also some of the *imagines maiorum* of the unlucky family of the Plautii came to light and it is tempting to try to identify them in the Corsini collection. The collection is actually not very large, only fifty-three pieces of sculpture in the round, and is quite homogeneous in its composition; a closer inspection easily reveals the existence of groups of sculptures constituting proper little 'galleries'. Some are pieces meant to embellish a rich villa garden, such as three early first-century

---

[71] The betrothal took place in AD 20 (Tac. *Ann*. 3. 29; cf. also Suet. *Claud.* 27, and Cass. Dio, 60. 32. 1); Drusus' death belongs to a period between 23 and 30 (cf. *RE*, III (1899), col. 2703 no. 138, s.v. Claudius).

[72] On this social and political phenomenon, see Wiseman, *New Men*.

[73] Cf. Torelli, *Storia degli Etruschi*, 190 f., with a special reference to Clusium, Volaterrae, Perusia, and Arretium.

[74] See most recently M. Lolli Ghetti, 'Un documento ottocentesco sul mausoleo dei Plautii a Ponte Lucano', *Archeologia Laziale*, 7 (1985), 167 f. (with prev. bibl.); for the inscriptions see *CIL* XIV, 3605–8 = *Inscr. It.* I² (1952), 122–5 = *ILS* 921, 964, 986.

[75] See *PIR*, I², A 205, and M. Cébeillac, *Les 'quaestores principis et candidati' aux ier et iie siècles de l'Empire* (Milan, 1972), 37 f.

[76] Although the inscription from the Etrusco-Umbrian town of Urvinum Hortense *CIL* XI, 5171, a dedication to the senator [—] Plautius [L.f. Aelius La]mia Silvanus [Aelianus ?]—on whom see *PIR*, I², A 206— might give us to think of the transfer to the Aelii Lamia of some of the properties acquired by the Plautii Silvani through the marriages fostered by our Urgulania.

Plate 56. Rome, Galleria Corsini. Portrait-head of a mature man, *c.*50 BC (courtesy of the Gabinetto Fotografico Nazionale).

Plate 57. Rome, Galleria Corsini. Portrait-head of a mature man (the so-called 'Cinquantenne', the '50-year-old Man'), 40–30 BC (courtesy of the Gabinetto Fotografico Nazionale).

herms with heads copied from famous sculptures—the portrait of Euripides, the so-called Pseudo-Seneca (in reality the portrait of Aristophanes) and the head of the scopaic Lansdowne Herakles,[77] constituting the complete decoration of an exedra like that discovered in the villa of the Volusii near Lucus Feroniae.[78] Other sculptures are instead portraits of Roman emperors, which seem to form three quite coherent groups. The first group consists solely of a portrait of Tiberius;[79] of the other two groups, the first includes five heads, one of Antoninus Pius, one of his wife Faustina, two of Marcus Aurelius (one of the young and one of the adult

type), and one of the young Commodus,[80] while the second group shows the portraits of Julia Mamaea, Bassianus, Julia Maesa, and Gallienus.[81] The head of Tiberius, an emperor who had ostensibly improved the fortunes of the Plautii, could easily be a portrait belonging to the original decoration of the Laterani villa, since we know that it was not uncommon to display imperial portraits in private houses for obvious political reasons.[82] The second group might instead be considered the series of cult images of the Antonine

[77] De Luca, 29 no. 11 (Euripides); 47 no. 19 (Pseudo-Seneca); 23 no. 6 (Herakles): one of these could be the 'bella testa di filosofo' (Valesio) found in the dig of 1732.

[78] See M. Torelli, 'Una "galleria" della villa. Qualche nota sulla decorazione del complesso', in *I Volusii Saturnini* (Bari, 1981), 97 f.

[79] De Luca, 60 no. 26, pl. LII.

[80] De Luca, 70 no. 35, pl. LXI (Pius); 69 no. 34, pl. LX (Faustina Maior); 71 no. 36, pl. LXII (young Marcus); 72 no. 37, pl. LXI (Marcus); 72 no. 38, pls. LXIII–LXIV.

[81] De Luca, 81 no. 45, pls. LXVIII–LXIX (Julia Mamaea); 82 no. 46, pls. LXX–LXXI (Bassianus ?); 82 no. 47, pls. LXXII, LXXVI (Julia Maesa); 86 no. 50, pls. LXXVI–LXXVII (Gallienus).

[82] Remember the trial referred to us by Tacitus (*Ann.* 1. 74) against Granius Marcellus for having turned into a portrait of Tiberius the head of a statue of Augustus exhibited in his own house.

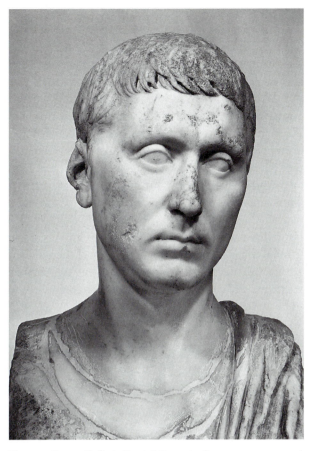

Plate 58. Rome, Galleria Corsini. Portrait of a young man, central years of the Augustan age (courtesy of the Gabinetto Fotografico Nazionale).

Plate 59. Rome, Galleria Corsini. Portrait of a young man, AD 40–50 (courtesy of the Gabinetto Fotografico Nazionale).

dynasty, of the second Severan dynasty, and of Gallienus, to be connected with the presence of an imperial estate and of a large group of imperial slaves and freedmen.

Completely isolated among the pieces of the Corsini collection are four male portraits, which share certain physiognomic features in common and appear to be datable in a tight chronological sequence between the years 50 BC and AD 40. It is really tempting to place these portraits in conjunction with the throne and the *imagines maiorum* of the Plautii discarded in the ominous year of AD 64 and to try to fit them into the genealogy of the family we have previously examined.

We would have the following possible identifications:

1. Portrait of a mature man, datable to around 50 BC (Pl. 56):[83] he can be the head of both lines of the house, A. Plautius *pr.* 51 BC.

2. Portrait of a mature man (the so-called Cinquantenne, the '50-year-old Man'), to be dated in the decade 40–30 BC (Pl. 57):[84] he can be either M. Plautius A.f. Silvanus, the husband of Urgulania, or his cousin, A. Plautius, the father of the namesake *cos.* I BC.

3. Portrait of a young man in his late twenties–early thirties, sculpted in the central years of the Augustan age (Pl. 58):[85] it must be a portrait executed on the

[83] De Luca, 51 no. 21, pls. XL–XLI.

[84] De Luca, 58 no. 25, pls. L–LI. Here I correct my earlier views on the chronology of this portrait, which is not datable between the Julio-Claudian and the Flavian period, as De Luca thought (ibid.) and I was induced to believe, but belongs to the final days of the Republic. Such an earlier date is supported by most of the same comparisons given by De Luca, from the portrait in the Kaulbach collection in Munich to the right hand bust of the Barberini Togatus or the so-called 'Pompey' in the Louvre (bibliography in De Luca, loc.cit.).

[85] De Luca, 82 no. 22, pls. XLII–XLV. The draped herm to which the portrait is attached could belong to it (De Luca, loc.cit.); the herm however finds a perfect pendant—in terms both of iconography and style—in a feminine herm, similarly draped, whose head appears to represent not a portrait, but an ideal goddess (De Luca, 31 no. 12, pls. XXI–XXII). The simplest solution to the problem appears to consider the male head as a piece separate from the herm; the artistic quality of the two draped herms is extremely high, so that they would not look out of place in the decoration of the Plautian gardens.

occasion of accession to the consular office, a *statua consularis* of our sources,[86] the highest of the magistracies *cum imperio* and the sole one giving the right to receive and exhibit an iconic portrait. We could therefore assign it either to A. Plautius *cos.*1 BC from the Laterani branch or to M. Plautius M.f. Silvanus *cos.* 2 BC from the Silvani branch.

4. Portrait of a young man of the same age as the previous one, carved in the 40s of the first century AD (Pl. 59):[87] we could think, again moving from one branch to the other, either of Q. Plautius *cos.* AD 36 or of P. Plautius Pulcher *pr. c.* AD 36; the latter is the only Silvanus of his generation to have reached a higher magistracy and to have remained free from the *nota* of infamy attributed to his suicide brother (who seems to have not even been buried in the family mausoleum of Ponte Lucano).

In offering this suggestion, we have to admit that there are very few hopes of obtaining from the evidence in our possession any further confirmation of the identifications proposed for these fine portraits. New excavations at Ciciliano, where we know there was a magnificent villa of the Plautii Silvani,[88] could perhaps retrieve portraits belonging to members of the Plautian family which may or may not support the present hypotheses. To judge from its stylistic quality, the small gallery here reconstructed would however by all means be worthy to figure amongst the ornaments from a glorious past, *monumenta triumphalia* and *imagines maiorum*, which we have postulated as a setting for the unique copy of an Etruscan throne known as the Corsini throne, created for the pride and the political advancement of a Roman family from an obscure *municipium* of Latium in the momentous climate of the upheaval of the Augustan *tota Italia.*

---

[86] For the *ius statuarum* see most recently M. Torelli, 'Statua equestris inaurata Caesaris: "mos" e "ius" nella statua di Marco Aurelio', in *Marco Aurelio. Storia di un monumento e del suo restauro* (Milan, 1989), 83 f.

[87] De Luca, 58 no. 24, pls. L–LI.

[88] The villa was partially excavated by the Soprintendenza (D. Faccenna, *NSA* (1948), 249 ff.) and published by C. F. Giuliani, in *Tibur*, ii (*Forma Italiae*, I. 3. ii) (Rome, 1961), 137 f.; most recently, see F. Sciarretta, *Trebula Suffenas, la città dei Plautii Silvani, presso l'odierna Ciciliano* (Tivoli, 1974).

EPILOGUE

TOTA ITALIA: AT THE ROOTS OF AUGUSTAN NOSTALGIA

'TOTA ITALIA IN MEA VERBA IURAVIT': THESE famous words of the emperor Augustus, exploited also in Italian Fascist propaganda, have become synonymous with the great contemporary consensus gained by Augustan policy and culture. In the previous pages we have seen what a long and bloody process the construction of Roman Italy was and we have explored some particular examples of the complex economical and ideological routes it took. *Tota Italia* and its culture, the Augustan culture, are the refined, final product of that tortuous, centuries-long itinerary.

The recent spate of studies on Augustan culture, culminating in the important exhibition in Berlin 'The Emperor Augustus und the Lost Republic',[1] has helped to clear much of the controversy regarding the nature, the forms, and the diffusion of that culture, but has also, as is plain, opened up new areas for debate. Among these, and of great importance and topical interest, is precisely the issue of the formation of *tota Italia*, a social structure which I myself, using a term developed by Antonio Gramsci, believe could be defined as a real 'historical block'. It raises some delicate questions concerning mental attitudes and, more generally, concerning history of long duration, well before any analytical definitions of a sociological nature.

Such an historical block does indeed presuppose a long period of formation and sophisticated ideological manipulation, during which the conceptual bonds, the cultural affinities and the great propagandistic themes of that future social reality were slowly created. As the previous pages have shown, the intricate task of tracking down the significant moments in this fascinating chapter of the history of ideas, identifying the changes in official religion and the figurative evidence in which it is possible to read the progressive articulation of this ideology, concerns the archaeologist no less than it does the historian.

There is no doubt that one of the key themes in Augustan ideology was the Trojan legend,[2] sung so superbly in Augustus' days in the verses of Virgil. The *princeps* uses and abuses it in the official iconography, in the figurative allegories of the regime, in the symbolic concept of architecture and urban space, in literary propaganda, to the point where some modern opinion —above all that of many archaeologists—has ended up believing that Augustus' insistence on Trojan themes was the exclusive emblem or even a prerogative of the dynasty. However, a closer analysis of the reception of the Trojan myth by the Romans in the long term, an analysis which through all the chapters I have tried to pursue in a fairly concise way and above all from a prevalently archaeological viewpoint, readily demonstrated that the 'Trojan message' had other and perhaps more important functions in the construction of a collective ideology, by all means linked to the dynastic issue, but none the less of a collective kind. In other words, the success of Augustan propaganda grows precisely from these deep and ancient roots, firmly established in the collective *imaginaire*. However, let us examine the question in detail.

The archaeological discoveries of the last twenty years have shown that the process of 'Italicization' of

---

[1] W.-D. Heilmeyer (ed.), *Kaiser Augustus und die verlorene Republik*, Catalogue of the exhibition; Berlin, 1988 (Mainz a.R., 1988).

[2] Cf. G. Binder, *Aeneas und Augustus* (Meisenheim, 1971), and above all, A. Momigliano, 'La leggenda di Enea in Italia fino all'età imperiale', in id., *Studi di storia della religione romana* (Brescia, 1988), 281 f.

the myth of Aeneas, far from being the schematism outlined in Andreas Alfoldi's superb book almost forty years ago,[3] had its beginnings in the first half of the seventh century BC, in that crucial period when the growth of the city and of the great aristocracies in southern Etruria and in Latium was accompanied by a rapid and selective acquisition of Greek cultural processes, among which myth holds a position of extraordinary importance and centrality, forming a well-established instrument of cultural and social regulation and also, in all likelihood, a forged 'link' between local aristocratic genealogies and a system of other admired and envied genealogies.

Among the most significant data to have emerged from the new discoveries should certainly be numbered the fact that the 'Italic' version of the myth of Aeneas conceals, in more than one particular, real facts and figures belonging to the era in which the myth was being developed in detail, that is, the safe decades between the first and second quarters of the seventh century BC. This was obviously a heroic phase of the history of the region between Latium and Etruria, something comparable to the age of Charlemagne in the medieval *imaginaire*. In Rome it is the era of Tullus Hostilius (who is appearing to us as less and less myth), of the destruction of Alba Longa and of the reorganization of the *curiae*, a time of intense development and of extreme economic and social trouble.[4] Indeed the princely grave covered by a substantial tumulus at Lavinium dates back to these years,[5] and barely one hundred years later a real *piaculum* was offered for its reopening,[6] which must have taken place for the pious quest for the bones of the deceased, by that time already identified at local level (and it may be supposed at the pan-Latin level, given the significance of those places) with the hero Aeneas. On that same site, already consecrated in the sixth century BC, some two hundred and fifty years later, possibly in 338 BC following the dissolution of the Latin alliance, a *heroon* was built (Figs. 60–1), a χωμάτιον οὐ μέγα as Dionysius of Halicarnassus would describe it the Lavinian tomb

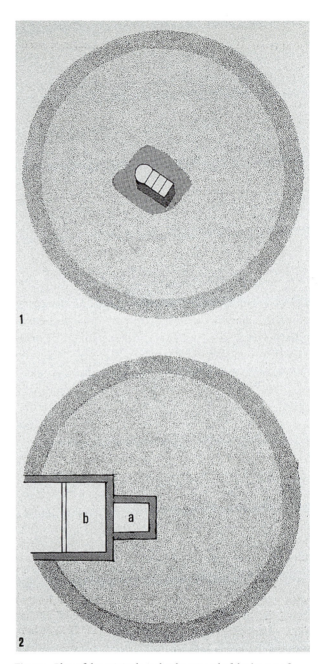

Fig. 60. Plan of the original tomb (above) and of the *heroon* of Aeneas below at Lavinium (after Sommella).

of Aeneas, based on his personal observation or on that of his source Timaeus.[7] In essence, by 570 BC the identity and mythical adventures of Aeneas had already been transferred to the figure of a *princeps* or a *rex* of Lavinium who died around 680. Figured monuments of wholly Italian production, such as the beautiful Etrusco-Corinthian *oinochoe* in the Bibliothèque Nationale in

[3] A. Alföldi, *Die trojanische Urahnen der Römer* (Basle, 1957), a very important book whose ideal continuation is the less specific *Early Rome and the Latins* (Ann Arbor, 1965).

[4] M. Torelli, 'Tre studi di storia etrusca', in *DArch* 8 (1974–5), 3 f. (= *La società etrusca. L'età arcaica, l'età classica* (Rome, 1987), 35 f.)

[5] P. Sommella, 'Heroon di Enea a Lavinium. Recenti scavi a Pratica di Mare', *RPAA* 44 (1971–2), 47 f.; M. Torelli, *Lavinio e Roma* (Rome, 1984), 11, 173 f.; see also F. Zevi, 'Il mito di Enea nella documentazione archeologica: nuove considerazioni', *Atti Taranto* (1978), 247 f.

[6] As I first pointed out in *DArch* 7 (1973), 400.

[7] Dion. Hal. 1. 64. 5.

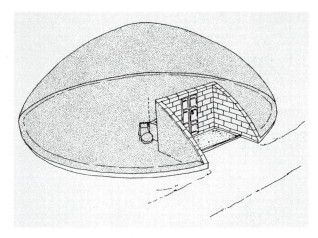

Fig. 61. Reconstruction of the *heroon* of Aeneas at Lavinium.

of wine. As the national Latin myth remembered, this wine had been 'freed' by Aeneas, who used it to make the first libation in the Lavinian sanctuary of Aphrodite.[10] Not many years before the rediscovery of the inscription, I proposed to identify this sanctuary with the one known as 'of the thirteen altars', very close to the aforementioned *heroon* of Aeneas (Fig. 15). Yet again we are dealing with a real person who lived *c.*680–670 BC, maybe the same ruler of the dominion concealed by the Lavinian myth or anyhow someone of the same *gens* as the *rex–tyrannus*. That is, *laucies mezenties*, an individual who actually existed and, from the name,[11] one identical to that of the mythical tyrant of Caere, could constitute a pendant, albeit antithetical, to his anonymous contemporary, the *princeps* buried in Lavinium, who was very soon to be identified with the mythical hero Aeneas.

This process of myth formation is not at all unusual and shows how deeply the Trojan legend was rooted in the collective psychology of Latium: the Greek stereotype which labelled all foreign peoples who were not entirely barbarians as 'Trojans' was a valuable picklock to establishing cultural, political, and mercantile relationships with important *ethne* in the west such as (besides the Etruscans and the Latins) the Elymians or the Veneti, but only among the Latins did the Greek myth very soon, at the beginning of the sixth century BC, become national legend. Consequently, people quickly became aware of its political uses. In this archaic phase, in which society does not yet recognize or does not want to distinguish ethnic membership of gentilicial groups, public from private, personal from political, the myth of Aeneas can have a large audience in the Etruscan area, as Alfoldi's classic research has

Paris showing an Ilioupersis and the flight of Aeneas dating *c.*610–600 BC, already reveal a definite interest in Trojan themes particularly in relation to Aeneas.[8]

Yet another discovery, made just a few years ago, serves to confirm the picture just outlined. It consists of an inscription on a goblet in impasto preserved in the Louvre like the rest of the former Campana Collection to which it belonged and, being part of that collection, almost certainly originating in Caere.[9] The inscription (Fig. 62), redeciphered when the vessel was being cleaned, is worded thus: *mi laucies mezenties*, that is 'I (belong to) Lucius Mezentius', the first and only documentary evidence of a *gens* to which the famous king of Caere belonged, incorporated in the Italic saga of Aeneas from early antiquity, characterized as a tyrant at the head of a whole empire over Latium and a collector of hefty tributes on the Latin production

Fig. 62. Paris, Louvre, former Campana Collection. Etruscan inscription *mi Laucies Mezenties* on an impasto cup, possibly from Caere (after Gaultier and Briquel).

[8] F. Zevi, 'I nuovi vasi del pittore della Sfinge Barbuta', *SE* 37 (1969), 39 f., and id. 'Note sulla leggenda di Enea', in *Gli Etruschi e Roma*, Incontro di studio in onore di M. Pallottino, Acts of Conference; Rome, 1979 (Rome, 1981), 145 f.

[9] F. R. Gaultier and D. Briquel, 'Réexamen d'une inscription des collections du Louvre: un Mézence à Caeré au VIIème siècle av.J.-C.', *CRAI* (1989), 99 f.

[10] See now M. Menichetti, '*Praenestinus Aeneas*. Il culto di Iuppiter *Imperator* e il trionfo su Mezenzio quali motivi di propaganda antiromana su una cista prenestina', *Ostraka* 3 (1994), 7 f.

[11] On the Etruscan name *mezenties* and its connection with the Italic **medj-ent-ios*, with a meaning not too different from the Etruscan *macstrna* in relationship to the Latin *magister*, cf. C. de Simone, 'Etrusco "Laucie Mezentie" ', in *Miscellanea etrusca e italica in onore di M. Pallottino* (= *ArchClass* 43 (1991), i. 559 f.

Plate 60. Tarquinia, tomb 'of the Bulls'. Achilles and Troilus (photo by M. Torelli).

shown, but exclusively in the Latin area comes to settle in a perhaps more complex and articulate way. Although we have evidence that the strong Hellenizing attitude of the Etruscans produced forged aristocratic lineages starting from Greek heroes, it is not infrequent that this or that noble Etruscan group incorporated one of the Trojan heroes at the head of its own genealogy (we are referring here to the diffusion, parallel to that of the myth of Aeneas, of the legend of Dardan in the land of Etruria)[12] as a memorial or a sign of the mythical origins of the *ethnos* from the Anatolian area. However, it is at Lavinium, and therefore in Latium, that Aeneas finds his own mythical–historic and religious place at a collective level, with the prestigious pan-Latin sanctuary of Aphrodite, called 'of the thirteen altars' by discoverers, and with the hero's tomb itself.

It is not by chance, therefore, that already about half-way through the sixth century, the complex and exceptional pictorial metaphor of the fresco[13] in the tomb 'of the Bulls' at Tarquinia (Pl. 60) enshrines, in a fairly clear

way to my mind, the first documented example of the political use of this myth: the occupier of the unusual two-room tomb, *Araθ Spuriana*,[14] is likely to be a member of the same gentilicial family who was supposed to honour the beautiful *tessera hospitalis* from the sanctuary of Sant'Omobono in Rome (Fig. 63) signed with the collective gentilicial name *Spuriana*.[15] The name of the individual in the role of *proxenos* or *hospes*, i.e. counterpart, of the *Spuriana* family and real owner of the *tessera* was a certain *Araz Silqetenas*, presumably a *Sulcitanus* of Sardinia[16] with a fictitious first name. (This last detail recalls the other famous Etruscan *tessera hospitalis* from Carthage,[17] where the owner is called *Puinel Karθazie*, i.e. a man showing a *gentilicium* derived from the placename Carthago and a *praenomen* derived from the ethnic *Phoinix* and subsequently modelled on Etruscan *praenomina* of the type *Venel*.) In the fresco of the tomb 'of the Bulls' we find the aristocratic and cruel Etruscan ritual of killing prisoners of war portrayed in the exact metaphorical form of Achilles' ambush of Troilus. Indeed Achilles appears

[12] Cf. G. Colonna, 'Virgilio, Cortona e la leggenda di Dardano', *ArchClass* 32 (1980), 1 f.

[13] On this tomb, more recently, see: E. Simon, 'Die Tomba dei Tori und der etruskische Apollonkult', *JDAI* 88 (1973), 27 f.; J. Oleson, 'Greek Myth and Etruscan Imagery in the Tomb of the Bulls at Tarquinia', *AJA* 79 (1975), 189 f.; L. Cerchiai, 'La "machaira" di Achille: alcune osservazioni a proposito della "Tomba dei Tori"', *AIONArch* 2 (1980), 25 f.; B. d'Agostino, 'Achille e Troilo: immagini, testi, assonanze', ibid. 7 (1985), 1 f.

[14] *TLE²* 78.

[15] Recognized as such by M. Martelli, 'Un sigillo etrusco', *QUCC* NS 9 (1981), 169 f.

[16] As interpreted by G. Colonna, in *Gli Etruschi e Roma*, 202 f.; though sceptical on this interpretation, C. de Simone, ibid. 98, connects the Tarquinian tomb with the *tessera*.

[17] *TLE²* 724.

0 _____ 3 cm.

Fig. 63. Rome, Capitoline Museum. *Tessera hospitalis* with the Etruscan inscription *Araz Silqetenas Spurianas*, from the sanctuary of Sant'Omobono (after *La Grande Roma dei Tarquini*).

there unusually armed with the sacrificial instrument of the *machaira*, probably in the role of the Greek ancestor of the *Spuriana*, whilst his victim and paramour Troilus seems an unveiled reference—his name in Etruscan, *Truile*, sounds like 'the little Trojan' —to the enemies of Achilles–*Spuriana*, i.e. to the Trojan–Romans, in whose triumphal sanctuary of Sant'Omobono the aforementioned *tessera hospitalis* was deposited. We do not know whether it was plunder of *idie prexis*, the still practiced aristocratic piracy,[18] or rather booty from the very same engagement of arms carried out on the Roman side with the dedication of the precious relic in the triumphal sanctuary of Sant'Omobono and on the Tarquinian side with the sacrifices of one or more 'sons of Priam' to the *manes* of the Achillean *Spurianas*.

If then, as I believe, the *Spurinas* of the fifth–fourth centuries BC, owners of the tomb 'of the Ogre I and II' and celebrated in the *Elogia Tarquiniensia*,[19] descend— possibly through a 'plebeian' branch—from the patrician *Spurianas* of the sixth century, the propagandistic Hellenizing motif in the tomb 'of the Bulls' finds confirmation to some extent in the decoration of the tomb 'of the Ogre II', whose political programme, expressed in the transparent veils of the *nekyia* of the Greek hero Odysseus and of the rescue of Odysseus' companions from the Cyclops (allusion to the Siceliote enemy) (Pl. 61) and with Theseus first in line (Pl. 62), appears to be centred on the Hellenic ancestry of the 'royal' *genos* of the *Spurianas* and their privileged

relationship with Athens, corroborated on the occasion of the siege of Syracuse in 414–413 BC.[20]

However, the tomb 'of the Bulls' is only the earliest and most significant instance of one of the favourite themes of political propaganda of a mythical kind in ancient Italy, which two centuries later returns in a fairly explicit form to adorn the walls of another famous painted tomb, the 'François' tomb in Vulci.[21] Once again here the sacrifice of the Trojan prisoners to the soul of Patroclus is the mythical allusion to the Etruscan ritual sacrifice of prisoners of war recurrent in some impressive monuments intended for the Tyrrhenian aristocracy, from the sarcophagus from Torre S. Severo belonging to a patrician from Volsinii[22] to the Faliscan stamnos in Berlin,[23] from the Tarquinian sarcophagus 'of the Priest'[24] to the crater of the *Turmuca* group in Paris, and in very distinct historical events, which range from the stoning of the prisoners from Alalia at Caere around 530 BC[25] to the killing of the 308 Roman prisoners in the forum of Tarquinia in 358

[18] As reconstructed by A. Mele, *Il commercio greco arcaico. Prexis ed emporie*, Cahiers Centre J. Bérard, 4 (Naples, 1979).

[19] M. Torelli, *Elogia Tarquiniensia* (Florence, 1975).

[20] M. Torelli, 'Ideologia e rappresentazione nelle tombe tarquiniesi dell'Orco I e II', *DArch* 3rd ser., 1 (1983), 7 f. (= *La società etrusca. L'età arcaica, l'età classica* (Rome, 1987), 161 f.).; F. Roncalli, 'Topographie funéraire et topographie de L'Au-Dela', *Les Plus Religieux des hommes*, Acts of Conference, Rencontres de L'École du Louvre, Paris, 1997, 37–43.

[21] F. Coarelli, 'Le pitture della tomba François a Vulci: una proposta di lettura', *DArch* 3rd ser., 1 (1983), 43 f.

[22] In spite of the accuracy of the *editio princeps* of E. Galli, in *MonAL* 24 (1916), 5 f. the sarcophagus deserves a more modern study, especially after the fanciful doubts advanced over its authenticity in *MDAI(R)* 70 (1977), 10 f.

[23] J. D. Beazley, *Etruscan Vase Painting*, 88 f., also 90, a useful list with analogous representations.

[24] H. Blanck, 'Die Malereien des sogenannten Priester-Sarkophage in Tarquinia', in *Miscellanea Archeologica T. Dohrn dedicata* (Rome, 1982), 11 f.

[25] M. Torelli, 'Delitto religioso. Qualche indizio sulla situazione in Etruria', in J. Scheid (ed.), *Le délit religieux dans la cité antique*, Acts of the Conference; Rome, 1978 (Rome, 1981), 1 f.

Plate 61. Tarquinia, tomb 'of the Ogre II'. Odysseus and the Cyclops (courtesy of the Museo di Villa Giulia).

Plate 62. Tarquinia, tomb 'of the Ogre II'. Theseus in the Hades (courtesy of the Museo di Villa Giulia).

BC[26] and on until the massacre of the Perugian notables that the young Octavian perpetrated on the altar of his deified father in 40 BC.[27]

Yet in the case of the 'François' tomb, the contrast between Etruscans portrayed as Greeks and Romans felt to be Trojan is made transparent by means of the placing of two analogous events in mirror-image—in perfect correspondence with the Etruscan cyclical conceptions of the history—on the two walls of the 'tablinum' of the tomb, where the Homeric action

[26] Liv. 7. 15. 10.

[27] App. *Bell. civ.* 5. 201 f., with the exhaustive commentary by E. Gabba, *Appiani Bellorum Civilium Liber Quintus* (Florence, 1970); Suet. *Aug.* 15. See S. Weinstock, *Divus Julius* (Oxford, 1971), 398 f., against the judgement of forgery passed on the episode by Blumenthal (*WS* 35 (1913), 283 f.). More difficult are other modern approaches to the consequences of the Perusine event, such as those formulated by I. Bitto ('Municipium Augustum Veiens', *RSA* 1 (1971), 109 f., where the foundation of the *municipium* of Veii—with the epitheton *Augustum!*—is placed immediately after the Perugian war [on the Veii municipium see now P. Liverani, *Municipium Augustum Veiens* (Rome, 1987)] or R. E. A. Palmer (*Roman Religion and Roman Empire: Five Essays* (Philadelphia, 1974), 32 ff.), who reconstructs an unknown *evocatio* to Rome from Perugia of Iuno Martialis (the goddess with this name appearing on coins of Trebonianus Gallus is precisely the Perugian deity and not the inexistent Roman one, since that emperor is notoriously of Perusine origins). The other argument put forward by Palmer is the name of the festival of Iunonalia given to the *nonae* of March by the late *Fasti Filocaliani*, patently a prolongation to the *nonae* of the *Matronalia* celebrated at the *kalendae* of March in the temple of Juno Lucina (whose *dies natalis* is precisely 1 March); note that the most erudite *Fasti Praenestini*, of the Augustan age, preserve the *nota* for 7 March with no mention of any *Iunonalia*.

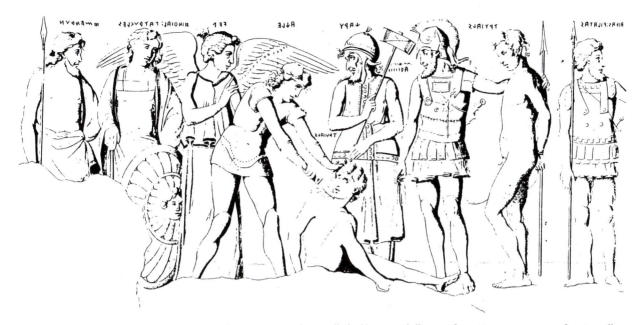

Fig. 64. Vulci, François tomb, so-called *tablinum*. Achilles sacrificing Trojan prisoners (after Coarelli).

Fig. 65. Vulci, François tomb, so-called *tablinum*. Episode of the saga of the Vibennae (after Coarelli).

—the massacre of Trojan prisoners at the hand of Achilles (Fig. 64)—of the *aetas heroica* (again Achilles is prot-agonist!) is conceptually repeated in the massacre of the members of the *coniuratio* of the *aetas regia* led by the Romans of *Cneve Tarχunies*, perpetrated by the *Volcientes fratres*, the *Vibennae*, and the *sodales* with *Macstrna*—Servius Tullius in charge (Fig. 65).

However, the Trojan myth is not only employed from a negative, anti-Roman viewpoint by non-Roman *gentes* or *ethne* of ancient Italy, who controversially define themselves as 'Greeks'; in point of fact the Romans also make use of it and in a fair variety of ways on both a conceptual and a sociological level. An example of this, perhaps the oldest documented, is that of the well-known statuettes (see Pl. 1) portraying Aeneas bearing Anchises on his shoulder, deposited in the three principal sanctuaries of the city of Veii by the Roman colonists brought there *viritim* in 388 BC.[28]

[28] M. Torelli, in *DArch* 7 (1973), 399 f.

These people identified themselves with Aeneas and represented themselves as such: just as Aeneas transported his father and the Penates from the burning city of Troy to their new home in the west and gave rise to the new Troy with the name of Rome, so too these colonists, leaving behind them a Rome destroyed by the Gauls and transporting to the site of Veii their own *lares* (and in the well-known inscription *ILLRP* 1271, contemporary with the statuettes, found at Tor Tignosa near Lavinium, Aeneas is called *Lar Aineias*),[29] will give life to a new Rome or, if you like, to a third Troy. The modest ex-voto, a frequent offering in the plebeian sanctuaries of Veii dedicated to Juno Regina, Minerva, and Ceres (as plebeian cults, enthusiastically taken up by the colonists), is not, nevertheless, merely an expression of the emotional state of the offerers, a psychological response to a separation from the homeland towards a new country (what certainly was felt to be painful and difficult), but it is above all an explicit declaration of political and social allegiance: indeed it is impossible to separate these statuettes from the heated political arguments over the reconstruction of Rome after the Gallic fire and from the stands taken by the plebs in favour of the transportation of the entire *urbs* to Veii.[30]

As we can see, the myth of Aeneas had penetrated so deeply that even the subordinate classes of Rome at the beginning of the fourth century BC manage to make use of it in controversy with the ruling classes. Even the latter, however, were aware of the disruptive energy which issued from the internal and international manipulation of the myth, by this time a national myth. I could give many examples, but for brevity's sake will select just one, sufficient to illustrate the range of different ways in which the phenomenon can be approached. We have seen in the previous chapters[31] how momentous the Romans' exploitation of the myth of the Palladium was in relation to Diomedes, a Greek hero worshipped from great antiquity among the Daunians. Excellent proof of this attempt to present themselves as good political allies of the Daunians can be seen in the Roman foundation in the Latin colony at Luceria where the temple dedicated to Athena Ilias, recorded by Strabo as the 'twin' of

the ones in Siris and Lavinium, was enthusiastically worshipped by the colonists with ex-votos of Latin type, for which some of the moulds are known only in Latium. The sanctuary is also celebrated, anything but accidentally, in a long excursus by Lycophron as the cult site of the 'Myndía Pallenís', i.e. of an Asiatic Trojan Athena, in the 'Dardanian' city, as he significantly calls Luceria. The cult of Athena Ilias, connected as it is to the history of the Palladium of Troy, appears to be located in two different places in the peninsula. On the one hand she is associated with the Colophonian colonization of Siris and the mythical figure of Diomedes, the Greek hero who hovers around the whole Adriatic basin; on the other, Diomedes is connected to the tradition of Aeneas and therefore in the widespread Tyrrhenian diffusion, to Latium in particular. I do not believe that more obvious proof of the 'active' use, in cultural and economic and social penetration, made by the Romans to of the myth of Aeneas could be found. The colonists, largely of Latin origin and bringing with them cult forms entirely unconnected to the local tradition, embodied in the anatomical ex-voto, none the less take over the local 'Trojan' cult of Athena Ilias and turn it to their own account in order to demonstrate both their established right to that land protected by the Trojan goddess and their considerable affinity, almost a *syngeneia*, with the indigenous peoples of Daunia, with whom they shared this very old and important 'Trojan' cult and whom they had come to save from the Samnite threat.

From this point of view, the Daunian aristocracy's response to the political proposal by the Romans seems almost more interesting, embodied as it is by the great temple, over which the early Christian church of S. Leucio was built, at Canosa (Fig. 66), rival to Arpi as capital of that same Daunia where the colony of Luceria was established. As we have seen, the very presence of a formal temple in Daunia is an exception, temple buildings in that region, dominated by forms of a domestic and gentilitial cult, being virtually nonexistent; but the temple's typology and decoration, dating from the end of the third century BC, make it absolutely unique. It has the plan of a perfect Etrusco-Italic (i.e. Roman) temple with figured capitals of very high quality and in terms of size is on a par with the largest of the mid-republican Etrusco-Italic temples outside Rome. Once again the dedication of the temple to Minerva, i.e. Athena Ilias, seems a detail worthy of note: the 'Diomedean' cult revived or restored as an

---

[29] Cf. J. Heurgon, '"Lars", "Largus" et "Lare Aineia"', in *Mélanges A. Piganiol* (Paris, 1966), 655 f. (= *Scripta varia* (Brussels, 1986), 203 f.).

[30] M. Torelli, 'Il sacco gallico di Roma', in *I Galli e l'Italia*, Catalogue of the Exhibition; Rome, 1978 (Rome, 1978), 226 f.

[31] See Chs. 2 and 4.

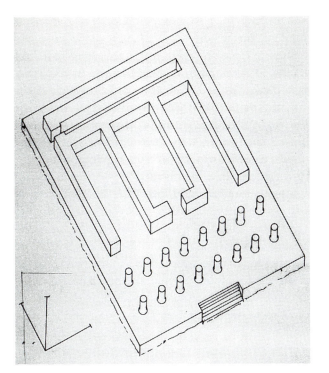

Fig. 66. Reconstruction of the temple of Minerva under the church of San Leucio at Canosa (after Pensabene).

'Aeneadic' cult of Roman type by the colonists from nearby Luceria, is exalted in the capital of Daunia in totally unaccustomed fashion, by means of a large temple and, as if that were not enough, of a purely Roman type (see Ch. 4).

At this point the Trojan myth, changes from being an ideological instrument of conquest, as at Veii or at Luceria, and becomes the cement bonding of the Daunio-Roman alliance, as at Canosa, amalgamating two quite distinct ethnic and cultural entities, poles apart from one another in both a geographical and a cultural sense: Romanization, at least in certain areas, proceeds apace with the evocation of Trojan ghosts, thus ensuring that in the course of the next two hundred years or so, cities of entirely different origins were able to feel no less 'Trojan' than Rome itself. The effect of the union, however, was felt almost immediately, as in the case of Beneventum, a Latin colony of 268 BC erected on the site of a Samnite settlement, but one positioned in an area which in the protohistoric period lay on the western borders of Daunia, and therefore claimed the usual mythical ancestor Diomedes. The Latin colony not only took over the same *oikistes*,[32] but

became the seat of another flourishing cult of Athena Ilias, still celebrated in the imperial age as Minerva Berecynthia significantly together with the Asiatic Magna Mater and her companion Attis.[33] The site of the sanctuary has not yet been identified, but on the basis of the findspots of some of the dedications to Minerva Berecynthia, I would propose locating it in the grandiose complex, almost 500 m. long, with substructures and cryptoporticoes in reticulate and brickwork, known as 'dei Santi Quaranta', spectacularly situated at the entrance of the city on the Via Appia beyond the Ponte Leproso.[34] The excavations now in progress will be able to confirm whether, as I suspect, this building too might be counted among those great local sanctuaries which were still being invested during the late republican and high imperial age, which I will come to shortly.

However, the conquest of Daunia and the final defeat of the Samnites goes hand in hand with other manipulations of the Trojan ideology, this time on the home front at Rome with the political struggle between Roman aristocratic groups. The other benchmark of the strategy for the control of the defeated Samnites, beyond Luceria and Beneventum, is the Latin colony of Venusia, founded in 291 BC. The colony is apparently the first to bear the name of a divinity and in so doing is one of the earliest attestations to the existence of a goddess named Venus in the Roman pantheon: the circumstance is too explicit to be accidental and a study of mine some years ago,[35] did, I believe, succeed in bringing to light the close connection between these two events, victory over the Samnites, the start of the cult of Venus (295 BC, Venus Obsequens on the slopes of the Aventine dedicated by Fabius Gurges, connected with the Aphrodite of Lavinium and seat of the great festival of the *Vinalia rustica*), foundation of Venusia and the strategies of the political faction led by the Fabii.

The dedication of the Roman temple by a Fabius on the plebeian hill par excellence, the Aventine, is an

[32] According to Solin. 2. 10 and Serv. *Aen.* 8. 9, Diomedes is the founder of Beneventum, while in Schol. Verg. *Aen.* 9. 246, Diomedes is even the

oikistes of Venusia and Venafrum; the further Adriatic exploitation of the Diomedean legend are discussed by M. Torelli, 'Spina e la sua storia', in F. Berti and P. G. Guzzo (eds.), *Spina. Storia di una città tra Greci ed Etruschi*, Catalogue of the Exhibition; Ferrara, 1993 (Ferrara, 1993), 57 f.

[33] R. Duthoy, 'La Minerva Berecynthia des inscriptions tauroboliques de Bénevent', *AC* 35 (1966), 548 f.; the inscriptions are in *CIL* IX, 1538–42.

[34] A. Meomartini, *I monumenti e le opere d'arte della città di Benevento* (Benevento, 1909), 307 f.

[35] M. Torelli, 'Aspetti storico-archeologici della romanizzazione della Daunia', in *La civiltà dei Dauni nel quadro del mondo italico*, Acts of the Conference; Manfredonia, 1980 (Florence, 1984), 325 f.

event of extraordinary importance for the many implications it carries as the first certain acknowledgement of the ancestral goddess of the Romans by the ruling aristocracy in a fairly complex interaction between gentilitial attitudes, political logic, and triumphal ideology.[36] The violent political battle between the group of the Fabii and the emerging plebeian Postumius Megellus is also fought with conflicting public works bearing propaganda messages. After the triumph of Sentinum (295 BC) Fabius Rullianus dedicates a temple of Jupiter Victor on the hill of 'origins', the Palatine:[37] Megellus' reply, on the same hill, is not long in coming, with a temple to Victory,[38] along with the legend of a previous foundation (of an altar) to the same goddess by the Arcadian hero Evander,[39] in obvious political contrast to the Trojan myth celebrated in the same year by Fabius Gurges with the temple of Venus Obsequens in Circo. The identification of Venus with Fortune, implicit in the Fabii's foundation, is rejected by the Megellus group: a well-known partisan of the latter, Spurius Carvilius, takes up the 'Servian' theme of Fortune again with the dedication of a second temple of Fors Fortuna (293 BC) next to the one of Servius Tullius,[40] and attacks the Jupiter Victor of Rullianus by building a colossus to Jupiter on the Capitol visible even from Mons Albanus, alongside his own portrait statue.[41] The Fabian group then reply to Megellus with a dedication made by the son-in-law of Rullianus, Atilius Regulus, again on the Palatine (294 BC) and once again to Jupiter with the epithet Stator,[42] in which we should read a transparent play on theonyms and epiclesis, Jupiter Victor—Victoria—Jupiter Stator, and a confrontation between Trojan myths and Arcadian legends, between 'Servian' traditions and those of patrician or Romulean emphasis; all this, take note, in a single year and at the centre of a political struggle in which the colony of Venusia, the alliance of the Fabii with the *principes* of Daunia, and strong popular participation, each plays a particular role with extraordinary reciprocal interconnections.

If it is the mid-republican era that produces the most astonishing evidence of the success of the Trojan legend as a unifying formula on the political level, capable of fulfilling the needs of patricians like the Fabii and emerging plebeians like the Postumii Megelli (or the Marcii, or the Genucii), of leading figures like the *triumphales viri* and of vast social strata such as the colonists sent to the four corners of the peninsula, then the late republican era (second–first century BC) represents the period when the principal 'national' legends with powerful propagandistic implications settled down and became consolidated.

The undoubted explosion of the Italic economy in that phase and the parallel emergence of local élites right up to senatorial rank, the expression of an enterprising class looking for ideological legitimization, contributed in a decisive fashion to the revival of the great themes of the national mythical past and of the native religious traditions embodied by the prestigious sanctuaries, guardians of that past and of those traditions: the thinking behind the Catonian *Origines* has its perfect counterpart on a monumental level in the laborious reconstruction of the most ancient and illustrious temples of the central-Italic cities.[43] It is not possible to understand the phenomenon of the colossal reconstructions carried out in the sanctuaries in Latium in the second and in the beginning of the first century BC or the spate of works centred on the ancient and not-so-ancient temples of Campania and of Samnium, of Picenum and of Umbria, without this need to prove, at a time of particular crisis for the traditional social structures and values, the antiquity of the individual *urbes* and therewith the legitimacy of the local ruling classes, so much the more necessary when these classes, as was often the case, lacked the appropriate pedigree and the prestige connected with it.

The late republican revival of 'national' legends is inextricable from the new thoroughly Hellenistic practice of taking a myth, often from an obscure and secondary tradition, and interpreting and recasting it in a subtle allegorical form, according to models circulating in the libraries of Alexandria, but especially of Pergamum. As we have seen,[44] the complex settings of pediments 'à imagerie' (the old Third Phase of Etrusco-Italic temple decoration), which we can follow throughout the second century BC, besides the paintings (unfortunately lost to us), were very important

---

[36] Discussion of this and related events by [P. Gros] and M. Torelli, *Storia dell'urbanistica. Il mondo romano* (Rome, and Bari, 1988), 99 f.

[37] Sources in S. B. Platner and T. Ashby, *A Topographical Dictionary of Ancient Rome* (Oxford, 1929), 306 f.   [38] Ibid. 570.

[39] Ibid. 569 f.   [40] Ibid. 212 f.   [41] Plin. *N.H.*, 34. 43.

[42] Again, sources in Platner and Ashby, *A Topographical Dictionary*, 303 f.

[43] [Gros] and Torelli, *Storia dell'urbanistica. Il mondo romano*, 151 f.

[44] See Ch. 5.

for the circulation of these themes. The examples could be many and detailed examination instructive, but I shall confine myself to outlining one proposition and adding one brief example to those examined in the preceding chapters. The opinion, started off by the important Colloquium held in Chianciano,[45] is based on the fact that often, if not always, the reformulated myths are those with Asiatic origins or settings, with a particular insistence on Trojan heroes and on Telephus, just as at Luni and Arretium: an extraordinary concurrence between the origins of the themes and the origins of the styles and at the same time a precious insight into the formative environment of the revived propaganda messages. The result is an even more sophisticated and complex use of the myth than in the past, with a series of oblique references to contemporary reality and to particularly 'problematic' concepts and allegories.

The example I want to cite in detail is the recently recovered pediment of the temple of Aesculapius outside the walls of the Latin colony of Fregellae,[46] dating from the second quarter of the second century BC, in whose fragments I believe we should recognize in all likelihood the outcome of the boxing match between Pollux and Amykos, a scene hallowed in the celebrated Ficoroni Cista from Praeneste of earlier date.[47] The absence of any obvious connection between the cult of the temple and the subject matter of its pediment is astonishing on first sight: Asclepius did not take part in the expeditions of the Argonauts. The explanations may be several. On one hand it could mean to celebrate an (otherwise unknown) mythical *origo* of the city and in this respect both the connection between Fregellae and the area of the *Aὐσονίη*, the coast between *promonturium Circes* and Minturnae, reached by the Argonauts,[48] and the parallel, still not fully explained, of the second-century BC pediment of the temple of Juno Curritis (rather than Albunea) at Tibur with a scene from the same cycle, the theft of the Golden Fleece, have a part to play:[49] the Argonauts, introducers

of the cult of Juno as at Paestum,[50] must have had an important role in the local tradition, which was perhaps mediated through Tibur, possibly the mother city of one part of the colonists.

On the other hand, however, this particular episode of the myth, relatively flourishing on Italic soil, has acquired here a particular embellishment in the celebration of the participation of the *turma Fregellana*, cream of the colonial aristocracy and the consul's mounted bodyguard in the Asiatic campaigns from Myonnesus to Magnesia, an event which deeply influenced local public opinion, judging by the 'historical' clay friezes with scenes of those battles (Pl. 63) found in more than one patrician house in Fregellae:[51] the victory of one of the Dioscuri over a king of Asia may represent a suitably eloquent reference to those feats of arms, so much the more so if Argonauts' ports of call (the Asiatic coasts above all and the Ausonian shores) clearly recalled the *turma*'s journey, and if the presence of Orpheus among the heroes celebrated by the myth (there is an Orpheus at the spring in the Ficoroni Cista, perhaps paralleled with the spring of the Asklepieion in Fregellae) and the very close connection between the Argonauts and the Cabiric mysteries in Samothrace[52] satisfy the widespread need of the age for the atmosphere of mystery cult and a certain esotericism of subject matter.

Myth, as we can see, though charged with more complex and intellectual values, continues to represent an instrument of powerful political propaganda, be it on the side of the *origines* or, we may now add, of the *syngeneiai* with the Greek world, or of political struggle in the *urbs*. Yet nothing could compete with the multifarious power of the Trojan myth. Once again just two examples will suffice to illustrate the spectrum of these powers. The recent recognition, in the 'Memmiusbau' at Ephesus,[53] of the *heroon* of C. Memmius C.f. the renowned *amicus* of Catullus and patron of Lucretius, *praetor* in 58 BC and *pro praetore* of Bithynia the following year, and of the homonymous young son, has not only given a monument of extraordinary

[45] Published in *Ostraka* 2: 2 and 3: 1; see above, Ch. 5.

[46] G. Manca di Mores and M. N. Pagliardi, 'Le terrecotte architettoniche', in F. Coarelli (ed.), *Fregellae. 2. Il santuario di Esculapio* (Rome, 1986), 51 f.

[47] Lastly T. Dohrn, *Die ficoronische Cista in der Villa Giulia in Rom*, Monumenta Artis Romanae, 11 (Berlin, 1972).

[48] See the traditions collected by J. Bérard, *La colonisation grecque de l'Italie méridionale* (Paris, 1957), 384 f.

[49] F.-H. Massa Pairault, *Iconologia e politica nell'Italia antica. Roma, Lazio, Etruria dal VII al I secolo* (Milan, 1992), 181 f.

[50] Strab. 6. 252; Plin. *N.H.* 3. 70; Solin. 2. 12.

[51] F. Coarelli, 'Due fregi da Fregellae: un documento storico della prima guerra Siriaca', *Ostraka* 3 (1994), 93 f.

[52] Sources and discussion by B. Hamberg, *Die Kabiren* (Uppsala, 1950), 158 f.; the relationship between the Samothracian Kabeiroi and the Argonauts is already in Aeschylus, *Κάβειροι*, fr. 37 Nauck².

[53] M. Torelli, 'Il monumento efesino di Memmio. Un capolavoro dell'ideologia nobiliare della fine della repubblica', *ScAnt* 2 (1988), 403 f.

(a)

(b)

Plate 63. Ceprano, Museum. Fragment of a frieze representing a battle of Romans against an army of a Hellenistic kingdom: (*a*) head of a Roman soldier; (*b*) Macedonian shield (courtesy of F. Coarelli).

the ancestors of some *familiae Troianae*, among whom are the Memmii.[54] The fictitious Trojan genealogy of the Memmii (how could we not remember the beginning of Lucretius' poem?), through a Mnestheus of the royal house of Assaracus and a Trojan Erichthonios, in obedience to the best principles of Pergamene philology, was connected on one side to Troy and on the other, very neoclassically, to Athens.

On the other side of the *domi nobiles*, there is a case of extraordinary interest which I managed to discover in my study of the cult practised in a very unusual extra-urban sanctuary of S. Venera near Paestum (Fig. 68), the site of joint excavations by the Universities of Michigan and of Perugia.[55] An ancient sanctuary, coexistent with the foundation of the Greek colony and only slightly altered in the Lucanian period, was radically restored between 50 BC and AD 10 at the expense of two women, who, judging by their lineage, are representative of the highest municipal aristocracy, a Sabina and a niece of hers called Valeria. The inscriptions[56]

architectural and stylistic importance its correct date (*c.*50 BC), but has helped us to comprehend its deep ideological significance. It is indeed easy to identify in the figures of heroes in Greek dress on the attic of the monument of C. Memmius, who are surrounding a man wearing a toga (Fig. 67) (obviously C. Memmius pater or his son) the pseudo-genealogy of the Memmii, senators of relatively recent nobility from the Roman colony of Tarracina; we are dealing with a lineage perhaps reconstructed with exquisite ζῆλος ὁμηρικός by our very own Memmius, friend of poets and himself *neoteros* poet, and preserved for us in the *excursus* of Virgil on the ships race at Anchises' funeral crewed by

[54] Verg. *Aen.* 5. 114 f.

[55] J. G. Pedley and M. Torelli (eds.), *The Sanctuary of Santa Venera at Paestum* (Rome, 1993).   [56] Torelli, 'Le iscrizioni', ibid. 195 f.

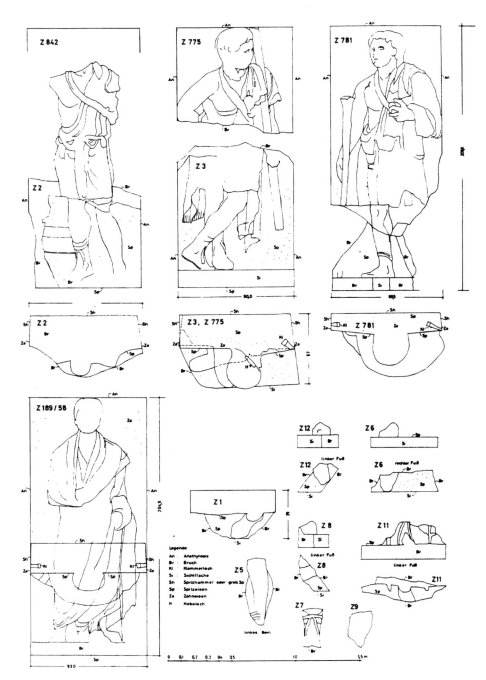

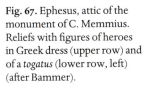

Fig. 67. Ephesus, attic of the monument of C. Memmius. Reliefs with figures of heroes in Greek dress (upper row) and of a *togatus* (lower row, left) (after Bammer).

describe the lavish rebuilding works, attributing to the former the reconstruction of the sacellum and the addition of the *opus tectorium*, of the *sedes*, and of the *pavimenta*, and to the latter the addition of a *culina* and of very mysterious *strongyla*: as luck would have it the excavations uncovered two pairs and a trio of these *strongyla*, low structures (Fig. 69) in the form of a circle (whence the Greek name, translatable precisely as 'the circles') one foot high and three feet in diameter, covered with *opus signinum* and with a column drum at the centre. Since the sanctuary was dedicated to Venus, apparently a Venus Erycina at whose service there were *hierodouloi*, documented by the inscription on a clay vessel maybe meant to contain flowers, it is highly likely that these *strongyla* (possibly used for the ritual *loutron* of the young girls during festivals of the

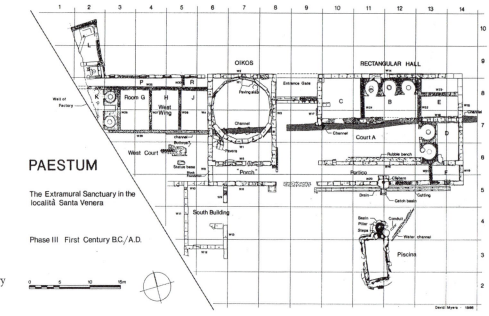

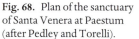

Fig. 68. Plan of the sanctuary of Santa Venera at Paestum (after Pedley and Torelli).

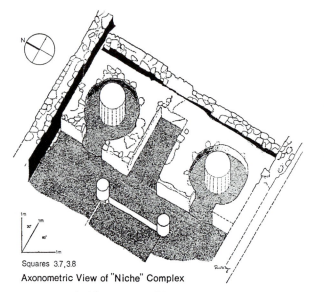

Squares 3.7, 3.8
Axonometric View of "Niche" Complex

Fig. 69. Detail of the *strongyla* of the sanctuary of Santa Venera at Paestum (after Pedley and Torelli).

goddess) were meant[57] to recall symbolically buildings of Cabiric sanctuaries in Thebes, but above all in Samothrace: this also explains why a *piscina* intended for breeding fish was built in the sanctuary too (we know that in Samothrace they practised a cult of fish called *pompilos*) and above all because, in addition to various statuettes of the marine Venus, a replica of the

[57] Discussion of the cult by M. Torelli, 'Donne, *domi nobiles* ed evergeti a Paestum tra la fine della repubblica e l'inizio dell'impero', in *Les Élites municipales de l'Italie péninsulaire des Gracques à Néron*, Acts of the Conference, Clermont Ferrand, 1992 (Naples and Rome, 1996), 153 ff.

Venus of the Tiepolo type has been discovered in the sanctuary (Pl. 64), with the easily recognizable Pothos flying on her shoulder. Both this type and the one known as Venus Genetrix[58] relate to the same religious sphere, that already being celebrated in the fourth century BC with the *Venerem et Pothon* executed by

[58] On these statuary types see A. Delivorrias, in *LIMC* II, nos. 293–8, pp. 41 f. and N. Blanc and F. Gury, ibid. III, nos. 589–92, 1024. Judging from both literary and iconographic sources, among these Aphrodite types the Venus Genetrix could represent a sort of prototype: as a matter of fact a precious inscription (*ILS* 5513: *signa Veneris Genitricis et Cupidinis ad theatrum posuit . . .*) and above all the coins show that it was Arkesilaos' masterpiece (on which see L. von Urlichs, *Arkesilaos* (Würzburg, 1887), and M. Borda, 'Arkesilaos', *BCAR* 73 (1949–50), 189 f.) that the eros made his appearance on the shoulder of the goddess, as is also shown by the Ravenna relief and on the pediment of the octostyle temple of the Medici–Della Valle reliefs. This type (we should remember that the cult statue in the temple of the *Forum Iulium*—Plin. *N.H.* 35. 156—was exhibited unfinished) had possible variants showing the eros on the back (as in coins contemporary with the display of the statue to the public or on our Paestan statuette) or on top (as in aforementioned reliefs) of the shoulder of the goddess and was certainly the inspirer of 'official' replicas of the Genetrix placed in the temple of Mars Ultor (cf. Ov. *Trist.* 2. 295 f.; *Feriale Cumanum*, in *Inscr. It.* 13. 2, 280 and 481 f.) and in the Pantheon (see Cass. Dio 53. 27. 2; Plin. *N.H.* 9. 121). The same type is represented in an extremely important portrait-statue of Antonia Minor—who was *sacerdos divi Augusti* and mother of the emperor Claudius—from the Baiae nymphaeum, part of the imperial palace there (B. Andreae, in *Baia—Il ninfeo imperiale sommerso di Punta Epitaffio* (Naples, 1983), 54 f.). This particular replica from Baiae is extremely important for the typological origins of Aphrodite accompanied by Eros: as Andreae recognized, the statue of the goddess is a replica of the Albani Kore (bibliog. in W. Helbig, *Führer*⁴, 4 (1972), 316 f., no. 3342), considered a work of Pheidias' circle of about 440–430 BC, while (and Andreae acknowledged it only marginally) the Eros is a replica of Skopas' Pothos (treatment of the type by G. Becatti, 'Il Pothos di Scopa', in *Le Arti* 3 (1941), 401 f. = *Kosmos. Studi sul mondo antico* (Rome, 1987), 63 f.). I wonder if the Baia group is in fact a replica of the Skopas' cult statue of Samothrace, considering the popularity of the type of the Albani Kore among the Roma public: but the argument deserves more detailed study.

Plate 64. Paestum, Museo. Statuette of Venus of the Tiepolo type, from the sanctuary of Santa Venera (photo by L. De Masi).

Skopas for Samothrace[59] which the Venus Genitrix by Arkesilaos[60] did no more than duplicate and update,

since the Asiatic Trojan Venus is one and the same as the Venus of Samothrace and the one in Eryx,[61] of whose sanctuaries the Paestum cult may consider itself a derivation. The sudden interest taken in this Paestan sanctuary, peripheral and up till that time of fairly negligible importance, by the Paestan aristocracy, and in particular by a group of local aristocrats directly or indirectly linked to one of the *quaestores adlecti* by Caesar in 44 BC, C. Cocceius Flaccus, founder of the triumviral colony of Apamea,[62] can be explained only in the light of a deliberate *repêchage* at local level for the greater glory of local 'Trojan' families, for the necessary adjustments to the models of the capital and for the political benefit deriving from the imitation of those models, and all of this certainly taking place before the great Augustan propagandistic campaign.

The Trojan mythical and ideological referent, celebrated not by chance in the years of the dying Republic with Varronian erudition in the *De familiis Troianis* (alongside historical–genealogical researches such as Pomponius Atticus' *Libri de gente Iunia* and others), is not, however, the only bonding device of *tota Italia*, but is simply its main ingredient. The pan-Italic culture of the *Origines*, ever since Cato's masterpiece, had exploited legends, traditions, and mythical-historic genealogies other than the Trojan ones. As we saw just now regarding the function of the myth of the Argonauts (or better some of its functions), the tale of the Odyssey becomes a pretext for long genealogies of *domi nobiles*: remarkable archaeological proof of this could be the portrait-statues of heroic type discovered over sixty years ago at Formia and never adequately published,[63] which could be related to the fictitious genealogy of the aristocratic family of the Aelii Lamiae, of secure Formian origin, who, as we learn from the

[59] Plin. *N.H.* 36. 25.

[60] It is difficult to verify the connections between the Genetrix, the Victrix *ad theatrum Pompeianum* and the Victrix *Capitolina*, known from Suetonius (*Calig.* 7; *Galba*, 18. 2) and from the calendars (*Inscr. It.* 13. 2, 494, 518) and whose iconography has not yet been reconstructed. It could be interesting to identify the Victrix type with the Victory of Brescia, associated with the Capitolium of that town (see now M. Denti, *Ellenismo e romanizzazione nella X regio. La scultura delle élites locali dall'età repubblicana ai Giulio-Claudi* (Rome, 1991), 279 f.), but I think that , in view of its setting (the local *Capitolium*), it could equally well be a replica of the Victrix *Capitolina*, Caesar's triumphal offering in Rome copied in Brixia on the occasion of the

complete enfranchisement of the Transpadani in 49 BC. The other opinion (mantained by Denti, loc. cit.), that links the Brixia statue with the concession of the *ius Latii* (and therefore, as Denti seems to disregard, with the Victrix *ad theatrum Pompeianum*, work of Pompeius Magnus, and in Brixia thinkable in relationship with the *clientelae* of Pompeius Strabo, the author of the grant of *ius Latii* to the same Transpadani) conflicts with the use of the type in official monuments of later age, such as the Column of Trajan.

[61] The Sicilian and Eastern connections of the myth of Aeneas are considered (but outside a real historical perspective) by G. K. Galinsky, *Aeneas, Sicily and Rome* (Princeton, 1969).

[62] M. Torelli, 'C. Cocceius Flaccus, Senatore di Paestum, Mineia M.f. e Bona Mens', *Annali della Facoltà di Lettere e Filosofia di Perugia—Studi Classici,* NS (1980/1), 105 f.

[63] After the excavation report by S. Aurigemma, in *NSA* (1926), 309 f., in *BA* (1922), 309 f., (1926), 424 f., (1930), 216 f., first, but only partial modern analysis of the great complex by P. Zanker, 'Zur Bildnissrepresäntation führender Männer', in *Les 'Bourgeoisies' municipales italiennes aux II et I siècles av.J.-C.*, Acts of the Conference; Naples, 1981 (Rome, 1983), 259 f.

Plate 65. Vatican Museum. Terracotta oil lamp-filler in the form of a Capitoline she-wolf, from Vulci (courtesy of the Musei Vaticani).

lips of Horace,[64] claimed to be descendants of Lamus, king of the legendary people of the Lestrigones,[65] which Hellenistic antiquarianism located precisely on the Formian stretch of coast.

Thus, beside the dominant Trojan model, in the propaganda, in the self-representation, in the expression of individual and collective hopes of groups of different origin and social position, a way is subtly cleared for alternative models, which can express either harmony, or polemic, or resistance to the socio-economic and cultural burden of the integration imposed by Rome.[66] The existence of these counter-acculturative thrusts is attested now and then by explicit reassertions of the dominant ideology. We could cite the aforementioned case of Vulci and the presence in the ancient Etruscan metropolis of Gracchan colonists: the latter's encroachment on public and private space might be embodied in the occupation of the tomb 'of the Inscriptions' (originally intended for the burial of

Etruscan gentlewomen distinguished by the title of *hatrencu*, perhaps in some way similar to the Roman Vestals) by a group of Sempronii, maybe *clientes* of the tribune and founder of the colony. Another tomb discovered in the last century, but whose contents have only recently been reconstructed, yielded a Megarian bowl associated with an unusual oil lamp-filler in the form of a Capitoline she-wolf (Pl. 65):[67] in other words we are confronting the proud reassertion of the identity of one of the Gracchan colonists in the face of a prevailing atmosphere of Etruscan origin and certainly anything but favourable. The choice of the symbol, the she-wolf, is highly evocative: not by chance are we dealing with the same symbol that a few years later will figure on the coinage of the Italic rebels[68] crushed by the *viteliu*, the bull which embodies the *coniuratio Italiae*. The same symbol yet again will come to embody the Roman spirit of Sulla's colonists in Faesulae, where we actually meet a replica in bronze of the Capitoline statue,[69] or of the *Iulienses* colonists in

[64] Hor. *Carm.* 3. 17. 1.

[65] T. P. Wiseman, ' "Domi nobiles" and the Roman Cultural Elite', in *Les 'Bourgeoisies' municipales italiennes*, 299 f. offers a useful appreciation of the employment of such traditions by the Roman *nobilitas*.

[66] A good evaluation of such phenomenon by C. Moatti, 'La crise de la tradition à la fin de la République Romaine à travers la littérature juridique et la science des antiquaires', in M. Pani (ed.), *Continuità e trasformazioni tra repubblica e principato. Istituzioni, politica, società* (Bari, 1991), 31 f.

[67] F. Buranelli, *Gli scavi a Vulci della società Vincenzo Campanari-Governo Pontificio (1835–1837)* (Rome, 1991), 168 f.

[68] Discussion in D. Briquel, *Le regard des autres. Les origines de Rome vues par ses ennemis (début du IVᵉ siècle / début du Iᵉʳ siècle av. J.-C.)*, (Besançon, 1997), 174–95.

[69] A large fragment of this replica, also in bronze, comes from the area where modern scholarship tends to place the ancient Capitolium of the colony: cf. *NSA* (1879), 108; (1883), 418 ff.

Arretium, who depict the myth of the she-wolf on the well-known marble altar discovered at Porta Crucifera,[70] perhaps the site of a great sanctuary of the imperial cult, which has also produced copies of the *elogia* of the *Forum Augustum* of Rome.[71]

On the other hand, the Trojan symbol, precisely because of its penetration deep into the ethnic and social fabric of the peninsula, could no longer express variety, distinction, contrast from a cultural viewpoint: in this respect it will suffice to mention the remarkable cippi discovered in the valley of the Uadi Milian in Tunisia (Fig. 70), incised in Etruscan and commemorating the creation of a transient colony of refugees from central Etruria, maybe from Cortona, founded by a certain M. *Unatas Zutas* in the heart of Africa on the example of Sittius the well-known knight from Nuceria,[72] cippi on which ownership is indicated symbolically by the ethnic *tartanium,* that is 'of the Dardanians'.[73] Trojans when all is said and done could even be Etruscans, as we saw at the beginning of our enquiry.

Wherever memorials exist capable of demonstrating the variety or even simply the longed-for *antiquitas*, that is where those realities are taken, utilized, exploited, even at the price of visible historical falsifications.[74] There is the case, for example, of the actual reinvention of the Tarentum clay statuette with 'Totenmahlfigure', which, after a silence of more than two centuries, is reproduced in the Augustan age—as D. Gräppler has demonstrated[75]—to be placed in tombs of Tarentum (Pl. 66), which had absolutely nothing in common with the culture which had produced and utilized those statuettes. With this funerary gift we are in the presence of a *pietas* expressed in usurped, but highly conscious forms, which manage to reproduce archaeologically an ancient cultural context and, therefore, in itself valuable: there is no doubt that with this act the citizens of Augustan Tarentum which had passed from

free Greek city to Gracchan colony and then *municipium*, meant to emphasize that the whole story of the city, even the Greek past with its rites and its customs, belonged to them.

After the terrible economic and social upheavals of the late Republic, the massive emigrations, the ruthless confiscations operated by Sulla and by the triumvirs and by Augustan recolonizations, very few of the old ethnic patterns of Italy at the time of the Roman conquest remained intact: the ingenious feature of Augustan politics lies in having sensed this overpowering 'desire for roots', the need of the new classes emerging from the disorder of the previous hundred years to give themselves a measure of respectability, and in amply quenching the increasing thirst for the past, that the antiquarian culture of the *Origines* had encouraged and spread during the whole late republican period. One of the characteristics of the charismatic leader, as Max Weber has pointed out, consists precisely in not inventing anything new and in giving the people exactly what the people expect to receive.

Attention is thus diverted from myth, by now reduced to a purely symbolic instrument, to antiquarianism, in which it is possible to recover both the legendary element and prestige, not only of the past as such, but also that of the classes who were originally guardians or protagonists of the past. The cities are then in a position to regain the collective past capable of legitimizing the collective present: Tarquinia celebrates its leader Tarchon,[76] Iguvium produces the transcription of the venerated rituals belonging to the religious brotherhood of the *fratres Atiedii* in the Latin alphabet,[77] Interamna Nahartium counts the years *ab Interamna condita* (i.e. from 672 BC).[78]

Even more discriminating, however, becomes the use of private documents with a view to social promotion and show of prestige by those who are the legitimate heirs to those documents. The case of the *elogia* of

---

[70] P. Bocci Pacini and S. Nocentino Sbolci, *Museo Nazionale Archeologico di Arezzo—Catalogo delle sculture romane* (Rome, 1983), 31 f., no. 42.

[71] *Inscr.It.* 13. 3, 57 f.

[72] On this episode, cf. L. Teutsch, *Das Städtwesen in Nordafrika in der Zeit von C. Gracchus bis zum Tode des Kaisers Augustus* (Berlin, 1962), 65 f.

[73] J. Heurgon, 'Inscriptions étrusques de Tunisie', *CRAI* (1969), 526 f. (= *Scripta varia* (Brussels, 1986), 433 f.); id., 'Les Dardaniens en Afrique', *REL* XLVII (1969), 284 f.

[74] As is shown in an exemplary way by M. Hobsbawn (ed.), *The Invention of Tradition* (London, 1986).

[75] Tomb no. 52: D. Gräppler, *Tonfiguren im Grab. Fundkontexte hellonistischer Terrakotten aus der Nekropole von Tarent* (Munich, 1997), 140–2, 236 (inventory of the tomb: 263).

[76] Most recently G. Colonna, 'Una proposta per il supposto elogio tarquiniese di Tarchon', in M. Bonghi Jovino and M. C. Chiaromonte Trerè (eds.), *Tarquinia: ricerche, scavi e prospettive*, Acts of Conference; Milan, 1986 (Milan, 1987), 158 f.

[77] See the discussion by A. L. Prosdocimi, 'Redazione e struttura testuale nelle tavole iguvine', in *ANRW*, I, 2 (Berlin and New York, 1975), 593 f. On the double redaction of part of the Tablets, cf. id., *L'umbro*, in *Lingue e dialetti dell'Italia antica* (Rome, 1978), 594 f., and *Le Tavole iguvine* (Florence, 1984), 121 f.   [78] *ILS* 157.

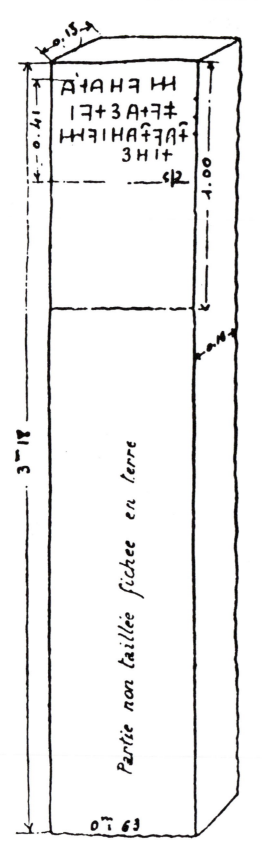

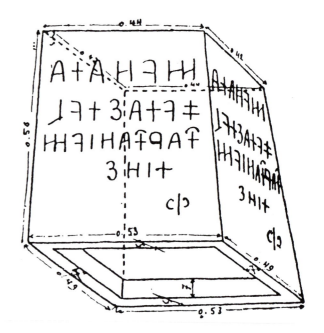

Fig. 70. Tunis, Bardo Museum. Drawings of the cippi with the Etruscan inscription *tular tartanium* | *M. Unatas Zutas*, from the valley of the Uadi Milian in Tunisia (after Heurgon).

Plate 66. Taranto, Museo. Terracotta statuette with 'Totenmahlfigure' of the Augustan age, from a tomb of Tarentum (courtesy of the Museo di Taranto).

the Spurinnae[79] is so well known as to need further comment here; I am anxious, rather, to stress that it is not an isolated instance, as is demonstrated by another case of extraordinary interest, the so called 'Corsini throne', which I have have dealt with in Chapter 6, that of a marble chair of typical Etruscan shape, but purposely copied in the first century BC.

We have seen the meaning of this exceptionally unusual work. In the light of what has been said so far and the spirit so evocatively described by G. A. Mansuelli as *ultima Etruria*,[80] it is not only easy to define the cultural and ideological setting of the 'Sedia Corsini', but we are obliged to do so: it is a copy of a real Etruscan throne executed between the end of the Republic and the beginning of the Empire to glorify the lineage of a family of Etruscan descent, which was in social ascent in the period of the civil wars, that of the notorius Urgulania, an aristocrat from Caere or Clusium, who

married into the ancient family of the Plautii Laterani of both Latin and Sabine origins. We may imagine that this 'copy' of a precious relic of a glorious Etruscan past and royal descent, displayed in the tablinum of Plautius Lateranus' house, had the same functions for the Plautii as the renowned Horatian verse 'Maecenas atavis edite regibus . . .' had for the *Cilnium genus*. However, having recognized its owner we are led to reflect not so much on the question of the formation of *tota Italia*, of which this monument, like the others hitherto discussed or noted, is an integral part, but on its end, the end of that historical block we described in these pages according to Antonio Gramsci's thought. The fate of the 'Sedia Corsini', rubbish thrown out with much else following confiscation, finishing up in the fill of the Severan *castra nova equitum singularium* and then of the *basilica Salvatoris* of Costantine, almost sums up the history of the Empire and the ephemeral fortunes of the aristocracies of old Italic stock, who had been the core of Augustus' *tota Italia*, the most vigorous support for the rise of a long-lasting regime.

---

[79] M. Torelli, *Elogia Tarquiniensia* (Florence, 1975).
[80] G. A. Mansuelli, *L'ultima Etruria* (Bologna, 1988).

Sources of Illustrations

Figures

1, 3, 5, 7, 9, 10, 11, 12, 13, 14, 26, 27, 28, 29, 30, 32, 37, 38, 39, 41, 52, 54. The author; 2. *Da Leukania a Lucania*; 4. *La civita di Artena*; 6. *Archeologia Laziale*; 8. *Notizie degli Scavi*; 15, 60, 61. *Enea nel Lazio*; 16. G. Calza et al., *Ostia*; 17, 18, 19, 20. J. Mertens, *Alba Fucens*; 21. *Sannio*; 22, 23, 24, 58. F. Brown, *Cosa*; 25, 34, 35, 36, 40. E. Greco and D. Theodorescu, *Paestum*; 27. E. Greco, *Paestum*; 31. *Metaponto*; 33. Sestieri, *Poseidonia-Paestum*; 42. A. Bottini, *Forentum*; 43, 45, 57. A. Russo Tagliente, *Edilizia domestica*; 44, 47, 48, 49, 50, 53. J. Mertens, *Herdonia*; 46. Drawing by Banucci (19th cent.); 51, 66. M. Tagliente, in *Italici in Magna Grecia*; 55. A. La Regina, *Pietrabbondante*; 56. D. Adamesteanu, *Rossano di Vaglio*; 62. F. Gaultier-D. Briquel, in *CRAI*; 63. *La grande Roma dei Tarquini*; 64, 65. *Monumenti dell'Istituto*; 66, 67. F. Coarelli, in *DA*; 67, A. Bammer, *Forschungen in Ephesos*; 68, 69. J. G. Pedley and M. Torelli, *The Sanctuary of Santa Venera*; 70. J. Heurgon, in *CRAI*.

Plates

1, 34, 35, 36, 37, 38, 39, 40, 41, 43, 43, 44, 45, 60. Museo di Villa Giulia, Rome; 2. J. Mertens, Brussels; 3, 4, 5, 6, 7, 8, 9, 10, 11, 12, 14, 15, 16, 17, 20, 21, 22. L. De Masi, Rome; 18, 19, 22, 23, 24, 26. Istituto Italiano di Numismatica; 25. Museo Nazionale, Naples; 27, 31, 33. M. Mazzei, Foggia; 28. after *Italia, omnium terrarum alumna*; 29, 30. Soprintendenza Archeologica della Basilicata; 32. Soprintendenza ai Beni Artistici e Storici della Puglia; 46, 49, Soprintendenza Archeologica della Toscana; 47, 48. Museo Civico, Bologna; 50, 51, 65. Vatican Museums; 52, 53, 54, 55, 56, 57, 58, 59. after G. De Luca, *La Galleria Corsini*; 63. F. Coarelli, Perugia; 66. Soprintendenza Archeologica della Puglia.

Index